DEADLY PARADIGMS

D. Michael Shafer

Deadly Paradigms
The Failure of U.S.
Counterinsurgency
Policy

▲

PRINCETON UNIVERSITY PRESS

Portions of Chapters 5 and 10 appear in the author's article, "The Unlearned Lessons of Counterinsurgency," *Political Science Quarterly* 103 (Spring 1988), copyright by the Academy of Political Science.

Published by Princeton University Press, 41 William Street,
Princeton, New Jersey 08540
In the United Kingdom: Princeton University Press, Guildford, Surrey

Library of Congress Cataloging in Publication Data will be
found on the last printed page of this book

ISBN 0-691-07774-6

This book has been composed in Sabon

Clothbound editions of Princeton University Press books
are printed on acid-free paper, and binding materials are
chosen for strength and durability. Paperbacks, although satisfactory
for personal collections, are not usually suitable for library rebinding

Printed in the United States of America by Princeton University Press,
Princeton, New Jersey

In Memory of Beth Shafer

CONTENTS

PREFACE AND READER'S GUIDE

When I started this project in late 1980, many people told me that counterinsurgency was passé. They warned that a book on the subject would never be more than a footnote to a rapidly fading and best forgotten moment in American foreign policy. Even today there lingers a certain Vietnam-induced public skepticism about Third World military entanglements and a healthy caution about them on the part of politicians. But after the brief hiatus of the mid-1970s counterinsurgency is back. Unfortunately, we are no better prepared to assess insurgencies and their implications for American interests or to undertake counterinsurgency operations now than we were ten, or twenty, or forty years ago.

This simple, sobering observation sparked both my personal and professional interest in the subject. As someone who has spent his life exploring questions of Third World development, counterinsurgency is a natural research topic. It is, after all, the "sharp end" of American involvement in the Third World. Professionally, two things intrigued me. On the one hand, given the importance—and contentiousness—of Third World military operations, I found it extraordinary that there was as yet no broad assessment of counterinsurgency's place in U.S. foreign policy equivalent to Robert Packenham's study of American development assistance, *Liberal America and the Third World*. On the other, as a political scientist and a citizen I found it extraordinary that—despite the high human, political, and economic costs of counterinsurgency operations and their regular failure to achieve their ends—current discussions of the subject are indistinguishable from those held twenty-five years ago. This double puzzlement led, in turn, to the two central questions around which this book is built: What is the place of counterinsurgency in U.S. foreign policy? And why has American thinking on the subject remained virtually unchallenged and unchanged throughout the postwar period despite its failure in practice?

These questions ought to interest academics, policymakers, and concerned citizens alike, and I have written the book with each in mind. Inevitably, however, it has not been possible to disguise entirely my concern with international relations theory and, in particular, the question of the sources of foreign policy. Thus, I suggest that nonacademic readers may wish to skip Chapter 2, "Possible Explanations: Sources of Policy Content and Continuity," Chapter 3, "Flight, Fall, and Per-sistance: Political Development Theory," and Chapter 6, "Not So Exceptionally American" (a look at French counterinsurgency doctrine and practice). I do suggest, however, that you glance at the introduction to Part II which lays out the argument and defines several essential terms.

Like all books, and especially first books, this project began as a voyage with only the hint of an end in sight. I steered, but without the help of many others in charting the course, parting the fog, avoiding the rocks, and bolstering morale, this intellectual vessel would have foundered far from port. The debts I owe my guides cannot be repaid; but even if unpayable, they demand acknowledgment. To three early mentors I owe the project itself: Joel Migdal who gave me a way of seeing the Third World, and Jorge Dominguez and Joseph Nye who patiently read and reread chapter drafts, inevitably concluding their comments, "But cut it in half!" To Richard Ullman and my colleagues Robert Kaufman and Roy Licklider I owe thanks for their unfailing support and well-intentioned criticism (however hard to take). To Lloyd Gardner, Stanley Hoffmann, Benedict Kerkvliet, Tony Smith, and Lawrence Wittner I owe special thanks for having taken the time to read, assay, and criticize in detail a stranger's trespassings on their areas of expertise. To Sandy Thatcher, my editor, I owe thanks for staying with this project despite early setbacks and for helping to make the final product a much better—and shorter—book than the manuscript he first received. Finally, to my father I owe the deepest intellectual debt of all, for to him I owe my love of distant lands, teaching, and a good argument.

But writing a book is not just an intellectual endeavor; it can also be a draining emotional experience. Without the support I received, it would not have been possible. So many thanks to Louise, Jessica and Allison McLane, and Cathy and Peter Anders who never ceased to make me think about more important things. But most of all, thanks to my wife, Evelind Schecter, for the savage way she wielded her editorial pencil, the style in which she kept me, the encouragement she gave, and the ever more insistent tone in which she asked: "How much longer?"

ABBREVIATIONS

AID	Agency for International Development
AMAG	American Mission to Aid Greece
AMT	Aguman ding Malding Talapagobra, or General Workers' Union (Philippines)
APSA	American Political Science Association
ARVN	Army of the Republic of Vietnam
CENIS	Massachusetts Institute of Technology, Center for International Studies
CIA	Central Intelligence Agency
CIC	Counter-Intelligence Corps
CIP	Counter-Insurgency Plan
DA	Democratic Alliance (Philippines)
EAM	Ethnikon Apeleftherotikon Metopon, or National Liberation Front (Greece)
ECA	Economic Cooperation Administration
EDES	Ethnikos Dimokraticos Ellinikos Syndesmos, or National Republican Greek Army
ELAS	Ethnikos Laikos Apeleftherotikos Stratos, or National Popular Liberation Army (Greece)
FLN	Front pour la Libération National, or National Liberation Front (Algeria)
GNA	Greek National Army
GVN	Government of Vietnam
HAM	Hearts and Minds
HMB	Hukbong Mapagpalaya ng Bayan, or People's Liberation Army (Philippines)
ICA	International Cooperation Agency
IDS	Inter-Departmental Seminar on Counterinsurgency
IMET	International Military Education and Training Program
INR	Department of State, Bureau of Intelligence and Research
JCS	Joint Chiefs of Staff
JUSMAG	Joint United States Military Advisory Group (Philippines)
JUSMAPG	Joint United States Military Advisory and Planning Group (Greece)

KKE	Kommounistikon Komma Ellado, or Greek National Communist Party
KPMP	Kalipunang Pambansa ng mga Magsasak sa Pilipinas, or National Society of Peasants in the Philippines
MAAG	Military Assistance Advisory Group
MACV	Military Assistance Command, Vietnam
MAP	Military Assistance Program
NATO	North Atlantic Treaty Organization
NSAM	National Security Action Memorandum
NSC	National Security Council
OLAS	Organization of Latin American States
OSIP	Overseas Internal Security Program
OPS	Agency for International Development, Office of Public Safety
PC	Philippine Constabulary
PKP	Partido Kommunista ng Pilipinas, or Philippine Communist Party
OSS	Office of Strategic Services
PKM	Pambansang Kaisahan ng mga Magubukid, or National Peasants Union (Philippines)
PL 75	Public Law 75, Aid to Greece and Turkey
SAN	Syndesmos Axiomatikon Neon, or League of Young Officers (Greece)
SAPI	Service d'Action Psychologique et d'Information (France)
UNRRA	United Nations Relief and Rehabilitation Agency
USIA	United States Information Agency
USOIDP	United States Overseas Internal Defense Policy
USOM	United States Operations Mission, or AID overseas office
VC	Viet Cong (Vietnam)

NOTATION FOR FOOTNOTES
AND BIBLIOGRAPHY

All document citations include a location key for readers interested in obtaining copies of their own. The following abbreviations are used:

DDRS, Retro:page   Carrollton Press, *Declassified Documents Reference Service*, materials from the initial Retrospective volume

DDRS, year:page   Materials from subsequent DDRS volumes

FR, year, volume:page   *Foreign Relations of the United States*

NADB, collection   National Archives, Diplomatic Branch

NAMM, collection   National Archives, Modern Military Branch

OPS Archives   Agency for International Development, Office of Public Safety Archives

PP/volume   *The Pentagon Papers: The Defense Department History of United States Decision-Making in Vietnam.* Senator Gravel edition. 4 vols. Boston: Beacon Press, 1971

PVI:page or PVII:page   Gareth Porter, ed. *Vietnam: The Definitive Documentation of Human Decisions.* 2 vols. Stanfordville, N.Y.: Earl M. Coleman, 1979

To save space, the following abbreviations of journal titles are employed:

APSR   *American Political Science Review*
AS   *Asian Survey*
CP   *Comparative Politics*
CSSH   *Comparative Studies in Society and History*
DSB   *Department of State Bulletin*
EDCC   *Economic Development and Cultural Change*
ISQ   *International Studies Quarterly*
MR   *Military Review*
RDN   *Revue de Défense Nationale*
WP   *World Politics*

PART I

▲

1

INTRODUCTION:
DOGS THAT DIDN'T BARK

This book explores the sources of American foreign policy. Like John Lewis Gaddis in his pioneering reassessment of postwar American national security policy, *Strategies of Containment*,[1] I argue that although the international, domestic political, and bureaucratic contexts of action are essential to understanding foreign policy, they are insufficient without reference to policymakers' "strategic codes," their "assumptions about American interests in the world, potential threats to them, and feasible responses."[2] But where Gaddis examines the "successive mutations, incarnations and transformations" of containment,[3] I focus on the continuity in policymakers' assessments of the sources of insurgency and prescriptions for assisting governments threatened by it during the period 1945–1965.

There is no mistaking postwar American concern about Third World insurgency. From the Truman Doctrine to the debate on Central America, the suppression of insurgent challenges to friendly Third World governments has received recurring, high-level attention. The United States has committed billions of dollars in economic aid to preempt insurgency and in military assistance to deter or defeat it. The counterinsurgency campaigns waged by Americans in support of Third World allies and by those allies with American help have killed and injured millions. Whether or not Americans were involved directly, they have been among this country's most important and contentious foreign policy undertakings. Yet American counterinsurgency advice to others and even direct involvement in counterinsurgency operations have often failed to achieve their aims.

This book is an effort to understand why not. Like *Strategies of Containment*, it inverts the standard practice in political science of focusing on variables producing change in policy. The problem here is to explain continuity *despite* changes in the international distribution of power, presidential administrations, bureaucratic coalitions and capabilities, the locale of conflict and the nature of the insurgencies, and the govern-

---

[1] John Lewis Gaddis, *Strategies of Containment: A Critical Appraisal of Postwar American National Security Policy* (New York: Oxford University Press, 1982).

[2] Ibid., p. ix.

[3] Ibid., p. viii.

ments they threaten. Thus, this book poses two questions: Why, given the importance accorded to defeating insurgency, have these assessments and prescriptions been so inaccurate, even counterproductive? And why, despite failure, have they remained virtually unchanged? The answers are straightforward: American counterinsurgency policy did not change because policymakers' faulty understanding of insurgency did not change; and their understanding did not change because of the nature and functions of the ideas underlying it.

Defining counterinsurgency requires care since the term is commonly used so laxly. Counterinsurgency is one element in postwar American national security policy toward the Third World. That policy, writ large, addresses the problems of managing a tight bipolar confrontation in an era marked by three essential characteristics: a relatively stable nuclear balance between the superpowers which has shifted confrontation to the periphery; a normative attachment to self-determination which has constrained traditional imperial forms of that competition; and tumultuous change in the Third World which has made it a tempting target for superpower meddling. For the United States, the challenge has been to define and implement a containment strategy for the Third World appropriate for a hegemonic, but not imperial (colonial) power. The generic solution might be called "security and development"; counterinsurgency is a form of it applicable when "blood is their argument."[4]

This security and development solution addresses the perceived strategic problem posed by weak, would-be modern Third World allies. It aims to provide security for the development process and generate popular support for the regime by promoting better government and economic progress without violating recipients' often newly won sovereignty. Counterinsurgency is a subset of security and development for problem cases. "As a strategy," declared a State Department counterinsurgency coordinator, it is "a technique for tiding weak and unstable governments over periods of internal upheaval until the constructive forces of political and economic development are strong enough to control the situation without external assistance."[5] It is a politico–military strategy to prevent latent insurgencies from breaking out by reinforcing the weak spots in threatened societies and, where this fails, to minimize the risk that American troops will have to be sent to suppress them. As such, counterinsurgency is limited to neither the brief coun-

[4] William Shakespeare, *Henry V*, 4: 1, line 137.
[5] Charles Maechling, Jr., "Our Internal Defense Policy—A Reappraisal," *Foreign Policy Journal* (January 1969), p. 19.

terinsurgency era from the advent of the Kennedy Administration to the Nixon Doctrine in 1969 nor to the formal doctrine spawned during it. In a variety of guises counterinsurgency has been preached and practiced by Americans since 1945.

Policymakers have touted counterinsurgency's prophylactic powers where insurgencies have not appeared and its curative powers where they have been defeated. Both claims are exaggerated. By and large, American counterinsurgency policy has failed, although this may seem a preposterous claim. After all, Vietnam aside, there is considerable evidence of success. In Greece, the Philippines, Thailand, Venezuela, and Bolivia active insurgencies were beaten back. Moreover, contrary to expectations, they have not broken out in other apparently insurgency prone areas. But appearances are misleading. Where insurgencies fell to defeat, victory was not the result of American efforts but of circumstances and actions largely unrelated to them.

Two problems haunt American counterinsurgency policy and programs: irrelevance and counterproductivity. Policymakers have misunderstood the sources of insurgency, underestimated the constraints on allies' willingness and capacity to make suggested reforms, and overestimated the United States' role as an outside promoter of security and development. As a result, their analysis of the potential for Third World insurgency is self-frightening while their claims for success are self-congratulatory. In fact, even where insurgencies were defeated, the United States failed to achieve the reforms deemed essential for counterinsurgency as they defined it. Instead, leaders of insurgency-threatened regimes used American aid to reinforce elements of their rule Americans considered sources of insurgent strength. In Greece and the Philippines this was irrelevant; in Vietnam it had disastrous consequences. In no case, however, did American policy achieve its aims: victory and defeat must be attributed to different factors.

Put differently, the problem has been the nonapplication and inapplicability of counterinsurgency policy. On the American side, nonapplication is a matter of domestic and bureaucratic politics. Despite agreement on what ought to be done, American counterinsurgency programs have suffered from political manipulation, managerial weakness, and sabotage by implementing agencies. Similar, though more exaggerated, problems have plagued the programs of countries the United States has attempted to assist. As a result, counterinsurgency as understood in theory has never been practiced. And the problems are deeper than this observation suggests since it implies that better management would improve counterinsurgent fortunes. This is not the case.

5

CHAPTER 1

Counterinsurgency is inapplicable as well as unapplied. It miscon-
strues American relations with insurgency-threatened governments,
the constraints facing leaders of those governments, and the relationship between governments and their subjects, as well as between them
and the insurgents. Thus, counterinsurgency programs may place impossible demands on those expected to carry them out. Worse, misas-
sessments of government–population relations and the sources of insurgency may produce inappropriate prescriptions, some of which
aggravate the very problems they are designed to alleviate. Similar
problems plague insurgency-threatened governments' efforts. American counterinsurgency prescriptions may be politically impossible to
implement or inapplicable to the problem as defined by the government, and so be ignored. Either way, the key is not the American program per se, but the nature of the target government, the insurgency,
and relations between them. Programs such as those suggested by the
United States can work—witness Ramon Magsaysay's success in the
Philippines. But they are not necessary to success—witness the Greek
victory by means antithetical to American prescriptions. Finally, success may be impossible, U.S. program or no—witness Vietnam.

At fault is a pervasive, compelling, but distorted vision of the Third
World state as beleaguered modernizer and the United States as manager of modernization. In this way, American counterinsurgency thinking obscured critical distinctions among threatened governments and
in American relations with them. Instead, it offered lumpen assessments and lumpen prescriptions as a result of which counterinsurgency
involvements were undertaken blind, without a clear measure of the
prospects for victory in any given case.

This assertion raises further issues: when and under what conditions
will threatened governments be able to defeat insurgencies? The questions go to the heart of the explanation of counterinsurgency's failure
and the lessons to be drawn from studying it. The essential lesson is
straightforward. Before undertaking any more such involvements, the
United States requires an analytic capacity to distinguish among cases
in terms relevant to its actual ability to shape events in accordance with
American interests and values. We still lack such a capacity. Indeed, we
still assume that if correctly managed, counterinsurgency can succeed
anywhere. It is a dangerous assumption, for it may lead policymakers
to commit American lives, lucre, and prestige to causes better analysis
might have revealed to be chimerical. Thus, the final chapter of this book
offers the outline of a more discriminating approach to assessing insurgency-threatened governments and the prospects of American involvement.

6

The aim of this book, however, is not only to investigate American counterinsurgency doctrine and past counterinsurgency involvements but also to explore the sources of foreign policy. After all, a focus on policymakers' assessments of insurgency and prescriptions for countering it presumes that what they think affects how they act in ways not reducible to situational factors. This may seem obvious to laymen, but few analysts defend such a position and disagree over which situational factors predominate. Indeed, debate rages over why governments do what they do overseas when they do it. This book contributes to that debate by systematically weighing alternative explanations of American counterinsurgency involvements against one another.

Chapter 2 outlines the claims of four approaches to understanding foreign policy in order to clarify their competing assertions and allow a structured comparison. In brief, realists explain counterinsurgency policy as a direct response to a particular security threat and the timing of its development by changes in the international arena. Observers of presidential politics attribute it to the interests of the president's team, and predict a four–year electoral cycle to major policy changes. Conversely, analysts of bureaucratic politics argue that policy content derives from the interaction of the agencies of the national security bureaucracy and the interests of their nonelected leaders. Such explanations discount the role of international events and politicians, and instead they attribute policy change to power shifts within and among organizations. Finally, American exceptionalists derive policy content from the American national style and suggest it will thus be unchanging, at least in its essentials.

None of these is wholly satisfactory. Realists offer no explanation for inappropriate policy or its failure to adjust to changing international situations. Presidential and bureaucratic politics analysts can explain poor policy implementation but not the continuity of perceptions and prescriptions over eight administrations and innumerable organizational changes. American exceptionalist explanations do account for policy fixity, but they fail because, when American counterinsurgency is compared to French revolutionary war doctrine, it is clear there is nothing exceptionally American about it. In fact, to explain both content and continuity, it is necessary to ask how policymakers assess insurgencies, develop prescriptions for coping with them, and conceptualize the United States' role in the process. Answers to these three questions are best understood in terms of the systematic, distorting impact of a coherent set of widely shared and unchallenged assumptions concerning the sources, nature, direction, and potential consequences of political change in the Third World.

7

To say as much is not to discard alternative explanations. This cognitive content approach is a bounded rationality approach and, as such, is modest in its claims. It recognizes the importance of international conditions and domestic constraints, as well as how changes in these may cause changes in policy (for example, in the relative importance of counterinsurgency in national security doctrine or in the level of resources devoted to it at any given time). Still, policymakers' ideas underpin the very definition of American national security interests, threats to them and possible responses. Changes in these ideas may result in a redefinition of American interests and so in a change in policy without a change in circumstance. Conversely, their failure to change with events may lead policymakers to fail to adjust policy as needed.

Testing the proposition that "where you stand depends on what you think" poses methodological difficulties. On the one hand, however judicious, all assessments of intention and perception are suspect. On the other, the tidal wave of bureaucratic politics literature has swept away all simple connections of intention, executive decision, and actual foreign policy action. Thus, analysts of ideas' impact on foreign policy face a twofold task: identifying actual links between specific analytic frameworks and foreign policy actions; and assessing how much explanatory power a focus on policymakers' ideas offers. Do ideas constitute a necessary condition or merely accompany antecedent situational, organizational, and role variables which provide more parsimonious explanations?

Failure to address this question explains much of the scepticism with which studies employing the cognitive content approach are met. This need not be the case, but avoiding it requires a three-step methodology.[6] First, a tight match between policymakers' ideas and their actions must be shown. Second, the analyst must assess other, antecedent explanatory variables to determine if unresolved questions remain or, conversely, if these variables explain policymakers' ideas (which hence lack independent causal weight). Finally, it is necessary to trace the actual process by which policymakers' ideas shape their assessment of a situation and choice of responses to it. The cognitive approach is useful only if analysts can show that credible assessments and policy prescriptions inconsistent with policymakers' analytic framework existed but were not considered because of their preconceptions.

This approach is applied in each of the case studies comprising part

[6] Modified from Alexander George, "The Causal Nexus Between Cognitive Beliefs and Decision-Making Behavior: The 'Operational Code'," in *Psychological Models in International Politics*, ed. Lawrence S. Falkowski (Boulder, Col.: Westview Press, 1979).

III of this book: French counterinsurgency, Indochina and Algeria; Greece, 1947–1950; the Philippines, 1946–1953; and Vietnam, pre-1965. The aim is, in Alexander George's phrase, a "structured, focused comparison" among them consistent with the method outlined above. First, I analyze each case from the perspective of alternative models to determine whether there is any call for cognitive content analysis. Second, I examine each to demonstrate the congruence of foreign policy action and policymakers' assumptions about the Third World (identified in Part II). Finally, I analyze all four to identify alternative assessments and prescriptions not consistent with those assumptions and to show how (and how much) analysis and action were distorted by those ideas and the failure to modify them.

This endeavor requires answers to several questions concerning the content and characteristics of policymakers' ideas: What are policymakers' assumptions concerning political change in the Third World? Why are they so widely shared? And why are they so inaccurate and yet so resistant to change? These are the subjects of Part II of this book. In brief, these chapters argue that policymakers share with other Americans a set of ideas deriving from the long tradition of Western social analysis and *histoire raisonnée*. This analytic framework functions for the United States in the postwar period as it did for the European powers during their hegemonic phases. It provides simple explanations for the complex challenges posed by the Third World, simple prescriptions for coping with them, and an ideological justification for doing so. This familiarity and the explanatory, prescriptive, and ideological utility explain why these assumptions live on despite academic attacks and real world failure. Furthermore, these ideas are so deeply embedded in our common knowledge and world view that we are both unaware of them and unlikely to doubt them. Any fan of Sherlock Holmes will recognize them immediately: they are the dogs that didn't bark.

This, then, raises some final questions: where did policymakers get their ideas, and, in particular, what role did social scientists play as a source? This issue is unavoidable in the counterinsurgency case, since during the 1960s social scientists played such a visible and controversial role in drafting and implementing doctrine. There are two perspectives on their contribution: One argues that academics played an important role as policy technicians and scientific legitimizers of policy; the alternative dismisses academics as irrelevant to the policy process and actual policy outcomes. As with all crude dichotomies, however, this one obscures more than it reveals.

Those stressing academics' importance in policymaking come from the left and right. The pairing is neatly embodied in Noam Chomsky's essay "Objectivity and Liberal Scholarship."[7] In it, he cites Zbigniew Brzezinski's claim for an "increasing role in the key decision-making institutions" of "organization-oriented, application-minded intellectuals," and Ithiel de Sola Pool's assertion that it is through the efforts of these "mandarins of the future" that "men of power are humanized and civilized."[8] For his part, Chomsky observes that "the Vietnam War was designed and executed by these new mandarins" who, he notes elsewhere, have led "in designing and implementing policy, interpreting historical events and formulating an ideology of social change that in part falsifies, in part restricts and subverts it."[9] Either way, the assertion is plain: academics are important.

Alternatively, many contend that little links social science, policy, and government action. Social science research, they argue, is too abstract to be "policy-relevant"; and besides, policymakers are unaware of it. As E. Raymond Platig, director of External Research for the State Department, put it, social science is "long on abstract and esoteric theory" but short on "theory easily applicable to the analysis of concrete situations, and almost devoid of problem–specific conclusions or convincing forecasts or projections."[10] By the same token, there is little evidence policymakers pay attention to social science. As one study concludes, "The extent to which the behavioral disciplines have been ignored in the conduct of our foreign relations is . . . much more impressive than the degree to which they have been used."[11] Where there is an impact, moreover, it is often that of an outmoded scholarship.

Others suggest that a similar chasm separates policy and practice in government action. Policy (or doctrine), they argue, is irrelevant except as an assertion of what ought to be done while the constraints imposed by bureaucratic politics and crisis preclude social science– or policy–informed decisionmaking and promote seat-of-the-pants ad hocery. The problem is embodied in I. M. Destler's two competing definitions of "policy": "an authoritative statement . . . prescribing general criteria for action"; and "what the government actually does." In fact, he notes, "broad policy decisions seldom provide effective guidance for

[7] Noam Chomsky, "Objectivity and Liberal Scholarship," in Noam Chomsky, *American Power and the New Mandarins* (New York: Pantheon, 1969). See, too, "Intellectuals and the State" and "Foreign Policy and the Intelligencia" in Noam Chomsky, *Towards a New Cold War* (New York: Pantheon, 1982).

[8] Cited in *American Power and the New Mandarins*, pp. 31, 26.

[9] Ibid., pp. 8, 26.

[10] E. Raymond Platig, "Foreign Affairs Analysis: Some Thoughts on Expanding Competence," ISQ 13: 1 (March 1969), p. 23.

[11] W. Phillips Davison, "Foreign Policy," in *The Uses of Sociology*, ed. Paul Lazarsfeld, William Sewell, and Harold Wilensky (New York: Basic Books, 1967), p. 394.

specific operational situations. . . . A large number of operational decisions are made by harassed bureaucrats who treat each issue as it comes and resolve it mainly on its own terms."[12] (Hence Senator Hugh Scott's quip: "Mercifully, this is mere policy and therefore not binding!")[13]

The irrelevance of social science theory and general policy to action seems obvious in the handling of Third World crises involving potential American counterinsurgency intervention. First, crisis leads to closure of the policy process through the exclusion of lower ranking experts and the concentration of decisionmaking in the hands of the president and his aides. This, however, may exclude essential information from the decision process, as well as those competent to assess it. Lacking any real knowledge of the situation or its context, decisionmaking may be reduced to judgments based on the assumption that, in Harry Truman's words, "if you understand Jackson County, you understand the world."[14] Second, under pressure, decisionmaking finesse is further reduced by the need for ideas which allow action without imposing impossible information requirements. The ambiguity and high stakes which give crisis its special character place a premium on the analytic framework with the highest explanatory, prescriptive, and ideological utility (i.e., appears the most parsimonious, offers the easiest solutions, and conforms best to decisionmakers' gut values). In short, crisis thinking favors not complex, social science theory but "first principles" and preconceptions. Finally, in the case of Third World crises the ignorance and attitudes of senior policymakers aggravate both general problems. For presidents and their advisers are likely to view the Third World as the object of superpower competition, not a subject of interest in itself, while if they possess foreign policy expertise they are likely to be Europeanists concerned with East–West and transatlantic issues.

Convincing as it may appear, this dismissal of academics' contribution to policymaking is as misleading as its opposite. In fact, academics may play three overlapping roles between the two extremes: the deep source of policymakers' perspectives; legitimizers of their actions; and,

[12] I. M. Destler, *Presidents, Bureaucrats and Foreign Policy: The Politics of Organizational Reform* (Princeton: Princeton University Press, 1972), p. 21.

[13] Cited in ibid., p. 22.

[14] Cited in Jonathan Daniels, *The Man of Independence* (New York: W. B. Lippincott, 1950), p. 285. George Kennan puts the problem more generally, noting of the president and his advisors, "The heart of their problem lies—and will always lie—in the shaping and conduct of policy for areas about which they cannot be expert and learned." *American Diplomacy, 1900–1950* (New York: Mentor Books, 1951), pp. 37–38.

at certain junctures, articulators of specific versions of widely believed notions which, in this specific form, have an independent impact. This triple role is obscured, however, by the false dichotomization of social science and policymaking, social scientists and policymakers. Neither the assumption that ad hoc decisionmaking is "theory-less" nor the claim that "harassed bureaucrats" respond to crisis "intuitively" stand scrutiny. Similarly, the notion that social scientists and policymakers engage in fundamentally different activities betrays a naive view of the social scientific endeavor and social scientists' relationship to society. In fact, what is striking is the embeddedness of policymaking in the intellectual milieu and social science in the policy concerns of the day. Both employ the same paradigms, according to Thomas Kuhn's broader sociological definition: "the entire constellation of beliefs, values, techniques and so on shared by the members of a given community."[15] Their relationship is recursive, not dichotomous.

The tie between even the most pragmatic policymaker and theory is there, though hidden. Policymakers may "reject the complex reasoning, numerous qualifications, and generally experimental and searching attitude of a . . . scientific approach" and believe that "truth is obvious once all the facts are known."[16] Yet without theory, facts are meaningless and analysis impossible. Where do policymakers' theories come from? Although they bear little resemblance to formal scholarly theories, academic pens have left their mark. There may be differences in emphasis, but policymakers' basic understanding of the world seldom differs fundamentally from social scientists' and derives from the same source.[17] Ironically, this is confirmed by the important supporting roles of outside social scientific experts to whom policymakers often turn for reassurances that their assessment of a problem and response to it are correct. As a result, social scientists are heard and do affect policy, albeit because they confirm policymakers' preconceptions and not because they offer profound new insights.

This relationship cuts the other way, too, thus reinforcing the observation that in practice social science and policymaking are not funda-

[15] Thomas Kuhn, *The Structure of Scientific Revolutions*, 2d ed. (Chicago: University of Chicago Press, 1970), p. 175.

[16] Roger Hilsman, Jr., "Intelligence and Policy-Making in Foreign Affairs," WP 5: 1 (October 1952), pp. 11–13.

[17] As Charles Lindblom and David Cohen note, "Even if policy-makers do not turn to [social scientists] in many of the ordinarily expected ways—for specific data, hypotheses, evidence or policy evaluation—they may take the whole organizing framework or perspective for their work from academic social science." *Usable Knowledge: Social Science and Social Problem Solving* (New Haven: Yale University Press, 1979), pp. 78–79.

mentally different endeavors. Social scientists also legitimize their work by shaping it to policy concerns. In part, this reflects dependence on government funding which "is not allocated in conformity with the priorities of the social science disciplines" but has "significantly shaped" social science paradigms to conform to government priorities.[18] More important, in the postwar period many American social scientists have defined their function in terms of policy relevance. Thus, for example, Gabriel Almond argued that

> our foreign policy must be informed . . . by a sound theory of social and cultural change. . . . Our diplomatic, military, propaganda, and foreign aid programs must be based on such a theory and must operate the interdependent levers of change with virtuosity. Without this kind of social science thinking, we will be unable to effect the course of change in the non-Western world in directions favorable to the preservation and spread of our own culture.[19]

In short, for many social scientists social science is instrumental; they are problem solvers in a political game, and their work is valued for how much it advances political ends.

The problem goes deeper, however, for the very nature of the social scientific endeavor confounds its distinctness from policymaking. There is no sharp division between the content and context of science. The aim of science is systematized knowledge, but science itself is still "first and fundamentally . . . a social activity." By taking it as such, "we can perhaps see the determinate connections that it has with the different parts of a society, for example, with political authority . . . and with cultural ideals and values. . . . Still further, when we take this view . . . we can see how its products . . . are the products of a process that has essential social characteristics."[20] How much this is the case depends on the state of a discipline, but as Philip Melanson observes, "One need not attribute technical purity and absolute 'objectivity' to the 'hard' sciences in order to strike a real contrast with the state of political science."[21] In fact, the lack of a well developed conceptual scheme means

[18] Michael Useem, "Government Influence on the Social Science Paradigm," *Sociological Quarterly* 17 (Spring 1976), pp. 159–60.

[19] Gabriel Almond, *The American People and Foreign Policy* (New York: Praeger, 1965), p. xxx.

[20] Bernard Barber, *Science and the Social Order* (London: George Allen & Unwin, 1953), p. 4. See, too, Stephen Jay Gould, *The Mismeasure of Man* (New York: W. W. Norton, 1981).

[21] Philip Melanson, "The Political Science Profession, Political Knowledge, and Public Policy," *Politics and Society* 2 (Summer 1972), p. 493.

that external influences will be acute in the social sciences. Thus, argue Peter Berger and Thomas Luchman, "Put a little crudely, it is essential to keep pushing questions about the historically available conceptualizations of reality from the abstract 'What?' to the sociologically concrete 'Says who?' "[22]

Though such efforts are critical, it is equally important not to ignore those moments when widely held, but diffuse, ideas are crystalized in specific, consequential forms; when "what?" makes a difference. The most striking postwar example of this was George Kennan's articulation of "containment." The notion was not new, but Kennan's formulation defined the terms of the debate about the Soviet Union and actual policy. Similarly, this book argues that, although the ideas embodied in the formal counterinsurgency doctrine drafted in the 1960s shaped earlier counterinsurgency involvements, the form they were given by its civilian, academic drafters had an important, independent impact.

THE CHOICE AND USE OF CASES

The case study approach to more general explanation prompts questions concerning the choice of cases and how they are used. As for the first, any choice of a few cases from among many raises the possibility that proof is the product of a tendentious selection process. I see no answer to this objection but to explain the grounds for my choices and allow the reader to judge their adequacy.

Cases were chosen according to three criteria. First, they had to be "critical cases," those in which my explanation was either least or most likely to hold. By this logic, if the explanation applied where least likely, then it had promise; conversely, if it could be disproved where most likely to fit, then it offered little. Second, cases had to be manifestly important and of some duration. One reason for this is obvious: to say big things about little events may be to say nothing about issues of consequence. More important, quick "in and out" operations requiring little mobilization of support may be mounted for idiosyncratic political reasons. Big, extended operations, however, require deep commitment and clearly articulated justifications which make assessment of policymakers' motives and methods possible. Such cases also become the basis for future "lessons of history" which may influence other, similar (or not so similar) cases. Third, where possible, cases were sought which differed on critical variables—e.g., presidential

[22] Peter Berger and Thomas Luchman, *The Social Construction of Reality: A Treatise in the Sociology of Knowledge* (Garden City, N.Y.: Anchor, 1967), p. 116.

administration, domestic political concerns of the day, the bureaucratic politics of involvement, and the nature of the threatened governments, the insurgency, and government–populace, government–insurgent, and insurgent–populace relations. I aimed to show that models based on these variables do not explain policy continuity across cases, while my focus on policymakers' insensitivity to variation among cases does.

These criteria should be evident in the selection of the four case studies that comprise Part III: French counterinsurgency policy and practice in Indochina and Algeria; and American involvement in Greece (1947–1949), the Philippines (1946–1953), and Vietnam (until 1965). The first case stands alone and serves but one purpose: to test the American exceptionalist model by comparing French and American counterinsurgency policies. In this instance, only two possibilities existed: the postwar counterinsurgency wars of the French and British. Of the two, the French case fit the critical case criterion better. British counterinsurgency successes in Malaya and Kenya, as well as the shared Anglo–American heritage would have confounded a test of the American exceptionalist claim of the uniqueness of American perceptions and prescriptions. Conversely, a demonstration that American counterinsurgency doctrine mirrored its French counterpart despite differences between the two countries and the failure of French counterinsurgency efforts would seriously challenge exceptionalist assertions.

Considering the three American cases, the choice of Greece, the Philippines, and Vietnam turned on the importance and critical case criteria. While the United States has offered counterinsurgency aid in many places, no other instance rivals these three cases in the size, visibility, and duration of the American commitment or in the broader purview of postwar foreign policy. As for the critical case criterion, these three again stand out. Greece and the Philippines have long been taken as models of counterinsurgency success. Thus, to demonstrate that in these cases American policy was irrelevant or counterproductive for the reasons I predict constitutes the strongest possible test of my explanation. Conversely, because failure in Vietnam is so often attributed to the causes I suggest, it is essential to demonstrate that other models do not offer better explanations and that mine applies.

This final point raises two issues: differences among cases on key variables, and the way in which the case studies are used. While there are significant differences among the cases, the limits imposed by the first two criteria did not allow the kind of "controlled experiment" suggested by the third. Rather than abandon it, I applied a two–step process in each case study. First, as much as possible of the origins, character, and consequences of American policy and practice is explained by means of the alternative models, thus permitting assessment of their utility and intercase differences. Only then is the case subjected to my own approach to see what it adds and what, if anything, it illuminates that the others cannot. The aim is to stack the deck against my preferred explanation to assure insofar as possible an uninflated assessment of both its absolute and relative importance.

CAVEATS

Several caveats are in order. First, the concern here is something broader than ideas as idiosyncracies or recipes for a given contingency. As Ernest May observed:

> Just as a distinction may be made in warfare between tactics and strategy, so a similar distinction may be made in politics. On the one hand, there is the choice between the alternative courses of action that are open in a particular place at a particular time. On the other, there is the broad formulation that fixes priorities and provides standards by which the appropriate choices among alternatives may be made.[23]

Ideas in this more stable, strategic sense are my subject. Second, references to social scientists and American policymakers notwithstanding, I do not deny differences among and between members of both groups. But these differences are less important than the similarities that bind them. Third, I hope to live up to Jacques Barzun's injunction that "the history of ideas cannot be written like an invoice of standardized goods. It is a subject requiring infinite tact. . . . Diversity must be reduced to clear patterns for the sake of intelligibility; [but] the meaning of each idea must be preserved from falsification by constant reference to its place and purport in history."[24] And finally, since much of this book is so critical of social scientists, policymakers, and foreign policy, it is necessary to underline my purpose: I do not seek to denigrate but to identify problems which mar the performance of all three. To join Stanley Hoffmann in borrowing a nice metaphor from André Gide, I am "concerned with the lion's fleas, not with denying that there is a lion under the fleas."[25]

[23] Ernest May, "The Nature of Foreign Policy: The Calculated versus the Axiomatic," *Daedelus* 91 (Fall 1962), p. 659.

[24] Cited in Leon Bramson, *The Political Context of Sociology* (Princeton: Princeton University Press, 1961), p. 4.

[25] Stanley Hoffmann, *Gulliver's Troubles, Or the Setting of American Foreign Policy* (New York: McGraw-Hill, 1968), p. 212.

2

POSSIBLE EXPLANATIONS:
SOURCES OF POLICY CONTENT
AND CONTINUITY

"The facts of foreign . . . policy will not organize themselves," observes John Odell,[1] and different would-be organizers of them may sort and join them in quite different ways. Take the case of counterinsurgency. It is possible to construct several very different, but equally plausible explanations of what inspires counterinsurgency policy and why its relative importance in national security policy has varied over time. One such account, for example, explains both in terms of unambiguous external threats. As the authors of NSC 68 put it in 1950, "risks crowd in on us, in a shrinking world of polarized power, so as to give us no choice, ultimately between meeting them effectively or being overcome by them."[2] In this context, counterinsurgency is the means of mustering and applying a variety of power appropriate to one aspect of the East–West conflict, and its relative importance changes with the changing circumstances of that conflict. Looking back, there is much to support such an explanation.

In the late 1940s and early 1950s insurgencies in Greece, the Philippines, Indochina, and Malaya forced counterinsurgency on policymakers. For example, NSC 90, "Collaboration with Friendly Governments on Exchange of Information Concerning Operations Against Guerrillas," begins: "Communist–controlled guerrilla warfare represents one of the most potent instrumentalities in the arsenal of communist aggression on a worldwide basis. It is therefore in the important security interests of the United States to take all practicable steps . . . to prepare to counter such guerrilla warfare on a coordinated world-wide basis."[3] At the same time, the Truman administration struggled with the underlying issues of rising nationalism and continued European colonialism. The invasion of South Korea, however, pushed such con-

---

[1] John S. Odell, *U.S. International Monetary Policy: Markets, Power, and Ideas as Sources of Change* (Princeton: Princeton University Press, 1982), p. 15.

[2] NSC 68, "United States Objectives and Programs for National Security," April 14, 1950, p. 34. NAMM, NSC file.

[3] NSC 90, "Statement of Policy Proposed by the National Security Council on Collaboration with Friendly Governments on Exchange of Information Concerning Operations Against Guerrillas," draft, May 8, 1951, p. 1. Truman Library.

cerns to the back burner and reemphasized conventional military options even in the Third World. The Eisenhower administration extended the process by adopting a strategic doctrine focused exclusively on superpower deterrence at the nuclear level—massive retaliation.

Massive retaliation had a twofold rationale. First, it was to stop conventional aggression through threatened use of nuclear weapons, the one area in which the United States possessed a "comparative advantage." Second, it promised cheap protection over the long haul. The same logic extended overseas by way of the Mutual Security Program. To complement a strategic doctrine of massive retaliation at the center, the Eisenhower administration increased military assistance to allies. NATO countries received the most, but the Third World got its share, and a growing one at that.

Massive retaliation did not last long. Although critics did not doubt the threat that drove it, they argued that massive retaliation was a penny wise–pound foolish response. In 1954, then Senator John F. Kennedy warned that massive retaliation reduced American credibility because "it would be difficult," for example, "to commence atomic retaliation against Communist aggression in Burma."[4] Indeed, noted others, despite the nuclear stalemate, conventional and subconventional wars continued, in part because the nuclear-dependent American military was too "muscle-bound" to act.[5] A limited war strategy for the limited use of military force for limited political objectives was required, but meeting the Soviet threat required weapons appropriate for each milieu and each level of conflict.

The Suez and Lebanon crises brought these issues into sharp focus. Despite academic warnings, the national security implications of events in the Third World had gone largely unheeded until Nasser's 1956 seizure of the Suez Canal raised the spectre of East–West confrontation over control of the emerging Third World nationalisms. Then in 1957 President Eisenhower sent the Marines to Beirut to save the government of Camille Chamoun and show American willingness "to secure and protect the territorial integrity and political independence of . . . nations requesting such aid against overt, armed aggression from any

[4] Speech to the Cathedral Club, February 1, 1954. John F. Kennedy, *A Compilation of His Statements and Speeches During His Service in the United States Senate and House of Representatives* (Washington, D.C.: 1964), p. 993.

[5] William Bundy, for example, reports "I can personally recall . . . several high-level meetings [at the CIA] in 1956 that bemoaned the problem, thought of it in worldwide terms, and recognized how little of the American military posture . . . was relevant to it." Foreword to Douglas Blaufarb, *The Counterinsurgency Era: U.S. Doctrine and Performance* (New York: Free Press, 1977), p. x.

nation controlled by International Communism."[6] At one level, the intervention worked: Chamoun survived. But at another, it demonstrated the irrelevance of American policy and capabilities vis à vis the dynamics of Third World nationalism which underlay events in the Middle East and seemed to offer the Soviets an opening.

The Third World thus reentered the superpower confrontation. In 1957, for example, the Joint Chiefs reported that one of three "fundamental long-term trends" in international relations would be "the growth of nationalism and the desire for an improved lot among backward and dependent peoples." As a result, "a major prize in the continuing conflict . . . will be the adherence of wavering peoples to the Soviet or the Western democratic cause. The Soviets can be expected to exploit their favorable opportunity of championing the causes of colonial peoples, to whom nationalism and communism may temporarily be made to appear synonymous."[7] Furthermore, the mobilization of Third World peoples made obsolete the simple CIA coup with which the Eisenhower administration had undone Mossadegh in Iran and Arbenz in Guatemala. This and the new appreciation of the Third World's import for American security led to new policy formulations.

The Eisenhower administration began to focus on the possible subversion of nationalist movements and the threat of indirect aggression. As Under Secretary of State Douglas Dillon warned the Draper Commission, national security would only "be served as our ground, naval and air forces are capable of waging limited war . . . ; [and] are susceptible of prompt movement to the Asian and African areas where limited wars are most likely to be fought."[8] The administration also made tentative moves to develop policies for coping with the new political dimension of global power. Thus, President Eisenhower enunciated the beginnings of a preemptive political strategy, declaring that in Latin America, for example, the choice was between "social evolution or revolution." It was therefore "imperative that institutions be developed and strengthened sufficiently to permit the peoples' needs to be met

[6] "President Asks for Authorization for U.S. Economic Program and for Resolution on Communist Aggression in Middle East: Message of the President to Congress," DSB (January 21, 1957), p. 86.

[7] JCS, Joint Strategic Plans Division, "Estimate of Probable Developments in the World Political Situation Up to 1957," JSPC 814/3, December 11, 1955, appendices 7, 13. NAMM, JCS list 1946–1947 CCS 092 (10–9–46). See, too, NSC 5440, "Basic National Security Policy," December 13, 1954, p. 12. NAMM, NSC file.

[8] Letter to William H. Draper from Douglas Dillon, Under Secretary of State for Economic Affairs, February 20, 1959, enclosure 1, "Objectives of Long-Term Foreign Policy," p. 20. DDRS, Retro: 962A.

through orderly processes of change."[9] Efforts to develop policies to achieve these ends had not progressed very far, however, by the time of the November 1960 elections.

The advent of the Kennedy administration marked a sharp increase in the relative importance of counterinsurgency in American national security policy. The very sharpness of the change, however, also indicates a possible new explanation. After all, the preceding account suggests that in the 1960s, as in the 1950s, changes in the international arena should have produced a smooth process of analytic adjustment followed by an equally smooth adjustment in policy. Instead, when change came it was rapid, discontinuous, and linked not to international events but to the electoral cycle. Counterinsurgency came to Washington with Kennedy and reflected presidential interests, the composition and interests of the presidential team, and the President's impact on policy.

President Kennedy made counterinsurgency a priority, giving it the prominence only sustained presidential interest can bestow. As General L. L. Lemnitzer, then chairman of the Joint Chiefs of Staff, put it in July 1962, Kennedy wanted "nothing less than a dynamic national strategy—an action program designed to defeat the Communists without recourse to the hazard . . . of nuclear war; one designed to defeat subversion where it has already erupted, and, even more important, to prevent its taking initial root . . . a strategy of both therapy and prophylaxis."[10] To get it, the President launched studies by the Joint Chiefs and an interagency group that in 1962 produced an ambitious statement of counterinsurgency doctrine, the "United States Overseas Internal Defense Policy."[11] Kennedy also wanted a counterinsurgency apparatus capable of providing "therapy and prophylaxis." Thus, in January 1961 National Security Action Memorandum 124 created the Special Group (C-I) to educate policymakers about the insurgency threat and ensure that government resources, agencies, and intragovernmental coordination capabilities could meet it.[12] Located in the White House, and including General Maxwell Taylor (then the presi-

[9] Statement by President Eisenhower, DSB (August 1, 1960), p. 161.

[10] "Summary Report, Military Counterinsurgency Accomplishments Since January 1961," Memorandum for the Special Assistant to the President for National Security Affairs, CM–843–62, July 21, 1962, p. 1. DDRS, Retro: 242C.

[11] (USOIDP), prepared by an Interdepartmental Committee consisting of representatives of State, Defense, Joint Chiefs of Staff, CIA and AID. Transmitted August 24, 1962, NSAM 182. Kennedy Library.

[12] The Pentagon Papers, Senator Gravel ed., vol. 2 (Boston: Beacon Press, 1971), p. 660. Hereafter in notes references to The Pentagon Papers will be cited as PP/volume number (e.g., PP/II).

dent's military adviser), McGeorge Bundy (national security adviser), and Robert Kennedy (attorney general), the Special Group gave the president direct control over the rapidly expanding counterinsurgency effort and the ability to impose both his vision of counterinsurgency and his sense of urgency throughout the government.

One of the most striking aspects of the Kennedy administration's assault on the problems of insurgency and counterinsurgency was its effort to understand both. Counterinsurgency doctrine put academic specialists to work marrying the most up-to-date theories of Third World development to a government doctrine for coping with its consequences. To supplement such efforts, the president read—and ordered his advisers to read—Mao, Giap, and other architects of revolutionary theory. Kennedy was particularly taken by Mao's famous aphorism that "Guerrillas are like fish, and the people are the water they swim in. If the temperature of the water is right, the fish will thrive and multiply." This made managing the water temperature critical and required a new social "oceanography."[13] To develop it, the government turned to outside research organizations and the academic community which geared up to study the social, political, and economic problems of "threatened areas" for the military and other government agencies.

Under President Kennedy there was also a big effort to spread the word about counterinsurgency. A 1961 memo, "US Counter-Guerrilla Operational and Training Capabilities," reflects the breadth of the training program considered necessary. "We need an institution(s) capable of running a comprehensive course in counter-guerrilla operations . . . , supplying instructors to . . . other service schools, the National War College and the Foreign Service Institute, and serving as a parent institution for satellite counter-guerrilla training centers maintained abroad." There should also be available, the memo argued, a "well-developed body of texts . . . devoted to the whole spectrum of problems, military and non-military, involved in deterring and defeating guerrilla insurrection, particularly in the context of transitional societies where 'wars of national liberation' . . . pose threats to friendly governments." Students should come from State, AID, USIA, CIA, and the military "to insure that we have sufficient properly-trained personnel to deal with the relevant range of problems." The memo concluded, "The final objective should be a US capability to give adequate, across-the-board advice and assistance to foreign governments . . . in creating

[13] Seyoum Brown, *The Faces of Power: Continuity and Change in United States Foreign Policy from Truman to Johnson* (New York: Columbia University Press, 1968), pp. 164–65.

an environment inhospitable to mass subversions; and dealing promptly and effectively with guerrilla insurrection."[14]

Plans for how to achieve these ambitious aims were bandied about during the first year of the administration. NSAM 131 called for "a school at the national level to offer instruction on the entire range of problems posed to the United States in dealing with developing countries, to include special area counter-insurgency problems."[15] Several plans for a national "Modernization Institute" were even proposed. Eventually, however, the administration decided to rely on decentralized training by the respective services supplemented by an "Inter-Departmental Seminar on Counter-Insurgency" under the auspices of the Foreign Service Institute.

But the power of the president to push and persuade had its backside, too. Energy could not guarantee quality. The president and his advisors forced upon operators a still half-baked counterinsurgency doctrine too general to provide workable guidelines for policy, let alone practical action in the field. Driven by high-level pressure, however, the doctrine swept all resistance before it. The top-down imposition of counterinsurgency stifled feedback, legitimate criticism, and doctrinal modification, observes Douglas Blaufarb, "and so the apparatus carried on with the approach . . . unthinkingly perpetuating the original errors."[16] Similarly, presidential enthusiasm for the development of a limited war capability opened the door to previously impossible Third World entanglements. For where the lack of such capabilities had helped keep the United States out of Indochina in 1954, for example, their rapid development under Kennedy soon set the stage for their use.

Conversely, lack of support among succeeding presidents helps explain the end of the counterinsurgency era. Elected to find "peace with honor" in Vietnam and faced with widespread resistance to further involvement in "limited wars," President Nixon reversed field. With the declaration of the "Nixon Doctrine" at Guam in 1969, the United States began the reduction of counterinsurgency capabilities by shifting the burden to our threatened allies. As Elliott Richardson put it, counterinsurgency "must be conducted by the government concerned, making use of its popular support, its resources and its men."[17] Thus, the

[14] George C. McGhee, Undersecretary of State for Political Affairs, "U.S. Counter-Guerrilla Organizational and Training Capabilities," memorandum for General Maxwell Taylor, Special Advisor to the President for Military Affairs, August 7, 1961, pp. 1–3. DDRS, 1981: 97A.

[15] PP/2, pp. 667–68.

[16] Blaufarb, *Counterinsurgency Era*, pp. 87–88.

[17] "The Foreign Policy of the Nixon Administration: Its Aims and Strategy," DSB (September 22, 1969), p. 258.

United States virtually eliminated the organizational structure and cadre of counterinsurgency experts built up since 1961.[18] No one suggested that a way to help allies lacking popular support, resources, and men was needed. This was the role counterinsurgency doctrine had failed to fill; without presidential support, it was impossible to develop an alternative.

But again there is reason to doubt the accuracy of such an account of counterinsurgency. After all, it suggests that counterinsurgency doctrine came and went with presidents and was implemented as they desired. Yet too many different agencies had too many axes to grind for counterinsurgency to work as doctrine required. Moreover, despite active presidential support, counterinsurgency was marginal to the main tasks of the agencies concerned or even threatened to them. Thus, they shrugged off political pressure and implemented their own repertoires. Counterinsurgency never had a chance.

This is most evident in military resistance to counterinsurgency doctrine and sabotage of its implementation.[19] That doctrine required major changes in military organization, flouted the military's definition of its mission, and violated institutional norms. The American armed forces are designed to fight in Europe and planning, doctrine, tactics, and organization focus on all-out conventional war in this essential theater. The military has emphasized violent line combat by general purpose forces armed with high technology, high fire power weapons. Conversely, Kennedy's civilian counterinsurgency strategists called for decentralized, political, low intensity, low technology warfare by specially trained "guerrilla-style" fighters on the furthest reaches of the globe. It was not a match made in heaven.

Resistance derived from the threat to the military's ability to carry out its primary mission to defend Europe. Most military men thought counterinsurgency irrelevant to that mission and argued that it should be resisted lest it divert time, energy, and resources from Europe. Thus, when President Kennedy demanded "a wholly different kind of force, and therefore a new and wholly different kind of military training,"[20] the military sidestepped. It left its essential unit, the combat division,

[18] H. Heymann, Jr., and W. W. Whitson, "Can and Should the United States Preserve a Military Capability for Revolutionary Conflict?" R–940–ARPA (Santa Monica: RAND Corp., January 1972), pp. iii, 32.

[19] For an excellent study of the subject, see Andrew F. Krepinevich, Jr., *The Army and Vietnam* (Baltimore: Johns Hopkins University Press, 1986). See, too, Robert W. Komer, *Bureaucracy at War: U.S. Performance in the Vietnam Conflict* (Boulder, Col.: Westview, 1986).

[20] Graduation Address, West Point, *The Public Papers of the President, John F. Kennedy, 1962* (Washington, D.C.: GPO, 1963), p. 454.

23

unchanged and simply declared that under counterinsurgency conditions its massive firepower would be used "discriminatingly." As a result, "the counterinsurgency forces of the United States were . . . ordained . . . to be dependent upon roads, to use weapons which would of necessity harm civilians caught in their fire while causing little harm to the nimble guerrillas, and to impact massively upon the host society in a way which could not but arouse nationalistic feelings."[21] Firepower remained the military's central icon, and old General Forrest's "Git that fustest with the mostest" its motto.

Resistance also derived from the threat counterinsurgency posed to institutional norms. The United States armed forces distrust such elite units as the Green Berets. They possess limited utility, drain material and human resources from the general purpose forces, damage the morale of other units, and resist tight discipline. More important, the armed forces, long-resistant to involvement in politics, believe in drawing a clear boundary between military and political affairs. As an explicitly *politico*-military doctrine, counterinsurgency violated this distinction.

Finally, when confronted for the failure to adopt counterinsurgency, the inability to win in Vietnam, and its eventual loss, the military reinforced existing conventional doctrine. Senior officers denied that suggested innovations would work; they asserted during the war that existing doctrine was working and after the war that it had worked, North Vietnamese victory notwithstanding. During the war the military argued that all the situation required was the unfettered application of more of what was already being done; and now it argues that the war was lost for having done too little of it. During the war the military did not develop a doctrine appropriate for Vietnam or elsewhere in the Third World and has since chosen to forget the "episode" entirely.[22] Indeed, it has reacted to critics with a purely institutional definition of national security. As one general put it, "A conventional military force, no matter how bent, twisted, malformed, or otherwise 'reorganized' is *still* one hell of a poor instrument with which to engage insurgents."[23] Thus, because it is difficult for the military as currently conceived to fight insurgents, insurgency and the ability to counter it were defined as irrelevant, attention shifted back to Europe and such

---

[21] Blaufarb, *Counterinsurgency Era*, pp. 81–82. See, too, Department of the Army, Field Manual FM 31–16, March 1967.

[22] Ernest Evans, "The U.S. Military and Low-Level Conflict" (Unpublished manuscript, Center for International Affairs, Harvard University, 1981), p. 113.

[23] Cited in Brian Jenkins, *The Unchangeable War*, RM–6278–1–ARPA (Santa Monica: RAND Corp., September 1972), p. 6. Emphasis in original.

quasiconventional responses to Third World problems as the Rapid Deployment Force.

SORTING OUT THE POSSIBILITIES

Here, then, are three very different, equally plausible accounts of the inspiration for counterinsurgency policy, its content, and its changing significance in American national security planning. More generally, these three versions of the same story suggest how, by asking different questions of different kinds of evidence, analysts can reach very different conclusions about the sources and content of foreign policy, and why and when it changes. But how does one choose among the alternative explanations? The first step is to specify the essential elements of each. Thus, this chapter outlines five competing types of explanation—realist, presidential, and bureaucratic politics, American exceptionalist, and cognitive content—to make possible comparisons of their relative utility in analyzing material presented in subsequent chapters. Attention focuses on their claims concerning the appropriate unit of analysis, the motivation of policy, the source of policy content, and the causes of policy change. In each case, too, possible weaknesses are identified, again with an eye to later testing.

Realism

The account of counterinsurgency policy which opens this chapter belongs to a class of explanations that focus on international events and states' responses to them. As a class, such explanations make two simplifying assumptions. First, they assume that events in the international system provide an unambiguous imperative to which the policies of individual states respond. Second, they assume that all states and their leaders respond in similar and predictable fashion. The two are inextricably linked: the presumed interchangeability of states and leaders allows analysis to focus exclusively on the international environment, while the presumed imperative of international events allows predictions about how states will act without reference to their domestic politics. International relations are thus an aggregate of the purposive actions of states as unified actors in response to one another and their external environment.

Like Adam Smith's vision of perfect market competition, such explanations leave causation to an "invisible hand" that guides state's responses to changes in "underlying market conditions"—whether the currency is military might, economic requirements, or whatever. Fur-

25

thermore, they reduce assessments of policy to questions of the exactness of fit between the imperatives posed by the international environment and states' actions. Similarly, the notion of international politics as an efficient, self-regulating market also explains policy change and the content of new policies. Thus, the unit of analysis is the state; its motivation is self-interest; policy is the rational course of action to achieve desired ends in a given international context; and policy change follows changes in the international system affecting the state's capacity to achieve its ends.

The most powerful variant of this genre is realism. Realism begins with the view that "war lurks in the background of international politics."[24] Furthermore, argue the realists, this is but evidence of the perpetual, anarchical state of war among the sovereign units which make up the international system. From this "Hobbesian situation" derives the realist explanation of foreign policy: states do what is necessary to survive in the face of changing threats from abroad. Thus, in this fundamental way, all states are alike, and their policies can be analyzed without reference to their domestic structures, ideology, or leadership. What matters is their capacity for self-preservation—their power. Indeed, in international politics, declares Hans Morganthau, "power is pitted against power for survival and supremacy."[25]

The beauty of realism derives from its simplicity and the parsimonious, powerful explanations it offers. It asserts that the stronger will prevail and hence that at the heart of foreign policymaking and analysis must be careful assessment of states' relative position in the power hierarchy. Since war is the *ultima ratio* in international politics, rank in this hierarchy is measured in military power. By the same token, realist explanations of change in international relations focus on shifts in the international distribution of military power. As a result, the realists argue for the necessary primacy of the high politics of national security over the low politics of all other affairs of state. Turned outward on a postwar world dominated by a single, bilateral power contest, realism thus also ignores the low politics of lesser powers and issues except when they affect the East-West contest.

POSSIBLE OBJECTIONS

There are two types of objections to realism: those that accept the primacy of international events and those that do not. Both can be ap-

[24] E. H. Carr, *The Twenty Years' Crisis, 1919–1939: An Introduction to the Study of International Relations* (New York: Harper Torchbooks, 1964), p. 109.
[25] Hans Morgenthau, *Scientific Man vs. Power Politics* (Chicago: University of Chicago Press, 1946), p. 71.

proached via consideration of the "power paradox," or how weak states prevail against the strong—and against the realist claim that the distribution of power determines outcomes in international relations.[26] Criticisms of the first sort suggest that the power paradox is illusory, the artifact of an oversimplified understanding of power. Here the commonest approach challenges the fungibility of power, specifically military power, and suggests instead that power is issue specific. But such criticisms are not fatal. Indeed, as the first version of the counterinsurgency story suggests, states regularly change their policies and develop new power capabilities in response to the changing requirements of a changing international arena.

Two other explanations of the power paradox, however, challenge the simplifying assumptions of this class of explanation as a whole: the clarity of the policy imperatives imposed by the international system and similarity of all states and statesmen before them. First, some explanations attribute the power paradox to problems in the domestic "conversion process" by which potential power is mustered and applied. The second and third versions of the counterinsurgency story are of this sort. Denying the autonomy of high politics, such explanations argue instead that a state's performance in the international arena is determined by the character of its domestic political structure or national security bureaucracy. Thus, strong states may lose to weaker ones because they are crippled by bureaucratic infighting or domestic politics. Second, other explanations attribute the power paradox to policymakers misunderstanding a situation and so applying power in the wrong form or against the wrong target. These stress not the clear policy imperatives posed by the international system, but the ambiguity that characterizes its "messages." Thus, they focus on policymakers' analytic frameworks and the possibility that these may distort reality and result in policy failure.

Domestic Level Explanations

This class of explanations focuses on how events inside states determine their foreign policy. The shift of analytic focus is prompted by two observations: foreign policy is often internally incoherent and logically inconsistent with the dictates of the international system; and it is inextricably bound to low politics. Such explanations note that states are not unitary actors as realists assume but complex conglomerates of in-

[26] David Baldwin, "Power Analysis and World Politics," WP 31: 2 (January 1979), pp. 161–94.

dividuals and organizations, each with their own interests, capabilities, and definition of the national interest. Thus, foreign policy may be neither what is required by the international situation nor a reasoned prescription for coping with it. Policy may be merely the outcome of the political process of coalition and compromise among various policymakers. (Hence, the first law of bureaucratic politics: "action does not presuppose intention.")[27] Furthermore, policy change may reflect shifts in this domestic political or bureaucratic balance of power, not new imperatives from without.

Presidential Politics

A powerful variant of the domestic political structure explanation of American foreign policy—illustrated by the second version of the counterinsurgency story—targets the role of the president and the characteristics of the presidency. Presidents, incontestably the center of foreign policy formulation, often consider it their particular prerogative. The president's unique position allows him to structure and manipulate the foreign policy process. He has no superior to report to, stands at the center of the foreign policy process through control of the executive agencies, and serves as the surrogate for the national interest. As a result, however, foreign policy bears the clear imprint of presidential role requirements and the interests of the presidential team. The president must attend not only to foreign policy, but he must also oversee the totality of his program, keep an eye on his party's and his own fate at the polls, and worry about his place in history. Such concerns may have a sharp impact on what policy initiatives are pursued and when, thus making analysis of foreign policy in isolation from low politics impossible. Finally, the presidential politics approach suggests that the electoral cycle, not international events, explain policy changes which occur as a new president and presidential team take over, imposing new perspectives and programs.

Bureaucratic Politics

The bureaucratic politics approach—illustrated by the final version of the counterinsurgency story—focuses on "how politics within a government influence decisions and actions ostensibly directed out-

[27] Graham Allison, "Conceptual Models and the Cuban Missile Crisis," APSR 63: 3 (September 1969), p. 711.

ward."[28] It, too, denies the unity of the state as an actor in international politics and its utility as an unit of analysis. It argues, however, that attention to elected officials is misplaced. What matters is the national security bureaucracy staffed by career officials whose tenure and professional interests are relatively unaffected by electoral politics. Politicians may come and go and with them their appointees to the policymaking levels of the executive agencies. But the bureaucrats remain, able to control their controllers through command of the upward flow of information, analysis and options, and implementation of the downward flow of policy. Thus, attention shifts to the structure and functioning of these organizations and the interests and behavior of those who staff them.

Analysts stress that the bureaucracies are not mechanical devices, but complexes of individuals in varying roles. "Where you stand," notes Graham Allison, "depends on where you sit [and] for large classes of issues . . . the stance of a particular player can be predicted with high reliability from information about his seat."[29] Role requirements, however, may lead to behavior only indirectly related to international imperatives. Bureaucrats may equate the national security with the interests of the organization to which they belong, or even their own professional interests. No less important, the nature and limits of the organizations comprising the national security bureaucracy may also distort policy. Foreign policy, after all, requires finesse and delicate timing, while as James Thompson notes, "Organizations are . . . blunt instruments that tend to mash rather than slice."[30]

The problem is size and its concomitants, for size introduces the deadly logic of Murphy's law, i.e., that anything that can go wrong, will go wrong—and at the worst possible moment. The complexity of the issues requires that they be factored into their constituent parts for treatment by the appropriate pieces of the bureaucracy. This, in turn, requires the subsequent coordination of their solutions, generally in the absence of an overarching authority. But since the resultant conflicts are often irreconcilable, "officials reach consensus by designing an ambiguous policy which . . . avoids making choices on priorities and leaves organizations free to continue operating as they have in the past

[28] Morton Halperin, *Bureaucratic Politics and Foreign Policy* (Washington, D.C.: Brookings, 1974), p. 5.

[29] Graham Allison, *Essence of Decision: Explaining the Cuban Missile Crisis* (Boston: Little, Brown, 1971), p. 176.

[30] James Thompson, *Rolling Thunder: Understanding Policy and Program Failure* (Chapel Hill: University of North Carolina Press, 1980), p. 21.

and to control their own operations."[31] Finally, because of the size and complexity of the tasks they perform, large bureaucracies must develop standard operating procedures (SOPs) in advance. In crisis, however, these determine what information policymakers receive, the options they consider, and what they can do. Thus, administrative feasibility, not substance, shapes action.

Organizational essence or mission may also constrain responsiveness to international imperatives. This mission—the conception the staff holds of the organization's primary role[32]—serves an important function. (Each element of the national security bureaucracy is supposed to be a specialized instrument for doing *something*.) But bureaucrats may come to view their organization's mission as a surrogate for the national interest. Indeed, they may actually pursue actions contrary to the national interest because they serve the interests of the organization or sabotage others because they threaten those interests.

The bureaucratic politics approach thus suggests that neither shifts in the international situation nor of administration cause policy change. Instead, policy follows the iron law of bureaucratic inertia: "bureaucracies at rest tend to stay at rest; . . . bureaucracies in motion tend to stay in motion."[33] Furthermore, insofar as policy reflects the outcome of bargaining among organizational actors in terms of organizational concerns and the SOP's available to them, it will change as a result of changes in this process or in organizational SOP's.

POSSIBLE OBJECTIONS

Despite their power, domestic politics explanations of foreign policy content and change are also open to criticism. Two assumptions are particularly problematic. First, all such explanations assume that policy positions are defined by players' roles. But as Frances Rourke observes, "interorganizational competition . . . over jurisdictional matters is not the same as debate over issues of substantive policy."[34] Indeed, often what allows competition to remain at the jurisdictional level is the existence of shared assumptions and goals among organizations. Although seldom discussed because assumed, these assump-

[31] Morton H. Halperin, "Why Bureaucrats Play Games," *Foreign Policy* (Spring 1971), p. 74.

[32] See Halperin, *Bureaucratic Politics*, pp. 26–51, and Morton Halperin and Arnold Kanter, eds., *Readings in American Foreign Policy: A Bureaucratic Perspective* (Boston: Little, Brown, 1973), p. 10.

[33] Francis Rourke, *Bureaucracy and Foreign Policy* (Baltimore: Johns Hopkins University Press, 1972), p. 50.

[34] Ibid., p. 24.

tions and goals may structure and limit the policy debate. This, however, weakens the claim that role predicts policy position. Furthermore, insofar as shared ideas affect policy, analysis must account for what, and how accurate, these ideas are. Second, domestic politics analysts explain policy as the outcome of *inter*organizational bargaining and *intra*organizational interests and capabilities, both of which are insensitive to the international environment and may produce policy incoherence. Thus, they suggest that greater insulation of the presidency from crosspressures, more bureaucratic coordination, or better implementation would improve policy. They assume, in short, that the problems lie in the conversion of thought into action, not in the thought itself. But policymakers may misunderstand the challenges they face and may respond inappropriately, in which case better implementation may be counterproductive. Without reference to their assumptions and intentions, however, there is no way to tell whether the aim or implementation of policy is at fault.

Here objections to domestic politics explanations cross those aimed at realism. Realism assumes that states respond logically to the imperatives of the international system; yet neither these nor the national interest in the face of them are self-evident. States may have some aspects of their foreign policy imposed upon them, but in most states, most of the time, policy choices reflect leaders' interpretations of the environment and conception of alternatives. As Henry Kissinger notes, "the conjectural element" is the heart of foreign policymaking, "the need to gear actions to an assessment that cannot be proved true when it is made."[35] After all, international events are interpreted not by crystal balls but by policymakers who bring to the task their own assumptions. Their final visions may be meaningless without reference to these intellectual prisms.

Three issues underlie this general criticism. First, there are no unambiguous facts in international relations. Facts are the product of the analytic framework observers bring to them. For example, though on June 25, 1950, American policymakers had no doubt that South Korea was being attacked, debate raged over what it meant and hence what to do. Moreover, the assumptions underpinning analysis may change over time such that similar events provoke dissimilar responses. Second is the problem of policy choice. It is in part determined by the threat and institutional or political capabilities, but the limits are wide, and within them imagination and analysis shape policy content. (Observes

[35] *American Foreign Policy*, expanded ed. (New York: W. W. Norton, 1974), p. 14.

CHAPTER 2

Hugh Heclo, "governments not only 'power'; they also puzzle.")[36]
Again, understanding particular policy choices demands examination
of policymakers' assumptions. Finally, behind such calculations lie
questions of value. As Stanley Hoffmann observes, "The decisive question
is: what is it wise to risk, and what for?—a question to which the
reply is never completely provided by always ambiguous and somewhat adjustable data."[37] Nor is it possible to respond that policy is
merely a means to achieve a single, universally valued end: security. For
in all but the most extreme cases, the purposes of policy—what governments seek and why—are more complex. Without an ear for these, international politics is a ballet for the deaf.

Analysis at the Level of the Individual

Such objections suggest the need for explanations of foreign policy
which argue, in effect, that "where you stand depends on what you
think." This entails a double shift of focus: from attention to events and
organizations to individuals and from the objective world to the sub-
jective world perceived by key players. Such explanations do not imply,
as Arnold Wolfers suggests, that nations are "governed by mad men
who decide and act on the basis of inner impulses in response to a
purely imaginary world." They do argue, however, that it is wrong to
conclude, as does Wolfers, that "policy-making can, as a rule, be assumed to constitute a relatively rational response to existing and fairly
correctly perceived external conditions."[38] Instead, they contend systematic biases may influence policymakers' perceptions of reality and
their responses to it.

There are two basic varieties of analysis at the level of the individual.
First, some focus on the effects of individuals' psychiatric and psychological peculiarities on perception and policy choice. Such approaches
offer insights where particular individuals have played critical and idiosyncratic roles. Because of the focus on *an* individual and daunting information requirements, however, they offer little systematic explanation of policy and policy change. Consequently, this book treats only
the second variety of individual level analysis. These stress not idiosyncracies, but widely shared assumptions and analytic frameworks that

[36] Hugh Heclo, *Modern Social Politics in Britain and Sweden: From Relief to Income Maintenance* (New Haven: Yale University Press, 1974), p. 305.
[37] Stanley Hoffmann, *The State of War: Essays on the Theory and Practice of International Politics* (New York: Praeger, 1965), pp. 138–39.
[38] Arnold Wolfers, *Discord and Collaboration: Essays on International Politics* (Baltimore: Johns Hopkins University Press, 1979), pp. 43–44.

systematically affect how policymakers understand and respond to the international environment. To avoid confusion with the first variety, these explanations will be referred to as societal.

Societal explanations recognize that the operational environment (the international situation and bureaucratic or political role requirements) defines the bounds of decisionmaking. Within these bounds, however, they argue that policy choice and content are determined by how policymakers perceive, analyze, and respond to them. In the words of Michael Brecher, "the operational environment affects the results or outcomes of decisions directly but influences the choice among policy options, that is, the decisions themselves, only as it is filtered through the images of decision-makers. The link between Image and Decisions is indeed the master key to a valuable framework of foreign policy analysis."[39] This "image's" accuracy defines the prospects for policy success; changes in it may produce policy changes independent of changes in the operational environment.

Two types of societal explanations stand out: political culture and cognitive content. The former contends that "attitudes and opinions toward foreign policy questions are not only to be understood as responses to objective problems and situations, but as conditioned by culturally imposed qualities of character. These largely unconscious patterns of reaction and behavior strongly influence the perceptions, selection and evaluation of political reality."[40] As implied by the term culture, these psychocultural characteristics are presumed to be stable, pervasive, and peculiar to a given nation. In the American case, this means a long-lived, uniquely American way of seeing and responding to the world with uniquely American results. Thus, American exceptionalist analysts contend that American culture and our peculiar history explain why American foreign policymakers seem to "ask the wrong questions, turn to the wrong analyses and . . . in the end provoke the wrong result."[41] This explanation also suggests such mistakes will continue because these cultural characteristics are relatively immutable.

[39] Michael Brecher, *The Foreign Policy System of Israel* (New Haven: Yale University Press, 1972), pp. 4–5.

[40] Almond, *The American People and Foreign Policy*, p. 29. As defined in Gabriel Almond and Sidney Verba's *Civic Culture*, "The political culture of a nation is the particular distribution of patterns of orientation toward political objects among the members of the nation." Thus, they claim, "We can relate specific adult political attitudes and behavioral propensities to the manifest and latent political socialization experiences of childhood." "In other words, the connecting link between micropolitics and macropolitics is political culture" (Boston: Little, Brown, 1965), pp. 13, 32.

[41] Stanley Hoffmann, *Gulliver's Troubles*, p. 126.

Cognitive content models shift attention from cultural to intellectual factors. Cognitive content analysts derive policy content and change from the shared ideas and analytical frameworks with which policymakers analyze the international situation, generate policy options, and choose among them. They aim not to analyze what John Odell calls individuals' "causal map of the immediate situation"[42] but to identify the assumptions defining the evidence examined, the questions asked, and the range of "plausible" answers. Finally, such explanations suggest that policy change may be caused not only by shifts in the international or domestic environment but also by changes in these assumptions. And even when "situational factors may explain the rejection of an old policy, the timing of a policy change, or the degree of policy coherence," paradigm change alone may explain "the choice of a new policy from among the alternatives."[43]

The Modelmaker's Dilemma

At the heart of the cognitive content approach is the problem of paradigm and perception, or the modelmaker's dilemma. It begins with what T. H. White called "the obscurity of total detail" and so the necessary *prior* choice of a sorting mechanism. This has important implications for policymakers' understanding of events and responses to them. Without a paradigm—a set of rules and standards for evaluating data—the policymaker is lost: all problems, approaches, facts, and possible courses of action seem equally plausible. But with a paradigm, he or she can sort the relevant from the irrelevant, link new situations to past experiences, predict the future, and assess possible solutions. Furthermore, this paradigm may limit the policymakers' options by obscuring possible interpretations of events and blocking consideration of possible policies. Thus, to understand the course and content of policy, it is necessary to analyze not only the operational environment policymakers face but also their analysis of events and how it affects their actions.

This observation raises the two issues that drive cognitive content approaches: the accuracy of policymakers' paradigm and its amenability to modification. The importance of the former is self-evident, but the latter is often overlooked. In fact, the possibility of perfectability turns on a paradigm's explanatory, prescriptive, and ideological utility. First, since the point of paradigms is to make reality accessible, the fail-

[42] Odell, *U.S. International Monetary Policy*, p. 62.
[43] Ibid.

ure to provide convincing explanations should stimulate change. Second, as prescription is the application of explanation to achieve a desired end, its failure should raise questions about the standing explanation. Finally, since paradigms legitimate the status quo policy or distribution of prestige, authority, and repute, challenges to this status quo, possibly completely unrelated to the paradigm, may either contribute to its demise or legitimize its successor.

Against these potential sources of change, however, stand impressive barriers.[44] First is the very familiarity of the reigning paradigm. As Michael Howard observes, "History does not repeat itself; historians repeat one another."[45] The paradigm is embedded in texts, curricula, other disciplines, general knowledge, and public policy; thus, change will be no faster than the incremental process by which these are revised. (In fact, Bernard Barber suggests that new paradigms come from the young who have no stake in the old and thus that change may be generational.)[46] Similarly, organizations established to fulfill a certain function develop an institutional inertia which may result in policies outliving their utility.

Second, explanatory utility can work against paradigm change as well as for it. Precisely because it has worked so well, a paradigm's proponents are loath to let it go. In part, this reflects a psychological tendency toward cognitive consistency. ("Human beings are quick to categorize the miraculous," note Manfred Eigen and Ruthild Winkler; "they attach an adjective to it and assign it a place in their world view.")[47] But there are also strong practical reasons to force new observations into old molds or ignore them altogether. Michael Polanyi argues that "if every anomaly observed in my laboratory were taken at its face value, research would instantly degenerate into a wild-goose chase after imaginary fundamental novelties."[48] Scientists, policymakers, and others thus attempt to manage anomalous data by adding bells and whistles to existing theory or explaining it as the exception that proves the rule.

[44] See Bernard Barber, "Resistance by Scientists to Scientific Discovery," in *The Sociology of Science*, eds. Bernard Barber and Walter Hirsch (New York: Free Press, 1963) for one study of such barriers in the natural sciences.

[45] Michael Howard, "The Use and Abuse of History," *Parameters* 11: 1 (March 1981), p. 11.

[46] Barber, "Resistance," pp. 554–55.

[47] Manfred Eigen and Ruthild Winkler, *Laws of the Game: How the Principles of Nature Govern Chance* (New York: Knopf, 1981), p. 166.

[48] Michael Polyani, "The Unaccountable Element in Science" in *Knowing and Being, Essays by Michael Polanyi*, ed. Marjorie Green (London: Routledge & Kegan Paul, 1969), p. 114.

The difficulty goes deeper, however, to the very nature and function of paradigms. Paradigms determine what *are* facts, what arrangements of facts are made, and how plausible each arrangement is considered.[49] A paradigm "helps determine what phenomena are important and . . . marks out areas to be ignored either because they can shed no light on problems defined as interesting or because the paradigm indicates that there can be nothing there. Indeed, instruments built on these assumptions may not be able to detect unexpected phenomena."[50] As a result, we may miss discoveries that are literally right before our eyes, while because paradigms define events, it is difficult for events to reshape them. The information necessary to confirm a new theory will be categorized according to the old one. Thus, the information seldom appears for what it is, and is often hard to retrieve and reorder. Moreover, the reigning paradigm determines which explanations of the new data make sense. Indeed, even in the natural sciences, "direct experimental tests of hypotheses are often given less weight than the conformity of the hypotheses with a general theoretical superstructure."[51]

Similar problems inhibit failed prescriptions from producing paradigm change. Because everyone shares the same paradigm, it is seldom considered a possible source of failure. Instead, failure of a particular prescription is likely to provoke questions relating to its implementation (and hence bureaucratic analysts' belief that better management means better policy).

Finally, a paradigm's ideological utility may also hinder its change. After all, "every game has its rules that set it apart from the surrounding world of reality and establish its own standards of value. Anyone who wants to 'play' has to follow those rules."[52] And, as Kuhn notes, paradigms determine the "rules and standards" of the game that define play and, by extension, the players.[53] The rules are embodied in an authority structure built upon, legitimized by, and reinforcing the reigning paradigm. In fact, in government the function of presidential advisors "is to insist on . . . the accepted paradigm, and to refine, extend and articulate it. One should not expect authority to perceive and act

[49] Kuhn, *The Structure of Scientific Revolutions*, p. 52.
[50] Robert Jervis, *Perception and Misperception in International Politics* (Princeton: Princeton University Press, 1976), p. 156.
[51] S. G. Brush, cited in André Courand and Michael Meyer, "The Scientist's Code," *Minerva* 14 (Spring 1976), p. 86.
[52] Eigen and Winkler, *Laws of the Game*, p. 4. In *End Game* Samuel Beckett puts the thought more bluntly: "Since that's the way we're playing it . . . let's play it that way."
[53] *Structure*, p. 11.

against its accepted cognitions."[54] Thus, a paradigm's role in defining and justifying the status quo may inhibit change for reasons unrelated to content.

Here lies a final question critical for the cognitive content approach: which paradigms under which conditions will display more or less dysfunctional continuity? Although the categories overlap, three kinds of variables explain differences in adequacy and perfectability: substantive, institutional, and ideological. Two substantive issues stand out: the nature and definition of the subject matter and supporting evidence. As for the definition of the subject, a paradigm's falsifiability will be affected by its breadth, aim, and degree of reification. The broader a paradigm's domain, the more difficult the development of tests of or alternatives to it. Similarly, the greater the extent to which a paradigm defines a "central tendency," the more difficult it will be to falsify since by definition "outliers" will be just that. Finally, the more reified the subject matter, the more difficult it will be to test or falsify; and, in the extreme, falsification will be reduced to a matter of semantics.

The unavoidable reification problem becomes critical in interaction with the nature of the subject matter. Evidence from the natural sciences suggests that, even in such matters as the conservation of energy, falsification is difficult. Paradigms of political behavior, however, pose greater problems. Since the subject matter exists as an object of study only by prior definition, the assumptions on which reification is based are beyond discussion. In fact, exploration within political paradigms may be no more than an elaboration of the preconceptions from which they were fashioned.

Ambiguous data further complicate this picture. Clear evidence is rare anyway, but at the fringes of paradigm where new paradigms develop ambiguous data are inescapable. Thus,

> One's theoretical model becomes simultaneously more necessary and potentially more dangerous. There is an increased tendency to interpret the very data which would lead one to change one's model in such a way as to preserve that model. Without the model one could not say if change had taken place, but with the model one is less likely to see the evidence for change.[55]

[54] Amos Perlmutter, "The Presidential Political Center and Foreign Policy: A Critique of the Revisionist and Bureaucratic-Political Orientations," WP 27: 1 (October 1974), p. 106.

[55] Raymond Bauer, cited in Joseph de Rivera, *The Psychological Dimension of Foreign Policy* (Columbus, Ohio: Merrill, 1968), p. 29.

Furthermore, the more confident the analyst and the greater his commitment to the established view, the less skeptical he will be. By the same token, the more reified the subject matter, the more daunting are the problems of ambiguous data. Indeed, "in most political questions it is . . . impossible to separate judgments about the validity of specific inferences from the larger question of the merits of contending theories and images that both support and are supported by the inferences."[56] Under such circumstances, the room for the injection of societal or ideological prejudices increases, further reducing the likelihood that external evidence alone will promote paradigm change.

The institutional setting in which a paradigm operates also affects the likelihood it will be modified. At one extreme the laboratory exists to push the limits of existing paradigms and embodies scientists' commitment to the effort. At the other revealed religions demand followers' devotion to *the* paradigm to which there is no alternative. Policymakers fall in between. They would like to be right, but the White House, for example, is neither a forum for discussion of the underlying assumptions of foreign policy nor a lab for testing ambiguous data from the field.[57] Indeed, notes Morton Halperin, policymakers "bend over backwards to show that they support shared images, particularly those with strong support within the society as well as the government."[58]

Finally, the greater the ideological utility of a paradigm, the less likely its modification on merit—particularly if the subject matter is highly reified. It was ultimately possible, for example, to overcome the Church's opposition to the ideas of Galileo and Copernicus; the earth does go around the sun. But in the reified realm of social and political paradigms, where subject matter and evidence are imbued with ideological coloration, the prospects for such demonstrations of truth are far less sanguine. Here the ideological utility of a paradigm may outweigh concern for whether it is right.

POSSIBLE OBJECTIONS

The problems of paradigm adequacy and perfectability also suggest the possible objections to societal explanations of foreign policy content and change. If policymakers' paradigms, cultural or cognitive, are tightly reality-related, then such approaches offer little. Conversely, the

[56] Jervis, *Perception and Misperception*, p. 171. See, for example, Thompson, *Rolling Thunder*, p. 87.

[57] As Dean Acheson observed, the farmer who pulled up his plants every morning to see how much their roots had grown during the night would not be very productive. Cited in Gaddis, *Strategies of Containment*, pp. 87–88.

[58] Halperin, *Bureaucratic Politics*, p. 152.

greater the paradigms' continuity and the more marked the changes when they occur, the more powerful they are as explanatory tools. More important, the more dysfunctional the continuity and/or non-reality-related the change, the greater the prospects that such explanations will elucidate otherwise inexplicable twists of foreign policy.

Societal approaches must thus demonstrate that policymakers' paradigms are bad enough to merit attention. Specifically, American exceptionalists must prove there exists a uniquely American, unchanging, significantly distorting way of perceiving and responding to the world which has systematic, identifiable consequences. Cognitive content analysts need not show a fixed paradigm, but they must produce one sufficiently out of step with the flow of events to have systematic, identifiable consequences otherwise inconsistent with the expectations of more parsimonious models.

Conclusion

In sum, this chapter has both outlined five alternative types of explanation about why governments do what they do overseas when they do it and suggested possible objections to each. Realists assert that foreign policy is a state's reasoned response to international imperatives and changes as they do. Presidential politics analysts contend that responses to international imperatives are shaped by presidential interests and role requirements and therefore change with the electoral cycle. Defining policy as "what happens," bureaucratic politics analysts explain how the characteristics of the national security bureaucracy and the interests of career bureaucrats determine the content, timing, and implementation of policy. Finally, those favoring societal explanations argue that policymakers' assessment of international imperatives and prescriptions for managing them depend on the cultural or cognitive framework they employ; thus, continuity and/or change in it may explain the course of policy.

It is impossible to choose among these five alternatives except by testing them simultaneously in specific circumstances. I will do so in the case studies comprising part III of this book. Before undertaking this task, however, it is necessary to examine the sources, content, and characteristics of policymakers' ideas.

PART II

▲

Appeals to reason or to the nature of the universe have been used throughout history to enshrine existing hierarchies as proper and inevitable. The hierarchies rarely endure for more than a few generations, but the arguments, refurbished for the next round of social institutions, cycle endlessly.

STEPHEN JAY GOULD

The difficulty lies not in the new ideas, but in escaping from the old ones.

JOHN MAYNARD KEYNES

Part II focuses on the intellectual underpinnings of postwar American counterinsurgency policy. These three chapters examine Americans' assumptions concerning the Third World and their assumptions' characteristics as ideas, as opposed to their substance. Chapter 3 studies the ideas behind counterinsurgency in their most abstract form—academic political development theory—traces their historical development, and explores their links to other disciplines and common knowledge. Chapter 4 then treats these same ideas as embodied in security and development doctrine, the United States' basic policy approach to the Third World. Finally, chapter 5 analyzes the marriage of these two strains of thought in the counterinsurgency doctrine of the 1960s.

Two caveats are in order. First, this unabashed focus on ideas is not a dismissal of alternative explanations of foreign policy. Rather, part II provides the necessary groundwork for the structured comparison of competing explanations offered in the case studies of Part III. To do so, chapters 3, 4, and 5 examine the two issues essential for cognitive content analysis: the adequacy and perfectability of policymakers' paradigms. If it can be established that policymakers' cognitive framework for analyzing and choosing responses to revolutionary change in the Third World is inaccurate and, moreover, resistant to improvement, then there is a case for considering a cognitive content approach to explaining why American policymakers have acted as they have when

43

confronted by insurgent challenges to friendly Third World governments. Part II builds just such a case. Second, the chapter order of Part II does not imply that social scientists' ideas determine the course or content of American foreign policy. As suggested in chapter 1, academics play three overlapping roles: the deep sources of policymakers' ideas, legitimizers of their actions, and, at certain junctures, articulators of policy-relevant versions of widely shared but inchoate notions. Each of these varieties of academic–policymaker ties is explored in the chapters of Part II.

THE ARGUMENT IN BRIEF

In 1945 Americans faced a new, complex, and threatening world. From self-imposed isolation, the United States had emerged a world power; and, on the opposite side of the globe, so had the Soviet Union. Europe lay in ruins between, its empires already slipping away. Suddenly Americans had to understand not only the narrow world as it had been but also a world of peoples whose names they could not pronounce and whose cultures baffled them. The hitherto ignored Third World stood at the center of attention, but Americans knew little about it. To cope with the new challenge, they needed an analytic lens through which to view the confusing dazzle, a means of sorting the important from the insignificant and identifying trends against the background. They needed to know who held power and who would, where politics were and where they were going. They needed to know what policies the United States should pursue to defend and promote its interests in this new arena of conflict.

Here, as in many other areas, the requirements of world leadership stimulated a frantic scanning of old ideas for those which might meet novel needs, a scramble to develop new ones, and no small measure of soul-searching. Yet out of the ferment just one coherent set of ideas concerning Third World change prevailed, while many others were ignored. Moreover, despite limited contact between social scientists and policymakers, the same set of ideas came to reign in both the ivory tower and the halls of government. And it has endured, remarkably unscathed by academic criticism, empirical falsification and the failure of policies based upon it. This is the puzzle of Part II: what explains the similarity of academic and governmental responses to the Third World, the potency of these notions, their inadequacies, and the failure to perceive or correct them?

The answers lie in the content and characteristics of this dominant set of ideas and its political, social, and intellectual role. This role can-

44

not be analyzed in a vacuum; these ideas can be understood only in their historical context. Rather like a business, they must meet the market test: no market, no theory; no market, no doctrine. Yet as in the real world, the market is a notoriously bad indicator of objective worth. High sales are no proof of quality; bad ideas, like bad products, may be sold for a long time and may do serious damage before they disappear from the shelf. To comprehend this set of ideas' success and endurance requires going beyond content to consideration of their intellectual antecedents and characteristics as ideas. The following chapters thus analyze the sources, substance, normative conclusions, and embeddedness of American political development theory, security and development, and counterinsurgency doctrine from the dual perspectives of intellectual content and characteristics. In brief, it argues that the nature, popularity, longevity, and failure of the ideas underlying them can best be explained in terms of their familiarity, utility, and method.

Familiarity, Utility, and Method

At one level, academics' and policymakers' ideas appear to be directly connected to their circumstances. They are supposed to be responses to reality, whether efforts to understand or manage it. The three chapters which follow thus explore what both groups thought, how accurate their ideas were, and how much those ideas have changed. Yet while critical, such an inquiry is insufficient since it cannot explain the endurance of ideas which distort reality or cripple efforts to respond to it. To account for this requires exploration of the other characteristics which make these ideas so appealing—even though wrong.

The first characteristic is familiarity. Despite claims of novelty, the supposedly new notions proposed after the war owe much of their meteoric rise and subsequent durability to their comfortable homeyness. In their method and major assumptions, conclusions and implicit value scheme, they replicate the main lines of traditional Western social analysis. As a result, these new ideas proved immediately accessible to all, were reconfirmed in other fields, and rang true even to nonspecialists. This gave these ideas a distinct advantage over others in the intellectual ferment. Familiarity allowed an intellectual incrementalism which made the new ideas easier to peddle since consumers immediately recognized them. There are institutional differences in the extent to which this applies in academia and government, but they are differences of degree, not kind. For academics and policymakers alike, brand recognition offers the same benefits it offers soap manufacturers, benefits which accrue irrespective of product quality. Conversely, the familiar-

45

ity which gave these ideas their market share also posed a high barrier to entry for truly new ideas, again irrespective of their quality.

But more than familiarity is needed to explain longevity, for many a popular product has ended a mere museum piece. A full explanation also requires reference to ideas' utility, or rather utilities: explanatory, prescriptive, and ideological.

The explanatory utility of the familiar ideas academics and policymakers cling to is obvious: they offer a powerful and parsimonious explanation of the complex politics of change in the Third World. Nor is this a matter of raising parsimony to artificial prominence. To the contrary, as Mancur Olson notes, "Since it is costly to acquire and remember information, parsimonious or concise and simple explanations must, other things being equal, be preferred."[1] This is perhaps especially true for hard-pressed policymakers who have neither the time nor the resources to use complex explanations and who must depend on simple, broadly applicable rules of thumb, but it clearly applies to academics, too. Conversely, alternatives not possessing explanatory utility may as a result be ignored, even though they provide a more accurate explanation of events.

Extending this logic, a set of ideas will gain in utility in proportion to its applicability to action. This prescriptive utility is critical to policymakers for whom explanations which do not produce unambiguous policy guidance will be academic. Yet prescriptive utility is also important for academics, especially those who desire a public function or depend on government support. Again, the postwar intellectual ferment bred many ideas, yet those lacking prescriptive utility, like those lacking explanatory utility, have done less well in the marketplace of ideas than those with them, irrespective of absolute accuracy.

Finally, the dominant explanation of events in the Third World served ideological ends. After all, few comfortably embrace ideas antithetical to their values and beliefs. Most select those that conform to them and support action in pursuit of them (i.e., those with ideological utility). Thus, not surprisingly, American explanations of change in the Third World justified direct developmental involvement just as the *mission civilatrice* and "white man's burden" justified French and British imperialism. For American society, it justified the self-satisfaction of the 1950s and early 1960s by proving that the United States had reached the terminal station of modernity. Best of all, it served its purveyors. The model of modern man is the rational, secular, achievement-

---

[1] Mancur Olson, Jr., *The Rise and Decline of Nations: Economic Growth, Stagflation and Social Rigidities* (New Haven: Yale University Press, 1982), p. 12.

oriented social scientist, the social cryptographer of the new world, while the policymaker is stage manager of the revolution of modernization.

One additional aspect of the dominant explanation requires comment, although unlike familiarity and utility it is not a necessary attribute of successful ideas in general. This might loosely be called its method. The dominant explanation of Third World change is couched in strictly universal terms. In its academic form, its concepts are highly reified, its variables vaguely specified, and its claims seldom operationalized. It is thus largely unfalsifiable. Moreover, because it is intentionally a theory of the central tendency, a theory of summarization not specification, its methodological armature denies the process by which the slow accumulation of anomalous data generates pressure for paradigm change. The governmental version is also universal in its explanation and tends prescriptively toward universally applicable recipes for action. In each case, the dismissal of specifics inhibits competition from more subtle explanations and has extended its shelf life.

In this way, familiarity and utility operate in conjunction with context and content to shape ideas' success in the marketplace. The latter are important, but, other things being equal, ideas with more of the former will prevail over others which are merely accurate. Familiarity and utility thus explain this particular assessment of Third World politics' safe market niche and the lack of acclaim for a new one despite falsification of the old and failure of policies built on its prescriptions. Alternatives meet none of the criteria for market success. The new explanations are unfamiliar—indeed assault familiar assumptions—and suffer from anti-utility. They offer not parsimony but explanations as nuanced as the world itself. The variables they identify are beyond manipulation such that they offer no practical policy prescriptions. Ideologically, they suggest that the West's self congratulation is unmerited, that the First World–Third World dichotomy is overstated, and that neither social scientists nor policymakers have much to boast about. It is not a winning combination. In short, Part II argues that there are solid grounds to doubt the adequacy and perfectability of academics' and policymakers' understanding of political change in the Third World. This being the case, there are also solid grounds for adopting a cognitive content approach to understanding American counterinsurgency involvements. Indeed, it may explain both the actual content of policy and the otherwise incomprehensible continuity of policy over forty years despite failure and very different conditions in the target countries.

3

FLIGHT, FALL, AND PERSISTENCE:
POLITICAL DEVELOPMENT THEORY

This chapter examines the content and characteristics of American political scientists' view of change in the Third World. While most of the
book focuses on governmental consumers of ideas, here attention rests
on the production of ideas and the process by which a specific set of
them came to market. This attention to social scientists does not imply
that they exercised a determinitive influence over policy. Rather, this
chapter examines political development theory not for itself but for the
lens it offers through which to view the sources, assumptions, and analytic consequences of the intellectual tradition shared by policymakers
and political scientists. As a result, the analysis necessarily slights political development theory's diversity and downplays the debates that
have raged in the field since its inception. But neither the diversity nor
the debate are important for understanding policy. Where policymakers employed political development theory directly, they drew on
the mainstream outlined here and where they thought the ideas were
their own, they resonated with it.

In the twenty five years after World War II, political development
knew an extraordinary vogue. From Icarus-like flight, however, it tum-
bled back to earth in the late 1960s. It was not, unfortunately, for having flown too close to the truth but because of shoddy workmanship,
an overweight of hidden baggage from the past, and structural flaws in
wing design. Critics found political development theory value-laden
and often marred by ignorance and flights of fancy. They found its concepts vague and its variables misspecified, poorly operationalized, and
seldom causally connected. Although intended to explain rapid political change, its models proved static, ahistorical, and even apolitical.
Where it was supposed to differentiate among cases, it muddied distinctions; where it was to be methodologically innovative, it proved to
be a refurbished version of eighteenth- and nineteenth-century ideas.
But despite these criticisms, no alternative has achieved widespread acceptance. Moreover, in its absence, the key substantive and normative
claims of the old continue to hold sway. The question is: Why? Why
the sudden and lavish attention? Why the abject failure? Why the delay
in recognizing failure? Why no acclaim for new, improved theories?
And why the endurance of the old? The easiest way to answer these

questions is to examine political development theory's content and characteristics, its familiarity and utility.

FAMILIARITY

Familiarity provides the simplest explanation for the rise, durability, and widespread acceptance of political development theory. Despite the theory's largely American habitat, its origins lie deep in the western European tradition of social analysis exemplified by Hegel, Marx, Darwin, Weber, Tönnies, and Durkheim.[1] Political development's key inheritance from this tradition was eighteenth-century histoire raisonnée or natural history and its nineteenth-century version, the Comparative Method. Histoire raisonnée is an ideal type, history as it ought to be. It is a logical construct, deduced from a set of universal axioms abstracted beyond the realm of human and temporal contingencies. From the axioms, historians assembled a smooth, universal, evolutionary continuum of logically linked stages—a historical Great Chain of Being—through which humankind and history proceed, propelled by equally universal forces of change.[2] The forces of change, however, seldom possessed causative power; they were descriptive labels attached to characteristics of society believed to change from one stage to another. The authors saw progress as inevitable and inevitably directional from lower to higher forms of society, knowledge, religion, and so on. Inevitably, too, the higher forms possessed what they took as the defining characteristics of their own society.

Writers of the nineteenth century took over and embellished histoire raisonnée. As exploration and imperialism brought new cultures into view, they were classified and placed in the appropriate niches along the presumed progression from primitive to civilized. Where there appeared to be gaps, searches began for transitional types, the most famous of which was, of course, the missing link between man and ape (a position early naturalists thought might be filled by Hottentots).[3] Charles Darwin then contributed the seductive imagery of growth. Where previous versions of the Great Chain of Being were static sys-

[1] This tradition has taken on different disciplinary faces with each subsequent hegemonic system. In the Spanish empire, it wore a legal and theological mask, in the French and British empires it wore historical and anthropological masks respectively, and in the United States the masks are economics and political science. These differences have important implications, but the underlying tradition remains largely unchanged.

[2] Robert Nisbet, *Social Change and History: Aspects of the Western Theory of Development* (New York: Oxford University Press, 1969), p. 157.

[3] Ali Mazrui, "From Social Darwinism to Current Theories of Modernization: A Tradition of Analysis," WP 21: 1 (October 1968), p. 70.

tems of classification, Darwin's embodied a dynamic process of change. It also had implications for the analysis of society. To some, Darwin's work provided a biological basis for differences among individuals and cultures, to others it supplied an analytic approach.[4] Either way, "survival of the fittest" both justified Western imperialism and offered an optimistic vision of the future for primitives who, through discipline and development, might be saved.

But social theories of evolution could not replicate the theory of biological evolution. The biological theory was populational and statistical. Its social variant was and is, to this day, a typological construction.[5] Moreover, it preceded the evidence used to support it. Rather than constructing a system of classification on observable characteristics of cultures, nineteenth- and later twentieth-century comparativists typed them in terms of logically deduced categories provided by histoire raisonnée. The accumulation of evidence merely reconfirmed preconceptions.

Classical sociology, particularly the work of Tönnies, Weber, and Durkheim, provided one of the two main conduits through which histoire raisonnée flooded into political development theory. All share the major assumptions of histoire raisonnée. Most important, the predominant mind-set of individuals composing a society determines everything from social mores to political institutions. Moreover, this mind-set and the social relationships derived from it come in modes—coherent wholes of interdependent values, beliefs, and attitudes on the one hand, and laws, institutions, forms of economic organization, and social structures on the other.[6] Ideal type modes (each a "terminus of history" in Sir Henry Maine's phrase) define the poles of human behavior, social organization, and history. Movement from one to the other results from the inexorable pressure of the superior mental mode and the social structures deriving from it. Once started, change is inevitable, total, directional, and imminent within the minds and structures of society.

This view of societies as unified wholes was both apolitical and inherently conservative. In fact, politics as normally understood had no place in such a picture, nor did power. Since all institutions derive from the shared values of society, all are, by definition, legitimate and au-

---

[4] Thus, according to Fredrick Engels, "As Darwin discovered the law of evolution in . . . nature, so Marx discovered the law of evolution in human history." Cited in ibid., p. 81.

[5] Nisbet, *Social Change*, p. 162.

[6] Ferdinand Tönnies, *Community and Society*, trans. and ed. Charles P. Loomis (New York: Harper Torchbooks, 1963) pp. 4–5, 231–32.

thoritative. As Max Weber put it, the "basis of every system of author-ity, and correspondingly of every kind of willingness to obey, is a belief, a belief by virtue of which persons exercising authority are lent pres-tige."[7] Thus, for Emile Durkheim, the state is "the collective type in-carnate" and crimes are "acts universally disapproved of by members of each society [and which] shock sentiments . . . found in all healthy consciences."[8] Similarly, Tönnies defines the law as "nothing but com-mon will" and declares that public opinion has "decided tendencies to urge the state to use its irresistible power to force everyone to do what is useful and leave undone what is damaging."[9] The very existence of the status quo vouches for its legitimacy and reduces all differences with it to evidence of an unhealthy conscience.

Psychology and particularly anthropology provided the second ma-jor source of similar assumptions for political development theory. In-deed, its proximate roots lie in the psychocultural approach, a hybrid that flourished in the 1940s and 1950s. Two things accounted for po-litical scientists' attraction to these two disciplines: their successes dur-ing the war and what they seemed to promise—all encompassing, value-free explanations for the behavior of widely differing peoples.

Social science achieved its first political recognition during World War II. Earlier, economists had played a limited role in government, but with the war interest blossomed. Political scientists went to work in various agencies, but anthropology and psychology caught officials' imagination. They did not win the war—indeed, many felt they had no impact at all—but it offered the first taste of the excitement of being there.[10] Political scientists felt left out, betrayed by what Gabriel Al-mond later called their "primitive theoretical and methodological tools."[11] In response, they reached out to steal back a bit of the fire. The 1944 APSA Panel on Comparative Government called for a "bold and sweeping" conception of the "lebensraum of comparative govern-ment" that "must bring into play economics and statistics, social psy-chology and political philosophy, cultural anthropology and intellec-

[7] Max Weber, *The Theory of Social and Economic Organization*, trans. and ed. A. M. Henderson and Talcott Parsons (New York: Free Press, 1964), p. 382.

[8] Emile Durkheim, *The Division of Labor in Society* (New York: Free Press, 1964), pp. 73–74.

[9] Tönnies, *Community and Society*, pp. 190, 230.

[10] Gene Lyons, *The Uneasy Partnership: Social Science and the Federal Government in the Twentieth Century* (New York: Russell Sage, 1969), pp. 83, 111–22, 174–80, and Leonard Doob, "The Utilization of Social Scientists in the Overseas Branch of the Office of War Information," APSR 41: 4 (1947), pp. 649–67.

[11] Gabriel Almond, "Anthropology, Political Behavior, and International Relations," WP 2: 2 (January 1950), p. 282.

tual history."[12] The call was repeated by the 1953 APSA Seminar on Comparative Politics which laid the foundations of political development theory.[13]

Political scientists' pursuit of the "lebensraum of comparative government" had far-reaching results. In part, the spectacle simply provided amusement as an "old and tired political science offers herself in a comically traditional marriage, bringing her cumbersome dowry of data to be reduced and refined by psychology, the arrogant playboy of the Western mind."[14] But the "systematic looting of the conceptual thesaurus of social science"[15] also resulted in the unquestioning, often unwitting, acceptance of the underlying assumptions of anthropology and psychology, reinforced the legacy of histoire raisonnée, and added new problems, too.

On the surface, few things link twentieth century functionalist anthropology and its evolutionist precursors. The latter imagined a single evolutionary path along which all societies move toward Western forms, each replicating the features of all others at a given stage of development; functionalist anthropologists, on the other hand, stressed the uniqueness of each culture. Universality reentered by the back door, however. Functionalists countered the atomism of cultural relativism with a theory of universal human needs to which all societies must respond. Cultures could thus be compared in terms of how they responded and then be placed accordingly on a developmental continuum from primitive to advanced. The characteristics used to type responses to universal needs were the same as those used earlier by the adepts of histoire raisonnée and the Comparative Method.

At the level of the individual a similar, hierarchical scheme of classification also marked the work of leading psychologists of the day. Where functionalist anthropology stressed universal social needs and processes, psychological theories stressed universal psychological needs and processes. Thus, Abraham Maslow, for example, imagined a hierarchy of needs ranging from survival to self-actualization. Individuals, he theorized, must meet lower-level needs before occupying themselves with higher-order needs, and both their mental set and behavior

[12] Karl Loewenstein, "Report on the Research Panel on Comparative Government," APSR 38: 3 (June 1944), p. 542.

[13] Roy Macridis and Richard Cox, "Research in Comparative Politics: Seminar Report," APSR 47: 3 (September 1953), pp. 641–57.

[14] Philip Rieff, "Psychology and Politics: The Freudian Connection," WP 7: 2 (January 1955), p. 304.

[15] Herbert Goldhamer, "Fashion and Social Science," WP 6: 3 (April 1954), p. 398.

are determined by which need they confront.[16] Implicitly, often explicitly, these formulations made clear that higher is better. It was but a short step to attribute lower-order needs to primitives and traditional societies as a whole, while defining modern societies as self-actualizing.

Here anthropology's and psychology's substantive contribution to political development theory met that of classical sociology, again in the form of an inherently conservative bias toward the status quo. Once more, the key was the "unity assumption"; that individuals are unified wholes whose values, attitudes, and behavior form a coherent system; that their societies are also coherent wholes of interdependent values and institutions; and that the values, attitudes, and behavior of individuals in a society and the values embodied in its institutions replicate and reinforce each other. Thus, for anthropologist Ruth Benedict,

> The life history of the individual is first and foremost an accommodation to the patterns and standards traditionally handed down in his community. . . . By the time he can talk, he is the little creature of his culture, and by the time he is grown and able to take part in its activities, its habits are his habits, its beliefs his beliefs, its impossibilities his impossibilities.[17]

Continuity of the status quo follows directly. As Margaret Mead noted approvingly, societies are "a circular system within which the newborn child . . . receives, perpetuates, and stimulates behavior in others in terms of the entire cultural tradition, so that the method of child rearing, . . . religious beliefs, the political system, are all conditions within which a given kind of personality develops."[18] In short, the status quo exists because people believe in it (and can imagine nothing else), and it will continue because they and the institutions of the status quo will teach future generations to believe. Conversely, not to believe means to be a deviant.

This culturally determined standard of behavior seemed to avoid ethnocentrism. A society could be regarded as "an ethical system . . . a set of signposts to the good and virtuous life."[19] For the outside observer, common practice in any society is ethical by definition; it can be

[16] Abraham Maslow, *Motivation and Personality* (New York: Harper & Row, 1954).

[17] Ruth Benedict, *Patterns of Culture* (New York: Mentor, 1960), p. 18.

[18] Margaret Mead, "The Study of National Character," in Daniel Lerner and Harold Lasswell, eds., *The Policy Sciences: Recent Developments in Scope and Method* (Stanford, Calif.: Stanford University Press, 1951), p. 74.

[19] Robert Redfield, *The Little Community: Viewpoints for the Study of a Human Whole*, The Gottesman Lectures, Uppsala University (Stockholm: Almquist and Wiksells Boktryekeri, AB, 1955), p. 46.

no other way. Thus, for example, Everett Hagen argues that "the authoritarian hierarchical traditional social structure must have persisted because submitting to authority from above . . . was satisfying and . . . because the conditions of life recreated personalities, generation after generation, in which it continued to be so."[20] Similarly, Harold Lasswell declares that in "caste societies the serf identifies himself with a master–serf group . . . in which the primary ego symbol of the individual serf is permanently reconciled to occupying a subordinate position."[21]

But anthropologists had to explain change as well as continuity. To do so, they turned to "cultural diffusion," a process consisting of external stimulus and internal adjustment. In its crudest form, change is "a process of reaction" by lower civilizations to a dynamic higher civilization that disrupts the stable, self-reinforcing circle of values, behavior, and institutions that characterize them in their pristine state. The disruption produces cognitive and cultural dissonance, setting off a process of readjustment which ends when the affected society approximates the higher civilization. In practical terms, argued Bronislaw Malinowski, this means that "Europeans contribute the initiative and driving force. . . . They largely determine the form of the new cultural realities." The result, he concluded, is "one of the most significant phases in human history, that is, the present Westernization of the world."[22]

The beneficial consequences of cultural diffusion notwithstanding, anthropologists and psychologists feared for the individual and society in the "no-man's-land of change" between "tribalism" and "Western culture." Many came to see their role as that of manager of modernization and advisor on "the big practical problems [of] constructive colonial statesmanship." After all, "the practical man is interested in culture change, the administrator in political and legal adjustments, the missionary in the change of religion and morals, the settler and the entrepreneur in the possibilities of labor, indigenous production and consumption." As for the native, "in order to progress, [he] often has to pass through a stage of chaos and disorientation, and . . . would have to be tided over this stage."[23]

---

[20] Everett Hagen, "How Economic Growth Begins: A Theory of Social Change," *Journal of Social Issues* 19: 1 (January 1963), p. 23.

[21] Harold Lasswell, "Personality, Prejudice, and Politics," WP 3: 3 (April 1951), p. 405. Condorcet observed that such claims "make nature herself an accomplice in the crime of political inequality." Cited in Gould, *The Mismeasure of Man*, p. 21.

[22] Bronislaw Malinowski, *The Dynamics of Cultural Change: An Inquiry into Race Relations in Africa* (New Haven: Yale University Press, 1961), pp. 64, 3.

[23] Ibid., pp. 64, 6, 71.

UTILITY

Explanatory Utility

From these familiar roots grew political development theory. Its potency, however, derived from more than its old-shoe fit. No less important was its explanatory utility, for it provided a classification system which placed all societies along a single normal growth curve from tradition to modernity. The system was not only directional but explicitly teleological. " 'Modern' means being Western," declared Edward Shils, and modernization, echoed Reinhard Bendix, is "all those social and political changes that accompanied industrialization in . . . Western civilization."[24] This classificatory system offered political development theorists the same advantages its earlier versions had offered their predecessors. On the one hand, it allowed them to ignore the diversity of traditional cultures and concentrate instead on the crosscultural regularities defining a society's position on the developmental continuum. On the other, it provided a powerful predictive tool since "the utility of the developmental approach . . . is not merely that it groups systems according to factors of normative or historical interest, but that it groups them according to the kinds of *futures* which they face."[25]

Political development theory also adopted the simplifying "unity assumption" and its concomitants. The analytic boundaries between the individual and society or state are rubbed out, as is the significance of material or power positional factors. Politics are not ways of "organizing and doing," but of "thinking and feeling," a "kind of mentality."[26] Thus, political development theory depoliticized politics. Politics became a dependent variable, and analysis shifted from content to process. Like its precursors, political development theory assumed political activity and institutions to be the epiphenomena of stable, society-wide value, belief, and attitude structures. Theory turned a blind eye to interests and power, and "de-odorized" politics, eliminating the cigar smoke and stink of fear that accompany the vulgar understanding of politics. More important, the attendant "politics of order" bias gave political development theory, too, an inherently conservative bent.

The status quo orientation of political development theory shows in its very definition of politics. As the 1953 APSA Seminar on Comparative Politics put it,

[24] Edward Shils, *Political Development in the New States* (The Hague: Mouton, 1962), p. 10; and Reinhard Bendix, *Nation Building and Citizenship* (New York: Wiley, 1964), p. 5.

[25] Gabriel Almond and G. B. Powell, Jr., *Comparative Politics: A Developmental Approach* (Boston: Little, Brown, 1966), p. 302.

[26] Robert Bellah, "Meaning and Modernization," *Religious Studies* 4 (1968), p. 39.

The function of politics . . . is to provide society with social decisions having the force and status of legitimacy. A social decision
has the 'force of legitimacy' if the collective regularized power of
the society is brought to bear against deviations and if there is a
predominant disposition among those subject to the decision to
comply. As for the means of enforcing decisions, every society . . .
has a determinate organization which enjoys a monopoly of legitimate authority (or *political ultimacy*).

The aim of political analysis, the seminar report concluded, is to un-
cover the value structures that account for political institutions, the different "legitimacy myths" by which "people justify coercion, conformity, and the loss of political ultimacy to some superior groups or
persons, as well as the ways by which a society rationalizes its ascrip-
tion of political ultimacy and the beliefs which account for a predispo-
sition to compliance with social decisions."[27]

This definition of politics and its implications echo through the political development literature. "The political system," wrote Almond,
"is that system of interactions to be found in all independent societies
which performs the functions of integration and adaptation . . . by
means of the employment or threat of employment, of more or less legitimate physical compulsion. The political system is the legitimate, or-
der-maintaining or transforming system in the society." Indeed, "legitimate force is the thread that runs through the inputs and outputs of the
political system, giving it its special quality and salience, and its coherence as a system."[28] Leonard Binder defined the study of politics as "the
study of the legitimation of social power," while David Easton's definition focused on "the authoritative allocation of valued things."[29] In
each case, the key to what states and politicians do is legitimacy. The
definitions assume, in other words, the inverse of a classic phrase: right
makes might.

[27] Macridis and Cox, "Research in Comparative Politics," pp. 648–49. Carl Friedrich
commented of "legitimacy myths": "Rousseau, in the famous opening passage of his *Social Contract*, stated that he could explain what might make legitimate the chains in
which man found himself as a member of organized society. But unlike the members of
the Seminar, he did not think of this problem exclusively as one of 'mythology.' " Comments on ibid., p. 658.

[28] Gabriel Almond, "Introduction: A Functional Approach to Comparative Politics,"
in Gabriel Almond and James S. Coleman, eds. *The Politics of Developing Areas* (Princeton: Princeton University Press, 1960), p. 7.

[29] Leonard Binder, *Iran: Political Development in a Changing Society* (Berkeley: University of California Press, 1962), p. 16; and David Easton, *A Framework for Political
Analysis* (Englewood Cliffs, N.J.: Prentice-Hall, 1965), p. 50.

These definitions also imply that the continued existence of a regime proves its legitimacy. Talcott Parsons asserts that a " 'politically organized community' is clearly a 'moral community' " and he declares, "I start with a view that repudiates the idea that any political system that rests entirely on self-interest, force or a combination of them, can be stable over any considerable period of time."[30] David Easton found this "so obvious . . . that it may be overlooked"; indeed, "it is the premise upon which the continuation of any political system depends."[31] Furthermore, since political systems are stable "moral communities," violence against them is not evidence of internal cleavages but of a pathological anomaly. In short, like its precursors, political development declared not only that "right makes might," but that "what *is* is right" and so rightfully mighty.

But political development theorists also needed to explain change. After all, interest in the subject derived from the tumult in the Third World. To explain it, they too turned to cultural diffusion and a beachhead model of change. It began with an initial contact with modernity, generally in the form of colonialism. Thereafter modernity spread as modern ideas and institutions demonstrated their superiority to the old. Eventually a modernized local elite developed making modernization a self-sustaining process by which the modern center sought to penetrate and absorb the passive, traditional periphery. While this process would be traumatic, theorists saw no serious obstacles. Fragile traditional societies would surely shatter on contact with modern states, while the dynamic modern mind-set would seem "a genuine liberation from the stuffy closets of theocratic traditionalism."[32]

Attention focused on the critical period of transition extending from modernity's breakout from the beachhead to its consolidation in a modern nation-state. In particular, scrutiny rested on the small cadre of modern elites and the "proto-centers" which would in time constitute the modern states of the Third World. Thus, declared C. E. Black, the consolidation of modernity depends on "the desire . . . of modernizing leaders . . . to mobilize and rationalize the resources of society with a

[30] Talcott Parsons, "Some Reflections on the Place of Force in Social Processes," in *Internal War: Problems and Approaches*, ed. Harry Eckstein (New York: Free Press, 1964), p. 34.

[31] David Easton, "An Approach to the Analysis of Political Systems," WP 9: 3 (April 1957), p. 391.

[32] David Apter, "Political Religion in the New Nations," in *Old Societies and New States: The Quest for Modernity in Asia and Africa*, ed. Clifford Geertz (New York: Free Press, 1963), p. 66.

view to achieving greater control, efficiency and production."[33] Likewise, asserted Yusif Sayigh, if the underdeveloped are to develop, they must be "shaken rudely by social and political shocks administered deliberately . . . by their social-minded leaders."[34]

It was but a short step to identify the actual regimes and rulers of Third World states with the abstract centers and modern elites of theory and endow them with the same values, intentions, and dynamism. Declared Edward Shils, the center "is central because it is espoused by the ruling authorities of the society."[35] Western educated intellectuals "are the sole modern class in their society; modernity rests on them." They "are often the creators of the new nation and not merely of the new state." Unlike the rest who are "pre-national," "pre-political" and live in "unthinking, sometimes obstinate attachment" to tradition, "they are 'nationalized' and 'politicized' and therein lies their chief novelty."[36]

The focus on the new elites of the Third World was sharpened by the identification of nationalism with modernization. Indeed, political development theory assumed that in modernity states and nations are coterminus. Thus, on the one hand, declared Rupert Emerson, "Nationalism wherever it manifests itself is in essence a response to the forces which in recent centuries have revolutionized the West and have penetrated in successive waves to the farthest corners of the world."[37] On the other, the state via nationalism, offers the logical panacea for the trauma of modernization, since it is, in Shil's phrase, "the ultimate significant entity."[38]

Not surprisingly, attention turned to nationalists as nation-builders and their problems converting protostates into fully actualized modern ones. At issue was "how to build a single coherent political society from a multiplicity of 'traditional societies'; how to increase cultural homogeneity and value consensus; and how to [develop] among members of a political system . . . a deep and unambiguous sense of identity with the state and other members of the civic body."[39] In this process legiti-

---

[33] C. E. Black, *The Dynamics of Modernization: A Study in Comparative History* (New York: Harper Torchbooks, 1966), p. 13.

[34] Yusef Sayigh, "Development: The Visible or the Invisible Hand?" WP 13: 4 (July 1961), p. 569.

[35] Edward Shils, *Center and Periphery* (Chicago: University of Chicago Press, 1975), p. 4.

[36] Edward Shils, "The Concentration and Dispersion of Charisma," WP 11: 1 (October 1958), pp. 6, 1.

[37] Rupert Emerson, *From Empire to Nation* (Boston: Beacon Press, 1960), p. 188.

[38] Shils, "Concentration," p. 4.

[39] Claude Ake, "Political Integration and Political Stability: A Hypothesis," WP 19: 3 (April 1967), pp. 486–87.

mation was critical since "if leaders are . . . to direct a society to higher levels of performance, their words and actions must carry an aura of legitimacy."[40] Theorists studied many ways of generating legitimacy, but all such studies embodied the diffusionist assumption that the ruling elites offered the only possible source of integration. This focus on legitimation granted de facto legitimacy to those elites, who thus by definition possessed the authority to shape their societies, if not yet the means to do so.

Finally, political development theory gained in explanatory utility by reducing the periphery to analytic insignificance. After all, declared Shils, it consists "of those strata . . . of the society which are recipients of commands."[41] Theory lumped all the peripheries of the Third World into one residual category on the assumption that the "characteristics common to [them] are more powerful determinants of their political behavior than the differences in their circumstances and outlooks."[42] Furthermore, theory declared the periphery's days to be numbered. Incrementally but inexorably, it would fall to the center, for in George Homan's words, "civilization has fed on the rot of the village."[43]

All did not go as expected. By the mid-1960s ruling elites faced difficulties throughout the Third World. The trappings of modern government were in place, and yet political instability, not development, prevailed. This, however, prompted not a reassessment of political development theory but its further elaboration. The problem, theorists argued, was that development was "blocked," and political instability was "the external manifestation of such blocking."[44] Attention thus shifted to either of two possible sources of blocking: threats from below or without.

The "breakdowns of modernization" literature stresses the overwhelming forces released by modernization and the comparatively underwhelming nature of still shaky new regimes. In one variant, the argument suggested that modernization had been *too* successful and unleashed a "revolution of rising expectations." Like the sorcerer's apprentice, the process of social mobilization had gone wild: "the rapid disorganization of traditional settings" had produced a "mob mental-

---

[40] Lucian W. Pye, "Identity and the Political Culture," in *Crises and Sequences in Political Development*, ed. L. Binder et al. (Princeton: Princeton University Press, 1971), p. 134.

[41] Shils, *Center and Periphery*, p. 39.

[42] Joan M. Nelson, *Access to Power: Politics and the Urban Poor in Developing Nations* (Princeton: Princeton University Press, 1979), p. 4.

[43] Cited in Redfield, *The Little Community*, p. 110.

[44] S. N. Eisenstadt, "Modernization and Conditions of Sustained Growth," wp 16: 4 (July 1964), p. 578.

ity and consequent political instability."[45] Rulers thus faced a "legitimacy crisis" for they were too new to command "an automatic and complete acceptance of the authority of governmental institutions."[46] At the same time, they could not satisfy rising expectations, limit popular demands, or even maintain minimal political order. Conversely, a second variant of the threat from below stressed antimodern backlash by traditional forces. "The problem," declared Clifford Geertz, is that "the new states are abnormally susceptible to serious disaffection based on primordial attachments" because of their "unaccountable absolute import" to the still traditional masses.[47] As a result, mobilized primordial identities may threaten national integration, while social mobilization raises demands on government.

The most influential version of the breakdowns in modernization argument is Samuel Huntington's *Political Order in Changing Societies*.[48] It upended the assumed connection of modernization (defined as urbanization, rising literacy, etc.) and political modernization (defined as democracy, stability, structural differentiation, and national integration). Progress toward the former might be inevitable, but it did not necessarily entail the institutional development required for the latter. Thus, like Malinowski, Huntington argued that analysis ought to focus not on the expected happy ending of modernization but rather on the "no-man's land of change" to be crossed getting there.[49] Moreover, he had no expectation that the transition from tradition to modernity would be successful, indeed quite the contrary.[50]

Despite this denial of developmental teleology, Huntington's book still embodied, and even revitalized, old assumptions. The destruction of traditional organizations and cultural diffusion produce social mobilization which leads to greater individual needs and desires. This, he argues, generates rapid increases in political participation and demands on the modern authorities. To aggregate and moderate these demands within the political system requires a level of political institutionalization commensurate with the level of political participation. But if political participation outpaces political institutionalization, the result is

[45] S. N. Eisenstadt, "Approaches to the Problem of Political Development in Non-Western Societies," wp 9: 3 (April 1957), p. 454.

[46] Lucian W. Pye, "The Legitimacy Crisis," in *Crises and Sequences*, ed. Binder et al., p. 141.

[47] Clifford Geertz, "The Integrative Revolution: Primordial Sentiments and Civil Politics in the New States," in *Old Societies*, ed. Geertz, p. 109.

[48] Samuel Huntington, *Political Order in Changing Societies* (New Haven: Yale University Press, 1968).

[49] Ibid., p. 35.

[50] Ibid., p. 4.

praetorian politics and political instability.[51] Given overwhelming social mobilization and expansion of political participation and underwhelming political institutionalization in the Third World, it is not surprising, Huntington concluded, that regimes everywhere seem threatened from below.

Arguments concerning the threat from without tie directly to the theory of totalitarianism, especially in its applied form, the "appeals of communism" literature. In fact, political development and totalitarianism mirror one another through the glass darkly. For modernization theorists, the destruction of traditional values, attachments, and institutions was the necessary and good first step in nation-building. For those writing not in the dazzle of decolonization, but the shadow of fascism, social mobilization threatened to produce mass society and mass politics—the bases of totalitarianism and the antithesis of democracy. For Hannah Arendt, Karl Mannheim, and others, social mobilization destroys not only the hierarchical social and political orders which once structured society but also the family, class, community, and ethnic identities which once gave peoples' lives meaning. Without them, these uprooted souls are "naturally susceptible to the temptations of revolutionary agitation" and ideologies promising a return to the safety of order and hierarchy.[52]

Here political development theorists identified the threat from without; development might be derailed by outside, specifically communist, influences. Thus, Gabriel Almond argued, for example, that communism draws on "the destructive energies and the desperate impatience" of the deracinated and "harnesses them in the service of a controlled and comprehensive destructiveness."[53] Similarly, Lucian Pye explained the appeal of communism in terms of the role it "has assumed in an acculturation process involving whole societies" and particularly for individuals "losing their sense of identity with their traditional ways of life and . . . seeking restlessly to realize a modern way. In this setting communism seems to gain the support of those who have already been affected by . . . the impact of the West."[54] In short, development might be "confiscated" by revolutionaries, and this added weight to the al-

[51] Ibid., pp. 78–80.

[52] Mancur Olson, Jr., "Rapid Growth as a Destabilizing Force," *Journal of Economic History* 23 (December 1963), pp. 532–33.

[53] Gabriel Almond, *The Appeals of Communism* (Princeton: Princeton University Press, 1954), p. 381.

[54] Lucien Pye, *Guerrilla Communism in Malaya: Its Social and Political Meaning* (Princeton: Princeton University Press, 1956), pp. 7–8.

ready dominant analytic focus on order and the attendant prescriptions for achieving it.

Prescriptive Utility

Political development theory had clear implications for policy prescription. Indeed, it derived great appeal from the ease with which its explanations could be translated into prescriptions for action. Moreover, because change was deemed inevitable, prescriptions for directing its course soon became many political scientists' chief concern. Thus, for Daniel Lerner, "the crux of the matter [is] not *whether* but *how* one should move from traditional ways toward modern lifestyles," and for Lucien Pye "the heart of the problem of nation-building is the question of how the diffusion of world culture can be facilitated while its disruptive consequences are minimized."[55] Of course, just as different theorists suggested different "critical variables" causing modernization, so too different advisors suggested different prescriptions. Some favored investment in education, others in modern communications and media, or vocational training, or industrialization. During the 1960s, however, rising concern with "breakdowns in modernization" and possible subversion of the development process shifted attention to institutionalization, order, state strength, and how to achieve them.

In keeping with the breakdowns in modernization model, prescriptions focused on one end or the other of the instability equation: overwhelming popular demands or underwhelming governmental capabilities. As for the former, if the "revolution of rising expectations" threatened to swamp the newly launched ship of state, argued Ithiel de Sola Pool, then development may "depend on somehow compelling newly mobilized strata to return to a measure of passivity and defeatism from which they have recently been aroused by the process of modernization."[56] Or, as Huntington put it, social mobilization will "produce political decay unless steps are taken to moderate or resist its impact on political consciousness or political involvement."[57] But, as he himself argued cogently, social mobilization was inevitable, and rising demands for political participation nearly unstoppable. Thus, pre-

[55] Daniel Lerner, *The Passing of Traditional Society: Modernizing the Middle East* (New York: Free Press, 1958), p. 405; and Lucien Pye, *Politics, Personality and Nation-Building* (New Haven: Yale University Press, 1962), p. 13.

[56] Ithiel de Sola Pool, "The Public and the Polity," in *Contemporary Political Science: Toward Empirical Theory*, ed. Ithiel de Sola Pool (New York: McGraw-Hill, 1967), p. 26.

[57] Huntington, *Political Order*, p. 86.

scriptive attention turned to the real targets of opportunity: the state, its institutions, and its leaders.

The resultant prescriptions are Hobbesian. They assume that development requires order which can be provided only by a modern Leviathan. As Pye put it, "we can conceive of political development as depending upon a capacity either to control social change or to be controlled by it. And, *of course*, the starting point in controlling social forces is the capacity to maintain order."[58] Huntington and others thus defined the public interest as "whatever strengthens governmental institutions . . . something created and brought into existence by the institutionalization of government organizations." (Indeed, Huntington suggested, "what's good for the Presidency is good for the country" and "what's good for the Presidium is good for the Soviet Union.")[59]

What's good for governments, advocates argued, is more, and more centralized, power. This is the key to both the assimilation of people newly mobilized by modernization and the innovation of policy necessary for political modernization and the destruction of the periphery. Thus, argued Neil Smelser, if "undifferentiated [traditional] structures . . . constitute the primary social barriers to modernization. . . . invariably a certain amount of political pressure must be applied to loosen these ties." This action requires a stronger state, and it

> creates conditions demanding a larger, more formal type of political administration. Thus, another argument in favor of the importance of strong government during rapid and uneven modernization is based on the necessity to accommodate the growing cultural, economic and social heterogeneity and to control the political repercussions of the constantly shifting distribution of power accompanying extensive social reorganization.[60]

More government would be better government, because more is better and because it would be more modern government which is also better.

Within this framework, it was easy to identify "allies in modernization." Those in the periphery were, of course, not eligible. They were the object of policy: their incorporation into the modern state was sought for the good of all, but they had no active role in the process. Conversely, it was assumed that as modern elites, Third World leaders

[58] Lucien Pye, "The Concept of Political Development," *Annals of the American Academy of Political and Social Science* 358 (March 1965), pp. 10–11. Emphasis added.

[59] Huntington, *Political Order*, pp. 25–26.

[60] Neil Smelser, "Mechanisms of Change and Adjustment to Change," in *Industrialization and Society*, ed. B. F. Hoselitz and W. E. Moore (The Hague: UNESCO-Mouton, 1966), p. 46.

shared the values and aims of the political development theorists themselves. The exact choice of modern allies, however, depended upon authors' choice of institutional prescription. For Myron Weiner, the aim of "the policy-oriented political scientist is to discover what political institutions and practices, commensurate with our belief in representative government and civil liberties, can best facilitate the emergence of a modern society."[61] Huntington focused on the political party ("a conscious and explicit answer to the problem of mobilization vs. institutionalization"),[62] and so favored party building. Others promoted development administration, institution building, and so on. But in each case, the aim was to increase the strength of the state and thus its ability to achieve its putative goal: development. Again, the bias for order took precedence with the "breakdowns in modernization" and apparent failure of democratic institutions and civilian elites that marked the 1960s. What mattered was neither the form of government nor the substance of state policy, but the amount of government,[63] defined as the ability to keep the lid on.

The bias for order shows clearly in support for the modernizing military. Of course, few analysts enjoyed championing military governance. Rather, they supported the military as the last hope agent of modernization—and political development theory offered apparently solid grounds on which to do so. According to Huntington, "officers are the most modern and progressive group in the society." They "promote social and economic reform [and] national integration, . . . assail waste, backwardness and corruption, and they introduce into society highly middle-class ideas of efficiency, honesty and national loyalty."[64] Moreover, because the military is a modern bureaucracy, "colonels can run a government [while] students and monks cannot."[65] Thus,

> In many societies the opportunity the military have for political creativity may be the last real chance for political institutionalization short of the totalitarian road. If the military fail to seize that opportunity, the broadening of participation transforms the society into a mass praetorian system. In such a system the opportunity to create political institutions passes from the military, the apostles of order, to . . . the apostles of revolution.[66]

[61] Myron Weiner, "India's Political Future," wp 12: 1 (October, 1959), p. 119.
[62] Huntington, *Political Order*, p. 340.
[63] Ibid., p. 1.
[64] Ibid., pp. 201, 203.
[65] Ibid., p. 239.
[66] Ibid., p. 262.

In short, under certain conditions, aid to Third World militaries, even encouragement of military coups, may be progressive.

Ideological Utility

Political development theory also promised important ideological rewards. "As America enters dynamically upon the world scene," declared Henry Luce in 1944, "we need . . . a vision of America as a world power," a vision of "America as the dynamic center of ever-widening spheres of enterprise . . . as the training center of the skillful servants of mankind . . . as the Good Samaritan, [for] out of these elements surely can be fashioned a vision of the 20th century."[67] Political development theory was not quite what Luce had in mind, of course, nor did policymakers and politicians need it to carry on. Still, it fulfilled a useful legitimizing role and made academics feel important.

Political development theory offered a vision of the United States' place in history based not on might but on right. America was definitive of modernity, and modern meant scientific, industrialized, and powerful. Modern also meant humane, participant, democratic; and democracy, the theory proved, is the "crowning institution" of history.[68] The American way was not merely a "manifestation of Western liberal parochialism," but it embodied "values of universal validity, and regimes that do not find a place for them . . . are less good than those that do."[69] In fact, political development theory proved that the United States, not the Soviet Union, was truly revolutionary and on the "side of history." Anticommunism thus was not reactionary, but a positive social doctrine. Moreover, it justified American penetration of the Third World just as its antecedents had justified European imperialism. It sanctioned the power asymmetries between modern and traditional societies and provided a socially acceptable new vocabulary for familiar racist characterizations of the "inferior races."[70]

No less important, political development theory bolstered American self-satisfaction of the 1950s and early 1960s. After all, wrote Max Millikan and Walt Rostow in 1957:

[67] Cited in Daniel Bell, "The End of American Exceptionalism," Reprinted in *Parameters* 10: 2 (June 1980), p. 6.

[68] Lerner, *Passing of Traditional Society*, p. 64.

[69] Edward Shils, "On the Comparative Study of the New States," in Geertz, *Old Societies*, p. 25.

[70] John F. Embree, "Standardized Error and Japanese Character: A Note on Political Interpretation," wp 2: 3 (April 1950), pp. 439–43.

> The United States is now within sight of solutions to the . . . issues which have dominated its political life since 1865 [including] social equality for the Negro, . . . equal educational opportunity, the equitable distribution of income. None of these great issues is fully resolved; but . . . if we continue to devote our attention [to them] we run the danger of becoming a bore to ourselves and the world.[71]

In fact, asserted Seymour Martin Lipset, "the fundamental political problems of the industrial revolution have been solved," and "this very triumph of democratic social revolution in the West ends domestic politics for those intellectuals who must have . . . utopias to motivate them to social action."[72] Utopia was *here*: evolution worked, and we were the proof.

Finally, political development theory let political scientists claim expertise on the big issues of the Cold War. In 1944 the APSA Panel on Comparative Government proclaimed that "in this period of total warfare . . . knowledge of foreign political institutions and ideologies has become of paramount importance. Comparative government has been transformed from a Cinderella-like academic discipline into a political instrumentality of the most immediate potency."[73] A new faith was abroad in the land, and political scientists were its priests, announced Gabriel Almond, "those who carry on the traditions of one of the most ancient sciences . . . intended to maximize man's capacity to tame violence and employ it only for the humane goals of freedom, justice and welfare."[74]

ICARUS IMPERILED

Familiarity and utility notwithstanding, political development theory had a serious problem: the promise of explanatory and prescriptive power was false. In fact, its success in the marketplace was the product of just those characteristics which assured its inadequacy and imperfectability as an analytic tool. As Jean Paul Sartre once observed, "Va-

[71] Max Millikan and Walt Rostow, *A Proposal: Key to an Effective Foreign Policy* (New York: Harper, 1957), pp. 149–50.

[72] Seymour Martin Lipset, *Political Man: The Social Bases of Politics* (Garden City, N.Y.: Anchor, 1963), pp. 442–43. Here is a point that provoked controversy not reflected in my presentation. Lipset's work met immediate criticism, much of it telling. However, few of the critics were heard beyond academic walls, while Lipset's thesis was seized upon and widely applauded.

[73] Loewenstein, "Comparative Government," p. 541.

[74] "Introduction," in *Politics of Developing Areas*, eds. Almond and Coleman, p. 64.

léry is a *petit bourgeois* intellectual, no doubt about it. But not every *petit bourgeois* intellectual is Valéry."[75] In so saying, he also fingers the key weakness of political development theory. For "the function of scientific concepts is to mark the categories which will tell us more about our subject matter than any other categorical sets."[76] Yet political development theory's success turned on "sufficient vagueness," not conceptual clarity. The resultant murkiness obscured reality and hampered efforts to develop more accurate approximations of it.

The sufficient vagueness problem appeared first, and fatally, in the very definition of political development. As Daniel Bell observed, "Says . . . the Talmud: 'If you don't know where you are going, any road will take you there.' "[77] Everyone took a different road. But what the many definitions did share was a tendency toward summarization, not specification. Theorists did not identify key variables—or even particularly political variables. Instead, they defined their topic as "manifestly multidimensional, involving all aspects of human society," "a multifaceted process involving changes in all areas of human thought and activity."[78] As a result, theoretical assertions often tended toward tautology, were self-evidently true, or could not be falsified, while empirical findings concerning them did not lead to modifications of the general theories.[79] Finally, theory suffered from its Olympian abstraction, for viewed from Parnassus, "the terrain of politics, its ridges and gullies, become flattened and the weary foot-traveler finds few guides to concrete problems."[80]

These weaknesses are not solely the fault of early practitioners, however, they are the heritage of histoire raisonnée. Hegel observed that what is reasonable is real, and a similar assumption underlies political development theory.[81] Much of the early, influential work in the field was done, as was histoire raisonnée, from an arm chair. Theorists ex-

[75] Jean Paul Sartre, *Critique de la raison dialectique* (Paris: Gallimard, 1960), p. 44.

[76] Abraham Kaplan, cited in Dean Tipps, "Modernization Theory and the Comparative Study of Societies: A Critical Perspective," CSSH 15 (March 1973), p. 199.

[77] Daniel Bell, "Ten Theories in Search of Reality: The Prediction of Soviet Behavior in the Social Sciences," WP 10: 3 (April 1958), p. 358.

[78] Lucian Pye, "Introduction," in *Communications and Political Development*, ed. Lucian Pye (Princeton: Princeton University Press, 1963), p. 11; and Huntington, *Political Order*, p. 32. For summaries of the many definitions of political development, see Pye, "Concept of Political Development" and Robert A. Packenham, "Approaches to the Study of Political Development," WP 17: 1 (October 1964).

[79] Joseph LaPalombara, "Macrotheories and Microapplications in Comparative Politics," CP 1 (October 1968), p. 55.

[80] Bell, "Ten Theories," p. 336.

[81] Ibid., p. 328.

plained what ought to happen as dictated by logical necessity and revealed by a fertile imagination. (Gabriel Almond, for example, whose theories shaped the discipline for more than a decade beginning in the mid-1950s, did not even visit the Third World until 1962.)[82] This is the "projective fallacy": that our experience describes the likely course others will follow.

The projective fallacy had two distorting impacts on political development theory. First, theorists grossly romanticized the natural history of the West to be projected on the Third World as normative. The result was ideologically gratifying but analytically disastrous. This problem was exaggerated by the second: given the a priori assumption that both the story and punch line were already known, analysts could ignore data. In fact, in view of its aim to unveil the mysteries of the Third World, political development theory is striking for its lack of supporting detail.[83] The problem was not a lack of data. Area specialists produced lots—and were dismissed as parochial. The complexity and geographical specificity of their work lacked the explanatory and prescriptive utility of grand theory. Thus, political development theorists denied its import, asserted that traditional societies lack politically salient differentiating characteristics, and recognized no change save in the direction of the Western experience. Since in theory the substance of a country's politics is determined by its position on the continuum from tradition to modernity, what mattered was process. Such resistance to scrutinizing reality understandably blunted theory's explanatory power, however.

Political development theory was ahistorical for similar reasons. If history reduces to a series of developmental stages through which all societies must pass, then when they do so chronologically it is immaterial and adds nothing to understanding the process by which they do. The resultant loss of a temporal variable again reduced theory's explanatory and predictive power. Ironically, homogenizing all modernization experiences into one modal experience without reference to history also "factored out" the impact of imperialism, the timing of decolonization, structural changes in the world economy, the balance of power, and so on—that is, precisely those issues which had aroused interest in the Third World.

As a result of the "projective fallacy," political development theory became a "gap theory." In fact, its explanatory and prescriptive utility

[82] Gabriel Almond, *Political Development: Essays in Heuristic Theory* (Boston: Little Brown, 1970), p. 21.

[83] See Emerson, *Empire to Nation*, p. 89; and Henry Bienen, "What Does Political Development Mean in Africa?" wp 20: 1 (October 1967), p. 129.

derive from the projected "normal growth curve" for all societies. Given such a curve, it is possible to plot all Third World countries on the same graph, identify the gap separating them from their future and thus prescribe the appropriate fix. Unfortunately, this appearance of prescriptive power obscures any clear notion of how to convert the necessary into action. "The situation," as Daniel Bell noted in a different context, "is reminiscent of two radicals in the 1920s debating the future course of Soviet politics. 'The objective situation,' said one, 'requires that Trotsky do so and so.' 'Look,' replied the other, 'you know what Trotsky has to do, and I know what Trotsky has to do, but does Trotsky know?' "[84]

The Tyranny of Method

Ironically, these limits on adequacy and perfectibility were exaggerated by unintended consequences of the contemporaneous effort to "scientize" the study of politics. The attempt began with the desire to escape the sterile historicism of legal-formal description and "extend the boundaries of the universe of comparative politics [to] include . . . the 'uncouth' and exotic systems of the areas outside Western Europe."[85] As Gabriel Almond told the APSA in his 1966 presidential address, "Like Rachel, Jacob's beloved but still childless bride, who asked herself and the Lord each morning, 'Am I?' or 'Can I?', so presidents of this Association . . . ask, 'Are we a science?' or 'Can we become one?' "[86] Many thought so, and agreed that a "scientific" approach would do the trick, for "casting our problems in terms of formal theory will direct us to the kind and degree of precision which are possible in the discipline, and will enable us to take our place in the order of the sciences with the dignity which is reserved only for those who follow a calling without limit and condition."[87] In Edward Shils's words, "We are not historicists. We aim at generalized categories and analytical propositions . . . because we regard them as among the highest intellectual achievements."[88]

The search for "science," as defined by social scientists, cost the understanding of Third World politics dearly. In part, the problems flow

[84] Bell, "Ten Theories," p. 359.

[85] Almond, "Introduction," in *Politics of Developing Areas*, eds. Almond and Coleman, p. 10.

[86] Almond, *Political Development*, p. 235.

[87] Almond, "Introduction," in *Politics of Developing Areas*, eds. Almond and Coleman, p. 64.

[88] Edward Shils, "Comparative Study," in *Old Societies*, ed. Geertz, p. 15.

from what an early critic labeled "an excessive preoccupation with the apparatus and language of social science rather than the social world" and a habit of reducing methodologies to "stylish irrelevancies . . . introduced more in the manner of magical wands than as scientific tools."[89] But the real problems lie in the failure to *be* scientific or to discriminate between the myth and the practice of science.

The authors of the seminal APSA report "Research in Comparative Politics" sought "to increase the awareness of the need for taking some kind of methodological position prior to or along with the collection and descriptive enumeration of facts."[90] Thus, researchers set out to develop a causally linked series of theoretical propositions with which to approach the world in the hope that "the system of analysis tentatively developed on a highly abstract level can be shown to offer useful concepts and relatively tenable theories."[91] This ultimate aim escaped them however, because they built not a model but a system of classification mirroring earlier histoire raisonnée and Comparative Method taxonomies. As Barrington Moore, Jr., put it,

> What emerges . . . is a collection of verbal categories, empty file drawers, as it were, that are arranged in a neat and, at first glance, imposing pattern. All that remains, supposedly, is to fill some . . . with facts, and the others will spring open with predictions. This would be quite true, and a tremendous achievement, if the relationship between the file drawers actually existed in the facts of social behavior. To permit valid inferences from one body of facts to another is the goal of any scientific theory. But in [this] case . . . the relationship does not derive from the objective materials examined, but . . . from the verbal symbols alone.[92]

Like its predecessors, political development theory was a set of boxes for data, not one derived from data. Moreover, having begun empirical research with an airtight system, political scientists denied themselves the ability to test either theory or reality.

The consequence was the "going with" syndrome derived from the

---

[89] Goldhamer, "Fashion," pp. 396, 394. As Gabriel Almond and Stephen Genco put it: "Our longing for full scientific status has led us to create a kind of 'cargo cult,' fashioning cardboard imitations of the tools and products of the hard sciences in the hope that our incantations would make them real." "Clouds, Clocks and the Study of Politics," WP 29: 4 (July 1977), p. 504.

[90] Macridis and Cox, "Research," p. 643.

[91] M. J. Levy, cited in Barrington Moore, Jr., "The New Scholasticism and the Study of Politics," WP 6: 1 (October 1953), p. 130.

[92] Ibid., p. 129.

"everything affects everything else" unity assumption. Theory identifies the supposed characteristics of, for example, modernity and connects them by asserting that they "go together," that is, are causally connected in a yet undetermined fashion. These descriptive characteristics, or indicators, are assumed to be attributes of change, while, in fact, they are attributes of classification. Theorists thus limited themselves to description of a society's current structure and failed to address the critical questions of where, specifically, it came from and how, specifically, it would change. In short, theory could not specify how which states under which conditions would do what.

Two additional methodological problems related to the drive for explanatory parsimony reduced the adequacy and perfectibility of political development theory still further. First, theorists were interested in the central tendency not the oddities of reality. In the words of the 1953 seminar report, "The problem of comparative method revolves around the discovery of uniformities."[93] As Gabriel Almond and Stephen Genco note, however, this led to "the enshrining of the notion of generalization as the *sine qua non* of the scientific aspirations of the profession."[94] The result was a field obsessed with generalities and positively uninterested in investigating specifics. (Harry Eckstein argued, for example, that revolutions cannot be considered a "theoretical subject" for investigation because there have not been enough of them.)[95] Furthermore, this focus on the central tendency discounted data not in conformity with it. Thus, the explanatory value of the theory was limited, as were the prospects that anomalous data could change it. This gave free rein to the familiar, a priori assumptions of histoire raisonnée.

Second, the related effort to adopt the "covering law" model of R. B. Braithwaite, Carl Hempel, and others reinforced these tendencies. The aim was to find and develop general laws to make Barrington Moore's "file drawers" actually "spring open with predictions." This required a powerful notion of determinism in political behavior, but causality is hard to come by in human affairs. In fact, more important are the *limits* of causality. To forget this is to forget Aristotle's warning: "Look for precision in each class of things just so far as the nature of the subject permits." And how can one speak of determinism in politics when so much political activity is devoted to changing the rules of the game? Yet in its absence, the essence of the covering law model is lost. Without the

[93] Macridis and Cox, "Research," p. 642.
[94] Almond and Genco, "Clouds," p. 498.
[95] Eckstein, *Internal War*, p. 10.

71

ability to specify conditions which necessitate a given outcome, its power evaporates.

Still, this methodological orientation had important consequences. As Almond and Genco argue, the problem is not that

> political scientists actually *see* the political world this way; no doubt we would all agree that it often *appears* to be quite porous, irregular and unpredictable. Rather . . . the arsenal of meta-methodological principles and procedures we have borrowed from the physical sciences—or, more correctly, from a certain philosophical perspective on the physical sciences —has come to us with an array of substantive assumptions that all proclaim the principle "all clouds are clocks."[96]

They tend "to convert the real into the rational or the contingent into the necessary," making reality "appear more solidly entrenched than before."[97] They also direct analytic attention away from many issues which consequently go unnoticed.

With these "meta-methodological principles," political development theorists also embraced the myth of science—that science itself is an objective enterprise. In fact, the two went hand in hand. Being sensitive to the risk of bias, they sought protection in the scientific method; but technique cannot preclude prejudice. Even the most rigorously scientific research is, as Stephen Jay Gould puts it, "a gutsy human enterprise."[98] Moreover, the issues raised by political development theory are by nature controversial, and there is precious little objective information about them. Under such circumstances, even scientific assessments may merely replicate social prejudice. Indeed, though they may be investigated with the utmost scientific rigor, the initial questions posed may be so narrow as to admit only answers resonant with the investigator's a priori assumptions. Such is the case with political development theory. Because its proponents believed in the myth of science, they did not notice how much their models recapitulated the familiar assumptions of histoire raisonnée. Furthermore, their faith in scientific objectivity added immeasurably to the ideological utility of their work, for the blinders they wore were, in Emile Durkheim's phrase, "like a veil drawn between the thing and ourselves, concealing them from us more successfully as we think it more transparent."[99]

[96] Almond and Genco, "Clouds," p. 504. Emphasis in original.
[97] Albert O. Hirschman, "The Search for Paradigms as a Hindrance to Understanding," WP 22: 3 (April 1970), p. 339.
[98] Gould, *Mismeasure of Man*, pp. 21–23.
[99] Emile Durkheim, *The Rules of Sociological Method* (New York: Free Press, 1965), p. 15.

The Fall

The challenge to political development theory went far beyond methodological concerns. The late 1960s saw an attack on all fronts: explanatory, prescriptive, and ideological. As for the latter, dissension over the Vietnam War led critics to assail social science's role in warmaking and policymaking in general. The war abroad and race riots at home also undercut the smug self-assurance which had supported the unexamined assumptions of the goodness and teleology of the modernization process. In fact, the western experience itself, now under scrutiny, was soon found to have been a less pleasant process than was imagined. Under fire from without and wracked by self-doubts, political development theorists pulled in their horns. With the new modesty came a reorientation toward specifics, not grand theorizing.

But ideological sea change was not alone in reorienting political development theory. The research boom of the late 1950s and early 60s had produced overwhelming evidence that all was not as expected in the Third World. Aristide Zolberg, for example, noted that given the continued existence of

> almost every "gap" ever imagined by scholars concerned with development . . . and in the absence of the requisites . . . posited for the maintenance of a political system, there is little place for countries such as these in the conceptual universe of political science. Yet [they] do persist. Hence we have little choice but either to play an academic ostrich game or come to grips with reality.[100]

But doing so involved undoing the fundamental assumptions that underpinned political development theory and its predecessors.

The first and most important to come under attack was the unity assumption. New evidence pointed to a syncretic individual capable of holding several different value structures, belonging simultaneously to different types of organizations, and behaving in different ways. He did not have just one mind-set, traditional or modern, but could be traditional and/or modern depending on context. This recognition of syncretism destroyed the entire explanatory structure of political development theory. On the one hand, it forced analysts to attend to the conditions of change in specific areas. With this, parsimony suffered a serious setback as did the notion that analysis could focus on abstract political processes without reference to policy substance or the world historical context of change. On the other, the psychological imperative of cognitive consistency presumed to underlie modernization, and

---

[100] Aristide Zolberg, "The Structure of Political Conflict in the New States of Tropical Africa," APSR 63 (March 1968), pp. 70–71.

73

the linkage of individual values and social or political institutions ceased to hold. Without it, adjustment, adaptation, and accommodation marked the Third World's response to the new. This, in turn, challenged the center–periphery model of Third World states, the beachhead model of change, and the related assessments of elites, "peripherals," and the sources of instability.

In particular, the new evidence challenged the notion that modern elites' behavior could be predicted by their modernity. Theory had assumed that they wanted to modernize their societies, if only they had the capacity to overcome peripheral passivity. Closer examination, however, revealed not a struggle pitting modern elites and states against passive peripheries, but it showed fragmented elites and faulted states muddling along in segmented societies. The problem was that in order to build anticolonial movements, nationalists cobbled together coalitions of autonomous localized organizations, both traditional and modern. Thus, at independence the central elites were not a distinct, cohesive social class, but displayed the same fault lines as society at large. Moreover, whatever they may have wanted to do, they have had to face the task of managing relations among the many, often antagonistic, groups on which they depend. As a result, ruling elites must give coalition management and self-preservation priority over development. In fact, they may have to pursue antidevelopment strategies to survive. They may eschew policies which hurt key constituency groups or reduce the state to little more than a means to divide national resources among insiders. More seriously, they may either deinstitutionalize government to eliminate autonomous sources of political power[101] or use societal fragmentation to strengthen their positions within or against the governing coalition.

But these regime maintenance strategies may ultimately destroy states' capacity to promote development. Corruption reduces the resources available for development. Without strong institutions, governments cannot raise revenues, implement day-to-day programs, or manage the social transformation necessary for modernization. Both the interpenetration of center and periphery and the dependence of ruling elites on substate groups block elite coalescence, political centralization, and national integration and shift resources to the state's rivals, further decreasing its capacity to govern. In fact, efforts to penetrate the periphery by sending officials into the

---

[101] See Alexander J. Groth, "The Institutional Myth: Huntington's Order Revisited," *Review of Politics* 41: 2 (April 1979); and John Waterbury, "Endemic and Planned Corruption in a Monarchical Regime," WP 25: 4 (July 1973).

countryside often backfire; rather than displacing local elites, the officials become dependent on them and, in effect, offer them direct access to the center.

This new picture forces reassessment of the analysis of instability. As for the threat of massification, the continued vitality of peripheral organizations indicates that the deracination process has not been total. Conversely, elite fragmentation, intraelite conflict, and competitive mobilization of the periphery by antagonistic elites suggest that the center itself is the source of much instability. As James Scott observes, "the problem of 'threatened institutions' . . . is not a problem of being swamped by 'socially mobilized masses of the unwashed' but of an artificial cloture or rigidity produced by incumbents."[102] Furthermore, outside resources supplied to increase government capacity to control the threat from below may either up the ante in intraelite competition for controlling the privilege to dispense spoils or simply increase the capacity of those in power to impose their preferences on others, irrespective of the national interest.

The consequences of this analytic shift are perhaps best illustrated by the changing treatment of Third World militaries and military coups. Earlier Third World militaries were seen as modern bureaucratic organizations led by development-minded nationalists, but reexamination revealed a bleaker picture. "Neat hierarchical command charts," notes Samuel Decalo,

> camouflage deep cleavages—an extension of wider societal chasms. . . . Indeed, many African armies bear little resemblance to a modern complex organization model and are instead a coterie of distinct armed camps owing primary clientelist allegiance to a handful of mutually competitive officers . . . seething with a variety of corporate, ethnic and personal grievances.[103]

This observation is not unique to Africa; the same can be said of those in many other areas as well. Moreover, in most cases, "a change in political style, a redistribution of political and economic power among elites (with the army assuring itself of the lion's share), and the satisfaction of the personal and group grievances of the dominant officer clique" are the consequences of coups, not social transformation.[104] Like their civilian predecessors, coup leaders face segmented societies

[102] Cited in Mark Kesselman, "Order or Movement? The Literature of Political Development as Ideology" WP 26: 1 (October 1973), p. 148.
[103] Samuel Decalo, *Coups and Army Rule in Africa: Studies in Military Style* (New Haven: Yale University Press, 1976), pp. 14–15.
[104] Ibid., p. 27.

with weak institutions, few resources, and the constant threat of coalitional collapse or countercoup.

The analytic consequences of this new orientation were as pronounced as the substantive ones. The most important has been a marked tendency toward specificity. "It is my firm belief," declares Theda Skocpol, "that analytic oversimplification cannot lead us toward valid, complete explanations." Thus, new theories will be complex, "involving varying and autonomous logics and different, though overlapping, historical times, rather than a single, all-encompassing system that comes into being in one stage and then remains constant in its essential patterns."[105] Similarly, Joan Nelson asserts that progress "depends on efforts to put together what is now known, piece by piece rather than in one grand stroke of theory." Research "should start not with bold intuitions about global tendencies, but with an attempt to identify key variables and recurring patterns. In other words, the starting point is not a search for uniformity, but an assumption of ordered variability. . . . Global theories, therefore, are at best premature."[106]

The analytic reorientation of political development theory led to the valorization of the periphery and the unpacking of the state. As for the former, the periphery was clearly not the passive object of central commands; it could resist and influence the center. Analysis thus focused on how individuals cope with events, not as abstract bundles of beliefs, but as persons "making choices out of a regard for [their] own interests."[107] These choices involve assessments of the critical features of the political, social, and economic environment, their likely impact on survival and betterment, and the available personal and organizational responses. For the analyst, understanding the choices entails three steps: differentiation of "classes" of peripherals depending on their circumstances and the available options;[108] identification of which elites and organizations control the resources they need;[109] and specification of

[105] Theda Skocpol, *States and Social Revolutions: A Comparative Analysis of France, Russia, and China* (New York: Cambridge University Press, 1979), p. 5; and Theda Skocpol, "Wallerstein's World Capitalist System: A Theoretical and Historical Critique," *American Journal of Sociology* 82: 5 (March 1977), pp. 1087–88.

[106] Nelson, *Access to Power*, pp. 13, 6–7.

[107] Robert H. Bates, "People in Villages: Micro-Level Studies in Political Economy," WP 31: 1 (October 1978), p. 136. As Eric Wolf commented, the new aim was "a concern with microsociology born of an understanding . . . that the transcendental ideological issues appear only in very prosaic guise in the villages." *Peasant Wars of the Twentieth Century* (New York: Harper Torchbooks, 1969), p. xi.

[108] Nelson, *Access to Power*, pp. 399–400; Wolf, *Peasant Wars*, pp. x–xi.

[109] Joel S. Migdal, "The Individual and Rapid Change," paper presented at the Annual

what determines whether they will challenge the status quo or remain passive.[110]

Analytic reorientation also produced a reconceptualization of the state. It could no longer be assumed to be the "ultimate significant entity" and the undifferentiated outcome of an universal development process; rather, it required study as a variable in its own right. Thus, on the one hand, analysts assess the timing and mode of a state's inclusion in the international system for clues as to its autonomy, differentiation, and control of the means of coercion.[111] On the other, they analyze the specific constellation of elites which constitute the state, the nature and strength of other social organizations competing with the state, and the state's resources for managing them. The relationship is recursive, not directional, for changes in competing organizations affect the autonomy and policies of the state, while state actions may affect individual organizations, the rules under which they operate, or the environment in which they do so. In short, how stately leaders can be—how far, fast, and precisely they can push social transformation—depend on this complicated mix which is affected, in turn, by the state of the periphery.

Perseverance

Reviewing these developments in a paper commissioned by the APSA, Joel Migdal came to a hopeful conclusion:

> Scholarship has been freed from the Procrustean notions that the future of the Third World is faithfully reflected in the mirror of Western history. Has the new vitality in the field also led toward some acceptance of new constitutive principles [and] challenged the assumptions of the earlier theorists and their dichotomous models about the nature of order and change? The answer . . . seems to be a qualified yes: qualified because so many of the ramifications coming from the new work are still inchoate and because important connections to past assumptions do survive.[112]

Conference of the International Society of Political Psychology, New York, September 2, 1978.

[110] As Theda Skocpol notes, "It is one thing to identify underlying, potential tensions rooted in objective class relations. . . . It is another thing to understand how and when class members find themselves able to struggle effectively for their interests." *States and Social Revolution*, p. 13.

[111] See ibid. and Charles Tilly, "Does Modernization Breed Revolutions?" CP (April 1973), pp. 425–27.

[112] Joel S. Migdal, "Studying the Politics of Development and Change: The State of the Art," in *Political Science: The State of the Discipline*, ed. Ada W. Finifter (Washington, D.C.: American Political Science Association, 1983), p. 327.

Certainly the ferment of the last decade and a half has given rise to some brilliant work, but it may be too soon to celebrate. The Procrustean notions Migdal and others would lay to rest have survived previous efforts to bury them. To paraphrase Mark Twain, news of their death may be exaggerated.

Optimists may argue that if not dead, political development theory is at least dying, its demise merely delayed by inertia. Despite large numbers of case studies, the absence of new theories has meant that outmoded ones persist in more general characterizations of political systems. But, argue the optimists, just as empirical falsification and ideological dissension led young scholars to challenge grand theory in the late 1960s, so this problem will be overcome as they and their students eventually dominate the field and impose their own theories. This evolutionary perspective on scientific change has its drawbacks, however. Even within the discipline, and all the more so beyond the confines of academic political science, the barriers may be higher and of a different nature than this view suggests.

Here we return to the marketplace of ideas. As I have argued, political development theory owes much of its success not to its content but to its familiarity and utility. These masked the theory's inaccuracy and slowed efforts to perfect it. At the same time, they will inhibit, and may even render impossible, the success of new explanations of political change in the Third World. Why? Because irrespective of their possible accuracy, the new theories of political development are not appealing products in market terms. Whatever the supposed benefits of novelty, their attack on the Procrustean notion of unilinear development must overcome both disciplinary inertia and, more daunting, these same notions as embodied in other academic disciplines and general knowledge. As for utility, the new theories have none. Self-conscious complexity, a focus on nonrecurrent events, and high information requirements reduce their explanatory utility and confound prescription. No less important, whatever the Vietnam-induced ideological distemper that helped provoke them, the new theories not only fail to provide a new ideological cause of their own but also offend against the old which has reasserted itself. As a result of this combined unfamiliarity and antiutility, it seems unlikely that the optimists will be borne out even in academia. Outside the ivory tower, where the canons of scientific investigation weigh less heavily and familiarity and utility bulk large, the prospects are still bleaker. And in no place does this show more clearly than in the most important nonacademic embodiment of the ideas underlying political development theory: security and development doctrine.

4

SECURITY AND DEVELOPMENT

Neither social scientists' concern over the Third World nor their understanding of it were confined to the ivory tower. Indeed, despite only limited contacts between professors and policymakers, academics' fundamental assumptions about the sources, nature, direction, consequences, and possible pathologies of political development are replicated in both public and classified government documents and official declarations. This chapter explores these notions in their governmental guise as the doctrine of security and development. My aim in this chapter is modest: to detail the intellectual content of security and development doctrine and note the explanatory, prescriptive, and ideological utility of the ideas underpinning it. Thus, the chapter neither examines roots of policymakers' ideas nor probes the doctrine's explanatory or prescriptive weaknesses. These are the subject of the following chapter which examines security and development's most important variant, counterinsurgency doctrine, and the role social scientists played in its formulation.

There are two conventional wisdoms on American policy toward the Third World. The first stresses economic development and the promotion of democratic institutions. It is reflected in the predominance of development among the stated goals of policy, the popularity of the Peace Corps, and even in conservative attacks on the American penchant for global nannyism. The second stresses American security and economic interests. It focuses on the need for Third World resources, markets, and investment opportunities, the predominance of security assistance over foreign aid, and the prominence of strategically placed anticommunists among aid recipients. But each view is incomplete. Doctrine emphasizes development *and* security, and provides a strong case for their interdependence. It addresses both ends of the "instability equation" explained in the preceding chapter: development policies seek to ameliorate the overwhelming demands unleashed by social mobilization, and security policies attempt to bolster the underwhelming capabilities of new states that they may manage disruptions while forging ahead with modernization. Without security, so the argument goes, development is impossible; without good government and economic progress, efforts to maintain it will be bootless.

79

INSTABILITY EXPLAINED

The standard explanation of Third World political instability offered in security and development doctrine is simple, universal, and provides unambiguous policy guidance. For hard-pressed policymakers, this parsimony and prescriptive power are a godsend and explain much of the doctrine's appeal. Unfortunately, the doctrine is too parsimonious and falsely universal. As we will see in the following chapter, the standard explanation blurs significant distinctions among Third World settings and so offers little guidance as to which policies under what conditions and in which countries will achieve what. For the moment, however, let us confine ourselves to doctrine itself.

For American policymakers, political change in the Third World seemed inevitable and, in the long run, a good thing. In the short run, however, the possible pathologies of development (or "breakdowns of modernization") dominated all other concerns. As Defense Secretary Robert McNamara put it,

> Roughly 100 countries today are caught up in the difficult transition from traditional to modern societies. . . . This sweeping surge of development . . . has turned traditionally listless areas of the world into seething caldrons of change. On the whole, it has not been a very peaceful process. . . . The years that lie ahead for the nations in the southern half of the globe are pregnant with violence. This would be true even if no threat of Communist subversion existed—as it clearly does.[1]

How policymakers assessed this threat of Third World instability determined the choice of policies for preventing or, if necessary, responding to it.

Like their academic counterparts, policymakers perceived the "shock of Westernization" as the initial source of turbulence in the Third World. As the State Department's Office of Intelligence Research (INR) reported in 1956:

> Western-introduced innovations have set off a chain reaction . . . which is resulting in prodigious social dislocation. The validity and importance of traditional . . . institutions and values have been directly challenged by . . . Western institutions and ideas which seem both more powerful and more promising. . . . For the individual . . . caught between the emotional pull of old cultural

[1] Robert McNamara, "Security in the Contemporary World," DSB 54 (June 6, 1966), 875–77.

patterns and the enticing rewards of modernization there is no easy answer. And even when he seems to have found the answer in modernism, the old ties continue to disturb him.[2]

Or as a senior AID administrator put it recently, the process of development is one of "destabilizing change, of wholesale disruption of traditional ways. . . . Inevitably there will be some measure of social and political rupture . . . and perhaps civil war or revolution."[3] Thus, the problem is one of identifying the sources of instability as a prelude to programming responses to them.

Policymakers focused on both ends of the instability equation identified in the preceding chapter: the underwhelming nature of Third World governments and the overwhelming demands upon them. As for the former, Third World governments were still weak, unstable and inexperienced, yet "if non-Communist governments cannot hold out any convincing prospect that rising aspirations will be even partially fulfilled, these governments' hold on the restless and increasingly influential urban 'middle groups' will weaken. These groups will then turn to extremist leadership, which may be prepared to work closely with the Communists."[4] As for the latter, the problem was the "revolution of rising expectations" unleashed by modernization. Because of "the spread of industrial civilization," declared Harry Truman, Third World peoples have acquired "democratic aspirations." But without development, new governments "will be unable to meet the expectations which the modern world has aroused in their peoples [who] if they are frustrated and disappointed . . . may turn to false doctrines which hold that the way to progress lies through tyranny."[5] Unfortunately, concluded a 1954 report to President Eisenhower, the tide of rising expectations "tends to extend far beyond the possibility of satisfaction within any reasonable period of time."[6]

Not surprisingly, policymakers have been nearly universally pessimistic. Despite the desirability of modernization, the perils of transition

[2] "Africa: A Special Assessment," I.R. No. 7103, January 3, 1956, p. 4. NADB, OSS file.

[3] Richard Hough, *Economic Assistance and Security: Rethinking US Policy* (Washington, D.C.: National Defense University Press, 1982), p. 70.

[4] Letter to William H. Draper from Douglas Dillon, Undersecretary of State for Economic Affairs, February 20, 1959, pp. 1–2. DDRS, Retro: 962A.

[5] Harry Truman, "The Point Four Program: Aid to Underdeveloped Areas," Message to Congress, in Department of State, *General Foreign Policy Series*, No. 18, p. 26.

[6] Joseph M. Dodge, "Fundamental Factors Related to the Economic Progress of Underdeveloped Areas, and in particular, South and Southeast Asia," Council on Foreign Economic Policy, Report to the President by the Chairman, 1956, p. 3. DDRS, 1977: 97D.

seemed overwhelming. As a 1959 Institute for Defense Analysis report put it,

> There are important differences in economic, social and political conditions in the underdeveloped areas, but virtually all countries are militarily weak, beset with serious political, social and economic instability, and vulnerable to unrest and dissension. . . . Most . . . are in the throes of deep and far-reaching . . . transformation, but few possess the kind of atmosphere in which changes can occur without violence and disorder.[7]

Indeed, the International Police Academy 1966 text book description of the "Background of Insurgency, Causes of Discontent" begins: "The seeds of potential unrest are sown whenever an undeveloped society comes into contact with a more highly developed country."[8] Since in Washington's view this applied to the entire Third World, the potential for unrest was universal.

So, too, was the threat of Soviet meddling. In a 1954 report on "Economic Problems and Long-Term Political Vulnerabilities in South and Southeast Asia," INR declared that "in recent years, Communist leaders appear to have directed their main drive . . . toward the underdeveloped areas of the world."[9] Indeed, argued Under Secretary of State Douglas Dillon in 1959, the Third World "is likely to be the major battlefield of the Cold War. . . . because newly independent states are unstable and uniquely vulnerable to pressure and subversion. Their very weakness invites intervention."[10] Nor has the perception of threat abated, for as an AID official noted in 1982, "The unstable, volatile nature of the modernization process itself . . . will no doubt offer future opportunities for the Soviet Union . . . to extend [its] power and influence."[11]

Policymakers' assumption that the premodern masses of the Third World are passive, malleable, and particularly susceptible to commu-

[7] Institute for Defense Analysis, *Studies for the President's Committee to Study the U.S. Military Assistance Program*, Study No. 2, "The Role of Military Aid in Promoting Internal Security in Underdeveloped Areas," March 3, 1959, p. 10–19. DDRS, Retro: 963A.

[8] AID, OPS, *The Police and Internal Security* (Washington, D.C.: International Police Academy, 1966), p. 1–4. OPS Archives, 286-75-172, Box 4.

[9] Department of State, I.R. No. 6737, October 28, 1954, p. 2.

[10] Letter to William H. Draper from Douglas Dillon, February 20, 1959. Enclosure 2: "Economic Growth in the Free World," pp. 4–5.

[11] Hough, *Economic Assistance*, pp. 3–4. See, too, U.S. House of Representatives, Committee on Foreign Affairs, *Soviet Policy and United States Response in the Third World*, Congressional Research Service report to Congress (Washington, D.C.: GPO, March 1981), pp. 121–22.

nist blandishments deepened their pessimism. Analysis replicated the modernization/massification paradox in the academic literature: the presumed defenselessness of traditional societies before modernity offered the possibility of development; but the attendant gullibility of their members provided a "window of vulnerability" through which the Soviets might lure the unsuspecting. As a State Department report put it in 1956, "the most challenging aspect of present day [Third World] lies in [its] social and political fluidity: here, potentially powerful forces are still malleable, and time still remains to influence the shape of things to come."[12] Policymakers' conception of the masses held little hope that the shape would be ours, however. They worried that uprooted from authoritarian traditional political orders, the masses would embrace a totalitarian ideology more readily than a democratic one. Thus, for example, the official statement of "U.S. policy toward Africa South of the Sahara" declared detribalization to be "one of the major problems of the area" since "until some new loyalty is provided, the detribalized African will be an easy target for elements eager to exploit his traditional need for leadership and guidance."[13]

From this position it was but a short step to the assertion that all Third World countries were, in fact, under some form of Soviet attack. As President Kennedy declared in 1961, "without exception" the countries of the Third World "are under Communist pressure. In many cases, that pressure is direct. . . . In others, it takes the form of subversive activity designed to break down . . . the new—and often frail—modern institutions."[14] Nor has this perception changed much since. Indeed, with Soviet interventions in Angola, Ethiopia, and Afghanistan, and perceived Soviet involvement in Central America, concern over Third World instability has once again moved to center stage. And so have the policy prescriptions that follow from the standard explanation of it.

PRESCRIPTION FOR COPING

"Our central task in the underdeveloped areas," declared Walt Rostow in 1961, "is to protect the independence of the revolutionary [modern-

[12] Office of Intelligence Research, "Africa: A Special Assessment," p. 1.
[13] NSC 5818, August 26, 1958, p. 16. NAMM, NSC file. See, too, Department of State, Office of Intelligence Research, "Economic Problems," I.R. No. 6737, p. 2, and "African Receptivity to Soviet Bloc Influence," I.R. No. 7650, January 24, 1958, p. 5. NADB, OSS file.
[14] Message on Foreign Aid to the Committee on Foreign Relations, March 22, 1961, *Congressional Record—Senate, 1961*, p. 4467.

ization] process now going forward."[15] Thus, he summed up the basic impulse of American policy toward the Third World in the postwar period. Initially, this meant, according to the 1956 statement of *Basic National Security Policy*, aiding nationalist movements in colonial areas, preventing their "capture" by communists, and convincing Europeans to allow "an orderly evolution of political arrangements toward self determination."[16] With the prospect of decolonization, the 1959 version prescribed "timely and appropriate political support to newly emergent states."[17] But even with intensified efforts, concluded a State Department study, "we cannot hope [to] prevent instability; we can only hope to moderate the effects of this instability, so that non-Communist elements . . . will retain power and continue to believe that their goals can be achieved in association with the free world."[18] Or as an AID official recently stated, "Given the dynamics of change . . . it makes little sense for us to stand aside. Our concern must be the character and pace of the change which is inevitable in any case. We must try to contribute to development and modernization which avoid the deterioration and eventual political turmoil . . . produced by . . . inequitable change."[19] The prescription for how to do so grew directly from the standard explanation of the sources of Third World instability. Similarly, policymakers' prescription for the Third World owes much of its longevity to its utility.

The first issue was choice of allies. The guidance was clear: if instability threatened because state institutions and elites could not cope, then they needed support. In part, this focus on leaders simply reflects the requirement that governments deal with governments. But more importantly, policymakers saw the postcolonial regimes as the source of most development in the Third World. They tended, too, to take Third World leaders at their word, believing that, because of their "Western education," they were the "driving force" of modernization while the masses were "naturally indifferent to political matters."[20] Policymakers viewed these leaders and the states they controlled as embodying the normative order of the future (even if, in practice, malin-

[15] Walt Rostow, "Guerrilla Warfare in the Underdeveloped Areas," DSB (August 7, 1961), p. 235.

[16] NSC 5602, February 8, 1956, pp. 16–17. NAMM, NSC file.

[17] NSC 5906/1, August 5, 1959, pp. 15-18. NAMM, NSC file.

[18] State Department, "Objectives of Long-Term Foreign Policy," included in letter to William Draper from Douglas Dillon, enclosure 1, Talking paper of Assistant Secretary Smith, "US Foreign Economic Assistance," p. 21. DDRS, Retro: 962A.

[19] Hough, *Economic Assistance*, p. 71.

[20] NSC 51, "U.S. Policy toward Southeast Asia," July 1, 1949, p. 4. DDRS, 1975: 276B.

tegration still reigned). This legitimized the status quo and reduced virtually all protests to evidence of bad conscience of either an anachronistic or subversive cast.

Thus, a method of aiding these elites was also implicit in the analysis of instability. It required a strategy to meet both sources of political instability, "to provide for an integral capacity to eliminate the root causes of disaffection and dissidence . . . and to cope with increased levels of violence."[21] This, in turn, required short-term programs to provide security for threatened elites and long-term ones both to build good government through strengthened institutions and to promote economic progress to defuse the revolution of rising expectations. While differences continue over the optimal mix of the two, they define the poles of debate on U.S. Third World policy.

Security

Security dominated policymakers' thinking. A 1971 RAND study summed up their assumptions as follows:

> domestic political violence can necessarily have only bad consequences for . . . development; the lower the level of domestic violence, the better necessarily the prospects for [it]; and therefore nations and governments need to be automatically "shielded" against violence . . . if they are to proceed with effective development.[22]

The perceived necessity of order became the necessary priority of security and security assistance programs which came to be defined as "developmental." Thus, Lauren Goin, director of AID's Office of Public Safety (OPS), insisted that the agency was "engaged in the development process. . . . There must be an adequate measure of internal order, internal stability, if a nation is going to progress in an orderly fashion in the social, economic and political arenas. The alternative is disruption, disorder, violence, and frustration of the aspirations of the people."[23] Indeed, like their academic counterparts, officials defined the maintenance of order as the first priority, for "if a government is to govern, it

[21] AID, OPS, "U.S. Police Assistance, 1955–1962," in "History of OPS, 1955–Present," January 1970, p. 45. OPS Archives, 286-75-090, IPS-1, Box 7.

[22] David Ronfeldt and Luigi Einaudi, *Internal Security and Military Assistance to Latin America in the 1970s: A First Statement*, R-924-ISA (Santa Monica: RAND Corp., December 1971), pp. 11–12.

[23] American Security Council, "Police Aid Program Under Attack," interview with Lauren J. Goin, Director, Office of Public Safety, *Washington Report*, n.d., p. 2.

must be able to enforce its edicts. . . . Compliance with the law or stability *must prevail*."[24]

Logically, the priority of order demands further justification. On the one hand, the assertion that a regime's security takes precedence begs the obvious questions of "defense against what" and "security for whom." On the other, the assertion that the law must prevail begs the questions of whose legality is being enforced and its legitimacy. That these questions are seldom asked reflects the strength of the standard explanation of Third World instability. This is neatly illustrated by AID chief David Bell's testimony on the 1963 Foreign Assistance Act which confounded "strengthening democratic institutions or liberalizing less democratic regimes" and "political stability" as interchangeable definitions of the "development" American programs promote.[25] Since instability arises from below or without modernizing governments, while conversely they are the source of progress, then even illiberal acts on their part are justifiable. Thus, despite a preference for representative government, the 1969 report of the Presidential Mission for the Western Hemisphere asserted, for example, that "the question is less one of democracy or a lack of it than it is simply of orderly ways of getting along."[26] In fact, to manage modernization and its discontents, an authoritarian regime may be required or even recommended to preclude the development of a totalitarian one.

POLICE ASSISTANCE

In the past, police assistance programs constituted the first element of the security prescription. Prior to World War II, the United States trained police units in Central America and the Caribbean, and established the Philippine Constabulary. During and after the war, the United States advised the Iranian Gendarmarie and observed the British police training program in Greece in the late 1940s. Then in 1954 the Eisenhower administration called for "recognizing the police as the first line of defense against subversion and insurgency."[27] The police as-

[24] AID, OPS, "History," p. 42. Emphasis in original. See, too, "AID Public Safety Assistance to Combat Criminal Violence and Terrorism," September 22, 1972, p. 1. OPS Archives.

[25] U.S. House of Representatives, Committee on Foreign Affairs, *Foreign Assistance Act of 1963*, Hearings, 88th Cong., 1st Sess., Part II, April 23, 24, 25, and 26, 1963, pp. 185–91 and ff. For a cogent analysis of Bell's testimony and the assumptions behind it, see Packenham, *Liberal America and the Third World*, pp. 64–68.

[26] Nelson A. Rockefeller, *The Rockefeller Report on the Americas*, The Official Report of the United States Presidential Mission for the Western Hemisphere (Chicago: Quadrangle Books, 1969), p. 58.

[27] AID, OPS, "History," p. 3.

sistance program began as the Civil Police Branch (later renamed the Overseas Internal Security Program, OISP) of the International Cooperation Agency and started training operations in 1955. The program grew rapidly for the remainder of the Eisenhower Administration, was reorganized by Kennedy as a division within AID, and flourished throughout the 1960s as the Office of Public Safety (OPS). To complement overseas programs, OPS established the International Police Academy in Washington, D.C. to train Third World police officers. Ultimately, 10,700 officers were trained in the United States, 5,024 at the International Police Academy, and at one time or another, police training missions operated in fifty-two countries.[28]

Police assistance embodied security and development notions. According to the repeatedly cited Interagency Committee on Police Assistance Program's 1962 statement of the "Role and Function of Police Programs,"

> In recent years the Communists have increased their efforts to exploit the process of . . . modernization in the less-developed nations. . . . The US interest lies in the orderly development of these nations—not simply in political stability. Our goal—far from defending the *status quo*—is to help governments deal with the dislocations inherent in development in an orderly way, with minimum civil strife and injustice and with maximum responsiveness to reasonable dissent. But in the short-run, the governments under attack must be able to contain the internal threat to gain time for basic development. Thus, police programs also support directly our major effort to press the basic economic development of the emerging countries.[29]

Furthermore, because "the police constitute the first line of defense against subversion and terrorism," argued OPS, "the earlier the police can meet such threats, the less it will cost in money and manpower and the less interruption will occur in the vital process of orderly government."[30]

[28] General Accounting Office, *Stopping U.S. Assistance to Foreign Police and Prisons*, Report to the Congress by the Comptroller General, GAO ID-76-5, February 19, 1976, p. 10.

[29] White House, *Report of the Interagency Committee on Police Assistance in Newly Emerging Nations*, response to NSAM 146, July 20, 1962, pp. 1–2. OPS Archives, 286-75-074, IPS 5, Box 1; and AID, OPS, "AID Assistance to Civil Security Forces," statement prepared for presentation to the President's General Advisory Committee on Foreign Assistance Programs, October 4, 1965, p. 4. OPS Archives.

[30] AID, OPS, "The Role of A.I.D. Public Safety Programs during the Johnson Adminis-

The assertion that OPS did not serve the status quo notwithstanding, the agency did assume the legitimacy of governments being aided. Moreover, it assumed that they were the managers of the development process and that "vital in this process [is] the need to ensure that the government [has] the capability for enforcing its own edicts; enforcing its laws and maintaining order."[31] Public order was thus defined as obedience to the laws of whatever regime happened to be in power because it was, again by definition, the rightful government. In fact, the Johnson administration actually declared OPS programs to be the "international dimension of the . . . War on Crime."[32]

OPS programs had two ends: improve Third World police forces' technical capabilities and integrate them "more closely . . . into the community."[33] The former presented few difficulties; the latter did. Although American advisors complained about political hacks and low motivation among the police forces aided, it required little effort to provide batons, tear gas, water canons, and other equipment and train locals in their use. But it proved more difficult to teach Third World policemen a modern American public service "mind-set" and so make them a progressive force in development. Particularly with the passage of Title IX (see "Good Government" discussion later in this chapter), OPS placed "major emphasis" on "the vital role of the police as a builder/protector of democratic institutions" and stressed "democratic institution building and popular participation." OPS sought to "orient the police to function as an important community service and to develop a sympathetic identification with the citizenry." ("This concept," the OPS history admitted, "is new to most political and police leaders, and attitudes must change—and are changing.")[34]

OPS programs also aimed to further development by molding Third World policemen into modern role models for the citizenry. OPS asserted, for example, that the International Police Academy "has contributed to U.S. goals in the broadening of the insight and *understanding* of its participants to the *traumatic* change which is affecting the environment in which they live and must work—*and has provided* them with *new ideas, new tools, and a revitalized pride* in their profes-

tration," document marked "Security Assistance Chap IX (FY1964-FY1968), n.d., pp. 5–6. OPS Archives, 286-75-090, IPS-3, Box 7.

[31] AID, OPS, "History," p. 1. The International Police Academy taught, for example, that "in almost all developing nations throughout the world, insidious elements are endeavoring . . . to undermine legitimate governments." *The Police*, p. I–1.

[32] AID, OPS, "The Role," p. 2.

[33] AID, OPS, "Civil Security Forces," p. 2.

[34] AID, OPS, "History," p. 40.

sion."[35] Thus, at the Academy, "maximum emphasis is placed on developing democratic leadership potential,"[36] since "the civilian police can help support the democratic process by fair treatment of the citizenry without discrimination, teaching respect for authority, and establishing rapport with the population. It should constitute an intimate point of contact between government and citizen."[37] It was a nice but naive hope, for as we will see in the following chapter, the political constraints on the police often kept even well-intentioned officers from performing as expected.

By 1968, OPS, focused on Vietnam, had become a target of congressional critics of U.S. policy. OPS claimed that it aided only countries "where the US can avoid being identified with a repressive and unpopular police force or with one deeply involved in domestic factional maneuvering" and that "police assistance is not given to support dictatorships."[38] But in 1973 when press and congressional investigators discovered the "tiger cages" at Con Son and other South Vietnamese prisons, as well as evidence that OPS had supported their construction, many in Congress were outraged.[39] Indeed, for many, OPS and this sort of OPS program came to symbolize what was wrong with American foreign policy. Thus, the Congress moved quickly to eliminate OPS by amending the Foreign Assistance Act of 1974 to prohibit police training programs after July 1, 1975. It is important to note, however, that debate at the time never addressed the underlying security and development rationale for police assistance. Instead, it focused entirely on the highly publicized abuses carried out by certain OPS supported police forces with apparent OPS acquiescence.[40] As a result, the unchal-

[35] Ibid., p. 44. Emphasis in original.
[36] AID, OPS, "The Role," p. 7.
[37] AID, OPS, The Police, p. I-2.
[38] White House, Report of the Interagency Committee, p. 3, and AID, OPS, "Civil Security Forces," p.4.
[39] See the testimony of Sen. James Abourezk, U.S. Senate, Committee on Foreign Relations, Foreign Economic Assistance Act, 1973, Hearings, 93rd Cong., 1st sess., June 26 and 27, 1973, pp. 244–50; and U.S. House of Representatives, Committee on Foreign Affairs, Subcommittee on Asian and Pacific Affairs, The Treatment of Political Prisoners in South Vietnam by the Government of the Republic of South Vietnam, Hearings, 93rd Cong., 1st sess., September 13, 1973.
[40] The Senate report on the Foreign Assistance Act of 1973, for example, refers to the "highly sensitive" nature of police assistance which "unavoidably invites criticism" that may "stigmatize the total United States foreign aid effort." The report recommends that police programs "are better left to be underwritten from local resources," while U.S. aid is "directed toward less sensitive areas." U.S. Senate, Committee on Foreign Relations, Report No. 93-377, 93rd Cong., 1st sess., August 17, 1973, p. 17.

lenged developmentalist arguments for police assistance were allowed to lie dormant until needed again.

In 1985 such arguments were reawakened to justify a Reagan administration effort to circumvent the prohibition against aid to foreign police forces. They again proved persuasive as Congress accepted exceptions to the prohibition that allowed training assistance to the police forces of Costa Rica, Honduras, and El Salvador in order to make them a more effective first line of defense against subversion. As a senior staff member of the Pentagon's Office of Special Planning put it, the essential prerequisite for preventing insurgency is good local intelligence, and the best source of that is "the cop on his beat"—provided, of course, that local cops "wear a white hat." And the role of police training, he concluded, is to teach both the techniques of modern police work and, more important, the public service orientation necessary to win popular trust and support.[41]

MILITARY ASSISTANCE

Military assistance programs are, as Andrew Pierre observes, "foreign policy writ large."[42] As such, it is not surprising that they cover a multitude of activities—from the gift of weapons to training tours for foreign officers—and serve both short-term tactical ends and long-term strategic ones. Officials offer three basic justifications for Third World military assistance, however. First, it aims to provide "the necessary means for internal security against Communist subversion" in order to reduce the number of "targets of opportunity" that might invite problems and so risk direct American involvement.[43] In 1980 Lt. General Ernest Graves, then director of the Defense Security Assistance Agency, explained, "If we . . . were not prepared to provide the equipment and training needed by others, we would have to be prepared to take the graver step of using U.S. forces to defend our interests."[44] Second, military assistance is supposed to provide political influence in recipient countries, including leverage to induce political reform. As testimony

[41] Telephone interviews with George Talbot, Office of Special Planning, International Security Affairs, Department of Defense, March 31 and April 1, 1986.

[42] Andrew Pierre, *The Global Politics of Arms Sales* (Princeton: Princeton University Press, 1982), p. 3.

[43] U.S. Senate, Special Committee to Study the Foreign Aid Program. *Report on Military Assistance and the Security of the U.S., 1947–1956*, prepared by the Institute of War and Peace Studies, Columbia University (Washington, D.C.: GPO, 1957), pp. 157–58.

[44] Lt. General Ernest Graves, Director, Defense Security Assistance, testimony, April 6, 1980, U.S. Senate, Committee on Appropriations, *Foreign Assistance and Related Programs Appropriations for Fiscal Year 1981*, Hearings, 96th Cong., 2nd sess., 1980, p. 286.

to the Draper Committee in 1959 put it, "where U.S. support allows us to exert a constructive influence . . . , it may in time affect the 're-pressive' character of the forces concerned."[45] Accordingly, officials of the Carter and Reagan administrations have argued that military aid to such countries as Zaire and El Salvador is producing significant im-provements in governmental and military behavior. Finally, military assistance justifications stress the benefits of reducing the defense bur-den on limited government budgets and the contributions of military investments and training to economic development.

Behind each category of justifications lie the assumptions of security and development doctrine. Military assistance prescriptions call for providing the state with the coercive capabilities to meet threats to its security and hence that of the development process. Security for the de-velopment process is, in turn, critical to the achievement of the specific aims of military aid since political instability invites Soviet meddling, regional imbalances, and competitive attempts to gain influence while preventing economic development. Moreover, besides merely defend-ing the development process, as "modern elites" Third World militaries are also supposed to have an independent development role of their own.

Military assistance justifications assume that development generates instability and hence enhances the need for security capabilities. Noted a report to the Draper Committee,

> The ideal would be . . . prevention. Social cohesion, economic well-being, political stability, governmental vigor and efficiency—these are the basic cures [of instability]. If they could be effected, such measures could probably forestall the development of a seri-ous . . . threat. They are tantamount, however, to developing the underdeveloped countries. The prerequisites would be time, meas-ured in decades and generations, large-scale programs, and the people to carry them out. Time is not available. . . . Preventive ac-tion through economic, technical, and related programs is, there-fore, not enough. Since Communists have the capability to create or intensify conflicts . . . almost at will, a countermeasures pro-gram must also include the readiness to deal with a revolutionary situation when and if it arises.[46]

The prescription was and remains simple. In 1970 General Robert Warren, then chief military aid administrator, described the require-

[45] Institute for Defense Analysis, *Studies*, No. 2, "Military Aid," pp. 10-34 to 10-35.
[46] Ibid., pp. 10-13, 10-15.

ment as "forces capable of providing . . . internal security essential to orderly political, social, and economic development."[47]

This theme runs through justifications for military aid to the Third World from 1945 to the present. In Truman's phrase, "Freedom cannot grow and expand unless it is protected against the armed imperialism of those who would destroy it."[48] And in 1960 President Eisenhower observed that

> Unaided, none of these countries can . . . simultaneously protect themselves from internal and external threats while pursuing the long and difficult road of economic development. To assist them to deter and counter, if necessary, the aggressive expansion of communism and to support them in their pursuit of the affirmative goals of creating free nations . . . the United States proposes to continue . . . its Mutual Security Program.[49]

The 1969 Defense Department's Military Assistance Program (MAP) funding justification declared it imperative to "contain the forces of international communism which seek to disrupt and enslave the nations and peoples the United States is trying to help toward orderly development and freedom from fear of external attack or subversion."[50] And as a recent congressional report asserts, "In providing military assistance . . . the United States has attempted to enhance the ability of friendly governments to defend themselves from external aggression or internal subversion from Communist . . . powers."[51]

But military aid programs extend far beyond the provision of military hardware and professional training. Indeed, policymakers assert that they promote economic, social, and political development. As a report to the Draper Committee declared, "The United States should, as a matter of policy, encourage the use of the armed forces of underdeveloped countries as a major 'transmission belt' of socio-economic reform and development." In fact,

[47] U.S. House of Representatives, Committee on Appropriations, *Foreign Assistance and Related Agencies Appropriations for 1971*, Hearings, 91st Cong., 2nd sess., 1971, Part I, p. 389.

[48] Cited in Major Edward L. Katzenbach, Jr., "Indochina: A Military-Political Appreciation," WP 4: 2 (July 1952), p. 212.

[49] Department of State, *The Mutual Security Program, Fiscal Year 1961: A Summary Presentation*, March 1960, p. 96.

[50] Department of Defense, *Military Assistance Facts: May 1969* (Washington, D.C.: Office of the Assistant Secretary of Defense for International Security Affairs, 1969), p. 1.

[51] U.S. House, *Soviet Policy and United States Response*, p. 195.

MAP represents one of the most useful available instruments . . . for meeting the challenges of the systemic revolution in the underdeveloped areas. . . . [which] cannot be successful in the long run unless the recipient countries undergo significant changes—organizational, sociological, economic and sometimes political. MAP should be looked upon not solely as a military program, but as a broadly gauged sociological and organizational undertaking.

The report thus urged that military assistance be used to build infrastructure, train dual military-civilian use units, improve officers' effectiveness as "agents of social change," and convert the military into an "instrument for unifying nascent countries and . . . breaking down archaic tribalism."[52]

IMET and the Modernizing Military

Behind the belief that Third World militaries are a force for development lies the familiar assumption that modernity is a matter of mindset. As Walt Rostow told Third World members of the first class of Green Berets graduated from Fort Bragg, "You are not merely soldiers in the old sense. . . . Your job is to work with . . . your fellow citizens in the whole creative process of modernization. From our perspective in Washington, you take your place side by side with those others who are committed to help fashion independent, modern societies out of the revolutionary process now going forward."[53] As with academic arguments for the "modernizing military," military aid justifications assumed that unlike civilian political institutions, Third World militaries were national, nonethnic, meritocratic, united, organizationally strong, technically sophisticated, development oriented, and incorruptible.

These characteristics made Third World militaries appear to be the ideal target for assistance. In 1969, for example, INR reported that Latin American militaries have a strong propensity to lead their countries toward modernity, because officers'

> occupational interests promote a concern sometimes bordering on obsession with the state of the nation and a conviction that they have an important role to play in realizing national destinies. . . . In their professional capacities . . . the officers are sensitively

[52] Foreign Policy Research Institute, University of Pennsylvania, *A Study of U.S. Military Assistance Programs in the Underdeveloped Areas (Final Report)*, report to the Institute for Defense Analysis, March 3, 1959, pp. 10–11, 4 and 11-2. DDRS, Retro: 963A.
[53] Rostow, "Guerrilla Warfare," DSB, p. 237.

93

aware of their national deficiencies and . . . they are highly motivated to progress from this low status to fuller development of national resources and command of modern technology.[54]

In the words of General Lemnitzer, chairman of the Joint Chiefs, this recommended a program aimed " at developing a new breed of foreign military men—respectable men whose ultimate purpose is to stabilize their local societies and to create an environment in which freedom has a chance to flourish."[55]

This view also justified aid to military regimes. As the CIA reported to the Draper Committee in 1959, such governments

> have come about, or may come about, primarily because of failures of civilian governments . . . to cope with basic social and economic problems besetting their states, or provide strong political leadership in inherently unstable situations. In most underdeveloped . . . states the armed forces have constituted the major institution-in-being capable of taking over and providing some kind of stability when existing civilian regimes could not.[56]

Having replaced "civilian governments run by self-serving politicians and inefficient bureaucrats," declared another report, "almost without exception these officer corps . . . have placed their countries on the road to stability and governmental efficiency."[57] Notes Brian Smith of the Alliance for Progress, "The dominant feeling in both Congress and in the State Department was that the armed forces in Latin America were not threats to democracy but . . . bastions against radical revolution as well as nation-builders."[58] Indeed, an analyst writing in the Army's *Military Review* claimed that "the military coup is *crucial* for the continuation and acceleration of nation-building."[59]

[54] Department of State, Bureau of Intelligence and Research, George C. Denney, Jr., "The New Militarism in South America: Agent for Modernization?" Research memorandum for the Secretary, RAR-26, August 28, 1969, pp. 8–9. DDRS, 1981: 214A.

[55] "Summary Report, Military Counterinsurgency Accomplishments since January 1961," Memorandum for the Special Assistant to the President for National Security Affairs, CM-843-62, July 21, 1962, p. 8. DDRS, Retro: 242C.

[56] CIA, Office of the Deputy Director (Intelligence), Robert Amory, Jr., "Certain Problems Created by the US Military Assistance Program," January 30, 1959. DDRS, Retro: 960A.

[57] Foreign Policy Research Institute, *U.S. Military Assistance*, pp. 70–71.

[58] Brian Smith, "U.S.–Latin American Military Relations Since World War II: Implications for Human Rights," in *Human Rights and Basic Needs in the Americas*, ed. Margaret Crahan and Brian Smith (Washington, D.C.: Georgetown University Press, 1982), p. 270.

[59] David Chang, "Military Forces and Nation-Building," MR (September 1970), p. 78.

Given faith in the modernizing military, the International Military Education and Training program (IMET) has always held a special position. It is supposed to teach not only professional skills but also modernity itself, by providing training tours for foreign military officers and NCOs at American facilities. In part, IMET serves obvious technical and diplomatic ends. IMET programs have long focused on such prosaic subjects as auto mechanics and civil engineering on the one hand, and the courtship of foreign officers on the other. (In Defense Secretary McNamara's words, it is "beyond price to the United States to make friends with these men. . . . They are the coming leaders of their nations.")[60] But justifications for IMET are seldom confined to such instrumental goals. Rather, Defense Department officials claim, that "inherent in training assistance" are critical attitudinal changes.[61] "Thrown into US society," declared the Army, "these men cannot escape having their thinking and their standards affected."[62] A 1973 RAND report claimed that "exposure to American training has . . . made many military officers in the Third World the driving force in their nations' quest for progress."[63] Indeed, a Special Study Mission to evaluate IMET concluded that although many IMET "training tours" are little more than "guided vacations" (to such installations as Disneyland), nevertheless they are "an important method of exposing a significant leadership group to American life and society as a crucial point in their intellectual development, thereby affecting their future philosophy and convictions."[64]

Not everyone agreed with the optimistic assessments of IMET's long-

[60] U.S. Senate, Committee on Foreign Relations, *Foreign Assistance Act of 1963*, Hearings, 88th Cong., 1st sess., 1962, p. 208. For a recent example, see Matthew Nimitz, Under Secretary of State, U.S. Senate, Committee on Appropriations, *Foreign Assistance and Related Programs Appropriations for Fiscal Year 1981*, Hearings, 96th Cong., 2nd sess., 1980, p. 275.

[61] Office of the Secretary of Defense, *Military Assistance Program, FY 1962, Congressional Presentation*, cited in Charles Windle and T. R. Vallance, "Optimizing Military Assistance Training," WP 15: 1 (October 1962), p. 93.

[62] U.S. Army, Office of the Secretary, "Evaluation of the Military Assistance Program," memorandum for the President's Committee to Study the United States Military Assistance Program, 1959, pp. 19–20. DDRS, Retro: 964A.

[63] Guy Pauker, Steven Canby, Ross Johnson, and William Quandt, *In Search of Self-Reliance: U.S. Security Assistance to the Third World under the Nixon Doctrine*, R-1092-ARPA (Santa Monica: RAND Corp., June 1973), p. 64.

[64] U.S. House of Representatives, Committee on Foreign Affairs, *Reports of the Special Study Mission to Latin America on Military Assistance Training and Developmental Television*, submitted by Hon. Clement Zablocki, James Fulton, and Paul Findley to the Subcommittee on National Security Policy and Scientific Developments, 91st Cong., 2nd sess., April 29, 1970, p. 7.

term effects. A 1971 INR study of military assistance to Latin America, for example, suggested that it "had a perceptible impact on the political leanings of the military in a few cases. But it was never a decisive ingredient when compared to overall US influence . . . and the basic tendencies of the national military institutions and societies themselves."[65] A decade later, a Congressional Research Service seminar investigating IMET programs' impact on foreign officer attitudes concluded that even sophisticated indoctrination efforts might produce at most a 5 percent change in trainee attitudes and that this would erode quickly upon their return home.[66]

Such criticisms notwithstanding, ambitious behavior modification justifications have maintained their currency. As Secretary of State Cyrus Vance declared in 1980, "IMET directly supports our efforts to advance the cause of human rights, as it exposes military officers in other countries to the role of our own armed forces in a democratic nation. I believe it has been a factor in the heartening moves toward democracy in a number of Latin American countries in recent years."[67] In fact, less than two years after criticizing IMET's effectiveness, the Congressional Research Service reported that IMET trainees

> are able to influence favorably the receptivity of their governments and their armed forces to American ideals and standards. In theory, their ability and willingness to use their positions . . . to influence the attitudes of their governments and military forces in ways favored by the United States has been enhanced by their exposure to the American political system.[68]

In short, IMET could teach officers the modern mind-set, thus making them not only the defenders of their would-be modern governments but also contributors to the modernization process.

Development

Beyond short-term security, policymakers were deeply concerned about the political and economic development believed necessary for

[65] Department of State, Bureau of Intelligence and Research, "Latin America: The Impact of Foreign Military Assistance," November 22, 1971, p. ii. DDRS, 1981: 215A.

[66] Smith, "U.S.–Latin American Military Relations," p. 229, fn. 62.

[67] U.S. House of Representatives, Committee on Foreign Affairs, *Foreign Assistance Legislation for Fiscal Year 1981*, Hearings, 96th Cong., 2nd sess., February 5, 1980. Argentina, Brazil, and Chile have been the major IMET program recipients in Latin American; elsewhere Iran and Pakistan have been among the largest recipients over the last twenty years.

[68] U.S. House, *Soviet Policy and United States Response*, p. 205.

long-term stability. Whatever modernizing leaders desired and whatever the future might hold, the present still posed problems. Policymakers worried that

> These countries, by and large, are not healthy democracies by
> Western standards, and power is not widely shared. In virtually all
> of them, power is in the hands of more or less narrow elites. . . . It
> is seldom that the ruling groups have a firm or widespread base of
> support at the grass roots level. Often they are divided into diverse
> cliques and factions competing for power. With few exceptions,
> they have been unable to give their countries efficient government.
> . . . In most of them civil administration is weak and underdevel-
> oped. Many . . . contain large areas in which national government
> authority is hardly established, and in which there are virtually no
> local government institutions. . . . Government agencies are
> staffed with personnel who lack the professional and technical
> skills . . . ; and in . . . many countries they are subject to corrup-
> tion and political manipulation.[69]

Thus, declared President Kennedy, Third World elites and their institutions of state required retooling to "lead the fight for those basic reforms which alone can preserve the fabric of their own societies. Those
who make peaceful revolution impossible will make violent revolution
inevitable."[70]

To make peaceful revolutions possible, policymakers have offered a
variety of prescriptions for aid to promote modernization. Despite the
complexity of the mission, they are certain of the basic process involved. As one AID administrator put it, "The problem for us today [is]
more practical than conceptual; more clinical than philosophical."[71]
Having specified the normal curve of development, the task is reduced
to fine tuning. Still, a hot debate rages over the most appropriate clinical procedure, and those charged with promoting development have
embraced many faddish approaches, including relief and recovery,
technical assistance, education and training, institution building, public administration, community development, internal security, political
development, basic human needs, and rural development. This profu-
sion reduces to two basic types, however, depending on which end of
the instability equation they address: weakness of the state or the revolution of rising expectations. The former consists of programs to build
good government, the latter to promote economic progress.

[69] Institute for Defense Analysis, *Studies*, No. 2, "Military Aid," pp. 10-10 to 10-11.
[70] "Fulfilling the Pledges of the Alliance for Progress," DSB, April 2, 1962, p. 541.
[71] Hough, *Economic Assistance*, pp. 2–3.

GOOD GOVERNMENT

Good government prescriptions have a double thrust: the promotion of *more* and *better* government. Prescriptions of the first variety derive from concern about the underwhelming nature of many Third World governments. If they cannot manage the demands provoked by modernization or meet the challenge of social transformation, policymakers argue, then the United States ought to help. This means, on the one hand, providing advice on public administration aimed at rationalizing and strengthening state institutions to increase their efficiency, honesty, and management abilities. These programs stress such action as controlling corruption, reforming the civil service to limit nepotism, reducing red tape, and improving revenue collection. On the other hand, they stress penetrating administration into the periphery in order to increase central control, overcome ethnic, communal, or regional resistance, promote national integration, and encourage further, more rapid modernization. Either way, efforts to increase the quantity of government assume states' legitimacy and that of their goals, despite policymakers' own testimony that many governments leave much to be desired.

Still, policymakers also worry over the quality of Third World governments' relations with their subjects. They worry because government-population relations are often so bad and because they contend that in the long run responsive, democratic government offers a durable bastion against instability. Moreover, policymakers believe that the United States "needs governments . . . which see things more or less like we do. Such governments can only arise from a set of reasonably well rooted, stable, democratic political institutions."[72] Although such long-term considerations often take a back seat to more immediate security and "quantity" concerns, they have had an enduring importance through the postwar period. Indeed, they have again become the focus of extensive activity as a result of the Reagan administration's initiatives to promote democracy abroad. The issue is perhaps best exemplified, however, by the 1966 Title IX amendment to the Foreign Assistance Act, "Utilization of Democratic Institutions in Development."

Title IX sought to refocus foreign assistance to assure "maximum participation in the task of economic development on the part of the people of the developing countries, through the encouragement of . . .

[72] Pat Holt, consultant to the Subcommittee on American Republics Affairs of the Senate Committee on Foreign Relations, in U.S. Senate, Committee on Foreign Relations, Subcommittee on American Republic Affairs, *Survey of the Alliance for Progress*, Hearings, 90th Cong., 2nd sess., Feb. 27, 28, 29, March 1, 4, 5, and 6, 1968, p. 198.

democratic private and public institutions at all levels."[73] Policymakers supportive of the Title IX initiative offered two approaches. Some favored support for the institutions of democracy per se—political parties, legislatures, legislative staffs—and assistance in the drafting of democratic constitutions, electoral laws, and so on. (Samuel Huntington even proposed an Office of Political Development, "a new style CIA, more skilled in building governments than in subverting them.")[74] Others stressed development of such organizations as cooperatives, unions, and community action groups to serve as training grounds for a more participant, ultimately democratic citizenry.[75] Both views were subsumed within the more general focus of Title IX on "popular participation" which grew out of a joint academic-government seminar chaired by Max Millikan and Lucian Pye at MIT in the summer of 1968. The seminar's final report declared participation in political decision-making "from the local community to the national center" to be the "central concept" because "more participation leads, through popular pressure, to improved governmental performance and to more equitable and useful distribution of resources. More economic growth provides both resources to make participation possible and a growing variety of institutions and organizations through which it can be practiced." Thus, aid ought to create or strengthen the institutions necessary to "enable people to articulate their demands effectively" and "enable government to respond effectively to those demands."[76]

Title IX had its problems, however. First, many criticized such efforts as dangerous because they threatened short-term efforts to maintain stability. Indeed, a former acting director of the Political Development Division of AID commented that Title IX faced objections precisely because it was an attempt to counter aid's (and AID's) emphasis on "actions which tended to strengthen central government institutions at the expense of grass-roots democracy."[77] Second, the Title IX focus on the quality of government suffered from the same debilitating weakness as its quantity counterparts: it assumed the legitimacy of the government. After all, the notion that more participation breeds stability assumes

[73] U.S. House of Representatives, Committee on Foreign Affairs, *Foreign Assistance Act of 1966*, House Report No. 1651, 89th Cong., 2nd sess., June 23, 1966, pp. 27–28.

[74] Samuel Huntington, *Military Intervention, Political Involvement and the Unlessons of Vietnam* (Chicago: Adlai Stevenson Institute of International Affairs, 1968), p. 28.

[75] Rep. Dante Fascell, "Behavioral Sciences and the National Security," in *Project Camelot*, ed. Irving L. Horowitz (Cambridge: MIT Press, 1974), pp. 194–95.

[76] See the seminar's final report, *The Role of Popular Participation in Development*, (Cambridge: Center for International Studies, MIT, 1968), pp. 1–3.

[77] John Schott, cited in Packenham, *Liberal America*, p. 160. See, too, Fascell, "Behavioral Sciences," in *Project Camelot*, ed. Horowitz, p. 194.

that those in power and those outside it share the same notions about the means and ends of state policy.

PROGRESS

Development prescriptions giving priority to economic progress begin from a familiar assumption: once exposed to modernity and the possibilities it offers for a better life, the masses will demand their share. In President Eisenhower's words, "Hundreds of millions of people throughout the world have learned that it is not ordained that they must live in perpetual poverty and illness, on the ragged edge of starvation."[78] To integrate them into the modern world and avoid the possibly violent consequences of thwarting their desires requires broadened opportunities in the modern economy and so broadened economic equality. Indeed, noted a 1959 Legislative Reference Service report, "The simple assumption that communism flows from poverty is so widely accepted in America that it is almost an article of faith."[79] It has not changed much since.

Variants of the progress prescription recur throughout the postwar period. Harry Truman described economic development assistance as "the most effective way . . . of helping to achieve the objectives of peaceful and democratic conditions."[80] As his successor put it, unless the poor "can hope for reasonable economic advance, the danger will be acute that their governments will be subverted by Communism."[81] Conversely, argued Senator Tom Connally, "A people with a rising standard of living and with hope for the future are immune to the preachments of communism. This is our most potent weapon and one for which the Kremlin can find no defense."[82] Thus, noted AID in 1962, "The long-range aim . . . of economic assistance . . . has been to create economic and social conditions of sufficient vitality to eliminate the

[78] Department of State, *The Mutual Security Program, Fiscal Year 1961: A Summary Presentation, March 1960*, p. vii.

[79] *U.S. Foreign Aid: Its Purposes, Scope, Administration and Related Information*, House Document No. 116, 86th Cong., 1st sess. (Washington, D.C.: GPO, 1959), p. 84.

[80] Special Message to the Congress Recommending Continuation of Economic Assistance to Korea, June 7, 1949, *Public Papers of the Presidents of the United States, Harry S. Truman, 1949*, p. 279.

[81] Special Message to the Congress on the Mutual Security Programs, May 21, 1957, *Public Papers of the Presidents of the United States: Dwight D. Eisenhower, 1957*, p. 373.

[82] Senator Tom Connally, "Reviewing American Foreign Policy Since 1945," Senate speech, September 22, 1950, in Department of State, *General Foreign Policy Series*, No. 35, p. 566.

causes of discontent and to sustain representative government."[83] And AID's position remains unchanged. The 1981 congressional presentation declares that AID specializes in programs that "attack the problems of poor people and help create the social infrastructures that make democracy work." An AID official adds, "We hope thereby to encourage greater distributional equity between groups and pluralistic social structures to counter economic and political instability and authoritarian governments."[84]

IDEOLOGICAL UTILITY

Finally, both the standard explanation of Third World instability and the prescriptions it generates derive no small portion of their pervasiveness and persuasiveness from their obvious ideological utility, shown clearly by American rhetoric about relations with the Third World. The standard explanation allowed policymakers to claim lofty detachment from the traditional rat race of international relations. As Harry Truman put it in his inaugural address, "The old imperialism—exploitation for foreign profit—has no place in our plans. What we envisage is a program of development based on the concepts of democratic fair dealing." Indeed, the United States has a calling "to stir the peoples of the world into triumphant action, not only against their human oppressors, but also against their ancient enemies: hunger, misery and despair." Thus, Truman expressed the modest hope that his Point 4 plan would "create the conditions that will lead eventually to personal freedom and happiness for all mankind."[85] Here, declared President Kennedy, was a worthy goal. "Democracy is the destiny of humanity," and thus Americans must face "our moral obligations as a wise leader and good neighbor in the interdependent community of free nations, our economic obligations as the wealthiest people in a world of largely poor people, . . . and our political obligations as the single largest counter to the adversaries of freedom."[86] Americans, he declared, must oppose the "powerful destructive forces . . . challenging the universal values which for centuries have inspired men of good will in all parts of the world."[87]

[83] "AID Supported Counter-Insurgency Activities," Memorandum for the Special Group (CI), July 18, 1962, p. 1. DDRS, 1981: 1B.

[84] Hough, *Economic Assistance*, p. 31.

[85] January 20, 1949, *Public Papers, 1949*, p. 113.

[86] Message to the Committee on Foreign Relations, March 22, 1961, *Congressional Record—Senate, 1961*, p. 4467.

[87] DSB, June 4, 1961.

Conversely, the standard explanation of Third World instability ties our rival for hegemony to the disruption of development. In the words of NSC 68, the Soviet Union has "pretensions of being the source of a new universal faith and the model of 'scientific' society." But this position is rightfully ours, its authors assert, for the "system of values which animates our society—the principles of freedom, tolerance, the importance of the individual and the supremacy of reason over will—are valid and more vital that the ideology which is the fuel of Soviet dynamism."[88] As Walt Rostow wrote, "Communism is best understood as a disease of the transition to modernization"; once that transition is past, the appeal of Communism passes, too.[89] Thus, declared President Kennedy, "the fundamental task of our foreign aid program . . . is not negatively to fight communism: Its fundamental task is to help make a historical demonstration that . . . economic growth and political democracy can develop hand in hand."[90] In sum, the standard explanation justified Americans' lofty mission to modernize the Third World along American lines and "proved" that the United States, not its ideological rival, held the torch of the future.

The standard explanation functions in similar ways for both American society and policymakers. After all, American society is held up as the model of modernity for others to emulate. Moreover, the standard explanation "scientifically" substantiated this self-proclaimed role as the "city on the hill," "the new Israel." By the same token, the duty of development it prescribed flattered Americans and harmonized nicely with the American missionary impulse. In particular, it flattered policymakers and practitioners. If the United States has the duty to develop the Third World and American society is to be the model, then they are the project engineers, ready to translate paper programs into real progress. At the organizational level, this of course provided the basis of bureaucratic self-justification, for instance in the annual budget battle. At the personal level, both explanation and prescriptions provide policymakers and practitioners an essential sense of purpose, of belonging to something important, worthwhile, good. And conversely, this same ideological utility also renders an attack on either explanation or prescriptions an attack on even more fundamental attachments: nation, way of life, and sense of self-worth.

[88] NSC 68, "United States Objectives and Programs for National Security," April 14, 1950, pp. 15–22. NAMM, NSC file.

[89] "Guerrilla Warfare," p. 235.

[90] Message on Foreign Aid to the Committee on Foreign Relations, March 22, 1961, *Congressional Record—Senate, 1961*, p. 4467.

CONCLUSION

This chapter has made no claims concerning causality or consequences; it has merely highlighted the parallels in content and characteristics between academic and governmental understandings of political change in the Third World. In particular, it has demonstrated how this set of ideas has benefited from the familiar, parsimonious explanation it offers of complex events, the clear prescriptions that derive from it, and the ideological comfort it provides. In other words, this chapter has explored the content and characteristics of these ideas as they relate to perfectibility, without seriously questioning their adequacy or possible alternatives.

Questions of the adequacy and perfectibility of policymakers' understanding of instability and their prescriptions for managing it lie at the heart of the following chapter which examines the most important expression of security and development: the formal doctrine of counterinsurgency elaborated during the 1960s. In brief, chapter 5 will show that familiarity and utility notwithstanding, the standard explanation of Third World instability suffers the same debilitating weaknesses as its academic counterpart. Unlike the failings of theory, however, those of counterinsurgency doctrine have had far-reaching consequences when expressed as policy. And here, too, the costs are higher; they are paid in human lives.

5

AMERICAN
COUNTERINSURGENCY
DOCTRINE

"What are we going to do about guerrilla warfare?" asked President Kennedy in the opening days of his administration.[1] He repeated the inquiry at the first meeting of the National Security Council; in response, it produced National Security Action Memorandum No. 2 ("Development of Counter-Guerrilla Forces") ordering the Secretary of Defense to "examine means of placing more emphasis on the development of counter-guerrilla forces."[2] Kennedy's question led to development of a formal American counterinsurgency doctrine and the institutional capacity for implementing it. It began, too, what one expert has dubbed "the counterinsurgency era." But to focus too tightly on the Kennedy administration is to risk missing many important features of counterinsurgency doctrine. Kennedy's counterinsurgents merely codified the assumptions and prescriptions of security and development and articulated the "theory" and practice of American counterinsurgency operations in the Philippines at the turn of the century, Nicaragua in the late 1920s and early 1930s, and Greece and the Philippines in the late 1940s. In fact, it is this that recommends counterinsurgency doctrine for study: it provides a fine lens through which to view a far wider, more turbid subject.

What stands out about the Kennedy effort was the role social scientists played. The counterinsurgency era was one of those critical junctures at which academics serve to reinforce policymakers' own ideas and reassure them by appearing to offer outside scientific sanction. Academics did not provide new perspectives which might have challenged the pat assumptions of security and development. Rather, they had a voice because they did not. Where academics had an impact, it was because they gave concrete form to extant but inchoate notions and because the legitimizing effect of their participation impeded the modification of counterinsurgency doctrine in the face of failure. Thus, this

[1] Roger Hilsman, *To Move a Nation: The Politics of Foreign Policy in the Administration of John F. Kennedy* (New York: Dell, 1967), p. 413.

[2] February 3, 1961, *Pentagon Papers*, Department of Defense ed. (Washington, D.C.: GPO, 1971), book 11, pp. 17–18.

chapter aims to explore social scientists' contribution to the counter-insurgency era.

Chapter 5 has two other goals. First, it details application of the standard explanation of political instability to the analysis of insurgency and the prescriptions for countering it, the *three great oughts*: security, good government, and progress. Second, it offers an initial analysis of the standard explanation and prescriptions in light of their failure to address the three issues critical to the United States as an outside provider of counterinsurgency assistance: the possibility of leverage; the prospects for governmental reform; and the nature of government-population (or insurgent-population) relations. These are discussed in general terms not entirely applicable to any given case. But the point is not to leap backward into a "counter universalism" as bland and featureless as that being criticized; rather, it is to lay the groundwork for the detailed analysis of the case studies that follow in Part III.

UNIVERSAL VULNERABILITY

For Kennedy era policymakers the presumably universal, traumatic modernization process caused concern that the threat of insurgency was also universal. As General Maxwell Taylor warned, the "symptoms of subversive insurgency . . . are found in virtually every emerging country in the world."[3] He and others promptly declared, however, that while insurgency may be universally potential, active insurgency requires an external source. Thus, for example, the International Police Academy training manual on insurgency notes that "the seeds of potential unrest are sown whenever an undeveloped society comes into contact with a more highly developed country. The strategy of subversive aggression is based on transforming passive unrest into active insurgency." Furthermore, "insidious elements" are attempting to do so "in almost all developing nations throughout the world."[4] The trauma of modernization may constitute the enabling condition for insurgency, but the causative factor is communist interference.

This conclusion had several consequences, the first of which was to reduce the local situation to analytic insignificance. Doctrine might declare that "a total program" for counterinsurgency requires accurate

[3] Cited in P. Kecskemeti, *Insurgency as a Strategic Problem*, RM-5160-PR (Santa Monica: RAND Corp., February 1967), p. 13.

[4] AID, OPS, *The Police and Internal Security* (Washington, D.C.: International Police Academy, 1966), pp. I-4, I-1. OPS Archives, 286-75-172, Box 4.

information concerning the country in question.[5] But if the preconditions for insurgency are universal, inevitable, and, by themselves, in-
nocuous, then analysis should focus not on the specific characteristics
of threatened governments or their relations with the population and
insurgents but on Communist tactics.

This analytic sleight of hand appears first in the definition of insurgency used in doctrinal statements, policy papers, and official training
materials. These assume insurgent illegitimacy, since the government is
defined as legitimate. Thus, insurgency is "an internal struggle . . . in
which a minority group attempts to wrest control from the duly constituted government. . . . The objective, as always, is the alienation of
the people from the government."[6] Moreover, despite the presumed necessity of governmental reform to undercut insurgent appeals, analysts
minimize such efforts' importance by proclaiming that all governments
have their faults.[7] But in assuming "duly constituted" governments, analysts assume away the very issues at the heart of the matter, questions
concerning the nature, authority, strength, and legitimacy of the threatened government.

Conversely, analysts dismiss insurgencies as the products of propaganda and coercion. Lt. Col. John McCuen argues that the "secret behind revolutionary successes in winning the people is to tell them what
they want to hear, irrespective of whether or not this happens to vary
from long-term rebel objectives."[8] Similarly, the International Police
Academy manual on insurgency declares that once insurgents "have recruited a solid base of adherents, they will frequently institute terrorist
tactics to bring the mass of people under control."[9] Thus, Douglas Pike,
then a senior government consultant on insurgency, contended that insurgent success depends on an ability to "coerce a passive and generally
apolitical peasantry."[10]

Analysts also delegitimize insurgency by discrediting the insurgents

[5] NSC, "U.S. Overseas Internal Defense Policy" (USOIDP), prepared by an interdepartmental committee consisting of State, Defense, JCS, CIA, and AID, transmitted August 24,
1962, NSAM 182, p. 13. Kennedy Library.

[6] AID, OPS, *The Police*, pp. I-6, I-15. See, too, the "Counterinsurgency Lexicon," JCS,
Office of the Special Assistant for Counterinsurgency and Special Activities, "Counter-
insurgency Bluebook for 1966 (U)," MJCS-331-66, November 15, 1966, p. 9 DDRS,
Retro: 242D.

[7] See, for example, AID, OPS, *The Police*, pp. I-4–I-5.

[8] Lt. Col. John J. McCuen, *The Art of Counter-Revolutionary War: The Strategy of
Counter-Insurgency* (Harrisburg, Penn.: Stackpole Books, 1966), p. 55.

[9] AID, OPS, *The Police*, p. I-6.

[10] Douglas Pike, *The Viet Cong Strategy of Terror* (Cambridge: MIT Press, 1970),
p. 3.

themselves. Many, they argue, are the losers in the modernization process, those uprooted from tradition but still out of place in the new order. Some are the temporarily discontented, and others simply criminals wanting a "cover" for their antisocial activities. Or they are the deceived, duped into actions from which there is no retreat or simply bamboozled.[11] In any case, they are not credible challengers to incumbent modern elites.

Finally, the tendency to discount local conditions shows in analysts' proclivity to explain the causes of insurgency by their anticipated results. For example, the Overseas Internal Defense Policy declared in theory that "the U.S. does not wish to assume a stance against revolution, *per se.* . . . Each case of latent, incipient, or active, non-communist insurgency must therefore be examined on its merits in the light of U.S. interests."[12] But, having said as much, analysts return to the prospects for communist meddling instability offers. A 1972 RAND study declares, for example: "A revolutionary conflict becomes unambiguously injurious to U.S. interests . . . if it lends itself to being exploited by Soviet or Chinese military power."[13] Communist involvement is a foregone conclusion, however. Thus, in effect, the United States has a security interest in opposing insurgency per se or, conversely, in supporting all insurgency threatened governments, regardless of local circumstances.

Universal Tactic

Given this reduction of insurgency to a communist tactic, it is not surprising that policymakers' efforts to understand revolution focused almost exclusively on the writings of the modern master theoreticians of revolution, including Mao, Giap, Guevara, and Debray. Still, one must ask just how useful a picture of Third World revolution they offer. It is an embarrassing question, for, on examination, there is less here than meets the eye. Indeed, the revolutionary masters' work suffers from weaknesses similar to those that dog their American counterparts.

Americans' reading of the revolutionary masters was both self-frightening and narcissistic; analysts took them at their word. When General Giap declared of Vietnam, "If we win here, we win everywhere," policymakers believed him. When Mao declared that his was a

---

[11] See, for example, Sir Robert Thompson, *Defeating Communist Insurgency: Experiences from Malaya and Vietnam* (London: Chatto and Windus, 1966), pp. 35–36.

[12] USOIDP, p. 12.

[13] Heymann and Whitson, *Can and Should the United States Preserve a Military Capacity for Revolutionary Conflict?*, p. v.

scientific, universally applicable revolutionary weapon, Americans took heed. As Stanley Hoffmann observed, Americans interpreted "Marshall Lin Piao's celebrated manifesto, *Long Live the Victory of the People's War*, as a new *Mein Kampf* rather than as a devious way of telling future liberation movements to rely primarily on themselves."[14] Conversely, the readiness with which Americans accepted the revolutionary masters' claims reflects the fact that mirrored in their writings was our own intellectual image.

Here, in the supposed clash of East and West, revolution and evolution, is the reunion of two branches of the histoire raisonnée tradition. Both revolutionaries and counterrevolutionaries assume that the Third World's shared experience with colonialism had everywhere produced a potentially revolutionary situation. Thus, Americans fret over the consequences of modernization—in particular, the possibility of Communists capturing uprooted peoples in the hiatus between tradition and a higher state, modernity. The revolutionary masters also focus on the inevitable, universal course of development, but in the deracination process they see the formation of classes, and so the fundamental dynamic of development. Each, however, assumes the malleability of the masses and, despite reference to an overarching process of change, focuses on tactical measures for "helping history." In other words, both revolutionaries and counterrevolutionaries identify their role as manager of modernization.

Like their American counterparts, the revolutionary masters assume a simple polarization between center and an undifferentiated, but universally frustrated periphery awaiting liberation. They, too, push local conditions into the background and make no serious attempt to analyze the complexity of politics at the periphery. They assume the preexistence of the preconditions for revolution: a large, malleable body of peasants, coolies, and other marginals fed up with their miserable condition and awaiting a catalyst. Indeed, inverting standard Western claims, they argue that creation of the preconditions for revolution, not development, is the inevitable result of European colonialism. And because this revolutionary situation is assumed, the masters of revolution limit themselves to the tactics of insurrection.

These characteristics are best exemplified by the two revolutionaries most studied by American counterinsurgents: Mao Tse-Tung and Ernesto "Che" Guevara. If the ultimate source and beneficiary of Third World revolution was Moscow, Mao provided the means. Both Mao's method and his person fascinated American counterinsurgents, al-

[14] Hoffmann, *Gulliver's Troubles*, p. 189.

though few understood him. Indeed, looking back it is hard to explain the hyperbole and fatuousness of the gushy outpourings about Mao. "Mao Tse-Tung," wrote two otherwise respectable specialists, "has done for war what Lenin did for imperialism and Marx for capitalism: he has given war 'scientific' schemata [and] presented the Communist revolutionary with a workable blueprint."[15] Another declared that "Mao Tse-Tung was the first to treat guerrilla battlecraft as a proper subject of military science and nobody has made a greater contribution to the guerrilla strategy than he."[16]

More important is the unquestioning acceptance of Mao's own grandiose claims about his work. Certainly, the conclusion that he had discovered a scientific, revolutionary master key did not derive from careful analysis of his writings. Even military writers praised such banalities as "Enemy advances, we retreat; enemy halts, we harass; enemy tires, we attack; enemy retreats, we pursue," which—cute style aside—would not have surprised Francis ("the Swamp Fox") Marion. Few noted that, notwithstanding the rhetoric of universalism, much of Mao's work served short-term political ends, not the dictates of systematic theorizing. Nor did they observe that his examples from other areas of the world were often wrong or that his analysis of China and his own campaigns was often self-serving. Many analysts also overlooked the caveats Mao attached to his work and the role of factors in his successes over which Mao had no control. Indeed, they simply ignored Mao's silence about the deep causes of revolution, and the mix of external intervention, political decay, social and economic change, and luck that underlay his victory. As a result, counterinsurgents left Mao believing that revolutionaries make revolutions.

If Mao was the master theoretician of revolution, Che Guevara personified the international revolutionary policymakers feared most. He also embodied the simplicities that made revolutionary doctrine a poor source for understanding insurgency or developing an antidote. In the bluntest terms, Che polarized the world into oppressors and masses, bad guys and good guys. He did note that the people may be unreceptive, passive, and dull; yet this resulted not in attention to why, but to even greater attention to *technique*. According to Che, good guerrilla tactics can literally make a revolution ex nihilo. Indeed, he asserts, "It is not necessary to wait until all conditions for making revolution exist; the insurrection can create them."[17]

---

[15] Edward Katzenbach, Jr., and Gene Hanrahan, "The Revolutionary Strategy of Mao Tse-Tung," *Political Science Quarterly* 70 (September 1955), pp. 322–23.

[16] Otto Heilbrunn, *Partisan Warfare* (New York: Praeger, 1962), p. 40.

[17] Ernesto Che Guevara, *Guerrilla Warfare* (New York: Vintage Books, 1961), p. 1.

Che lionizes the insurrectionary. Success depends on the guerrilla *foco*, the band of brothers who are, in Castro's words, "the embryo of liberation armies and constitute the most efficient way of initiating and carrying out revolutionary struggle."[18] At the heart of the *foco* is the romantic guerrilla hero, the revolutionary missionary who creates new revolutionaries from the inert mass of the peasantry. This "vanguard of the people," Che declares, must "be a true priest of the reform to which he aspires . . . a sort of guiding angel who has fallen into the zone." As such, "he interprets the desires of the great peasant mass" and serves "to explain the motives of the revolution, its ends, and to spread the incontrovertible truth."[19] What counts is the revolutionary—his vision and his bag of tricks.

Revolutionary doctrine, in short, provided a poor source for understanding insurgency. Like the greater intellectual tradition to which it belongs, it tends to two extremes: on the one hand, revolutionary theorists built their analysis on the presumed unfolding of a universal pattern driven by abstract, unspecified "forces"; on the other, their focus remains the revolutionary elite whose vanguard role is that of midwife to the inevitable. As a result, doctrine obscures critical intervening variables, suggests a false universality, and shifts attention to the activities of self-proclaimed "revolutionaries." Counterrevolutionary doctrine replicated these weaknesses, following as problematic a course as its revolutionary counterpart. Neither has delivered half of that promised, and successes have had little to do with doctrine.

Counterinsurgency: The Universal Countertactic

If insurgency was but a tactic, a countertactic was needed. As Walt Rostow told the Green Berets, "we are up against a form of warfare which is powerful and effective only when we do not put our minds clearly to work on how to deal with it."[20] Thus, "the most logical solution," argued Lt. Col. McCuen, "does lie in developing a counter-revolutionary strategy which applies revolutionary strategy and principles IN RE-VERSE to defeat the enemy with his own weapons on his own battle-field."[21] By such means, the Joint Chiefs declared, "the American mili-

---

[18] Fidel Castro, "Speech to the OLAS Conference," in *Guerrilla Warfare and Marxism*, ed. William J. Pomeroy (New York: International Publishers, 1968), p. 296.

[19] Guevara, *Guerrilla Warfare*, pp. 33, 5, 10.

[20] Walter Rostow, "Guerrilla Warfare in the Underdeveloped Areas," DSB (August 7, 1961), p. 237.

[21] McCuen, *Art of Counter-Revolutionary War*, p. 78. For an excellent operational statement of this, see Headquarters, 5th Special Forces Group (Airborne), "Letter of In-

tary can . . . defeat Communist subversive aggression *whenever* and *wherever* it arises."[22]

Analysts and policymakers reinforced this conclusion with "lessons" drawn from the counterinsurgency success stories: Greece, Malaya, and the Philippines. Training manuals and government documents were rife with references to them, RAND and other organizations studied them, and articles about them littered *Naval Institute Proceedings*, *Air University Review*, *Military Review*, and *Marine Corps Gazette*. The lessons taught were tactical and programmatic, however, emphasizing what was done, not in what circumstances. The conclusion was that "the key existed if it could be found and turned."[23] This master key, applicable whenever and wherever needed, was counterinsurgency.

The search for the counterinsurgency master key led to a burst of cooperation between academics and policymakers. It was a mutually beneficial collaboration, if benefit is measured in terms of the immediate interests of those involved. For many academics, "the Defense Department offered the essential lure . . . a pot of gold in the form of resources for . . . social research in connection with Vietnam and other 'wars of national liberation'; and . . . lent to the resources a sense of mission reinforced by the President."[24] Conversely, academics were able to convince policymakers that "defense management needs a technology of human behavior based on advances in psychology and the social sciences"[25] and created a demand for their services by inundating Washington with books and articles on the necessity of fighting guerrilla wars. For their part, policymakers already believed what academics were telling them. What they required, and received, was reassurance that their definition of the problem and responses to it were correct.

One document and one institution illustrate both the interaction of

---

struction Number 1 (First Revision): The Special Forces Counterinsurgency Program," January 1, 1965, Annex 5, Civil Affairs and Psychological Operations, p. 10. DDRS, 1975: 70D.

[22] W. R. Peers, "Counterinsurgency Bluebook, Fiscal Year 1966(U): Memorandum of Promulgation," MJCS 331-66, November 15, 1966, p. 1. DDRS, Retro: 242D.

[23] Bundy, Foreword to Blaufarb, *Counterinsurgency Era*, p. x.

[24] Seymour Deitchman, *The Best Laid Schemes: A Tale of Social Research and Bureaucracy* (Cambridge: MIT Press, 1976), pp. 133–34.

[25] Charles Bray, "Toward a Technology of Human Behavior for Defense Use," *American Psychologist* 17: 8 (August 1962), p. 528. The chairman of a Defense Department sponsored study told Secretary McNamara in 1961 that "while World War I might have been considered the chemists' war, and World War II . . . the physicists' war, World War III, which we might already be in, might well have to be considered the social scientists' war." Cited in Deitchman, *Best Laid Schemes*, p. 28.

academics and policymakers and its consequences better than any others: the "United States Overseas Internal Defense Policy" (USOIDP) and the Inter-Departmental Seminar on Counter-Insurgency (IDS). The USOIDP became the basic statement of U.S. counterinsurgency doctrine in August 1962. It was an effort to marry academic modernization theory and government resources to produce an antidote for insurgency. As McGeorge Bundy's cover memo made clear, it was "to serve as basic policy guidance to diplomatic missions, consular personnel, and military commands abroad; [and] to government departments and agencies at home."[26] It remained in force until 1968, when it was slightly modified, and lapsed only in the early 1970s.[27]

The USOIDP minces no words about the significance of insurgency. It begins: "A most pressing U.S. national security problem now, and for the foreseeable future, is the continuing threat presented by Communist inspired, supported, or directed insurgency."[28] At stake is "primary influence over the direction and outcome of the developmental process" (p. 5). Unfortunately, the threat of insurgency exists throughout the developing world because of the "stresses and strains of the developmental process brought about by the revolutionary break with the traditional past and uneven progress toward new and more modern forms of political, social, and economic organization" (p. 5). This "revolution of modernization," the authors contend, "can disturb, uproot, and daze a traditional society. While the institutions required for modernization are in [the] process of being created, this revolution contributes to arousing pressures, anxieties, and hopes which seem to justify violent action" (p. 3). Moreover, transitional societies may suffer from "lack of communication between the government and the countryside," "weak governmental institutions lacking administrative capacity," armed forces that are "estranged from the people and constitute a hindrance rather than a help in promoting nation-building and social cohesion," and ignorance of "how to battle the blandishments and false hopes" tempting the deracinated (pp. 6–8).

[26] NSAM 182, August 24, 1962, p. 1. Kennedy Library.

[27] Charles Maechling, Jr., chairman of the committee that drafted the USOIDP now describes it as "a somewhat simplistic document" which "defined the threat solely in terms of Marxist 'wars of national liberation' without discriminating between target governments or concerning itself with the domestic origins and root causes of internal turmoil." Furthermore, "It contained virtually no political guidance as to the circumstances in which it should be applied and no criteria laying down conditions that had to be met by the host country before the aid program could become operative." "Insurgency and Counterinsurgency: The Role of Strategic Theory," *Parameters* 14: 3 (Autumn 1984), p. 34.

[28] USOIDP, p. 1.

Complicating this situation are the Communists. The USOIDP argues that the "natural" stresses of the development process are a necessary condition for insurgency (p. 6). But because the potential for insurgency is presumed universal, attention focuses on external sources to explain its infrequent occurrence. Consideration of local conditions is minimized, as is attention to the character of specific governments, their relations with their subjects, or willingness and capacity to reform (p. 2). Instead, the USOIDP focused on the Communists' "comprehensive, tested doctrine for conquest from within" which "can be destructively applied to underdeveloped countries at almost all their points of vulnerability" (pp. 1, 9–10). In effect, the authors identified insurgent techniques with communism and then mistook those techniques for the causes of insurgency.

Under the circumstances, it is not surprising that the USOIDP's authors sought "to fashion on an urgent basis an effective plan of action to combat this critical communist threat" (p. 1). This required "a unified concept of operations based on a comprehensive plan tailored to the local situation" (p. 13) and the ability to "create situations of strength within the local society" by providing "an integrated capability to eliminate the root causes of disaffection and dissidence, to expose and counter communist efforts, and to cope with increased levels of violence" (p. 21). Thus, the USOIDP's authors proposed both to meet the "revolution of rising expectations" with land reform, community development, and education and to improve the "underwhelming" capabilities of threatened Third World governments (pp. 14–16).

This prescription turned on two assumptions. First, it assumed that Third World regimes would pursue development if given the necessary material support. Second, it assumed that popular support for insurgency is coerced or misled discontent about remediable local inequities. In other words, it assumed away the possibility that governments and their subjects might have insuperable differences while ignoring the possibility that governments might be incapable of meeting the demands of development and their subjects.

The USOIDP did recognize that such programs might require politically sensitive reform and generate resistance, "regardless of how unrealistic and short-sighted this stubbornness may seem objectively" (p. 17). But the force of this observation is vitiated by the pathetic measures suggested for overcoming the problem. Governments should be "persuaded" to show "political wisdom." The United States should train military and police officers to "create in them an awareness of the political process of nation-building" and make them "advocates of democracy and agents for carrying forward the developmental process."

And diplomats should use their "sympathetic personal rapport" with local leaders (pp. 16–17).

The ideas embodied in the USOIDP also found expression in the Inter-Departmental Seminar on Counter-Insurgency (IDS) taught at the State Department's Foreign Service Institute. The course was designed to help policymakers "understand and cope with the urgent problems in nations engaged in the difficult process of modernizing the economic and socio-political systems [and] is directed to those problems which may be encountered in any underdeveloped country, and to those civil or military disturbances which are occurring in some developing countries in Asia, Africa, and Latin America which are or may be exploited by the Communists."[29] Looking back, an early graduate observed that the course "reflected the deficiencies of the doctrine. It was highly generalized and often left the officers at a loss as to how to translate the generalities into policies and, even more difficult, into practical actions."[30] At the time, these deficiencies went unnoticed. In fact, the seminar embodied the interpenetration of academic and official thinking on the issues of modernization and insurgency and the high hopes held for the collaboration.[31]

The IDS first met in June 1962 and continued to meet eight to ten times a year thereafter for many years. Each class had forty to seventy students from State, Defense, USIA, CIA, AID, and the armed services,[32] among them ambassadors and other senior officials as well as auditors, such as Robert Kennedy and General Maxwell Taylor. The teaching staff was equally impressive. From the government came Ambassador W. Averell Harriman, U. Alexis Johnson, and Major General Edward Lansdale. Complementing them were academics from the Massachusetts Institute of Technology's Center for International Studies (CENIS). These men—Max Millikan, Lucien Pye, Everett Hagen, and Walt Rostow (already in Washington with the Kennedy administration)—had helped pioneer political development theory and champion the need for

[29] Department of State, Foreign Service Institute, "Problems of Development and Internal Defense," Country Team Seminar, A-700, June 11–July 13, 1962, p. 1. DDRS, Retro: 439A.

[30] Blaufarb, *Counterinsurgency Era*, p. 73.

[31] At a special Oval Office reception, President Kennedy told the first graduating class "we want to emphasize the necessity for the experience which you are going through, that it be shared by all the people in the National Government who have anything to do with international relations. . . . They all must concentrate their energy on what is going to be one of the great factors in the struggle of the Sixties." Cited in ibid., p. 72.

[32] JCS, Office of the Special Assistant for Counterinsurgency and Special Activities, "Bluebook," p. 146.

an American foreign policy sensitive to the "dynamics of modernization."

The IDS began with three weeks of lectures. The first week dealt with
"The Development Process and Its Hazards" and examined "the forces
unleashed by the development process which complicate the attain-
ment of U.S. objectives by generating disruptive influences, dissidence
and targets of exploitable Communist opportunity."[33] Lecturers focused on "the explosiveness of change," the threat of an overwhelming
"revolution of rising expectations," and, in particular, its importance
in the context of the "all-pervasive effort of Communism to confuse
and arrest modernization." The second week examined "The Development
Process, Policy Choices and Determinants for Minimizing Insurgency"
to highlight the "broad policy choices . . . open to the non-Communist elites of a modernizing nation which can determine its general
course toward modernity: whether it proceeds with minimum risks
of insurgency and Communist inroads or whether insurgency . . . will
seriously challenge the central government for leadership of the modernization process." Lecturers asked how elites can maintain control of
modernization, not whether they are committed to it. The week closed
with a lecture by Roger Hilsman on "The Dynamics of Insurgency," intended to tie the CENIS analysis to policy and specify "the causative
links between modernization and insurgency." In the third week practitioners took over to "set forth the doctrinal basis . . . and unified concept for applying U.S. resources in support of local efforts to counter
subversive insurgency." Finally, at the end of the third week the students separated into "country teams" and spent three more weeks applying their new knowledge to specific countries, often those to which
they were assigned.

THE PRESCRIPTIONS

Policymakers developed not one "unified concept" of counterinsurgency, but two basic package prescriptions: hearts and minds and cost-
benefit. These share fundamental assumptions, despite an acrimonious
debate among their proponents. In fact, they are distinguished from
one another only by the relative priority given their primary components. Hearts and minds stresses development over security; cost-benefit gives priority to security. In each case, however, similar misassess-
ments of Third World governments, their subjects, the sources of

[33] This and all subsequent IDS quotes are drawn from Department of State, F.S.I.,
"Problems," pp. 4–15a.

115

insurgency, and an outsider's ability to intervene result in misprescription.

Hearts and Minds

Hearts-and-minds analysts attribute insurgency to the trauma of modernization, the revolution of rising expectations, and Communist meddling. Thus, their prescriptions call for the rapid incorporation of the vulnerable periphery into the modern center. The aim is to transform the passive parochial into at least a subject, if not a true citizen, of a modern state. The means are measures to improve the state's capacity to affect the hearts and minds of its citizens. Once involved in the modern state and served by it, so the argument goes, the individual will be invulnerable to the blandishments of hardcore insurgents.

Under the rubric of winning hearts and minds fall a variety of prescriptions. All, however, address the problems of improving threatened states' performance in three key areas: physical control of territory and populace; penetration of authority throughout the country; and promotion of economic and social development. Thus, the hearts and minds prescriptions amount to three great *oughts*. Governments *ought* to secure the population from insurgent coercion. They *ought* to provide competent, legal, responsive administration free from past abuses and broader in domain, scope, and vigor. And they *ought* to meet rising expectations with higher living standards.

SECURITY

For hearts-and-minds analysts, the first problem is protection of the populace from insurgent predators. Without a modicum of order, they argue, nothing is possible. Besides, a government unable to defend its people cannot command their allegiance, while one that does will win their gratitude and support. Thus, threatened governments must receive assistance to strengthen the military and develop popular defense forces which actively involve the people. Analysts also recommend the physical relocation of people to defended villages. Indeed, many argue that population control can promote all three great oughts. By building "strategic hamlets" governments can achieve the essential first step to victory, the physical and political separation of the guerrilla from the population. Furthermore, bringing the populace under government control simplifies counterorganizing them to support the government. Such efforts, it is argued, help break down traditional parochialisms and lay the groundwork for a national community coterminous with the state. Finally, resettlement makes it easier to deliver development assistance to overcome peasant poverty and meet rising expectations.[34]

GOOD GOVERNMENT

Improved security, however, is but the prerequisite for the development programs necessary to drench insurgent fires forever. Thus, hearts-and-minds analysts suggest that insurgency-threatened countries ought to attack the two basic political problems behind insurgency: bad administration and underadministration. If past bad administration underlies popular support for insurgency, then reforms are essential. Insurgency-threatened governments should become what all modern governments ought to be anyway: law-abiding, administratively strong, and responsive. They also ought to address distributional, racial, and communal problems and remove corrupt or abusive officials. Besides measures to improve the quality of government, increases in the quantity of government are needed to fill "the gaping void of underadministration"[35] which leaves the field open to insurgent organizers and governments unable to cope with the revolution of rising expectations. Thus, a strong administration must be established and officials trained to staff it. In short, the aim is to deny insurgents room for maneuver, provide desired services more effectively, overcome the isolation of parochial communities, and speed penetration of national authority and values into them.

PROGRESS

While security and good government are critical, counterinsurgents (like old wives) believe the surest way to the hearts and minds of peasants is through the stomach. Thus, the final great ought is the simplest: governments ought to provide the benefits only promised by the insurgents. The logic is simple. First, if unrest is caused by bad living conditions or rising expectations of better ones, government benefits will be oil upon the waters. Second, if the government is viewed as distant and disinterested, analysts argue, such aid will help persuade the masses to abandon the insurgents and rally to the government. Third, along with the development of modern political structures, economic development

[34] See, for example, McCuen, *Art of Counter-Revolutionary War*; Thompson, *Defeating Communist Insurgency*; David Galula, *Counterinsurgency Warfare: Theory and Practice* (New York: Praeger, 1964); and Lt. Col. T. N. Greene, ed., *The Guerrilla: And How to Fight Him* (New York: Praeger, 1962).
[35] McCuen, *Art of Counter-Revolutionary War*, p. 96.

117

ought to eliminate the very threat of insurgency by making the material benefits of modernity available to all.[36]

The Unity Principle

Finally, to top off the three great oughts, analysts insist on the necessity of managing all three simultaneously: "The government cannot attack the guerrillas . . . unless [the people] feel some measure of sympathy . . . toward [it]. This attitude must be brought about through the economic, political and social actions that make the people's lives better. . . . And the government cannot take any steps unless the people, . . . the police stations, and all the rest can be protected."[37] A coordinated effort by military, political, and administrative leaders is required to insure balanced action on all fronts and at all levels. In fact, "perhaps the overriding principle should be the *unity principle.*"[38]

POSSIBLE OBJECTIONS

At first glance it seems a potent prescription; on closer examination it is transparently flawed. Managerial problems add to the difficulties, of course, but the deep reasons are analytic. Hearts and minds analysts' assumptions cloud assessment of the three issue areas critical to an outside power contemplating support of an insurgency threatened government: the constraints on leverage; intragovernmental limits on reform by the would-be ally; and the nature of relations between government and populace or, conversely, between insurgents and populace. The weaknesses derive from policymakers' basic assumptions about Third World politics and political change. The resulting misanalysis opens each of the three great oughts to criticism and vitiates many of their key components. Indeed, the prescriptions offered may be irrelevant, impossible, or worse.

LEVERAGE

For the United States as an outside power involved in counterinsurgency, the issue at the level of government-to-government relations is leverage. Specifically, the question is how to ensure that an ally does what American policymakers deem necessary to eliminate insurgency. This would appear to present no difficulties since the United States and

[36] For a detailed study of the "progress ought," see Packenham, *Liberal America and the Third World.*

[37] Seymour Deitchman, *Limited War and American Defense Policy* (Cambridge: MIT Press, 1964), p. 40.

[38] McCuen, *Art of Counter-Revolutionary War*, pp. 72–73.

the threatened government are both presumably interested in ending the insurgency and hence in doing what is necessary. And should leverage be required, the United States seems to have it all. As the USOIDP put it, governments facing extinction "have no practical alternative to accepting the U.S. recommendations, particularly if specific reforms become prerequisites to the continuance of U.S. aid."[39] But appearances may be deceiving.

There are two limits on leverage that stand in a paradoxical relationship to one another: capacity and willingness. In part, the former reflects the need for an arm's-length relationship between the United States and its endangered ally. Because the United States is not a colonial power, American counterinsurgents do not control the political, administrative, and military machinery of allied governments and cannot track either their policies or actions effectively, let alone fine tune them. The United States must thus depend on diplomatic exhortation in the absence of real authority. The problem goes deeper, however. Hearts-and-minds analysts' assertion that successful counterinsurgency depends on local development and/or reform precludes direct American involvement. The United States may advise and bankroll reform, but the programs must be 99 percent local if they are to win hearts and minds forever. In other words, policymakers' analysis of the requirements for success suggest that for both practical and diplomatic reasons the United States cannot exercise authority in counterinsurgency or reform efforts.

But here lies the willingness half of the paradox. For leverage to be meaningful, the possessor must be ready to exercise it. As Constantine Menges observed in a RAND memo, the "United States can exert significant influence on ally governments only if it can make credible to an ally regime that it has alternatives to collaboration. Such explicitly outlined alternatives are necessary . . . to preserve the capacity of the U.S. government to bargain with, and if necessary, coerce ally governments in a counterinsurgency effort."[40] Yet while they define counterinsurgency as a local concern, analysts define insurgency as a strategic issue for the United States. This heightens worry over threatened allies' efforts to achieve the three oughts, but it simultaneously reduces the credibility of the "alternatives to collaboration" necessary if the United States is to exert leverage. Perversely, the more critical the situation, the less leverage the United States can muster. Conversely, the more critical

[39] USOPID, p. 17.
[40] Constantine Menges, *Democratic Revolutionary Insurgency as an Alternative Strategy*, P-3817 (Santa Monica: RAND Corp., March 1968), p. 5.

the situation, the more "reverse leverage" nominal clients will exercise: the less likely they will undertake needed reforms, and the more tempted they will be to depend on American assistance and resources rather than reform and the mobilization of local ones. Ironically, leverage may be proportional to the problems facing the United States elsewhere. The greater the problems are, the higher the propensity to shift limited resources away from the threatened government, and hence the more credible the "alternatives to collaboration."

Leverage, in short, is more problematic than initially suggested. Indeed, the extent to which the United States can stage-manage counterinsurgency may turn as much, if not more, on the domestic politics of the threatened country as on the resources the United States devotes to the cause. Thus, the assessment of leverage at the government-to-government level requires assessment of the prospects for reform in the insurgency-threatened country. The accuracy of such assessments depend, in turn, on the quality of the analytic lens used. Here, however, American counterinsurgents were ill-served.

INTRAGOVERNMENTAL CONSTRAINTS

Will and capacity also define the prospects for leverage, reform, and achievement of the great oughts at the intragovernmental level. Each depends on leaders' desire to implement the necessary reforms and ability to carry through. Neither notion is new. Counterinsurgency analysts have long stressed the need for the will and capacity to undertake "reform in crisis." They have never, however, specified which governments under which conditions will be willing and able to do what. Yet without answers to these questions, policymakers cannot assess of the prospects for leverage over an ally or reform on its part.

Whether or not political elites will undertake needed reforms depends on the implications of reform for their interests. Hearts-and-minds analysts sidestepped this issue by assuming that the interests of "modernizing elites" are coterminous with the national interest. They were not entirely indifferent to the weaknesses of this critical assumption. Indeed, in an influential article in 1962, U. Alexis Johnson noted that

> To bring about some degree of social, economic and political justice . . . will invariably require positive action by the local government. In some cases only radical reforms will obtain the necessary results. Yet the measures we advocate may strike at the very foundations of these aspects of a country's social structure and domes-

tic economy on which rests the basis of the government's control.[41]

Johnson even conceded that the task might be "sometimes impossible." But this warning, like the observation that prompted it, went unheeded. Analysts largely ignored the possibility that, for certain elites, the aim of fighting is to defend power and privilege; thus, the prescribed "good government" may be even less palatable than toughing out the insurgency as long as possible before flying to exile in Miami or Monaco.

To assess this possibility requires analysis of the consequences of specific reforms for specific elites. It requires even more, however, for the questions of will and capacity involve not a homogeneous leadership but several often conflicting elites with different bases of power, resources, and interests. Indeed, the problem of capacity is that of coalition management in fragmented regimes. The issue is not whether reform is necessary: insurgency threatened governments *do* need greater legitimacy and more professional, public service–oriented armed forces if they are to defeat their rivals for power. Instead, the issue is whether the interests of key elites and necessary reforms are reconcilable. Analysts obscure this point by assuming that the long-term goals of defeating insurgency and development will eclipse short-term petty political concerns. But politicians are risk adverse; they discount future problems in the face of more immediate ones. Where the stakes of politics are high—possibly life or death—the risks of the present are paramount. And for cleavage-riven regimes threatened by insurgency, the risks of managing intragovernmental tensions dominate the present. This, however, may transform the call for reform into an insistence that regimes risk their hold on power to defeat the insurgents.

The dilemma appears most clearly in the area of military and police reform. A professional military is essential to defeat insurgents, and its tight control is essential for improved relations with the population. But insurgency-threatened regimes depend on the continued support of the military and police. Such support must be bought, not only with money but also with political power in the form of autonomy and veto rights over actions affecting the corporate and personal interests of officers. The consequences may be disastrous for counterinsurgency. Soldiers may become mercenaries neither interested in nor capable of facing the insurgents. Poorly disciplined, often unpaid and unaccountable,

[41] U. Alexis Johnson, "Internal Defense and the Foreign Service," *Foreign Service Journal* (July 1962), p. 23.

such troops are likely to prey on, not protect, the public.[42] For would-be reformers, internal and external, the prospects for success may be limited since the conditions that create the demand for reform indicate a political situation likely to render it impossible. If so, they will also render the prescriptions of the security ought counterproductive as these add to the armed forces' political weight and resources, making reform still more difficult.

Here it is necessary to stress the importance of not falling backwards into a counteruniversalism. These conditions do not apply everywhere. Whether they apply or not depends on the nature of the regime, insurgency, and required reforms. However, neither counterinsurgency doctrine nor the analysis of Third World politics behind it allow for such assessments. Bereft of this analytical acuity, prescription is blind.

GOVERNMENT-POPULACE RELATIONS

Last, and most important, are questions of the relations between government and population or, conversely, insurgents and population. The problems appear first in the security ought. The assumption of governmental legitimacy and the definition of insurgency as the product of outside meddling reduces the IFF—identify friend or foe—problem of counterinsurgency to a simple sorting process. It also justifies providing as much security assistance as governments desire. Analysts need never ask the obvious questions: "security for whom?" and "defense against what?" Failure to do so, however, obscures alternative explanations of insurgency and faults in the prescriptions of the security ought.

Two possibilities in particular stand out. First, support for the insurgency may derive from calculation that insurgent, not government, programs offer more. If so, it is unreasonable to expect people to feel more secure because the existing social order is better defended against efforts to change it. Second, support for the insurgents—or lack of support for the government—may derive not from the masses' capture by the insurgents but from the masses' abuse by the government. If true, security prescriptions may be counterproductive. If the government is abusive, or unable to control the agents of key constituents (e. g. "civil" guards, death squads), then increasing its coercive capabilities may increase attacks on civilians, not insurgents. Furthermore, such predatory behavior may increase with resettlement and the resulting subjugation of the population to direct control by the government. In short, the claim that improving the military capabilities of a government will increase security and so win the hearts and minds of the populace may

[42] Blaufarb, *Counterinsurgency Era*, p. 303.

be false. To the contrary, increasing the government's security may actually decrease that of the population, further alienating them and, in the extreme, forcing them to such self-defense measures as joining the insurgency.

Two elements of the security prescription partially recognize the need for better relations between the military and civilians: civic action and IMET. These, however, break down under the weight of other inappropriate assumptions. Civic action programs aim to buy popular support (or at least reduce support for the insurgents) by delivering material benefits.[43] They are, in effect, a public relations gimmick to improve the military's image, and as such, they represent an admission of the military's uncivic behavior. But civic action programs have their limits.

One set of problems relates to civic action by United States forces. Despite U.S. Army claims that civic action is highly efficacious,[44] projects within its capabilities are too small to be of much benefit and are no substitute for real national development programs. More important, American civic action projects are irrelevant to the task at hand. Although they may deliver benefits to the population and reduce hostility to a foreign presence, they cannot contribute to the improvement of government-population relations. Here lies a second, fatal set of problems. The quantity and quality of an ally's civic action operations depend on the local political and military system. If the government cannot control the military or the military preys on the population, then the prospects for achieving the discipline and public service orientation necessary for effective civic action seem poor. In short, civic action is least possible in those cases where it is most needed.

This is the problem IMET is supposed to address by creating, in the words of Gen. Lyman Lemnitzer (Chairman of the Joint Chiefs, 1961–1962), a "new breed of foreign military men—respectable men whose ultimate purpose is to . . . create an environment in which freedom has a chance to flourish."[45] But the prospect that a small minority of foreign trained officers will have a major impact is limited by the same constraints on reform mentioned earlier. The weaker the political system,

[43] Col. Irving Heymont, "Armed Forces and National Development," MR (December 1969), p. 51.

[44] See JCS, Office of the Special Assistant for Counterinsurgency and Special Activities, "Bluebook," p. 284; and Department of the Army, *Counterguerrilla Operations*, FM 31-16 (1967), p. 16.

[45] "Summary Report, Military Counterinsurgency Accomplishments Since January 1961," Memorandum for the Special Assistant to the President for National Security Affairs, CM-843-62, 21 July, 1962, p. 8. DDRS, Retro: 242C.

the more likely politicians are to worry about the threat from within than the threat from without. They will thus be leery of efforts to discipline or depoliticize the armed forces. To do so might prove fatal today, while the consequences of continued predatory behavior can be put off until tomorrow, especially if a powerful ally is committed to the cause.

Questions of the quality and quantity of the ties linking government and population explain the limits of good government prescriptions. Underlying the good government ought is a deep, unresolved tension between centralization and decentralization, between governmental control and responsiveness. Normatively, Americans prefer decentralized, democratic government as the ultimate goal of political development and a means of defeating insurgency. Conversely, their assumptions about the modernization process, the key participants in it, and its possible pathologies produce a prescriptive bent for centralized, paternalistic government. The assumptions underlying both these antithetical positions are flawed, however, and result in the misanalysis of national politics, relations between central government and provincial and/or local government, and local politics.

At the national level, politicians are not divorced from power bases, nor are those power bases directly related to popular support or participation. Instead, politics is often the outcome of military, police, administrative, economic, and other groups' maneuvering among themselves. Thus, political power and performance are likely to be tied to these preexisting, if fluid, arrangements and not to democratic legitimation by elections. As long as this is so, elections are unlikely to provide meaningful participation for the population and may increase popular cynicism.

Decentralization and democratization may even have a perverse impact on government-periphery relations. Central political elites often lack the means to mobilize voters or administer beyond the capital; therefore, they depend on local power brokers to do both. As a result, national politics and policy may be defined by those whose entrenched positions of power may be one of the causes of the distributional conflict underlying insurgency. Furthermore, decentralization increases their power because they are the only ones positioned to profit by the new resources and freedom of action let slip by the center. In short, rather than improving popular access to the system and raising popular support, democratization and decentralization may do just the opposite.

Last, and most important, are questions of the adequacy of arguments for decentralization at the local level. Here analysts have built a strong case for grass-roots democracy to give people a stake in government. Such arguments, however, turn on what Samuel Popkin has labeled "the myth of the village": a vision of the premodern village as a unified, consensual, "moral" community destroyed by the trauma of modernization and the "penetration" of central authority and the capitalist economy.[46] Thus, it is claimed, if the roots of instability and support for insurgency lie in "defensive" reactions by villagers seeking to reconstruct the safety of traditional village life, the solution is to return local autonomy and control.[47] But the argument fails on the assumption of a contented, traditional community and a desire to recreate it.

The issue is one of power. Contrary to myth, many traditional villages suffered sharp tensions arising from the powerfuls' ability to shift taxes to the weak, inflict the poor with forced labor drafts and conscription calls, and keep the lion's share of community resources for themselves. Colonialism aggravated this situation by providing external resources to local notables whose positions were thus greatly strengthened. Power within the village and access to external resources gave the notables control of village government and relations with the outside, despite democratic traditional forms of village government. These distributional tensions within the village, notables' external alliances and the appearance (real and imagined) of external support for the status quo provide insurgents a powerful package of grievances with which to mobilize support. Such conditions also suggest, however, that decentralization may hurt counterinsurgency efforts by offering local notables the opportunity to further enhance their power at the expense of those already prone to support the insurgents.

Here the argument joins the other major theme: the necessity for political control by the center. Analysts see insurgency-threatened allies as developers whose well-intentioned developmental efforts are the unintentional—if unavoidable—causes of their plight. Thus, they argue, counterinsurgency requires the ability to manage modernization. Governments must possess the will and capacity to make the hard decisions: invest not consume; rationalize administration; root out corruption; attack parochial political groupings, and so on. Conversely, the masses are supposed to be malleable, gullible, and vulnerable. They are

---

[46] Samuel L. Popkin, *The Rational Peasant: The Political Economy of Rural Society in South Vietnam* (Berkeley: University of California Press, 1979).

[47] In a report on the "other war" in Vietnam prepared for President Johnson, Robert Komer declared, for example, that "A major effort has begun to restore some authority and autonomy to the vital and traditional village/hamlet level government." Robert W. Komer, "The Other War in Vietnam—A Progress Report," Report to the President, September 13, 1966, p. 39.

the Achilles heel of the development process, easy targets of insurgent propaganda, because they have been uprooted from the traditional structures that once kept them out of trouble, have no grasp on issues of import beyond the village, and do not know their true self-interest. Together these arguments provide a strong case for paternalistic, possibly authoritarian governments able to do the dirty work and prepare the way for democracy.[48] However, there are problems with this approach.

The counterinsurgents assume that *more* government is *better* government. But this presupposes the very issues at question in a country threatened by insurgency: that government and populace share goals which will be advanced by greater government capabilities at the grassroots level. Yet elites' interests and those of the population may be very different. Greater government capacity to enforce the desires of the former on the latter may even worsen, not improve, conditions. In politics, as in romance, familiarity may breed contempt.

The problem shows starkly in the case of programs to increase government efficiency and administrative capacity. In the abstract, both are essential, but without attention to policy content they may be counterproductive. Indeed, improving administrative capacity has often meant, for example, greater governmental ability to collect taxes, enforce skewed land tenure arrangements, and raise conscripts. In short, improved administrative capacity may mean better enforcement of the status quo that is the insurgents' target and a primary cause of popular support for them. Nor can the resulting problems be avoided by means of apolitical, civil service administration. Although many analysts assume that administrative reforms are "primarily technical matters" and that "technically skilled and persuasive" American advisors will "readily succeed" in passing on their expertise,[49] notions of administrative impartiality are meaningless when *who* sets the rules to be administered lies at the heart of the conflict. Furthermore, despite the benefits of improved administrative capacity, governments may sacrifice reforms to the more immediate requirements of political loyalty and patronage politics on which the regime's very existence depends.

Similar problems plague the prescription that threatened governments ought to be scrupulously law-abiding. This assumes the legality

[48] U.S. Army, Office of the Secretary, "Evaluation of the Military Assistance Program," memorandum for the President's Committee to Study the United States Military Assistance Program, 1959, p. 19, DDRS, Retro: 964A; and Hough, *Economic Assistance and Security*, pp. 10-11.

[49] Blaufarb, *Counterinsurgency Era*, p. 86.

of the government in power. But if the insurgents have credible local roots, and the political system is not—as the counterinsurgents suggest—representative or responsive, then what is legality cannot be assumed. To the contrary, what is legality is a primary point of contention: whose legality, what laws, what are or will be the rules of the game, and who will define them, *these* are the subject of insurgency.

Nor can questions of governmental legitimacy be addressed with the simple prescriptions of the progress ought. These confuse absolute standards of living with opportunities for future betterment and imagine that peasants cannot distinguish between the two. They assume a population which will respond with gratitude to short-term changes in the level of benefits from government. It is true that the peasants attracted to insurgencies would like *more*: more food, money, health, and future security. It does not follow, however, that the simple promise of more explains peasant support for the insurgents or that providing food, medicine, and credit will win them back. In fact, such efforts may be irrelevant to peasants seeking not an added increment of welfare, but a redistribution of income, power, and prestige. For them, the issue may not be the absolute *quantity* of goods and services provided by a system controlled from afar; instead, it may be the *quality* of their relationship to that system and, in particular, their ability to shape the rules of the game.

Cost-Benefit Counterinsurgency

Formal doctrine did not remain frozen in its initial form. When the "other war" in Vietnam failed to progress, the criticism began, and with it came a new wave of analytic writing, this time from the West. Where before the Camelot academics of the Northeast had held sway, analysts from the RAND Corporation achieved prominence at the end of the Johnson years and held it through the Nixon administration. With this shift, the language of counterinsurgency changed from talk of hearts and minds to the jargon of cost-benefit economics, and the focus changed from concern about overwhelming popular demands to underwhelming state repressive capabilities. It was not a change for the better. Cost-benefit counterinsurgency kept, even exaggerated, the weaknesses of hearts-and-minds prescriptions and further muddled the issues of leverage, reform, and government-population relations.

The cost-benefit approach is best exemplified by the work of two RAND analysts, Nathan Leites and Charles Wolf, Jr.[50] They begin by

[50] See, for example, Charles Wolf, Jr., "Insurgency and Counter-Insurgency: New

criticizing hearts-and-minds analysis for its focus on poverty, income inequalities, and corruption and the need for economic betterment, redistribution, and good government. Hearts-and-minds, they contend, views insurgency

> as analogous to a popular election in which the progress of the conflict depends on, and reflects, the distribution of popular preferences. Indeed, the insurgents' emergence is itself often viewed as a reflection of the government's loss of a primary heat in a subliminal popularity contest. Progress of the conflict is analogous to progress of an electoral campaign: the 'people' judge the contest, and express the preferences that determine the outcome.[51]

Even in its "moderate version," they argue, hearts and minds identifies governmental malperformance with insurgency, and so "effective government" and "institution building" with successful counterinsurgency. These more moderate variants, they concede, are less "preferences oriented" but "the emphasis is still on the demand side of the insurgency problem, that is to say on the receptivity of the environment for insurgency."[52]

Leites and Wolf press their most successful attack against the progress ought. They argue cogently that there is no simple link between economic aid and support for the government. If modernization sows the seeds of insurgency, then more of the same may exaggerate, not alleviate, both the problem and the need for better, more centralized capabilities on the part of an already overextended government.[53] Furthermore, given limited control of the countryside, aid to peasants may actually help the insurgents without raising support for the government since they may use it to pay off the guerrillas.[54]

Leites and Wolf go further to argue that popular preferences simply do not matter. They come to this conclusion by inverting a now familiar thesis. They contend that all Third World countries are vulnerable and thus that mounting an insurgency should be easy anywhere. Having said as much, however, they add that they "are as enthusiastic as

---

Myths and Old Realities," *Yale Review* 56: 2 (December 1966); Charles Wolf, Jr., *Controlling Small Wars*, P-3994 (Santa Monica: RAND Corp., December 1968); Nathan Leites and Charles Wolf, Jr., *Rebellion and Authority: Myths and Realities Reconsidered*, P-3422 (Santa Monica: RAND Corp., August 1966); and Nathan Leites and Charles Wolf, Jr., *Rebellion and Authority: An Analytic Essay on Insurgent Conflicts* (Chicago: Markham, 1970).

[51] Leites and Wolf, *Myths and Realities*, pp. 4–5.

[52] Ibid., pp. 5–6.

[53] Wolf, "Insurgency," p. 228.

[54] Leites and Wolf, *Rebellion and Authority*, p. 19.

others are for 'effective' (democratically-oriented and progressive) government, and for economic and social development. But to say that this . . . has to be accomplished to deal with insurgency is . . . too ambitious . . . to be interesting or useful. Pies in the sky are too remote to be tasty."[55] What they suggest instead are direct efforts to "raise the costs of inputs" and "block the output" of the "insurgent system."

Leites and Wolf present a simple, mock-economic model: of inputs→process→outputs. As for inputs, Wolf argues that "what an insurgent movement requires . . . is not popular support . . . but . . . food, recruits, small arms [and] information at reasonable cost. . . . These costs may be 'reasonable' without popular support . . . ; and, conversely, . . . may be raised considerably without popular support having been acquired by the government."[56] On the output side lie what they define as the essentials of success: terrorist activities, disruption of government administration, demoralization, and defeat of its military forces.

Leites and Wolf suggest a four-part prescription. First, "counter-rebellion" efforts must change "the costs and amounts of the inputs that the insurgent system gets." Second, they must attack "the process by which these inputs are . . . converted into the activities of the insurgent 'system.' " Third, they must block the outputs of the insurgent system. Finally, they must undertake "the business of hardening . . . the insurgency's targets so that they can withstand more of the insurgent activities." Specifically, they suggest resource and population control, rewards for killing or betraying insurgents, a military strategy of attrition, improved area security, and such target "hardening" measures as strategic hamlets.[57]

But the heart of the cost-benefit approach is coercion. In fact, Leites and Wolf aim to demonstrate the political utility of force in attacking Third World instability. They assert that "limiting damage or enhancing gain may be a sufficient explanation for the behavior of the population, without recourse to more elusive explanations concerning putative preferences or sympathies."[58] Thus, counterinsurgents should worry not about popular allegiances, but about how to raise the costs to the peasantry of supporting the insurgents. And force, they con-

---

[55] Leites and Wolf, *Myths and Realities*, pp. 7–8.

[56] Wolf, "Insurgency," p. 227.

[57] Leites and Wolf, *Myths and Realities*, pp. 9–11, and Wolf, "Insurgency," pp. 232–35. For an application of Leites's and Wolf's approach, see Heymann and Whitson, *Can and Should the United States Preserve a Military Capability for Revolutionary Conflict?*, pp. 56–58.

[58] Leites and Wolf, *Rebellion and Authority*, p. 42.

clude, is the best and cheapest way, since "the contest between R [Rebellion] and A [Authority] is . . . a contest in the effective management of coercion."[59]

The cost-benefit approach has its flaws. Foremost among them is the potential immorality of a strategy based on coercion. Leites and Wolf acknowledge the problem explicitly. "While the cool analysis of coercion is morally repugnant," they note, "failure to analyze it should be even more odious, because such neglect magnifies the power of those who do." In fact, failure to analyze *and use* coercion will allow insurgents to "establish themselves impregnably with precisely those capabilities whose absence from the authorities' arsenal contributed to their arrival in power."[60] Theirs, in short, is a morality of consequences. But here is the rub: even within their definitional universe, the practicability of cost-benefit counterinsurgency is questionable.

In practice, the Leites and Wolf program replicates the great oughts and shares their limitations. Input control requires the administrative capacity to manage resource and population movements; targeting the insurgent's organization requires dedicated police and intelligence forces; and the need to harden "Authority's" structure sounds suspiciously like the good government ought. Wolf himself notes that

> One of the more crippling impediments to effective counter-insurgency programs lies in the wanton abuse of power by the government's military and paramilitary forces. . . . Military discipline must be . . . brought under firm control so that such harshness as is meted out . . . is unambiguously recognizable as a penalty deliberately imposed because of behavior by the populace that contributes to the insurgent movement.[61]

But all this is "too remote to be tasty." Such complex tasks are likely to be beyond the capabilities of weak, fragmented regimes dependent upon mercenary armed forces.

No less problematic is the relationship between external benefactor and ally. Leites and Wolf rightly note the limitations of strategies requiring reforms by threatened regimes in order to qualify for assistance. They observe, too, that the United States cannot expect allies in need to be politically pure. The problem, Wolf argues, "is that our disposition to accept the 'popular support' view of [insurgency] makes us too prone to look for overly broad and ambitious 'social transforma-

[59] Ibid., p. 155.
[60] Ibid., pp. 156, 158.
[61] Wolf, "Insurgency," p. 239.

tion' solutions, and to overlook the more modest, realistic, sometimes distasteful measures that may improve the situation step by step."[62] But this poses two problems. First, it raises the question of whether it is possible to distinguish between the coercive, short-term measures prescribed and later reforms which will eventually render them unnecessary. Second, because leverage is inversely proportional to involvement, by providing short-term assistance the United States reduces both leverage and the prospects for reform.

Beyond these practical issues lie crippling analytic flaws. There are, in fact, two related problems stemming from the assertion that popular preferences are immaterial. Both derive from the familiar notion that the periphery is the object of others' politics. First, despite claims of neutrality, Leites and Wolf assume the illegitimacy of "Rebellion" and the legitimacy of "Authority" (which Wolf defines as "a legal and legitimized right and capacity to command").[63] Similarly, Leites and Wolf delegitimize insurgents by insisting that they are foreign-inspired and dependent on coercion; then they deny by definition the possible legitimacy of insurgent counterclaims and popularity. (Such notions are meaningless, after all, if the masses are incapable of knowing or pursuing their real interests.) Thus, from the outset they prejudge what may be a contest to redefine the political rules of the game and legitimacy itself.

Here lies a second assumption: that politics can be analyzed as process devoid of substance. Wolf asserts that "what needs to be . . . made central to the discussion is the question of authority and control, and of instruments to effectuate this authority and control."[64] Since the legitimacy of "Authority" is assumed, this reduces to consideration of instruments and hence the ability to coerce compliance. This reduction of counterinsurgency to the exercise of coercion has the analytic advantage of eliminating questions of human costs and the political consequences for "Authority" of abusing its subjects. If insurgency thrives on coercion, then it is of no political consequence if "Authority" uses the same instruments. Conversely, even if the population perceives opportunities in the insurgency, sufficient force can make supporting the insurgents to win long-term benefits a pointless venture. This second as-

---

[62] Ibid., p. 233.

[63] Wolf, *Controlling Small Wars*, p. 2. In *Rebellion and Authority: Myths and Realities Reconsidered*, for example, Leites and Wolf attempt to "neutralize" their language by using "rebellion" for "insurgency," "authority" for "regime" or "government," and so on. If only it were possible to achieve scientific detachment by such simple-minded means. See pp. 2–3.

[64] Leites and Wolf, *Myths and Realities*, p. 3.

sumption holds only if the former does—that is, that the peasantry are the passive objects of other people's manipulation. But if the tenacity of the Viet Cong is any indication, some peasants under some conditions are willing to invest even their lives in an effort to remake their world. By denying the importance of context and content, however, Leites and Wolf also deny themselves the ability to identify which peasants under what circumstances will be willing to die for what causes.

CONCLUSION

Although the counterinsurgency era spans only the years from 1961 to 1969, counterinsurgency doctrine is older and longer-lived. It owes its rapid, widespread acceptance and main outlines to the security and development ideas it embodies and with which it shares the same familiarity and explanatory, prescriptive and ideological utility. These, too, help explain counterinsurgency doctrine's resistance to change and the superficiality of most critiques of it. For while there has been criticism, no one has challenged its intellectual bases or the fundamental problems built into its explanation-prescription formula. Like those who would bury the old notions of political development, Douglas Blaufarb is perhaps too optimistic in asserting that "the term 'counter-insurgency' conveys today, in the late 1970s, various impressions mostly having to do with cold war attitudes, now considered outdated, and . . . with U.S. intervention, now considered misguided, to prevent revolutions in distant lands."[65] Indeed, in the few years since those lines were written, policymakers have rediscovered counterinsurgency and begun programs which replicate those of the early 1960s.

Chapters 3, 4, and 5 have shown the content and continuity of the ideas underlying counterinsurgency doctrine, identified their key characteristics, and analyzed their weaknesses, at least in the abstract. But this is not enough. To demonstrate the utility of a cognitive approach also requires that it be tested against alternative explanations and that its explanatory weight be shown to merit the attention. It is thus necessary to establish how in specific cases policymakers' ideas had an important, independent impact. This is the aim of Part III.

[65] Blaufarb, *Counterinsurgency Era*, p. 1.

PART III

▲

6

NOT SO EXCEPTIONALLY
AMERICAN

Before analyzing three case studies which weigh the cognitive content explanation of foreign policy against realist, presidential, and bureaucratic politics alternatives, this chapter sets it against American exceptionalism. So far this book has argued that the ideas behind American policies toward the Third World owe their power and popularity to the intellectual heritage of western social analysis. American exceptionalists, on the other hand, contend that American foreign policy is, indeed, exceptional. They argue that it is "conditioned by culturally imposed qualities of character [that] strongly influence the perception, selection, and evaluation of political reality."[1] As the term culture implies, such characteristics are supposedly stable over time, shared by all Americans, and unique to them. They derive from a unique past as interpreted in a set of political principles and projected on the world as the American program. They also, suggests Stanley Hoffmann, make American policymakers "ask the wrong question, turn to the wrong analysis, and thus in the end provoke the wrong results."[2] As for counterinsurgency, such analysis suggests that the misperception and misprescription outlined in the preceding chapter are peculiarly American, born of a uniquely American blindness to the nature of political change in the Third World, and having uniquely American consequences.

On closer examination, the argument is less powerful than it appears. American foreign policy, like the rest of American life, has its oddities, of course. But the power of American exceptionalism derives from the claim that the distinguishing features of American foreign policy can be attributed to uniquely American factors. Yet when Europe is examined, explanation is confounded at both ends. Neither causes nor consequences are uniquely American. Thus this chapter examines the ideas underlying French colonial policy and revolutionary war (counterinsurgency) doctrine to demonstrate the parallels to American equivalents in content, function, and consequences.

---

[1] Almond, *The American People and Foreign Policy*, p. 29.

[2] Hoffmann, *Gulliver's Troubles*, p. 126. Similarly, George Kennan argues that American foreign relations are flawed by "mistakes of understanding" that are "deeply rooted in the national consciousness." *American Diplomacy, 1900–1950* (New York: Mentor Books, 1951), pp. 6, 77.

AMERICAN EXCEPTIONALISM

Stanley Hoffmann observes that "for a policy-maker, there is as much truth in Eliot's 'Hell is ourselves' as in Sartre's '*L'enfer c'est les autres.*' "[3] The uniquely American hell he and others describe is defined by a unique American past, set of principles, and program. Analysis begins with the uniquely *happy* character of the American past: its comparative value consensus, lack of political cleavages, economic opportunity, and absence of politically salient social class stratifications. This pleasant past, argue the exceptionalists, has led Americans to define the state as the embodiment of a shared normative order, view reform, not revolution, as the proper mode of political action and believe in the possibilities of bootstrap self-improvement. It has also, they contend, given rise to a special mode of "apprehending the world mentally for judgment and reform."[4] Thus, notes John Morton Blum, "confident of the superiority and the attractiveness of their culture, just as sure of the *ennui* and decadence of the old World, Americans . . . believed the spread of their . . . systems of government and social organization to be inevitable."[5] And this, American exceptionalists contend, raises the question of America's role in others' advancement. For while initially Americans encouraged inevitability by example, in the twentieth century they have harkened to the 1776 challenge of the only real American revolutionary, Tom Paine: "We have it in our power to begin the world again."

Critical to Americans' performance as expediters of peace and progress is the belief that politics is a matter of principle. (In Woodrow Wilson's words, "Politics is a war of causes, a joust of principles.")[6] It shows, the exceptionalists argue, in declarations that the United States has no interests abroad but the pursuit of "world order." It explains, too, the otherwise incredible grand strategies propounded by American leaders and their hurt when others doubt the purity of American motives. But most important, particularly for an exceptionalist explanation of the weaknesses of counterinsurgency doctrine, is the belief that politics within other countries are also a matter of principles, not power or interest. Here the United States has been blinded by its happy history. Thus, counterinsurgency doctrine's blindness to intragovernmental

---

[3] Hoffmann, *State of War*, p. 173.

[4] Hoffmann, *Gulliver's Troubles*, p. 94.

[5] John Morton Blum, *The Promise of America: An Historical Inquiry* (Boston: Houghton Mifflin, 1966), p. 151.

[6] Cited in Richard Hofstadter, *The American Political Tradition and the Men Who Made It*, 25th anniversary ed. (New York: Knopf, 1979), p. 235.

constraints on reform, for example, reflects American experience: without fundamental differences over ends, Americans think conflicts can be easily managed within the rules of the political game. Doctrine's blindness to government-population relations also reflects the American experience. Convinced that states embody a normative order embraced by all, Americans can neither imagine fundamental political differences between center and periphery nor understand that power, not preference, may explain the political order. Similarly, given economic opportunity and social mobility at home, Americans are blind to rigid class systems elsewhere and thus unsympathetic to violent efforts to overturn them. As a result, too, argue exceptionalists, "United States' policy-scientists and policy-makers have few answers to the problem of integrating dislocated communities."[7]

Finally, argue the exceptionalists, the American past and principles combine in a unique program marked by an instrumental view of the world. (After all, notes Louis Hartz, "when you take your ethics for granted . . . all problems emerge as problems of technique.")[8] Again, this seems clear in the legalism of counterinsurgency doctrine. Blessed with shared values and spared conflicts over ends, Americans focus on legality because our conflicts have been manageable within the bounds of due process. But as a result, argue the exceptionalists, Americans have failed to perceive that such is not the case in countries torn by insurgency. A similar blindness, they contend, explains the depoliticized technical determinism of the progress ought which stresses technical fixes, training, and the provision of goods and services. Again, so the argument goes, Americans are misled by the ease of their own economic development, the relative equality of economic opportunity, and lack of politically salient social stratifications. Thus, they fail to take account of both socially and politically imposed constraints on development and the possibility that some in the target society may be committed to blocking it.

But, according to the exceptionalists, the most characteristic feature of the American program is its violence, a tendency that shows distinctly in the security ought. Americans, notes Stanley Hoffmann, are torn by an "existential tension between an instinct toward violence to eliminate obstacles and the aspiration for harmony."[9] It is resolved in the logic of the security ought which assumes that, with extermination

---

[7] Stanley Hoffmann, "Restraints and Choices in American Foreign Policy," *Daedelus* 91 (Fall 1962), p. 683.

[8] Louis Hartz, *The Liberal Tradition in America: An Interpretation of American Political Thought Since the Revolution* (New York: Harcourt, Brace, 1955), p. 10.

[9] Stanley Hoffmann, *Primacy or World Order* (New York: McGraw-Hill, 1978), p. 6.

of external impediments, peace and progress are within reach. "In the name of such principles," observes George Kennan, "you could fight a war to the end. A future so brilliant would surely wash away the follies and brutalities of the war, redress its injuries, heal the wounds."[10] Indeed, the very notion that threats are external jibes neatly with the American belief that conflict and disorder are themselves alien and can be burnt off like warts, leaving a world restored. Given such a perspective, American counterinsurgents were blind to the potential problems of the security ought.

The question remains, however, whether these problems are uniquely American and so constitute an explanation of American foreign policy. The short answer is no, but a more satisfying one requires comparison. Thus, the rest of this chapter examines French colonial policy and counterinsurgency doctrine in the light of American exceptionalists' claims.

THE FRENCH AND REVOLUTIONARY WAR

The trauma of Vietnam has led Americans to regard the war as theirs and to ignore the ties that link our policy to foreign precedents. Yet the parallels between French and American doctrines and practices are undeniable. The resemblance is ironic but apt. Anglo-American cultural bonds and Britain's counterinsurgency successes would seem to make Britain a more suitable model than France which lost both of its counterinsurgent wars and with which relations have long been rocky. But France, like the United States, won many battles while losing, suffered military humiliation, and endured domestic political upheavals as a result. And they, like the Americans, developed a formal counterinsurgency doctrine. Furthermore, the very lack of ties between France and the United States makes it an excellent case for testing American exceptionalism.

At first glance, the ties between the French and American counterinsurgency doctrines seem superficial. True, the United States sent military observers to Indochina and Algeria, service publications ran translations of articles by French authors, and during the Kennedy administration translations of several French books on revolutionary war were popular. But American texts contain few references to French counterinsurgency efforts and draw no lessons from them. Instead, American analysts criticized them roundly and, as Douglas Blaufarb notes, "what was seen as the French failure to deal realistically with the

[10] Kennan, *American Diplomacy*, p. 60.

underlying political appeal of the insurgency was believed to vitiate the usefulness of French experience in either Vietnam or Algeria."[11] Why, then, the resemblance between French and American doctrines and practice?

French and American counterinsurgency programs resonate because they share the same assumptions and serve the same functions. Examined closely, the doctrine of revolutionary war reveals familiar notions about the origins, nature, direction, consequences, and possible pathologies of development in the Third World. It prescribed the same inappropriate responses to misunderstood problems and diverted attention from the three critical areas of leverage, constraints on intragovernmental reform, and government-population relations. And the ideological role of revolutionary war retarded its modification in the face of failure.

Revolutionary War: Background and Beginning

The proximate origins of revolutionary war lie in Indochina. It flared bright in the struggle for Algeria's sun-blasted *bled* and flickered out as France's empire burnt down to ashes. The doctrine began with disillusioned young officers in Indochina. Their ideas were ignored at first, but in the bitter debate that followed defeat they gained currency. By the late 1950s, their articles appeared in such prominent French military publications as *Revue de Défense Nationale* and *Revue Militaire d'Information* and their ideas surfaced with increasing regularity in unsigned pamphlets distributed clandestinely throughout France and the military. With advancing seniority, these officers also had occasion to put theory into practice in the villages of Algeria and alleys of Algiers' casbah.

Initially a simple effort to defeat nationalist movements, revolutionary war quickly became far more. For its proponents, the doctrine answered the frustration, humiliation, and betrayal they felt as incompetent leadership fumbled away victory, first in Indochina, then in Algeria. The problem, as they saw it, was their leaders' failure to grasp the fundamental change in the nature of war wrought by Mao. "We still persist," noted Roger Trinquier, a leading theoretician of revolutionary war, "in studying a type of warfare that no longer exists and

---

[11] Blaufarb, *Counterinsurgency Era*, p. 49. Recently, Charles Maechling, Jr., chair of the interagency committee that wrote the USOIDP, remarked on the "almost irrational bias" Kennedy Administration counterinsurgency planners held against France and the resulting "almost total dismissal of the French experience in colonial wars." Maechling, "Insurgency and Counterinsurgency," p. 33.

that we shall never fight again, while we pay only passing attention to the war we lost in Indochina and the one we are about to lose in Algeria."[12] Something had to be done, and they were convinced they had the answer. "There is nothing inevitable about our enemy's temporary successes," declared Jacques Hogard, another leading revolutionary war analyst, "victory is within our grasp and is certain, even if difficult."[13] The doctrine they propounded was to provide the necessary means. It failed.

The doctrine of revolutionary war was naive, intellectually thin, and oversold by avid proponents seeking higher impact with exaggerated threats and touted miracle solutions. But despite its flaws, revolutionary war provided a neatly packaged, internally coherent doctrine with the appearance of explanatory and prescriptive power and immense ideological utility. For many, it simplified and explained the world and the threats France faced in it, promised a means of coping, and suggested a heroic national mission for France and those who answered the call. Nor was revolutionary war an aberrant, purely military phenomenon. To the contrary, even in its final form as a putschist's ideology, the doctrine merely exaggerated notions long expressed in French discourses on colonialism and the debate over France's proper place in the postwar world. Indeed, it is, to borrow Tony Smith's phrase, the "ink-blot" where Frenchmen projected their "shared anguish . . . at the passing of national greatness, shared humiliation at a century of defeats, shared belief that France should retain her independence in a hostile world, . . . [and] shared fear that her inability to regain international rank would be the consequence of her own internal decadence."[14] Thus, revolutionary war doctrine offers a lens through which to examine the assumptions behind French policymaking in the face of insurgency. But before beginning, it is necessary to outline French colonial policy and the political context in which revolutionary war flourished.

FRENCH COLONIAL POLICY: PAST, PRINCIPLES, AND PROGRAM

French colonialism has always been close to Frenchmen's sense of self-esteem and France's place in the world. Economic and domestic political motivations figured in each expansion of the empire, but crit-

[12] Roger Trinquier, *Modern Warfare: A French View of Counterinsurgency*, trans. Daniel Lee (New York: Praeger, 1964), pp. 3–4.
[13] Jacques Hogard, "Guerre Révolutionnaire ou Révolution dans l'Art de la Guerre," RDN (December 1956), p. 1497.
[14] Tony Smith, *The French Stake in Algeria, 1945–1962* (Ithaca: Cornell University Press, 1978), p. 127.

ical, too, was the need to restore French prestige after setbacks in Europe. Suffering tribulations at home, France took Algiers—then all of Algeria—to demonstrate its virility. After Otto von Bismarck's armies had trounced its military and the Great Depression of 1873 had undone its economy, France reinflated its national ego through further colonial expansion. And in response to the humiliations of World War II, French leaders once again sought solace in empire, despite the rising tide of nationalism. But these setbacks and the need for colonial counterstrokes only gave urgency to a deeper French sense of superiority and mission.

The conviction of a national *mission civilatrice* underpinned both strains of French colonial theory. The first, *assimilation*, called on France to "civilize" the natives and ultimately incorporate them as full citizens in a greater France. Some, however, objected to the task's size and the logical consequence of success: the submersion of white Frenchmen by a rising tide of brown ones. Others objected that "inferior races" and "barbarians" could never accede to French standards. Together they proposed *association*, a permanent master-subject "partnership" in which France would lead and the natives would do whatever they were capable of. Association prevailed, but most Frenchmen and colonial officers clung to the ideals of assimilation. Either way, no one doubted France's mission to lead the colonial peoples toward an approximation of France's exalted status.

Both variants of colonial policy derived from histoire raisonnée.[15] In fact, they embody the two variants of the developmental great chain of being. Assimilation reflects the dynamic version which assumes that in time all societies will mount the stages of development to modernity; conversely, association assumes that, as in the evolutionary order, societies can be classed from least to most developed, but that like animal species, they are stuck at their rank. In either guise, French colonial policy applied a French standard of "reason," defined a French evolutionary plane, and posited a French tutelary role, whether to bring the native up to French standards or educate him to his natural station.

This French conceit resulted in a tendency to "apprehend the world for judgment and reform." France, the model of modernity, naturally judged the rest of the world inferior. (As Pierre Mille noted wryly, "The Chinese, having no railroads, no mechanical textile industry, no Napoleon . . . are extremely inferior to us.")[16] Unlike Americans, however,

[15] See, for example, Hubert Deschamps, "Et Maintenant, Lord Lugard?" *Africa* 33: 4 (October 1963); and Raymond Betts, *Assimilation and Association in French Colonial Theory, 1890–1914* (New York: Columbia University Press, 1961), pp. 165–76.
[16] Cited in Betts, *Assimilation and Association*, p. 170.

the French would not leave development of the inferior to historical inevitability. Rather, colonialism was to reform others in the French image, literally to civilize them.

The French, too, operated overseas with a notion of politics as principles. As in the American case, this appeared regularly in statements of grand purpose. In 1950, for example, General Jean de Lattre, French commander in Indochina, informed an American observer that "We have no . . . interests here. . . . The work we are doing is for the salvation of the Vietnamese people."[17] More importantly, however, French ideas shaped assessments of "the colonial situation" and produced a blindness similar to that afflicting American perspectives on the Third World.

The problems begin with the assumption that the French way is the uniquely best way. French colonial officers did not believe indigenous cultures or institutions offered anything of value. Their role was that of teacher and civilizer; it was unthinkable that the objects of their attentions should have grounds to complain. After all, declared Charles de Gaulle, "Because of us, people of all races, hitherto . . . plunged into a millenary torpor where history is not even written, discovered in their turn liberty, progress, justice. Because of us, new elites were born . . . whom we reared not that they would abuse others, but that they would lead them toward a better and more worthy fate."[18] The French, in short, believed that France embodied a normative order embraced by citizens and subjects alike. As a result, Frenchmen simply could not grasp that Asian and African interests might not coincide with their own. De Gaulle himself was puzzled, hurt, and angered by Sékou Touré's observation that France's subjects had no objections to partnership per se but did not care for the partnership of a horse with its rider. This being the case, however, it is not surprising that France's program for its colonies often stumbled.

Like its American counterpart, the French program encouraged emulation. As the Colonial Congresses of 1889 and 1890 resolved, French policy should "propagate among the natives the language, methods of work and, progressively, the spirit and civilization of France."[19] The superiority of French culture being assumed, French policy was "how-to" oriented—that is, how to inculcate the native with the Gallic essence. Here the French, like the Americans, argued that reform (or evolution through assimilation), not revolution, was the way. But as in

[17] PP/I, p. 67.
[18] Cited in Smith, *French Stake in Algeria*, frontispiece.
[19] *Recuil des délibérations du Congrès Colonial National, Paris, 1889–90*, Vol. 3 (Paris, 1890), p. 329.

the American case, French confidence in their mission also produced a penchant for vengeful violence against the ungrateful. As Arthur Girault explained in a major text for colonial officials, France sought "zealously to make [natives] into Frenchmen: they are educated, . . . dressed in the European mode, our laws are substituted for their customs. . . . But . . . if they show themselves refractory toward our civilization, then, to prevent them from injecting a discordant note in the midst of the general uniformity, they are exterminated or pushed back."[20] To echo George Kennan's caustic comment cited earlier, "A future so brilliant would surely . . . heal the wounds."

Postwar Politics of Decolonization

This is the backdrop to France's trials with decolonization and two ugly counterinsurgency wars. Although the French were not blindly optimistic about reestablishing their empire, they proceeded with a policy anachronistic even when announced, a policy as pathetic as costly and ultimately futile. The questions are obvious and inevitable: Why the gamble? Why the sorry misconception of the colonial situation and misprescription for coping with it? Why, in the end, the difficulty getting out?

Strategic and economic imperatives offer partial but insufficient answers. The colonies allowed France to claim world power status: Indochina gave France a voice in Asia; the Levant and North Africa secured France's Mediterranean position. The colonies were also economically important, at least to politically powerful economic elites. Imperial preference protected markets France could not have held otherwise and guaranteed supplies of raw materials. (Algeria was France's largest market and, with the discovery of oil in 1956, promised France energy self-sufficiency.) Shorn of its colonies, many argued, France faced economic disaster. But while widely accepted, many such arguments are simply wrong. The supposed economic stakes, for example, were exaggerated by the false claim that decolonization would end trade with the excolonies. Moreover, many of the supposedly externally imposed imperatives merely camouflaged an undiscussed vision of a greater France. Finally, none of these arguments explains the determination of actual policy. They are arguments about why France had to hold the colonies, not how. Given the supposed importance of

---

[20] Arthur Girault, *Principes de colonisation et de législation coloniale*, 3d ed. (Paris, 1927), p. 68.

the colonies, they leave unanswered the question of why France handled them so badly.

The weakness of the Fourth Republic offers the commonest explanation for the failure of postwar colonial policy. As commentators of all stripes agreed, the Fourth Republic was too weak to address as contentious an issue as decolonization. In Paris, the problem was governmental paralysis. General de Gaulle called it "a form of continual sabotage," while after Dien Ben Phu, General Henri Navarre explained that failure in Indochina was not military, but the result of "the very nature of the French political system."[21] Later parties of the center and right asserted that the key to North Africa lay in Paris, not in Tunis, Algiers, or Rabat. Moreover, in the colonies, Paris could not control local political elites, bureaucrats, or the military. French rule depended on local strongmen whose abuses raised popular resentment and whose interests led them to sabotage reform. Similarly, conservative civil servants, often drawn from local settler communities, opposed reform from within. Finally, in Indochina military officers often operated beyond government control, and in Algeria key units confronted Paris directly.

But these arguments, too, are insufficient, suggesting that the French fought two savage wars, back-to-back, in a fit of absentmindedness. Such analysis offers no explanation for the huge efforts necessary to field forces of as many as 500,000 for nearly fifteen years or to justify thousands of French dead. Moreover, they seem to suggest that policy content was determined by systemic weakness. Yet important as such weaknesses were, it is necessary to look elsewhere for the conception of France and France's role in the world that shaped policymakers' definition of and responses to the situation. It is necessary to look to the familiar and potent ideas embodied in French colonial policy.

"France cannot be France without greatness," wrote Charles de Gaulle, and by greatness he meant virility born of empire. As he told President Roosevelt, "I know that you are preparing to aid France materially, and that aid will be invaluable. . . . But it is in the political realm that she must recover her vigor, her self-reliance, and, consequently, her role. How can she do this if she is excluded from the or-

---

[21] Charles de Gaulle, *Discours et messages: dans l'attente, 1946–1958* (Paris: Plon, 1970), p. 279; and Navarre, cited in Raoul Girardet, *La crise militaire française, 1945–1962,* Cahiers de la Foundation Nationale des Sciences Politiques, No. 123 (Paris, 1964), p. 163 fn.

ganization of the great world powers . . . if she loses her African and Asian territories?[22] In a world dominated by the United States, the Soviet Union, and Britain, the empire was France's sole claim to importance. It was a position embraced by all but the Communists, a common ground upon which programmatic details were fought over. Thus, like de Gaulle, Prime Minister Edouard Faure asserted that

> The entire honor of France as well as her human mission oblige us absolutely, without equivocation and without reticence, to keep Algeria for France. . . . Without Algeria and without French Africa, what would become of our country? Her economy gravely menaced, her world-wide influence compromised, she would be no more than a reflection dimming daily of her former greatness.[23]

And on succeeding Faure, Socialist Guy Mollet declared that without the empire France "would become a diminished power of second or third rank, shorn of her world role."[24]

Nor did French leaders' claims for empire end with the colonies' importance to France. Even Socialist Party spokesmen identified defense of the empire with a global struggle against subversion, the Chinese peril, and communism. Still more important is the most common theme of party manifestos from the late 1940s to 1962, the *mission civilatrice*. Not only the Conservatives believed that "France is the only world power that can make any legitimate claim to be a civilizing influence." A Socialist manifesto of the same period asserted that "France has accomplished a truly civilizing task in her overseas territories." It denounced the "misconceptions of the reactionary ministers" and exploitation that the well-being of "native peoples" required "une veritable association" with France.[25]

This conception of the necessity of empire and France's imperial role proved doubly dangerous. First, by making the empire France's greatness, the French made colonial wars the measure of the nation. In the Quixotic struggles that followed, the resulting need for self-confirmation made circumstances irrelevant. France had to stand everywhere. Second, assurance about the *mission civilatrice* blinded understanding of the colonies and the options open to France. Indeed, assertion of

---

[22] Charles de Gaulle, *The Complete War Memoirs of Charles de Gaulle* (New York: Simon and Schuster, 1967), p. 574.

[23] Cited in Smith, *French Stake in Algeria*, p. 162.

[24] Guy Mollet, *Bilan et perspectives socialistes* (Paris: Plon, 1958), p. 59.

[25] Both are cited in Christopher Harrison, "French Attitudes to Empire and the Algerian War," *African Affairs* 82: 326 (January 1983), pp. 85–86.

the *mission civilatrice* killed analysis and determined policy in its absence.

The blinding effects of the mission civilatrice show clearly in French delusions about their subjects' affections. For the majority of Frenchmen, colonialism was *right*; and they translated this notion into the assertion that their subjects thought so too. As then Colonial Commissioner (later prime minister) René Pleven told the 1944 Brazzaville Conference on the future of the empire,

> In greater colonial France there are neither peoples to free nor racial discriminations to abolish. There are populations who feel French and who want to take, and to whom France wishes to give, a larger and larger part in the life and democratic institutions of the French community ... but who do not expect to know any other independence than the independence of France.[26]

Thus, throughout the trials of Indochina and Algeria, French observers returned with reports of "unforgettable signs of affection, loyalty and confidence" and public declarations of "love for France."[27]

The French also believed in the necessity of a continuing *in loco parentis* role. While many on the right denied that the colonies would ever evolve enough to merit independence, even the Socialists, who ruled France during much of the Indochina and Algeria wars, argued that for the foreseeable future the colonized would require French supervision. (Socialist Prime Minister Guy Mollet asked, for example, "How is it possible [that] the Algerian nationalists could be so absurd as to fight to the death ... to obtain the right to send their people back to a centuries-old misery?")[28] Like their American counterparts, French academics and policymakers believed that the colonized, lacking a modern mind-set, could not govern themselves. As historian Robert Aron explained in 1962, Muslims lack the "taste for order and clarity we have inherited [from Descartes]. . . . They do not know how to reason and argue like us. . . . The true nature of Muslim thought reappears—more emotional and sentimental than dialectical and logical."[29] At the same time, however, they argued that an increasingly important minority had been uprooted from tradition and now constituted a new, poten-

[26] *Brazzaville: 30 janvier–8 fevrier, 1944*, Ministère des Colonies, p. 22.

[27] President of the Republic Vincent Auriol, *Combat*, June 7, 1949. The converse of these pious claims was the denial of French racism and exploitation, despite the dominant settler fear of being "drowned" by an Asiatic or Arab "horde" and the constant references to the colonized as "voyous," "ratons," "bougnoules," "melons," etc.

[28] Cited in Smith, *French Stake in Algeria*, p. 145.

[29] Robert Aron, *Les origines de la guerre d'Algérie* (Paris: Fayard, 1962), pp. 11–12.

tially dangerous class in need of special care. Either way, many concluded, more and better French management of the modernization process was needed.

Such arguments also justified dismissing colonial protest movements as subversive. Nationalism, declared General de Gaulle, will result in "dreadful misery, terrible political chaos, general massacre, and soon after the bellicose dictatorship of the Communists."[30] Indeed, he and others switched attention from the trauma of modernization to communist interference in it and so concluded with a deputy addressing the National Assembly that "Nationalism in Indochina is a means, the end is Soviet imperialism."[31] From here it was but a short step to a communist conspiracy theory. Thus, many, and not only those on the conservative right, believed that Indochina and Algeria were connected steps in a Soviet drive at the "underbelly" of Europe.

Despite constant cabinet turnover, continuity, not change, marked French colonial policy from 1945 to 1960. General de Gaulle set the tone in March 1945 when he laid down the terms for French rule in Indochina: absolute French sovereignty. In 1949, he still branded negotiation with Ho Chi Minh "capitulation" and late in the Algerian conflict still insisted:

> We cannot let it be put in question in any form . . . that Algeria is in fact our domain. This means, moreover, that in no matter concerning Algeria can French public authorities—executive, legislative, judicial—alienate their right and their duty to be the last resort. This means, finally, that the authority of the French Republic must be exercised frankly and firmly . . . and that the governor general . . . will be responsible only before French public officials.[32]

The Socialist governments of Léon Blum and Paul Ramadier followed de Gaulle's lead. In January 1947, for example, Ramadier asserted that he would not tolerate attacks on "the historic work of eternal France," and in March, he reasserted that "France must remain in Indochina, . . . her replacement there is not open."[33] Ten years later, another So-

[30] Cited in Department of State, Bureau of Intelligence Research, "A Review of the Algerian Question Prior to Its Consideration by the 15th UN General Assembly," I.R. No. 8351, September 26, 1960, p. 2. NADB, OSS file.

[31] PP/I, p. 24.

[32] de Gaulle, *Discours et messages*, p. 107.

[33] *L'Année politique, économique, sociale et diplomatique, 1947* (Paris: Presses Universitaires de France, 1948), p. 322; and *Journal officiel*, March 18, 1947, pp. 904–6.

cialist, Guy Mollet, declared: "Let us then reaffirm the essential and demonstrate a unanimous will that France remain . . . in Algeria."[34] When his government left office in May 1957, France was fully mobilized with 500,000 men in Algeria—an increase of 300,000 since 1956.

Each government talked of reform, but a peculiar blindness marked the discussion. The French believed in the possibility of reforming the empire in order to preserve it. In Indochina, Algeria, and elsewhere, France would be more liberal but still sovereign, assuming the colonized wanted and needed continued French control. The position made perfect sense to the French, but not to their subjects. For them, French sovereignty was the target, not the aim. Consequently, this policy of liberalism and sovereignty produced contradictions similar to those plaguing American policies. These appear, for example, in the French equivalent of the good government ought. The French Union offered limited self-determination to colonial subjects, but it denied demands for real reform. The French president was president of the French Union; its parliament merely advised the National Assembly; and France retained full control of all diplomatic, military, and currency arrangements. Similarly, policymakers stressed the material progress colonialization had brought and insisted that further progress required continued colonial assistance. They ignored the fact that the primary beneficiaries had been French settlers, not colonial subjects, and that much of the progress had been achieved at the colonials' expense. In each case, incremental gains, whether economic or political, meant little to populations still subjected to French control while mobilized by nationalists to achieve a radical redistribution of power, wealth, and prestige.

But most important was the French variant of the security ought. Like their American counterparts, the French argued that security (that is, the security of the French presence) was the essential prerequisite for all else. As Léon Blum told the National Assembly in December 1946, "We must take up . . . the organization of a free Vietnam in an Indochinese Union freely associated with the French Union. But first of all, peaceful order, the necessary base for the execution of contracts, must be restored."[35] Thus Marius Moutet, Socialist Minister for Overseas France, declared days later that "before any negotiation, it is . . . necessary to have a military victory."[36] Given the unworkability of the rest of the French program, however, security became an all-absorbing aim.

[34] *Journal officiel*, March 27, 1957, p. 1909.
[35] Cited in Smith, *French Stake in Algeria*, p. 71.
[36] *L'Année politique*, 1947, pp. 426–27.

Unable to see an alternative, France equated its *mission civilatrice* with the repression of colonial nationalism. Revolutionary war doctrine formed a critical component of the effort and embodied the basic assumptions behind it.

Universal Threat, Universal Vulnerability

The theoreticians of revolutionary war sought to arm France with a strategic doctrine for the postwar era. They failed, largely because they confused the *methods* of insurgent movements with the *causes* of insurgency and then systematically mistook their own ethnocentric conception of the Third World for reality.

Revolutionary war doctrine embodied a French cold war world view as rigid as its American counterpart. The world had become a battleground for two fundamentally opposed camps, and this, in turn, produced "an even more radical transformation than that provoked by the French revolution: war has become permanent, universal and truly 'total.' "[37] Nuclear weapons merely changed the likely form and venue of conflict. As one analyst put it, "'The balance of terror' means that it is not in the nuclear realm that the conflict will be played out. It will be played out in that of political warfare"—that is, revolutionary war.[38] Indeed, for General Chassin and others, revolutionary war was "without the slightest doubt the *most* dangerous form of war for France, and perhaps for the West, . . . because it can be waged with the least risk by an opponent acting through intermediaries, who can gradually deprive us of every strategic position in the world."[39]

The theoreticians of revolutionary war saw the threat of Soviet sponsored revolutionary wars everywhere; indeed, the dominoes were already falling. The defeat of Chiang Kai Shek and the mounting attack on French Indochina, argued "XXX" in 1954, were but the opening moves, since "a French defeat in Indochina would be a defeat for the Western democracies. . . . Its repercussions would be profound vis-à-vis India, Burma, Malaysia, Indonesia, the Philippines and the . . . varied, uncertain world searching for its future, along the edges of the Pa-

[37] Hogard, "Guerre Révolutionnaire," p. 1498. See, too, Hogard's companion piece, "Cette Guerre de Notre Temps," RDN 27 (August–September 1958), particularly p. 1308.

[38] Suzanne Labin, "La Guerre Politique des Soviets," (Part I) RDN (June 1960), pp. 1028–29. Hogard, actually claims the "nuclear war is thus no more than a phase, a battle, in the worldwide revolutionary war." "Cette Guerre de Notre Temps," p. 1316.

[39] Gen. L.-M. Chassin, "Insuffisance de la stratégie nucléaire," RDN 16 (July 1960), pp. 1194, 1198–99.

cific and Indian Oceans."[40] Four years later, General Allard vainly attempted to convince France's NATO allies that the Soviet's revolutionary war strategy "has blinded many to the fact that its primary thrust is not a direct assault, but a wide encircling movement passing by China, the Far East, India, the Middle East, Egypt and North Africa, finally to strangle Europe." He concluded pessimistically: "it is now almost completed, all that remains is to tear Algeria away from France."[41]

Like their civilian counterparts, French counterinsurgents dismissed claims that the problem was nationalism, not Communist meddling. For example, Colonel Broizat declared Algerian nationalism to be "an artificial dialectical creation" designed solely to serve the purposes of Moscow.[42] And it served so well, argued the counterinsurgents, because of the vulnerability of the colonized to the Circean call of nationalism. This vulnerability derived from the same characteristics that necessitated colonialism: their passivity, malleability, and gullibility. Analysts portrayed the colonized as an undifferentiated collection of happy-go-lucky children of nature bound by mental chains of religion, tradition, and intellectual sloth, and purposely blurred distinctions among them. (They regularly referred to the Algerian *fellegha* as "Viets.")[43] Thus, Africans, it was argued, share a "collective emotionalism" and an "impulsive character . . . which, almost without transition, can switch from its normal childish good humor to irrational and violent frenzy," while the "natural nonchalance of aborigines blessed by a warm climate" explains African backwardness.[44] Similarly, Muslim countries are backward because "the modern scientific mentality is entirely foreign to Islam."[45] Without it, and "subject to religious pressures or a stifling traditionalism, the masses accept with fatalism life under a foreign civilization."[46] This passivity renders the "masses" vul-

[40] "XXX," "Pourquoi l'Indochine," RDN (June 1954), p. 649.

[41] Général J. Allard, "Vérités sur l'Affaire Algérienne," RDN 26 (January 1958), p. 10.

[42] Cited in John Ambler, *The French Army in Politics, 1945–1962* (Ohio State University Press, 1966), p. 313.

[43] Peter Paret, *French Revolutionary Warfare from Indochina to Algeria: The Analysis of a Political and Military Doctrine* (New York: Praeger, 1964), p. 25.

[44] Col. J. Muller, "La Subversion Menace-t-elle Aussi l'Afrique Noire Française?" RDN 26 (May 1958), pp. 763, 758.

[45] Cited in Pierre Rondot, "Les Musulmans et l'Islam devant le Technique," RDN (June 1960), pp. 1011–12. Rondot observes that "the technical ineptitude of Muslims, especially Arabs has become axiomatic."

[46] Guy-Willy Schmeltz, "L'Europe devant le Sous-Développement Economique," RDN 26 (May 1958), p. 734.

nerable to communist ideologues. What is more, their antlike lack of differentiation and willingness to follow orders mindlessly make them perfect subjects for totalitarian control.[47]

The critical period was the transition from tradition to modernity, and the key players were the "transitionals" poised between the two. "A veritable mental revolution" is necessary, "to push the [indigenes] from a magical and mythical conception of the world . . . to a rational one which alone will permit them to build modern states."[48] Yet while necessary and ultimately beneficial, this "mental revolution" may be dangerous in the short-term. Indeed, "European colonialism introduces the critical spirit and provokes dangerous social cleavages between modernized and traditional groups. By upsetting the ancestral structures, it has morally uprooted peoples in whom the ancient tribal fervor is now free-floating, ready to be unleashed by any extreme mystique or mystification."[49] "The result," explains another analyst, "is an inferiority complex and rancour inspired by envy" and, adds still another, "a mob mentality . . . which reveals a still unstabilized psychological tension, the characteristic indication of political underdevelopment."[50] It is the perfect seedbed for revolt.

For French counterinsurgents, like their American counterparts, rebels exemplify failed modernization. As "Captain Amphioxu" explains, rebel leaders in Algeria are "pseudo-intellectuals who have ill-assimilated the notions they were taught. Showing hatred for their masters, they want to dominate them and take power: not by reason of their competence, but pushed by their lust for pleasure." Their followers are "the dregs of the cities: pimps, thieves, killers," and the human refuse of the development process: "violent by nature, they are driven by vengeance, jealousy, rancour against the society in which they could not find a place. . . . They kill . . . for the pleasure of killing."[51] In fact, for many, nationalism itself, "this immoderate desire for independence," constituted "clear evidence of a lack of political maturity" and thus of a need for continued French tutelage.[52]

[47] Gen. L.-M. Chassin, "Guerre en Indochine," RDN (July 1953), p. 3.

[48] J. C. Froelich, "La Situation Politique Actuelle d'Afrique d'Expression Française," RDN (November 1960), p. 1800.

[49] Schmeltz, "Sous-Développement Economique," p. 734.

[50] Muller, "La Subversion," p. 758; and Froelich, "La Situation," p. 1789.

[51] Capitaine Amphioxu, "La Guerre en Algérie: Regards de l'Autre Côté," RDN 28 (January 1957), pp. 83, 85.

[52] Muller, "La Subversion," pp. 756–57.

CHAPTER 6

Universal Tactic: Mao Madness

If Moscow set the colonial tinder alight, Mao was the match. For the French, as for the Americans, Mao was a sort of demon-saint whose method evoked awe with its apparently all-encompassing scope and invincibility. But Mao served the French as badly as the Americans. Indeed, observed Edgar Furniss, "It was a tragic day for the French army, the Fourth Republic, and de Gaulle—to say nothing of countless Algerian Moslems—when some do-it-yourself military theoreticians stumbled across the writings of Mao Tse-Tung."[53] For the French, too, failed to discern the weaknesses of Mao's work, but they grasped instead what he was best at—guerrilla tactics. According to its French students, revolutionary war is a scientifically planned assault by a highly organized minority against the rightful rulers of a state. The key to success is not substance but method, since "we know," Trinquier declared, "that it is not at all necessary to have the sympathy of a majority of the people in order to rule them. The right organization can turn the trick."[54]

As they surveyed the world from Indochina to Algeria and found similar techniques being employed by insurgents, French counterinsurgents thought they had found similar revolutions. They thus shifted attention from the processes of development and local conditions to the tactics of external agitators. The former might be enabling conditions for revolution, but foreign agents using Maoist tactics caused it. This shift of focus shows in the very language used. Marvelous medical images of intoxication, infection, cancer, gangrene, rot, and putrefaction abound.[55] What matters are the cancer, microbes, paracites, or poison afflicting the body politic; the possibility that the body itself might be defective or prone to disease is ignored. Like Americans, the French *defined* revolutionary war as an attack on "established authority."[56] Such analysis, although comforting, provided little understanding.

The difficulties appear first in the tendency to define the causes of insurgency by its supposed consequence: Communist expansion. Thus, "Whether directed from inside or out," declared Lt. Colonel J. Roussel, "all subversive activities tend to the same end."[57] Moreover, insurgency

---

[53] *De Gaulle and the French Army: A Crisis in Civil-Military Relations* (New York: Twentieth Century Fund, 1964), p. 41.

[54] Trinquier, *Modern Warfare*, p. 4.

[55] See, for example, J. Perrin, "L'Algérie et l'Information," RDN 27 (December 1958), pp. 1935–36.

[56] Trinquier, *Modern Warfare*, p. 6.

[57] Lt. Col. J. Roussel, "A Propos de Subversion et d'Insurrection," RDN (March 1960), p. 500.

"is not a political or social or ideological movement, it is uniquely overt or covert assistance given to the foreign policy of the Soviet state."[58] Where local circumstances are recognized, it is only insofar as they provide opportunities for this external meddling. In the words of Colonel Lacheroy, "In the beginning there is nothing" until unrest is deliberately created by an omnipotent outside force.[59] Those less extreme still believed that "every political system has its opponents and internal enemies,"[60] but these matter only when exploited by the revolutionary whose "very calling . . . is to embitter all the 'internal contradictions' of his enemies."[61] The issue is *how*. Analysis emphasized psychological bamboozlement, ideological manipulation, and terror.

Psychological warfare fascinated the French. For many it was the heart of revolutionary war. Colonel Bonnet, for example, asserted that

Partisan Warfare + Psychological Warfare = Revolutionary Warfare.

This, he declared, is "a law valid for all revolutionary movements that today agitate the world."[62] Psychological warfare converts the gullibility of the masses into a weapon and leads law-abiding citizens to abandon their natural goodness, for "if the revolution wishes to succeed, it must pervert this moral sense."[63] The key to this perversion is ideology, for it alone "can bring to warfare that indispensable fervor."[64] But in Communist hands, ideology is a cynically manipulated product of verbal mirror play such that "modern crusaders," argued Hogard, "fight for ideas gone mad, ideas which their leaders do not believe . . . but instead judge attractive to the 'mass' they plan to conquer." [65]

Essential to this conquest is the "recruiting sergeant of modern revolution," the propagandist. "He knows how to mobilize entire populations, body and soul, in the service of a cause which is not only foreign to them, but against their true spiritual and material interests."[66] He promises to "fill the great emptiness left by abandoned ancient beliefs" and applies "the method" which "consists of calling upon the

---

[58] Labin, "Guerre Politique," I, p. 1032.

[59] Col. Charles Lacheroy, "La Guerre Révolutionnaire," in *La Défense Nationale* (Paris: 1958), p. 322.

[60] Trinquier, *Modern Warfare*, p. 106.

[61] Hogard, "Guerre Révolutionnaire," p. 1498.

[62] Col. Gabriel Bonnet, *Les guerres insurrectionnelles et révolutionnaires* (Paris, 1958), p. 60.

[63] J. Hogard, "Guerre Révolutonnaire et Pacification," *Revue Militaire d'Information* (January 1957), p. 15.

[64] Col. Nemo, "La Guerre dans le Milieu Sociale," RDN 22 (May 1956), p. 611.

[65] Hogard, "Guerre Révolutionnaire," p. 1502, 1508.

[66] Ibid., p. 1508.

miserable mass' sense of justice and equality on the one hand and, on the other, on racial sentiments: nationalism and xenophobia."[67] Thus, they argued, expressions of popular discontent must be ignored; they are evidence not of the peoples' true interests, but rather of Communist ventriloquy.[68]

Not everybody found "psychwar" enough to account for popular support of the rebels. Those who did not turned to terror as an explanation. General Allard, for example, described Vietnam and Algeria as countries "where a clandestine political organization was able, through the use of terror, to impose itself by force on the mass of the population."[69] Another officer declared that "it would be a mistake to attach too great an importance to the psychological factor, since fear of FLN sanctions . . . forces the people, however much they may want to abandon the insurgents, to submit to the law of those who reign by terror."[70] And for Trinquier, terrorism and revolutionary war were synonymous. "We know," he writes, "that the *sine qua non* of victory in modern warfare is the unconditional support of a population. . . . Such support may be spontaneous, although that is quite rare and probably a temporary condition. If it doesn't exist, it must be secured by every possible means, the most effective of which is *terrorism*."[71]

Universal Countertactic: French Doctrine

French doctrine reflected the counterinsurgents' conception of insurgency and suffered its many inadequacies and inaccuracies. Like the sharp reflection of a summer cloud in a still pond, the doctrine's hard-edged appearance belied both the airy indefiniteness of its subject and the fragility of its underpinnings. The counterinsurgents defined insurgency as a universally applicable technique using a limited repertoire of tactics and thus sought an equally universal repertoire of countertactics. "The counterguerrilla struggle," declared Trinquier, "is definitely a question of *method*."[72] But the French method responded only to the

---

[67] Nemo, "Milieu Sociale," p. 611; and Chassin, "Guerre en Indochine," p. 4.

[68] Besides, remarks Froelich, "So what? The dogs' howling doesn't keep the caravan from passing by." "La Situation," pp. 1788–89.

[69] Allard, "Vérités," p. 20.

[70] Lt. Philippe Marchat, "Rappelé en Algérie," RDN 26 (December 1957), pp. 1849–50.

[71] Trinquier, *Modern Warfare*, p. 8.

[72] Ibid., p. 92. In the words of Colonel Lacheroy, "As it is a question of techniques and only techniques, there is no reason why Franco-Vietnamese technicians cannot do it as well as those of the Vietminh—and more rapidly since they benefit from the experience of the enemy." Cited in Ambler, *French Army*, p. 317.

skewed understanding of insurgency; in the face of real insurgencies it proved ineffective or worse. Whatever other practical or political factors compounded the failure, fundamental conceptual flaws doomed the effort from the start.

Like any mirror image, French doctrine reversed the insurgents' presumed modus operandi. If they built a popular base and alternative administration and then attacked the regime militarily, the French would first destroy the insurgent organization militarily and then undertake the political, organizational, and administrative work needed to guard against "reinfection." French doctrine thus defined an ordered pair of missions: destroy and construct. In the words of General Allard, "These two terms are inseparable: destruction without reconstruction is entirely negative; construction without first having destroyed would be delusion."[73] In short, without security, good government and progress are impossible; without good government and progress, security is pointless.

PHASE ONE: DESTROY

The first mission is "to eliminate from the midst of the population the entire enemy organization that has infiltrated it and is manipulating it at will."[74] The army must, of course, destroy the insurgents' military wing. More important, however, the destroy mission is designed

> to expose, dismantle, and eliminate the rebel politico-administrative armature which is the veritable nervous system of the insurgency. It is through it that the population is entrapped willingly, but mainly by force, separated, indoctrinated, . . . terrorized, trapped in a fine mesh net from which it cannot escape. To tear away this net, destroy this tentacled organization, is to liberate the population, free it from moral and physical confinement, to strip it of this mantle of fear that paralyzes it. This is our first mission.[75]

PHASE TWO: CONSTRUCT

If victory is to be lasting, however, the destruction of the insurgent organization must be followed by "the construction of peace" and "establishment of a new order." Indeed, the heart of the matter was an experiment in social engineering. This meant, on the one hand, "resumption of human contact with the population, its protection and assistance to it of all sorts. . . . It also means organizing it hierarchically,

[73] Allard, "Vérités," p. 22.
[74] Trinquier, *Modern Warfare*, p. 43.
[75] Allard, "Vérités," p. 22.

that is to say substituting for the insurgent political and administrative system a new organization marking the beginning of the future colonial order."[76] On the other, it meant an intense propaganda effort to counter the insurgents' false advertising.

As in the American case, this construct ought involved more and better government. French counterinsurgents argued that insufficient government control allows the insurgent organization to grow while government abuses offer it issues for propaganda. Thus, greater control was needed to remove abuses and offer a broader array of goods and services. They also argued that given the gullibility of colonial populations more control was better; unless "organized in such a way as to side with the legal government," they will remain vulnerable to rebel propaganda.[77] "It is necessary that all forms of complicity, including those of abstention and silence, be rendered impossible or treated, in the same manner as the crime of treason, by special courts."[78] In short, the "establishment of a new order" meant the imposition of a frankly authoritarian society. "Call me a fascist if you like," Trinquier declared, "but we must make the population docile and manageable; everybody's acts must be controled."[79]

PERILS OF PRACTICE

When applied, French doctrine soon showed its flaws and those of French thinking on the colonies in general. The problems appeared first in the destroy ought. They sought, in Mao's phrase, to attack the guerrilla "fish" as they swam in the popular "sea." But "fishing" presupposes the analytic separateness of "fish" and the fisherman's ability to distinguish between "fish" and "water." By assuming that the insurgent organization is a distinct, foreign imposition upon the population, French theorists denied the problem. In practice, however, their prey proved elusive because the category "enemy" was more complex than their definition allowed and because, in fact, sea and fish were often indistinguishable. As a result, the French, unable to target their "destroy" campaigns accurately, destroyed thousands of innocent lives.

Some shrugged off the problem and merely demanded more of what was already being done. For them, the goodness of the end justified any necessary means. Indeed, their conception of revolutionary war provided, in Bernard Fall's words, "a Cartesian rationale for the use of tor-

[76] Ibid., p. 23.
[77] Capt. André Souyris, "An Effective Counterguerrilla Proceedure," translated from original and republished in MR 36: 12 (March 1957), p. 87.
[78] Col. Lacheroy cited in Ambler, *French Army*, p. 171.
[79] *Le Monde*, July 10, 1958.

ture."[80] They believed that despite being "manhandled, lined up, inter-rogated, searched" and subjected "day and night" to "unexpected intrusions [by] armed soldiers, . . . people who know our adversaries will not protest in submitting to inconveniences they know to be nec-essary for the recovery of their liberty."[81] Declared Trinquier of French activities in Algeria, "the firmness of repression was reserved only for our enemies. The population never doubted this."[82]

Many others refused to accept the logic of torture. "On the subject of torture," wrote General Pierre Billotte, for example,

> I am unequivocal: in whatever form, for whatever purpose, it is unacceptable. . . . The ideological character of modern warfare changes nothing. . . . On the contrary, in struggles of this kind, vic-tory . . . falls to the more noble ideology; the greater respect for moral and human values constitutes one of the most effective means of gaining victory, since it goes directly to the hearts of men who are temporarily hostile.[83]

Here, however, those in opposition were in a bind. The French had no "more noble ideology," nor did they have a better "sorting mecha-nism" for straining rebel fish from the popular water. Whatever the merits of opposing torture and indiscriminate violence, these officers could offer no more accurate way of targeting destroy missions.

Similar problems plagued French resettlement policies in both Indo-china and Algeria. In Algeria alone more than two million people—20 to 25 percent of the entire population—were herded into camps euphe-mistically called *centres sociaux*. Undertaken to protect the people from insurgent influences, relocation often had the opposite effect. In fact, most of those resettled were neither the target of attacks nor par-ticular supporters of the insurgents. But being uprooted, degraded, and subjected to subhuman living conditions radicalized many. In fact, re-location camps became important sources of insurgent support.[84]

The blindness of French policy shows most clearly, however, in the psychological warfare programs that were the centerpiece of the con-struct ought. The technicians of revolutionary war believed that "if subversion is provoked by an ideal, the remedy must be of the same na-

---

[80] Introduction to Trinquier, *Modern Warfare*, p. xv.

[81] Trinquier, *Modern Warfare*, p. 48.

[82] Cited in Paret, *French Revolutionary Warfare*, p. 114.

[83] Cited in ibid., pp. 73–74.

[84] George Armstrong Kelly, *Lost Soldiers: The French Army and Empire in Crisis, 1947–1962* (Cambridge: MIT Press, 1965), p. 188.

ture";[85] thus they needed an appealing vision of the future neatly packaged in catchy slogans. The aim was to out-advertise the insurgents in this war of rhetoric and golden phrases. To do so, the French military formed the *Service d'Action Psychologique et d'Information* (SAPI) in 1956. Psychwar swept the French military: a Psychological Warfare Instruction Center was established; Army staff headquarters got a Psychwar and Moral Section; chairs in psychological warfare were established at the Superior War College and other service institutions; special Loudspeaker and Leafletting Companies were formed; SAPI units were attached to all major commands; and SAPI's ideas achieved general acceptance in the military.

Psychwar, claimed "Ximenes," required the "latest resources of experimental psychology for sensitizing the indifferent portion of the population and for converting it."[86] In fact, the French used whatever fit their preconceptions. From Gustave Le Bon they took the notion that members of crowds suppress their individualism and respond instead to a "will of the group" easily manipulated by outsiders.[87] From Marxist Pavlovian Serge Tchakhetine they adopted a crude behavioral psychology explaining how such control might be achieved. They supplemented this with the claims of Nazi Eugen Hadamovsky that symbols, slogans, demonstrations, and violence could be used to keep the population regimented and docile. And from across the Atlantic they borrowed from Leonard Doob and Harold Lasswell—"the American technicians of public opinion."[88] ("Who says what to whom and how" was also *the* question for the French psychological warriors who brought Madison Avenue to the Algerian *bled*.)

But the essence of French psychwar is captured in a comment by Colonel Lacheroy: "That mass is for the taking. How do you take it?"[89] The technique is "psychological impregnation—the release of stimuli, the elaboration of slogans adapted to the situation, the incessant repetition of affirmations, and the systematic reiteration of biased information by all means of dissimulation."[90] Here the mirror-imaging of their own perception of insurgency was perfect: if skillful indoctrina-

[85] Muller, "La Subversion," pp. 755–56.

[86] "Ximenes, " "Revolutionary War," MR 37: 5 (August 1957), p. 104.

[87] In Algeria, SAPI offered a three-part program for prisoners: "Disintegrate the Individual"; "Creation of a Collective Consciousness: Reindoctrination"; and "Creation of the Collectivity: Reaction of the Collectivity on the Individual." *Le Monde*, January 23, 1958.

[88] Capt. R. Caude, "Propagande et Guerre Psychologique," RDN (August–September 1955), p. 181.

[89] Lacheroy, "La Guerre Révolutionnaire," p. 312.

[90] "Ximenes," "Revolutionary War," p. 104.

tion could create revolution from "nothing," then equally skillful counterindoctrination could create counterrevolution. In the words of General Chassin,

> The human soul is eminently receptive and malleable. With well chosen slogans and an intelligent, tenacious and methodical indoctrination program, it is possible to make people believe whatever you want. The human spirit is easily violated. It generally suffices to appeal to the base instincts and, above all, to repeat what you want them to believe loudly and incessantly.[91]

Through "psychological impregnation," counterrevolution could be immaculately conceived; no substantive issues need be addressed.

Immaculate conception did not take in Algeria. Although French motto was "in the face of lies, impose the truth," the French truth did not accord well with Algerian truth, and Algerians refused to give up theirs, even in the face of intense propagandizing. Often, the message was offensive. The Muslims—80 percent of the population—found little inspiring in the Army's claim that "it is the fate of the West and Christendom that are at stake in Algeria."[92] More often, the terms of reference were irrelevant. SAPI, for example, recommended the following format for propaganda speeches:

> Algeria, world stake: the Russians, leaders of Communism . . . want to tear Algeria from France and conquer Europe. . . . Insist on the key position of France, nation-leader of Europe, whose road from Paris to Brazzaville passes through Algiers. France: torch of liberty. Paris: center of world culture, final stake in the long struggle undertaken by Moscow.[93]

Such speeches warmed French hearts, but they held no charms for the Algerians who did not see their struggle as a battle between West and East and who had known only the French torch and none of the liberty. The countermyth remained a fantasy, and the masses were less malleable than supposed.

Ideological Utility: Continuity and Change

Two questions remain: how to explain revolutionary war's potency even in the face of defeat; and given this potency, how to explain its rapid demise when the fall came. The answer to the former lies in the

[91] Chassin, "Guerre en Indochine," p. 9.
[92] Cited in Kelly, *Lost Soldiers*, p. 143.
[93] Cited in Smith, *French Stake in Algeria*, p. 170.

doctrine's ideological utility for the French state and officer corps; to the latter, in changes in both.

The ideological ties between revolutionary war doctrine and the French state pull both ways. On the one hand, the doctrine justified policies already contemplated for other reasons and provided a defense against criticisms of them from at home and abroad. More generally, it reaffirmed the assumptions about France's role in the world that informed decision-making. On the other hand, the doctrine's authors intended it as an analytic and prescriptive tool for the state. As Frenchmen who shared the politicians' biases, however, they unwittingly built these into their work such that it mirrored not reality but their fondest patriotic beliefs.

Ironically, despite differences of national perspective, revolutionary war doctrine served the same sort of ideological functions for the French as its equivalent did for Americans. Where the latter justified postwar hegemony, revolutionary war doctrine sanctioned France's claim to an international role. It reasserted that France's greatness was the empire and put steel in Prime Minister Paul Ramadier's assertion that "We will hold on everywhere, in Indochina as in Madagascar. Our empire will not be taken away from us, because we represent might and also right."[94] The French counterinsurgents went even further, claiming that "Western civilization now faces a life or death situation" and that France alone held the key for survival, since it alone understood revolutionary war.[95] According to a CIA report, the French "tend to regard the US Army as 19th Century army with 20th Century weapons."[96] Indeed, French officers argued that American anticolonialism indicated that the United States was already "provisionally occupied,"[97] leaving France to carry the weight of the West, the greatness of its civilization, *and* the glory of God on its shoulders. It was a worthy role.

In an alliance dominated by Anglo-American nuclear monopoly, revolutionary war doctrine also justified France's lack of nuclear weapons. It was France's *riposte* to Anglo-American nuclear hegemony, a doctrinal counter to massive retaliation, and the basis for a positive French role in NATO. Noted Colonel Nemo, "The French Army is practically the only one to have encountered Communism in action. . . . It can, therefore, open . . . the debate on the form of future war."[98]

[94] JCS, Historical Division, Walter S. Poole, *The History of the Joint Chiefs of Staff*, Vol. 4, 1950–1952 (December 1979), p. 410.

[95] Chassin, "Guerre en Indochine," p. 3.

[96] CIA, "Report on the French Army Mutiny in Algeria and Its Consequences," May 22, 1961, p. 9.

[97] Hogard, "Guerre Révolutionnaire," p. 1508.

[98] Nemo, "Milieu sociale," p. 606.

Finally, revolutionary war doctrine justified the continued importance of France's *mission civilatrice*. It echoed the fanciful rewrites of history that were the staple of politicians' declarations on colonial policy and explained how France's antinationalist wars were "as different from old-fashioned colonial campaigns as from classic warfare."[99] Indeed, "in contrast to revolution and subversion, counterrevolution seeks to install a natural authority. [It] does not try to take hold of the population, but rather to liberate it, and engage it in the fight against a foreign power for the common national good."[100] France alone, they argued, not the so-called nationalists, could deliver true independence and the benefits of civilization. Thus, in Algeria France's generous vision of the future for the "different ethnic communities which history has called to cohabitate under the French flag" contrasted with "the fallacious notion of an Algerian nationalism with no standing in history" being flogged by "the fanatic champions . . . of an illusory pan-arabism."[101] Decolonization would mean simply "to abandon . . . populations we promised to lead toward a better future to the despotic rule of a ferocious dictatorship."[102]

Ideological Utility:
The Personal and Corporate Dimension

Revolutionary war doctrine possessed even greater ideological utility for the counterinsurgents and the French army. Just as it gave the state a world role, it gave its proponents a special position in the army, and the army a special position in France. Just as it justified the state's denial of blame for insurgency, it allowed the army to blame others for losses in Indochina and Algeria.

For its adepts, revolutionary war doctrine served two functions. First, it offered young officers a claim to power in the military. In fact, it was their brain child, born of the frustration of those who felt the war in Indochina was lost because their superiors' premodern notions had no place on Mao's revolutionary battlefield. Second, as experts on *the* threat facing France and the West, they felt they should have a privileged place in politics. They alone, they argued, saw the true peril to France; they alone could save it.

[99] Allard, "Vérités," pp. 18–19. See, too, Gen. Marchand, "Les Origins du Drame Indochinois," RDN (October 1952), pp. 311–12.

[100] Anonymous pamphlet circulated in the barracks, 1957, "Counter-Révolution: Stratégie et Tactique." Cited in Paret, *French Revolutionary Warfare*, pp. 117–18.

[101] Allard, "Vérités," p. 41; and Général d'Armée P. Ely, "Les Problèmes Francais de l'Equilibre Mondial," RDN 28 (November 1959), p. 1716.

[102] Hogard, "Guerre Révolutionnaire," p. 1510.

The doctrine of revolutionary war served the French army in similar ways. First, it justified the Army's traditional colonial roots and its attachment to the imperial France under attack. Second, it gave the army a role in the Cold War. After a decade and a half of humiliation, it was satisfying to declare that "this generous and exalting task to which the army consecrates itself with an admirable faith and dynamism is critical to the defense of the Free World and Western civilization."[103] And finally, the nature of revolutionary war and the requirements for combatting it seemed to require significant role expansion for the army. The logic of this argument soon pushed many beyond the political pale.

THE FALL OF GUERRE RÉVOLUTIONNAIRE

As the costs of the Algerian war rose with no end in sight, tension between the counterinsurgents and Paris rose apace. For the former, doctrine became the basis for a savage critique of French society and a platform for military intervention in politics.[104] For the latter, failure in Algeria and the political threat posed by elements of the colonial military prompted a redefinition of France's world role and a reformation of the military to marginalize the counterinsurgents. The final confrontation came in 1961 when Algerian-based paratroopers attempted a coup against de Gaulle.

For the counterinsurgents, the logic of revolutionary war suggested that to distinguish between "hot" forward areas on wartime footing and "cold" metropolitian rear areas on peacetime footing is fatal. Hot insurgencies are but one aspect of the total revolutionary war being waged against the West; no less important is the political war of subversion being waged at home. Failure to recognize this, they argued, explained why despite possessing the means necessary for victory, the French army kept losing. Civilians realized neither the gravity of the situation nor the sternness of the measures required to meet it. The army thus felt "abandoned by metropolitan opinion"[105] and even "stabbed in the back." As General Massu warned in December 1957, "in Paris an attempt is being made to discredit the Army in order more easily to reach an agreement with the FLN; it is an old tactic which I have known since Indochina. Now it must be known that the Army will no longer permit the intriguers to betray France."[106] It was ominous evi-

---

[103] Allard, "Vérités," p. 41.
[104] Jacques Hogard, "Le Soldat dans la Guerre Révolutionnaire," RDN 24 (February 1957), p. 214.
[105] Marchat, "Rappelé en Algérie," p. 1833.
[106] Cited in Ambler, *French Army*, p. 111.

dence of how much the military had come to regard itself as the *pays réel* and civilian France as an aberration.

The enemy was already within; the Communist "warfare system" had begun its subversive work. "The enemy is 'one' from Paris to Saigon, Algiers to Brazzaville," declared Hogard. "Everywhere he attacks the Nation. . . . Everywhere he demoralizes our compatriots, sabotages our National Defense, . . . empoisons our 'internal contradictions' and wages a revolutionary war [against us] by making use of the facilities we leave him, in the name of the 'liberty' he seeks to deprive us of."[107] The solution was simple: if France was too rotten to unite behind the Army, it had to be united by the Army. "It is time," declared General Chassin, "for the Army to cease being the *grand muette*."[108] "The democratic ideology has become powerless in the world today," asserted Hogard; France needs instead "a combative system of values strong enough to unite and stimulate national energies." But this would be possible, he noted elsewhere, "only if the enemy within is reduced to silence!"[109] To do so required the repatriation of counterrevolution and its authoritarian methods, including the Communist system of "parallel hierarchies"—the surveillance of all by all—which is "much more efficacious than traditional liberal organization."[110] Indeed, they implied, it is also more desirable.

Very different developments were underway in Paris. The monetary costs of the war were crippling, and the political pressures generated by full mobilization, conscription, and high casualties were irresistible. France, isolated internationally and preoccupied with Algeria, had little energy to defend its position in an increasingly American dominated Europe. France needed a sharp break with the past and a new definition of its world role.

In the past, France had sought recompense for its inferiority to its European neighbors in the colonies; in 1958 General de Gaulle began a campaign to make France the lynchpin of Europe itself. At the heart of the effort lay the reformation of the military and creation of the nuclear *force de frappe*. Development of the French atomic bomb had begun in 1956, but until 1958 many thought it was to solidify France's place in NATO. De Gaulle had different intentions. His aim was autonomy, a po-

---

[107] Jacques Hogard, "L'Armée Française devant la Guerre Révolutionnaire," RDN 24 (January 1957), p. 86.

[108] Général L.-M. Chassin, "Du Rôle Idéologique de l'Armée," *Revue Militaire d'Information* (October 10, 1954), p. 13.

[109] Cited in Paret, *French Revolutionary Warfare*, p. 28; and Hogard, "L'Armée Française," p. 88.

[110] Hogard, "Guerre Révolutionnaire," p. 1499.

sition for France independent from and on a par with Britain and the United States.

The *force de frappe* was also the General's trump card with the Army. As one officer put it, de Gaulle's "purpose is obviously to appease and win over the military by giving them a really ambitious program which will demand all their energies—energies which might find an outlet elsewhere if allowed to go unused. To those of us . . . afraid of a listless, boring life, he is offering brand-new techniques, enormous scientific toys, and a [new] theory of war."[111] No less important, the attendant restructuring of the military marginalized the increasingly suspect counterinsurgents and allowed de Gaulle to isolate them. The technicians of revolutionary war had no place in the high-tech army he envisioned.

These two contradictory trends came to an open confrontation in the abortive coup of 1961. Having (uneasily) coexisted from the creation of the Fifth Republic, Army–de Gaulle relations broke down after the General's September 16, 1959, announcement that Algerians would be offered the choice of independence, "association," or integration. Tension rose through both the barricades confrontation of January 1960 and the government's riposte, the explosion of France's first atom bomb two weeks later. When the coup attempt came, de Gaulle's reputation, authority, and defensive preparations carried the day: the bulk of the armed forces stood firm. In the treason trial that followed, the hardcore counterinsurgents were purged. Many others were retired or exiled to positions of insignificance. With independence for Algeria and France's remaining colonies, counterinsurgency, too, was marginalized. Revolutionary war was dead.

Conclusion

To come full circle, clearly there are important differences between French and American policies toward the Third World, differences born of each country's unique history and geopolitical position. For France, prewar great power status derived from its empire, and postwar revolutionary war doctrine reflected the desire to reclaim it and France's position in the world. Conversely, as a nonimperial hegemonic power in a time of Third World nationalism, the United States criticized French policies as anachronistic and aiding the Soviets. These differences are clearly demonstrated in American concern for an arm's-length relationship in the provision of counterinsurgency assistance,

[111] Col. Gilles Anouil, cited in Furniss, *De Gaulle*, pp. 212–13.

the demise of French revolutionary war doctrine with decolonization, and its perseverance in the United States. What is more important, however, are the marked parallels between the two.

These similarities confound American exceptionalism at both ends. While Americans have had a happy history and little experience with social dislocation, the French have had a singularly violent history marked by revolutionary conflict. Yet rather than producing distinct "psycho-cultural characteristics" with unique consequences for action, the French and American pasts seem largely irrelevant to policymakers' perceptions of and prescriptions for Third World insurgency. Instead, the same assumptions underpin both the French and American versions of security and development and counterinsurgency doctrine: policymakers on both sides of the Atlantic share the same analytic framework, born of the histoire raisonnée tradition, and make the same assumptions concerning the nature, source, direction, and consequences of both political change in the Third World and their own managerial roles. Thus, Stanley Hoffmann correctly observes that American policymakers "ask the wrong question, turn to the wrong analysis, and thus in the end provoke the wrong results."[112] But French policymakers, too, ask the same wrong questions, turn to the same wrong analyses, and thus in the end provoke the same wrong results. Nothing is exceptionally American here after all.

[112] Hoffmann, *Gulliver's Troubles*, p. 126.

7

GREECE:
THE TROJAN HORSE

The 1947 decision to aid Greece marked a turning point in American foreign policy. The bold rhetoric of the Truman Doctrine announced the coming of containment, the Cold War, and a new, activist world role for the United States. If Munich and Eastern Europe showed how not to manage the Soviet Union, "the success which has been achieved by the peoples of Greece," declared Dean Acheson, "is clear proof that the forces of aggression can be halted by invoking the proper measures at the proper time."[1] It seemed to confirm the belief that Soviet agents foment insurgencies but American aid can provide a low-cost antidote. It seemed, too, to confirm the efficacy of the three oughts: security, good government, and progress. Ever since, these "lessons" and the underlying assumptions they reinforce have reappeared in American policy toward other insurgencies around the world. They are dangerously misleading, however, another Trojan horse to entice—and betray—the unwary.

American involvement in Greece should be read not as a success story but as a cautionary tale. True, the Greek government defeated the guerrillas, and the United States benefited by their success. But contrary to the supposed lessons of Greece, the United States contributed little to the victory. American policymakers misperceived the crisis and prescribed irrelevant or even harmful solutions to it. Insufficient leverage, intragovernmental limits on reform, and abusive government-populace relations resulted in American initiatives being ignored or subverted. Nor did Greek policies remotely resemble counterinsurgency as preached by the United States. In fact, not only did the Greeks flout American wishes, turn American aid to their own ends, and pursue policies abhorrent to the United States, but they won under the leadership of a government Americans believed central to the problem and by means Americans declared counterproductive.

This chapter explores why American policy failed. After sketching the historical background, it turns to realist, presidential, and bureaucratic politics interpretations. Each contributes a piece of the puzzle:

[1] NSC 84/2, "The Position of the United States with Respect to the Philippines," report of the Secretary of Defense, September 14, 1950, p. 47. *DDRS*, 1978: 253A.

the first explains policymakers' sense of compulsion; the second the rhetorical overkill of the Truman Doctrine and its consequences; and the third the often muddled implementation of policy. But while each offers important insights, none is sufficient. To understand policy content and failure, it is necessary to explain how policymakers analyzed the situation and how analysis shaped action; this task constitutes the chapter's second half.

THE SETTING

Most analysts of American involvement in Greece focus on the East-West balance of power; Greece is but the venue of superpower conflict. At the time, too, decisionmakers ignored essential elements of the "situation on the ground." Yet in large measure these defined American allies and enemies, their room for maneuver, and even the possible outcomes of American efforts. They offer a foreboding backdrop for American engagement in the Greek civil war.

Prewar Greek politics was a winner-take-all struggle for power across a royalist-republican "National Schism" by two irreconcilable coalitions of military officers and their civilian allies. The contest began when the Military League called liberal politician Eleftherios Venizelos to office in 1909.[2] It quit politics in 1911, but thereafter members formed the core of the Venizelist, antiroyalist party. During World War I, the Venizelists backed Britain, while King Constantine and royalist officers backed Germany. In 1917 the King was forced to abdicate for his efforts. Three years later, royalist officers engineered a plebiscite which recalled Constantine to the throne and began a purge of Venizelists. In 1922 Constantine came a cropper as a result of the disastrous Asia Minor campaign. Venizelist officers mounted a coup, forced him to abdicate again, tried and executed the responsible royalist officers, forced Constantine's son, George II, to abdicate, and finally established a republic in 1924; it lasted a year before being undone by a rightist coup. Venizelist officers attempted a final coup in 1935. When it failed, there followed another purge of the military and bureaucracy. In thorough control of the government, the royalist army rigged another plebiscite and returned George II to the throne. A year later, General Metaxis persuaded the King to abolish parliament, invoke martial law, and suspend the constitution.

[2] The following is based on Bruce Kuniholm, *The Origins of the Cold War in the Near East: Great Power Conflict and Diplomacy in Iran, Turkey and Greece* (Princeton: Princeton University Press, 1980), pp. 73-82; and Richard Clogg, *A Short History of Modern Greece* (New York: Cambridge University Press, 1979).

For the next three years Metaxis pursued the Right's aims unimpaired. Trained in Berlin at the *Kriegsakademie* (where he was known as "the little Moltke") he sought to "discipline" the country and recast Greek society along Prussian lines. He shared Hitler's and Mussolini's hostility toward liberalism and communism, turned to nazism and fascism for models of the Greek future, and with the help of Heinrich Himmler and his own security czar, Constantine Maniadakis, built a Greek Gestapo to eliminate opponents.[3] A fierce nationalist, however, Metaxis led a spirited defense against the Italian invasion of 1940. But with Metaxis dead, the regime collapsed when the Germans attacked on April 6, 1941. When the Wehrmacht reached Athens three weeks later, they were met by Maniadakis who, observed the OSS, "is said to have handed over to the Gestapo his very complete dossiers of all persons suspected of Republican sympathies and . . . a number of [Venizelist] officers . . . detained for opposition to the regime."[4] So began the collaboration between many Greek rightists and the Germans and the near monopoly of the resistance by republicans and the left.

Against this background, the Greek government-in-exile established itself in Cairo. From the outset, three things sullied its legitimacy for most Greeks: the taint of Metaxis; dependence upon the British who insisted on the continued rule of King Constantine; and the failure to resist the Germans. None of these bothered the government-in-exile, however. It aimed to use the war years to prepare for its return after the Allies had removed the Germans.

The Cairo government was not interested in resistance. The royalist military's first message was not a call to arms, but a "code of conduct" for officers that "disapproved" of armed resistance and called instead for the organization of a military league "which would appear on the political stage immediately after liberation [and] assume authority to appoint a government." Thus, in Cairo royalist officers organized Syndesomos Axiomatikon Neon (SAN), the aim of which was "suppressing the remnants of leftism [republicanism] in the army and . . . promoting the royalist interest."[5] In Greece, too, government-in-exile eschewed action. As the OSS reported in 1943, "the Royalist underground . . . is not known to maintain a single guerrilla band nor to have achieved a single instance of sabotage."[6] By means just short of blackmail the Brit-

[3] Department of State, Office of Intelligence Coordination and Liaison, "The Role of the Army in Greek Politics," I.R. No. OCL-3745, August 15, 1946, p. 7. NADB, OSS file.

[4] Ibid., p. 9.

[5] General Ventiris, Deputy Chief of Staff and spokesman of the Greek National Army, Cairo, cited in ibid., pp. 10, 13.

[6] OSS, "Communist-Led Organizations Within the Free Greek Forces," R and A Report No. 1062, August 6, 1943, p. 14. NADB, OSS file.

ish eventually coaxed Colonel Zervas to form a resistance unit. Zervas's National Republican Greek League (EDES) never boasted more than 5,000 men and was "virtually a private army . . . limited to his native territory in North-West Greece."[7] For the rest of the war, moreover, well documented reports surfaced of EDES collaboration with the German "Security Battalions" established to hunt the nonroyalist Greek resistance, the EAM.[8]

Inside Greece, the National Liberation Front (EAM) fought the Germans and the EDES and prepared for the postwar contest to control the country. EAM was founded at the instigation of the Communist Party of Greece (KKE), but the Communists never formed more than a small minority of the membership. In fact, the OSS reported, "Its members are drawn from all political parties except the Royalists and former Metaxists."[9] EAM proved immensely popular, and both the OSS and British intelligence recognized it as "the largest and most formidable underground organization in Greece."[10] By late 1944, it counted 1.5 million of Greece's 7.5 million inhabitants as members and fielded forces of 50,000.[11] Moreover, unlike the Cairo government and EDES, EAM was militarily independent of the Allies, having armed itself with weapons dumped by the Greek Army in 1941 or captured from the Germans. In Egypt, too, EAM's "exile" wing commanded a wide following among the enlisted men and nonroyalist junior officers of the Greek armed forces.

The KKE's role in EAM was of constant concern to analysts, most of whom mistook the KKE's fondest hopes for reality without weighing its many weaknesses. Although the party's aim was a Communist dictatorship in Greece, between the KKE and this ambitious goal stood many obstacles it never overcame, including Moscow's lack of support. In fact, Moscow ignored the KKE until the middle of the war and then recognized it only to pressure EAM to join the government-in-exile. With liberation Moscow pushed the EAM to maintain order rather than take advantage of its numerical and military superiority to seize control.

[7] C. M. Woodhouse, *The Struggle for Greece: 1941–1949* (London: Hart-Davis, MacGibbon, 1976), p. 38.
[8] OSS "Resistance in Greece," R and A Report No. 1470, n.d., p. 4 (NADB, OSS file) and Clogg, *Short History*, pp. 146–147.
[9] OSS, "Communist-Led Organizations Within the Free Greek Forces," p. 12. It continues, "EAM is . . . opposed to the Metaxist regime and all its works, and in this it is at one with the rest of . . . political opinion in Greece."
[10] OSS, "Resistance in Greece and Its Relation to Allied Policy," R and A Report No. 1741, January 25, 1944, p. 2. NADB, OSS file.
[11] Lawrence Wittner, *American Intervention in Greece, 1943–1949* (New York: Columbia University Press, 1982), p. 3.

Later, Moscow signaled its disapproval by sending an ambassador to Athens at the height of the December 1944 clashes between EAM and the newly reinstalled government. For the Soviet Union, the Grand Alliance took precedence over support for the KKE. Similar considerations of Soviet interest helped undo the KKE at the height of the insurgency.

The KKE was also unable to control EAM members or offer them an appealing program. Initially, the KKE alone had a nationwide underground and through it gained an early advantage in organizing the EAM membership. As EAM grew, however, KKE control declined as the need to keep the Popular Front together required concessions to noncommunist groups. These groups had no interest in the KKE's revolutionary aims, but they sought instead to use the resistance to regain control of status quo politics.[12] Equally important, as more members joined the EAM, the KKE could maintain control only by offering the prospect of a better future. Here the KKE was ill-served by its ideology and leadership, for it was an urban-based party of middle class revolutionaries. Bound by its orthodoxy, the leadership devoted party efforts to the cities, ignored peasants problems, and subjected them—often brutally— to the party's vision of social organization. Where the peasantry rebelled, the KKE unleashed death squads which rivaled their right wing counterparts in nastiness.

The struggle for power after liberation raged throughout the war. In early 1943, EAM launched the first round of the Greek civil war, an effort to eliminate the EDES. Ignoring EAM's contribution to the war effort, the British responded by trying to destroy it. Zervas's forces were not up to the effort, however. As a result, reported the OSS, British policy was "instrumental in permitting the Germans and quislings to recruit from EDES and other nominally anti-German organizations members of their Security Battalions to fight the EAM–ELAS." In fact, many joined "wearing British uniforms and carrying sten guns," and the Ministry of National Defense of the government-in-exile gave "orders detaching a great number of officers of all ranks and units . . . for incorporation into the Security Battalions."[13] Out of these attacks of

[12] Noted the OSS, "In the enthusiasm of the moment, the Communist leadership . . . enrolled a number of members . . . not for ideological reasons, but because the EAM seemed to be far and away the most efficient of the resistance organizations. Once Greece is liberated . . . many, if not most, of those who now call themselves communists . . . will depart from the fold." "Resistance in Greece," p. 3.

[13] OSS, "The Greek Security Battalions," R and A Report No. 2165, May 18, 1944, pp. 5, 3–4. NADB, OSS file. For the story of British policy, see Phyllis Auty and Richard Clogg, eds., *British Policy Toward Wartime Resistance in Yugoslavia and Greece* (New York: Macmillan, 1975).

Greek upon Greek came a still more bitter political polarization. What few moderates remained were divided, strengthening the radicals at both extremes. By early 1944, the British had concluded that the divisions in Greece went so deep that "after the liberation . . . civil war is almost inevitable."[14] They were right, but by the time it began the United States was holding the bag.

In the final days before the liberation, both sides realized they were stalemated. Both the government-in-exile and British recognized that they lacked the forces necessary to defeat EAM. Conversely, EAM radicals recognized that British resolve would make a coup difficult, while moderates hoped that through politics they could win a place in power. Thus, in September 1944 all parties signed the Caserta Agreement. The guerrillas pledged allegiance to the Government of National Unity and recognized the authority of a British general. Following the Germans' withdrawal, these arrangements held for a time. Although government ministers found their writ limited to Athens, EAM proved cooperative. As Ambassador Lincoln MacVeagh noted, "for the moment, danger of a red terror seems to have been removed, with Communist leadership turning to political maneuver rather than direct action." He concluded correctly, however, that "this will certainly be a losing game for that leadership in Greece."[15]

Efforts to reestablish a political center were doomed from the start. True to his liberal background, Prime Minister of the Government of National Unity, George Papandreou, argued that EAM should be given a role in Athens in order to coopt EAM moderates and undermine the KKE. Other Greek leaders and the British rejected all accommodation with EAM, however; it had to be smashed.[16] Between the two sides stood the issues dividing all Greeks: demobilization and the fate of collaborators. Clearly the country could not continue with two armed forces answering to separate authorities. The logical solution would have been demobilization of the ELAS (EAM's military wing) and the Mountain Brigade (the rightist praetorian guard), removal of collaborators from the officer corps, and creation of a new National Army. But as the OSS reported,

> EAM's fear, and it is a real one, is that not only will ELAS be dissolved . . . but that there will be no popular national army in the

[14] Directive to Brigadier Myers, April 1943, cited in Woodhouse, *Struggle for Greece,* p. 38.
[15] Diary entry of November 5, 1944, *Ambassador MacVeagh Reports: Greece, 1933–1947,* ed. John O. Iatrides (Princeton: Princeton University Press, 1980), p. 640.
[16] Wittner, *American Intervention,* pp. 9–10; and Kuniholm, *Origins,* p. 223.

true sense. Not only are the ex-Tsoliadhes [Gestapo-controlled Greek secret police] and members of the Security Battalions being trained as units, but there is a strong tendency to place Royalist and ex-Metaxist officers in high ranking positions.[17]

For its part, the government had no intention of prosecuting collaborators (many of whom had acted under orders) or disbanding the Mountain Brigade which had been created as a "politically reliable" weapon against EAM. Lacking popular support, the government depended upon the collaboration-tainted gendarmerie and other police forces and actively recruited officers and enlisted men who had fought with the Security Battalions, without whom there would have been no counter to EAM.[18]

By November 1944, a pattern of provocation and reaction was leading to open conflict. On December 2, 1944, an EAM-sponsored rally in Athens ended in gunfire, beginning the second round of the civil war. EAM is blamed, but the OSS and other observers concluded that the "crisis . . . was precipitated by rightist determination to exploit to the full the opportunity offered by British support. They believed that a compromise solution would perpetuate the influence of EAM, whereas forcing the issue might make it possible to eliminate EAM from the political scene."[19] Churchill welcomed the conflict and opposed a political solution. In fact, he ordered General Scobie to act as if he were "in a conquered city where a local rebellion is in progress."[20] Once again, however, a definitive solution proved impossible. Just as the British began their counterattack, the Germans unleashed the Ardennes offensive, forcing a political accommodation in Greece. Thus, in February 1945 both sides signed the Varkiza Accords; the agreement promised: free expression of political opinion; trade union rights; an end to martial law; the removal of collaborators, elections, and a plebiscite; reconstitution of the armed forces without prejudice against ELAS; and legal status for the KKE and EAM in return for demobilization of ELAS forces. As with previous agreements, however, the proof was in implementation.

It was not long in coming: despite formal concessions, the eighteen months saw the Right's entrenchment and marginalization of the cen-

[17] OSS, "The Greek Political Crisis," R and A Report No. 2752, December 4, 1944, pp. 2–3. NADB, OSS file.
[18] Ibid., OSS, "The Greek Security Battalions"; and OSS, "The Present Balance of Political Forces in Greece," R and A Report No. 2862, February 27, 1945. NADB, OSS file.
[19] OSS, "The Present Balance of Political Forces in Greece," p. 1.
[20] Cited in Wittner, *American Intervention*, p. 23.

ter and left. EAM began by destroying its majority support by massacring 4,000 hostages at the end of the second round.[21] Then it boycotted the March 31, 1946 elections because of expected electoral fraud and rightist intimidation. There were both, but abstention gave the Right an absolute majority and complete control of the government. Five months later, a plebiscite (held under similar conditions) returned the King to power. In the arena of formal politics, the left had conceded everything, and the Right had achieved its maximal program. Behind the scenes, too, the Right rapidly consolidated its control. SAN stymied all efforts to purge collaborators, incorporated many veterans of the Security Battalions into the Mountain Brigade and kindred organizations, and ensured that Mountain Brigade officers would train the new "National" Army. They used the gendarmerie and secret police "to make wholesale arrests among those suspected of sympathy for the EAM,"[22] and purged the new National Army of all "unreliable" officers. Senior SAN members, including several exmembers of the quisling government, took control of the General Staff, and two Metaxist-collaborationist policemen took control of public order.[23]

The key was violence, however. The United Nations Study Commission reported "mass terrorism and persecution" and "punitive expeditions carried out by Greek gendarmes and Rightist bands against villages whose inhabitants took an active part in the struggle against the occupation forces."[24] In August 1946, Ambassador MacVeagh reported to Washington that "democratic activity on the part of both liberals and leftists is at standstill since this produces instant threats of destruction of property or death." They had, he noted, taken to the hills.[25] By the end of 1946, exguerrillas and their families were once again arming themselves, this time in self-defense against fellow Greeks.

The exact timing of the KKE decision to fight is unclear. Following the Varkiza Agreement, it adopted a conciliatory policy and publicly supported democratic, constitutional government. As the level of violence rose, the KKE waffled, and there is evidence that they actually restrained noncommunist EAM members from taking up arms.[26] Finally, in February 1946, the Central Committee declared its intention "to go ahead

[21] MacVeagh's January 15, 1945, letter to Roosevelt, *Ambassador MacVeagh Reports*, pp. 667–71.
[22] OSS, "The Present Balance of Forces in Greece," p. 12.
[23] OSS, "The Role of the Army in Greek Politics," pp. 14–16.
[24] UN, Security Council, "Report by the Commission of Investigation," UN doc. S/360, vol. 1, May 27, 1947, p. 230.
[25] August 28, 1946, in *Ambassador MacVeagh Reports*, p. 696.
[26] Wittner, *American Intervention*, pp. 32, 44–46.

with the organization of a new armed struggle."[27] Still, "no reliable source dates the formation of local headquarters in the field earlier than June 1946, nor the departure of Vafiades Markos [KKE military leader] for the mountains earlier than August."[28] And not until September 1947—five months after the Truman Doctrine—did the Central Committee decide to abandon political means and commit itself to civil war.

A REALIST EXPLANATION OF AMERICAN INVOLVEMENT

Realist analysis offers considerable insight into the reasons for which policymakers felt compelled to involve the United States in the Greek civil war. As they saw it, the issue was the postwar balance of power. Early in the war, American diplomats saw that more was at stake in Greece and the Near East than defeat of the Germans; at stake, too, was the outcome of the "great game" Britain and Russia had played for centuries from the Balkans to the Khyber. At the center of the board were the countries of the "northern tier," Greece, Turkey and Iran. For the British, control of them meant control of the imperial artery to India and beyond; for the Soviet Union (as for Czarist Russia) it would mean access to a warm water port and the influence a position on the Mediterranean would offer. The prospect of a clash between the two threatened the major American postwar interest—prevention of another world war. As Ambassador MacVeagh wrote President Roosevelt, "Realism requires that we consider . . . that if Great Britain remains in the forefront here, playing her old game of power politics with inadequate means, while we remain aloof, the whole area will eventually fall under the dominating influence of the only other great power in the vicinity, namely Russia." Thus, "to save . . . that for which we all have made such sacrifices, the one disinterested power among the three left standing should take the initiative where the interests of the other two clash."[29]

Policy thinking began to shift. As Churchill and Stalin approached the issue of postwar spheres of influence in Eastern Europe and the Balkans, public expressions of American policy continued to reflect the Wilsonian hopes of the Atlantic Charter. Roosevelt, however, tacitly accepted the balance of power logic and confidentially gave Churchill a free hand. With FDR's death, balance of power politics took another

[27] Cited in George Kousoulas, *Revolution and Defeat: The Story of the Greek Communist Party* (London: Oxford University Press, 1965), p. 231.
[28] Woodhouse, *Struggle for Greece*, p. 175.
[29] MacVeagh to Roosevelt, February 17, 1944, in *Ambassador MacVeagh Reports*, pp. 455–56. See, too, the letters of May and October 15, pp. 517–21 and 627–28.

step forward. Where Roosevelt had distrusted the State Department, Truman depended on it. His Secretary of State, Edward Stettinius, depended on his Under Secretary, Joseph Grew; Grew depended on the regional bureaus; and, as of January 1945, the Office of Near Eastern Affairs was headed by Loy Henderson, a persuasive advocate of balance of power politics. Henderson's influence only increased when a close friend, Dean Acheson, replaced Grew as Under Secretary in August 1945.[30]

The postwar period began with a new American activism. On the one hand, events in Eastern Europe seemed to confirm the primacy of power politics and the suspicion that force alone would blunt Soviet expansionism. At the same time, with Europe in ruins, Americans concluded that they stood alone against the Soviets. On the other, Americans had also emerged from the war confident of their mission. As President Truman put it, "The Old World is exhausted, its civilization imperiled. Its people are suffering . . . confused and filled with fears for the future. Their hope must lie in this New World of ours."[31] In sum, American interests were global, and global issues were American concerns.

In Greece, the change of attitude slowly increased American involvement. During the war and immediately afterwards, American official observers had looked on Greek politics with distaste and sought to avoid association with British initiatives. With the Varkiza Agreement, the United States began to offer more. Initially, assistance was limited to the provision of relief supplies through UNRRA. Then in January 1946, the Export-Import Bank extended a $25 million loan to the Greek Government and in February Greece received a further $10 million. In March, the State-War-Navy Coordinating Committee suggested the sale of military supplies to Middle and Near Eastern countries. The sale was approved in November.[32] Despite this gradual increase in involvement, however, policymakers continued to assume that Greece was Britain's responsibility and that the United States should stay at arm's length.[33] Moreover, assessments of Greece's prob-

[30] Kuniholm, *Origins of the Cold War*, pp. 234–42.

[31] Address to the Rio de Janeiro Inter-American Conference for the Maintenance of Continental Peace and Security, September 2, 1947, *Public Papers of the President, 1947*, p. 431.

[32] State–War–Navy–Coordinating Committee, "Policy Concerning Provision of United States Government Military Supplies for Post-War Armed Forces of Foreign Nations," SWNCC 202/2, March 21, 1946, FR, 1946, 7: 7, and November 1, 1946, FR, 1946, 7: 244.

[33] See Acheson to Winant, London, January 10, 1946, and Byrnes to Tsouderos, January 15, 1946, FR, 1946, 7: 89–90, 96.

lems continued to stress the need for action by the Greek government itself, strict adherence to the Varkiza Agreement, and better economic management.[34]

Then events in Azerbaijan transformed the context of policy toward Greece. In January 1946, Soviet troops and the Communist (Tudeh) Party of Iran threatened annexation of this Iranian province, Western access to Iranian oil, and Iran's very independence. Having faced a Soviet fait accompli in Eastern Europe, Truman was anxious to avoid one in the Near East, especially because "the analogies between Stalin's and Hitler's tactics were too strong to ignore."[35] Pressure was applied at the UN, the battleship *Missouri* was dispatched to Istanbul, and in his April 6 Army Day address President Truman referred pointedly to the area's strategic importance, called for extension of Selective Service, and pledged military support for UN efforts to protect all nations in the region. By December the Soviets had quit, and the administration drew the obvious lesson: firmness backed by power meant success in this great game. At the same time, reports from Greece took on a shrill note.

Throughout the Azerbaijan crisis, persistent voices had called for a deeper involvement in Greece. Loudest was Ambassador MacVeagh's, but Loy Henderson, too, lamented that at arm's length, the United States could not affect events in Greece.[36] By August, reported Acheson, the State Department was re-examining its "rather reserved attitude" toward the Greek government because "it might be that we would have no choice."[37] In October, his concern "over worsening internal conditions in Greece and increasing tension along northern Greek frontiers" led to the drafting of twelve possible U.S. initiatives toward Greece including advice on internal political and economic affairs, military assistance, and economic aid.[38] (When asked for comments, MacVeagh responded, "I feel now as Cassandra might, had anyone suddenly agreed with her!")[39] On October 21, 1946, these and other recommendations were included in a "Memorandum Regarding Greece" that laid out an activist American policy. Also in October, Secretary of State Byrnes sent journalist Mark Ethridge to report on con-

[34] See Merriam to MacVeagh, May 16, 1945, in *Ambassador MacVeagh Reports*, p. 679; Acheson to Truman, August 7, 1946, FR, 1946, 7: 187; and Wittner, *American Intervention*, pp. 47–50.

[35] Kuniholm, *Origins of the Cold War*, pp. 300–301.

[36] MacVeagh to the Secretary of State, January 11, 1946 FR, 1946, 7: 92; Henderson to Acheson, June 4, 1946, ibid., pp. 7–8.

[37] Dean Acheson, *Present at the Creation: My Years in the State Department* (New York: W. W. Norton, 1969), p. 195.

[38] Acheson to MacVeagh, October 15, 1946, FR, 1946, 7: 235–137.

[39] Letter to Henderson, in *Ambassador MacVeagh Reports*, p. 707.

ditions in the Balkans. Then in December, economist Paul Porter was dispatched to assess Greece's reconstruction and development needs.

By February 1947 the investigative efforts had produced alarming results. In Athens, Ethridge, Porter, and MacVeagh compared notes and sounded the tocsin. On February 20 MacVeagh cabled the State Department that "we feel situation here so critical that no time should be lost in applying any remedial measures. . . . Impossible to say how soon collapse may be anticipated, but we believe that to regard it as anything but imminent would be highly unsafe."[40] Loy Henderson was impressed and immediately drafted a memo to Acheson. Acheson gave it a new title—"Crisis and Imminent Possibility of Collapse in Greece"— and expanded on MacVeagh's argument that without assistance Greece might fall, taking with it "the whole Near and Middle East and northern Africa." On February 21 Acheson sent his memo and Mac-Veagh's recent cables to Secretary of State Marshall with the comment, "we recommend reconsideration of our policy and [a] decision to assist Greece with military equipment."[41] Hours later the British notes arrived announcing Britain's decision to quit Greece. As Marshall told Secretary of Defense Forrestal three days later, the British position was "tantamount to . . . abdication from the Middle East with obvious implications as to their successor."[42]

But as policymakers considered what to do, Greece per se slipped into obscurity. As implied by Acheson's famous analogy, Greece was irrelevant; it just happened to be the bad apple. The issues were position and power: the "inexorable facts of geography" and "the comparative power that the US and USSR are willing to expend." Indeed, the solution of the problem "will depend on the whole East–West conflict in all its global extent."[43] "The security of the whole Eastern Mediterranean and Middle East would be jeopardized" by Soviet control of Greece, concluded the NSC, as would the global security of the United States.[44] Thus, "the problem is not so much . . . saving the Greek people," argued Loy Henderson, as it is "preventing Greece from becom-

[40] MacVeagh to State, February 20, 1947, ibid., p. 712.

[41] Acheson to Marshall, February 21, 1947, FR, 1947, 5: 29–31.

[42] Kuniholm, *Origins of the Cold War*, p. 409.

[43] Acheson to the House Foreign Affairs Committee, March 20, 1947, in Department of State, "Aid to Greece and Turkey: A Collection of State Papers," Near Eastern Series, No. 7, May 4, 1947, p. 837; and Office of Intelligence Research, "Prospects for the Preservation of the Independence of Greece," OIR Report No. 4664, April 27, 1948, pp. 10, 28–29. NADB, OSS file.

[44] NSC 5, "The Position of the United States with respect to Greece," January 6, 1948, FR, 1948, 4: 2.

ing a Soviet base and permitting the impression . . . that the United States is lacking in resolution when faced with aggression."[45]

The imposition of an East–West perspective lent the decision to get involved the air of compulsion. Testifying to a doubting Congress, Secretary of State Marshall asserted that "the choice is between acting with energy or losing by default."[46] Consequently, observed John Iatrides, with the delivery of the British notes the locus of activity

> shifted dramatically to Washington. The American Embassy in Athens was now essentially confined to the task of providing supplementary information which was needed to respond to potential critics of the proposed programs of action, and to the task of implementing such policies, conceived by officials who had only the most general understanding of the real problems besetting Greece. Once the Greek crisis had come to be perceived as the work of the Soviet Union and its agents in the Balkans, the complex realities of Greece's particular situation appeared as minor details in the broader and all-important East–West confrontation.[47]

Furthermore, by defining Greece as an East–West test of wills, policymakers made it one. Argued Secretary of State Byrnes, "the world is watching the support or lack thereof which we furnish our friends at this critical time and the future policies of many countries will be determined by their estimate of the seriousness . . . with which the US upholds its principles and supports those of like mind."[48] Conversely, asserted the CIA, "far more disastrous than the loss of Greece itself would be the psychological and political repercussions [which] could result in international panic."[49] No less important, "success of this Communist technique in Greece would render almost inevitable its employment elsewhere."[50] Thus, issues unrelated to conditions in Greece required that the United States commit itself, and this commitment required continued commitment, also without regard to conditions on the ground.

In sum, the realist explanation of foreign policy as a logical response

[45] Henderson to the Secretary of State in re NSC 5, January 9, 1948, FR, 1948, 4: 12.

[46] In Arthur Vandenberg, Jr., and Joe Morris, eds., *The Private Papers of Senator Vandenberg* (Boston: Houghton Mifflin, 1952), p. 339.

[47] *Ambassador MacVeagh Reports*, p. 713.

[48] Byrnes to Acheson, September 24, 1946, FR, 1946, 7: 224. See also Henderson to Marshall, January 9, 1948. FR, 1948, 4: 12.

[49] CIA, "Possible Consequences of Communist Control of Greece in the Absence of US Counteraction," ORE 69, February 9, 1948, p. 1. DDRS, 1978: 329B.

[50] Rankin to the Secretary of State, December 21, 1948, FR, 1948, 4: 220.

to compelling international security risks offers a great deal. United States involvement answered the perceived need to respond to a security threat posed by the Soviet Union. As for timing, intervention marked the end of a slow process of adjustment to a new American role reflecting the United States's displacement of Britain as hegemonic power. Furthermore, the tight focus on the East-West balance of power helps explain the irrelevance of Greece per se in the choice to intervene while commitment itself helps explain the subsequent unresponsiveness of policy to conditions there. But such analysis also leaves much unexplained. Whatever the reasons for intervention, it offers no insight as to the policies pursued. It explains why, not how, the United States had to act. But the issue of how cannot be ignored. For despite the importance decisionmakers attached to the situation, actual policy was muddled and ineffective. A shift of analytic focus is needed to explain why.

Domestic and Bureaucratic Politics

However important issues of security and balance of power politics may have been, the packaging and implementation of policy reflected domestic political and bureaucratic concerns. For policymakers convinced of the necessity of involvement in Greece, the political worry was how to manage isolationist hostility toward foreign entanglements, especially after the Republican sweep of 1946. Immediately after the war, their fears dictated arm's-length involvements and a refusal to bring balance of power concepts into the public discourse on foreign policy. When events in Greece seemed to compel action, however, policymakers were forced to confront the issue directly and, as one State Department official put it, "electrify the American people."[51] They did so with the Truman Doctrine.

Truman's March 12, 1947, speech was a carefully orchestrated effort to shift the foundations of American foreign policy. American assistance was "imperative if Greece is to survive as a free nation," declared Truman. Moreover, "it is necessary only to glance at a map" to realize that its fall would threaten the whole Middle East and demoralize struggling countries even further afield. Indeed, at stake was the struggle between democracy and totalitarianism. Failure might "endanger the peace of the world—and we shall surely endanger the secu-

[51] FR, 1947, 5: 47.

179

rity of our own nation."[52] It was a call to a crusade, no half-measures allowed. Truman had taken to heart Senator Arthur Vandenberg's admonition that to get congressional support, he would have to "scare hell" out of the American people. It worked. Isolationist preferences notwithstanding, Vandenberg himself admitted afterwards that faced with "almost a Presidential request for a declaration of war . . . there is precious little we can do except say 'yes.' "[53]

Saying "yes" had distinct consequences for American policy, however. The crusading universalism reinforced the tendency to analyze events in Greece not on their merits, but as they were supposed to relate to the East–West struggle. At a more prosaic level, assurances built into the speech to meet domestic objections to involvement shaped the American role in Greece. For those concerned about intervention in the internal affairs of Greece, Truman stressed that his aid request merely responded to a similar request from the government of Greece. (In fact, the State Department drafted the Greek request; as Paul Porter, chief of the American Economic Mission to Greece, told Prime Minister Maximos, it was a "merchandizing tool" to sell Congress on aid.)[54] To calm congressional fears of a giveaway, Truman insisted on Greek accountability and pointed to the "request" that American administrators "insure that the financial and other aid . . . shall be used effectively."[55] Thus, the administration built into the aid package provisions for deep American penetration into the day-to-day operations of the Greek government.

But the toughest problem was selling the Greek government to a skeptical Congress and American public. To counter criticism of rightist abuses and the superficiality of "democracy" in Greece, Truman had to declare that the government's aim was "to become a self-supporting and self-respecting democracy." He admitted that "no government is perfect." But the problem, he insisted, lay not within but without and could be cured by removing foreign meddlers and the "evil soil of poverty and strife." Thus, the President and the U.S. government became

[52] *Public Papers of the President of the United States, Harry S. Truman 1947* (Washington, D.C.: GPO, 1963), Vol. 3, pp. 176–79. For an analysis of the making of the Truman Doctrine, see Wittner, *American Intervention*, chapter 3.

[53] U.S. Senate, Committee on Foreign Relations, *Legislative Origins of the Truman Doctrine*, Hearings, 80th Cong., 1st sess., 1973, p. 128.

[54] Porter Mission, *Tentative Report of the American Economic Mission to Greece*, Appendix B, Porter to Maximos, p. 1.

[55] March 12, 1947, *Public Papers*, Vol. 3, p. 177. In subsequent briefings by members of the administration, this point was hammered home. See, for example, Acheson before the House Foreign Affairs Committee on March 20 and Clayton to the same, March 24. Department of State, "Aid to Greece and Turkey," pp. 836 and 841–42.

hucksters for the Greek regime. While the administration pressed the Greeks to avoid public excesses that might offend American opinion, at home it denied Greek government wrongdoing and even mounted a public relations campaign to discredit its critics.[56]

Bureaucratic constraints also shaped policy. The first explains why, despite the perception of crisis, the United States did not send troops. The demobilization of American forces after the war and the strategic primacy of Europe left the military loath to commit troops in Greece. In March 1946, General Marshall declared that he would resist pressures, "however justifiable and understandable," to send even token forces "since it was necessary to conserve our very limited strength and apply it only where it was likely to be most effective."[57] Eventually, contingency plans for the use of American troops were developed, but the Joint Chiefs insisted that any use of force in the Eastern Mediterranean be accompanied by partial, perhaps general, mobilization.[58] This was so politically unpalatable as to kill consideration of an American troop commitment.

Bureaucratic politics affected policy in Greece, too. In early 1945, MacVeagh wrote Foy Kohler at the State Department that relief efforts were failing "because there are too many cooks and no chef." "If ever there was need for a 'czar,' " he concluded, "it is in this complex problem of relieving and reconstructing a completely ruined country under conditions imposed by a global war."[59] No "czar" was in the offing, however. To the contrary, with passage of the aid package (PL 75), authority was divided among three separate agencies with different perspectives and types of resources. As a result, policy lurched drunkenly, responding not to changing circumstances in Greece but to the shifting fortunes of bureaucratic players. The instability weakened American

[56] Lawrence Wittner, "The Truman Doctrine and the Defense of Freedom," *Diplomatic History* 4: 2 (Spring 1980), pp. 178–79.

[57] Henderson to Rankin, March 25, 1946, report on Marshall's secret testimony to the Senate Foreign Relations Committee, FR, 1948, 4: 64–65. See, too, JCS, "Future United States Support to the Armed Forces of Greece," report of the Joint Strategic Survey Committee, October 6, 1948, p. 4. DDRS, Retro: 248A.

[58] JCS, Joint Staff Planners, "The Greek Situation," PM-575, September 2, 1947, pp. 1–2 (DDRS, 1975:71C); NSC 5 (Policy Planning Staff redraft of January 10, 1948), FR, 1948, 4: 25; NSC 5/4, "The Position of the United States with respect to the Use of U.S. Military Power in Greece," Report to the President, June 3, 1948, pp. 4–5 (DDRS, 1977: 297B); and JCS, "The Position of the United States with respect to Greece," memorandum for the National Security Council, April 13, 1948, p. 2 (DDRS, Retro: 61E). See also Wittner, *American Intervention*, pp. 237–39.

[59] MacVeagh to Kohler, January 29, 1945, *Ambassador MacVeagh Reports*, pp. 683–84.

initiatives and let the Greeks play one piece of the American mission against another.

One such struggle pitted the Embassy against the American Mission for Aid to Greece (AMAG). Secretary of State Marshall's instructions to AMAG chief Dwight Griswold stated explicitly that "the external and internal problems of Greece are of DIRECT CONCERN to the Embassy" and that "the responsibilities of the Ambassador . . . include in particular the problem of bringing about changes in the Greek government."[60] But Griswold had different ideas and the resources to implement them. In fact, just two months later, Griswold reported success in establishing a new coalition government by using "the economic leverage of the Aid Program as a club." Unrepentant, he justified his action by arguing that Ambassador MacVeagh had no such club and thus could not have forced formation of the coalition.[61]

The battle continued for three years. In October 1947, Truman approved a directive on Embassy-AMAG responsibilities that made the embassy the "sole channel for dealing with the Greek government on matters of high policy."[62] Griswold replied the next day denying State Department authority and claiming a congressional mandate to enforce the PL 75 requirement of "strict controls over expenditure of American and Greek funds."[63] A month later, Truman reversed himself and approved Griswold's recommendation that the AMAG chief have both the power to intervene in "high policy" issues affecting AMAG and absolute power in economic matters. It did not help, and in January 1948 NSC 5 bemoaned the fact that "effective implementation of US policy has . . . been hampered by lack of centralized control" and recommended that the United States should "immediately designate" a "senior representative of the United States and director of all US activities in Greece."[64] Thus, the ambassador was made head of AMAG as well. The move was irrelevant, for at the same time the aid program was taken over by a newly established Economic Cooperation Administration (ECA) mission whose chief reported to ECA headquarters in Washington. The turf battle continued apace, aggravated by the growth of the ECA mission which soon dwarfed the embassy. Throughout, American policy suffered the confusion MacVeagh had warned about in 1945.

[60] July 10, 1947, FR, 1947, 5: 219.
[61] Henderson to Lovett in re Griswold's "flamboyant" account in the September 15, 1947 AMAG monthly report, in *Ambassador MacVeagh Reports*, pp. 725–26.
[62] Directive of October 23, 1947, in ibid., pp. 728–29.
[63] Griswold cable of October 24, 1947, in ibid., pp. 727–28.
[64] FR, 1948, 4: 3, 6.

Such domestic political and bureaucratic politics analyses add a further dimension of understanding. They explain the rhetorical overkill and crusading universalism of the Truman Doctrine, the policy shift from arm's-length to deep involvement, and the inconsistency of policy implementation despite the declared importance of the situation. But like realist analyses, they also leave questions unanswered. They do not explain why certain interpretations of events in Greece prevailed, the choice of responses to them, the consistency of understanding among agencies (despite turf battles), or the inaccuracy of this understanding and its consequences. Answers to these require another shift of analytic focus.

The Three Oughts in Greece

Policymakers' "shared image" of the Greek crisis stressed two remediable problems. They assumed, first, that Soviet meddling was the cause of Greece's problems. For example, a Policy Planning Staff analysis of "Possibilities for Relieving the Situation" begins: "Starting from the premise that Greece's difficulties arise principally and fundamentally from the objectives and policies of the Soviet Union."[65] Second, they believed that poverty and economic dislocation left Greece defenseless and drove many to heed the lure of totalitarian ideology. Few doubted they knew what to do to overcome both; as the head of the American military mission put it in October 1947, there was "nothing wrong with Greece that time, forceful U.S. guidance and American dollars will not correct."[66] Although priorities reflected bureaucratic affiliation, all agreed on the three great oughts: security, good government, and progress.

SECURITY

Security of the Greek state against external attack was policymakers' first concern. "As long as the USSR pursues its expansionist policies," argued the Joint Chiefs, "the security of the Eastern Mediterranean and Middle East is of critical importance to the future security of the United States."[67] Thus, "U.S. long-range strategic interests" required "a Greek

[65] Policy Planning Staff, "Report on U.S. Aid to Greece," November 24, 1948, FR, 1948, 4: 200.

[66] Col. Charles Lehner, Commander USAGG to Director, P & O Division, Dept. of the Army, October 30, 1947; cited in Wittner, *American Intervention*, p. 226.

[67] Cited in NSC 42/1, "U.S. Objectives with Respect to Greece and Turkey to Counter Soviet Threats to US Security," March 22, 1949, p. 5. DDRS, 1977: 43B.

military establishment capable of maintaining internal security"[68] because, as Under Secretary of State Lovett told the Greek Ambassador,
"the only way to beat the guerrillas [is] by fighting. . . . Every effort
should be made to wipe them out."[69]

Unfortunately, the Greek armed forces showed no inclination or capacity to do so. Criticism of their miserable performance runs through
embassy, CIA, and Joint US Military Advisory and Planning Group
(JUSMAPG) reporting. In January 1948, for example, NSC 5 noted that
the Greek military was hampered by "lack of offensive spirit, by political interference . . . and by poor leadership, particularly in the lower
echelons."[70] Eleven months later, a major Policy Planning Staff report
listed "the inefficiency of the Greek Army" as "by far the most important" cause of American aid's limited success. Greek soldiers were demoralized, their officers poorly trained, the officer corps "permeated
with distrust," political preferment outranked merit, and many officers
were "guided . . . by political ambitions."[71]

The primacy of security and Greek army incompetence produced a
strong military bias in American assistance. Initially, aid focused on logistics and training Greek soldiers to use American equipment, but this
proved insufficient. By fall 1947, Dwight Griswold recommended that
AMAG give "operational advice" to the Greek General Staff. He was
soon echoed by General Stephen Chamberlain who was sent to assess
the military situation.[72] In January 1948, Secretary Marshall informed
AMAG that

> Destruction guerrilla forces and establishment internal security
> . . . now have clearly assumed paramount importance as necessary
> preliminary for successful American aid to Greece. Until achieved,
> these aims should henceforth take precedence over any portions
> present program which do not directly support them. *Dept would
> therefore view favorably any program modifications you may rec-
> ommend after re-examining Mission projects in terms of their fur-
> therance, with least delay, of this basic objective.*[73]

[68] State-Army-Navy-Air Force Coordinating Committee, cited in ibid., p. 6. See, too,
JCS, Joint Strategic Survey Committee, "U.S. Assistance to Greece," JCS 1798/1, October
15, 1947, p. 50. NAMM, JCS list, 1946–47 CCS 092 (8-22-46) Sec. 8.
[69] Memo of conversation, August 10, 1948, FR, 1948, 4: 123.
[70] FR, 1948, 4: 3.
[71] Policy Planning Staff, "Aid to Greece," November 24, 1948, FR, 1948, 4: 198.
[72] Griswold, cited in Michael Amen, *American Foreign Policy in Greece, 1944/1949:
Economic, Military and Institutional Aspects* (Frankfurt am Main: Peter Lang, 1978), p.
179; and Chamberlain, FR, 1947, 5: 376.
[73] January 12, 1948, FR, 1948, 4: 26. Emphasis in original.

The resulting flood of military aid to Greece included training, equipment, and supplies. More important, it included efforts JUSMAPG hoped would "overcome political influence on the Greek high command" by providing high level operational guidance and "overcome inertia and stimulate aggressive offensive action" at lower echelons by assigning observers to field commands.[74]

THE GOOD GOVERNMENT OUGHT

Despite the primacy of security, policymakers were also concerned with the quality and quantity of government in Greece. But the perceived political problems, too, were considered temporary. Greece was defined as a "free, democratic nation" in need of aid merely "to restore [its] authority . . . throughout Greek territory."[75] Indeed, the Truman administration refused to tie aid to improved protection of citizens' rights since

> Greece's problems do not arise from lack of constitutional guarantees, but from disturbed conditions which impede the operation of constitutional government. . . . Our assistance will be instrumental in stabilizing the . . . situation and thus will assure the Greek people the full freedom to conduct their own affairs which they have traditionally enjoyed.[76]

The CIA noted that "excesses have taken place, but these have been the result of a reaction against Communist terrorism rather than any real tendency toward fascism."[77] Still, there were problems.

Policymakers expressed concern over a variety of governmental weaknesses. First, they worried about Greece's "historical difficulty in reconciling order with democracy"[78] and the government's tendency to consider all opponents Communists and treat them accordingly. Conversely, however, they lamented an excess of democracy—"the inerad-

[74] Report of Chamberlain, October 20, 1947, cited in JCS, Historical Section, Kenneth Condit, *The History of the Joint Chiefs of Staff*, vol. 2, 1947–1949 (Washington, D.C., April 22, 1976), p. 37. NAMM.

[75] March 12, 1947, *Public Papers*, Vol. 3, p. 177.

[76] U.S. Senate, Committee on Foreign Relations, "Questions and Answers Relating to the Greco-Turkish Aid Bill," April 3, 1947, in "Aid to Greece and Turkey," p. 888. The CIA asserted in 1948 that "given assurance of hope and stability through American aid, the people should eventually be able to reaffirm their democratic preferences." "Greece," Situation Report SR-10, March 1948, p. I-11. DDRS, 1977: 168A.

[77] CIA, "Current Situation in Greece," ORE 28-48, November 17, 1948, p. 5. DDRS, 1978: 331A.

[78] Acheson, *Present at the Creation*, p. 331.

icable individualism of the Greek"[79]—the prevalence of "petty politics," and the "unwillingness or inability of Greek leaders to work together for urgent needs [of] their country."[80] "Even in the face of national disaster," the CIA complained in 1948, "many politicians in Athens have refused to surrender their personal and party interests for genuinely national purposes."[81] Finally, Americans criticized governmental overcentralization, overcompartmentalization, overstaffing, administrative partisanship, and "resistance both to a sense of responsibility to the electorate and to administrative reform."[82]

The Greeks needed good government. They were told repeatedly that "in this critical time . . . all loyal political parties and leaders should unite to form most broadly based govt possible, dedicated to modernization, [and] all feasible conciliation to loyal opposition." The United States encouraged "political evolution" and "the formation of a broader government," and the American mission was ordered to "organize and recruit the civilian group to exercise control and direction in Greece."[83] The United States pushed changes "which would result in curtailing petty political maneuvering and improper political interference in military affairs, and consequently in more efficient handling of Greek civil and military affairs," and mounted a "comprehensive program to increase the administrative efficiency of the Greek government."[84] Policymakers suggested civil service reductions, merit promotion, and instruction for Greek officials "in modern techniques of government . . . to equip them for the great tasks ahead."[85] Finally, they counseled the regime to develop a "far-reaching propaganda campaign" to make the people recognize their "responsibility as Greeks" to support the government.[86]

[79] Policy Planning Staff, "Aid to Greece," November 24, 1948, FR, 1948, 4: 200.
[80] Byrnes to MacVeagh, November 2, 1945, *Ambassador MacVeagh Reports*, p. 687. MacVeagh called postwar Greek leaders "small men, old men, and men entirely lacking in the sense of realism which the situation requires." Letter to Cannon, October 14, 1946 (Ibid.).
[81] "Greece," Situation Report SR-10, March 1948, pp. I-10–I-11.
[82] Policy Planning Staff, "Aid to Greece," FR, 1948, 4: 199; CIA, "Greece," SR-10, p. I-5; and CIA, "Current Situation in Greece," ORE 28-48, p. 5.
[83] Byrnes to MacVeagh, January 3, 1947, FR, 1946, 7: 287; NSC 42/1, pp. 12–13; Central Intelligence Group, "The Greek Situation," ORE 6/1, February 7, 1947, p. 2 (DDRS, 1978: 222C); Acheson, *Present at the Creation*, p. 220.
[84] NSC 42/1, pp. 12–13.
[85] Department of State, "First Report to Congress on Assistance to Greece and Turkey," Near Eastern Series, No. 11, November 1947, p. 12 and Department of State, "The Greek Aid Program," Near Eastern Series, No. 10, October 1947, p. 3.
[86] Grady to Secretary of State, October 22, 1948, FR, 1948, 4: 170.

THE PROGRESS OUGHT

Finally, policymakers agreed with Truman that "the seeds of totalitarian regimes are nurtured by misery and want. They spread and grow in the evil soil of poverty and strife."[87] And if help was needed anywhere to keep them from germinating, it was in Greece. One of the poorest countries in Europe before the war, Greece had suffered more during it than any other country but the Soviet Union. Eight percent of the population had been killed, and six more left homeless. Once able to cover 60 percent of its imports with exports, Greece could cover less than 25 percent in 1945. Never able to feed itself, Greece had suffered terrible crop-land, herd, and orchard losses. The transportation system was so badly damaged that relief supplies could not be moved from Athens and instead passed into the black market.[88] Small wonder that Senator Vandenberg concluded that Greece was "primarily" an issue "for economic aid."[89]

The solution seemed self-evident and readily attainable. As Paul Porter reported to the House Foreign Affairs Committee in March 1947, "The majority of the people of Greece are . . . eager to perfect their democratic institutions if given the opportunity. They need material assistance and technical guidance if they are to function as a free, self-sustaining democracy."[90] Thus, the United States undertook reconstruction of transportation and communication facilities, land reclamation, the supply of housing materials, food, clothing, medicine, and so on. To complement these efforts, Porter told Congress,

It will be necessary for Greece to adopt a plan of vigorous fiscal and taxation reforms; to develop a tight system of control of imports, development of exports, control of foreign exchange, and such other measures as are necessary to assure that essential commodities flow through distribution channels to the farmers, workers, and producers who need them.[91]

And to ensure that these measures were adopted, policymakers insisted that American representatives "have complete authority" to advise on

[87] March 12, 1947, *Public Papers*, Vol. 3, p. 180.

[88] Woodhouse, *Struggle for Greece*, pp. 161–62, 208, 265–66; and the Porter Mission report, April 1947 in "Aid to Greece and Turkey," p. 899.

[89] Letter to Rep. John B. Bennett, March 5, 1947, in Vandenberg and Morris, eds., *Private Papers*, p. 340.

[90] Testimony of March 28, 1947, "Aid to Greece and Turkey," p. 842.

[91] Ibid., p. 845.

and veto plans, control the disbursement of funds and supplies, and even "participate in day-to-day government operations."[92]

The Limits of Leverage

Leverage constituted a regular theme in field reporting and policy papers throughout American involvement in Greece. From the beginning Ambassador MacVeagh, Mark Ethridge, and Paul Porter agreed, as MacVeagh cabled Washington, that American aid "should be clearly conditioned" on the Greek government's "acceptance and implementation of specific economic policies."[93] Indeed, later in secret testimony to the House Foreign Affairs Committee concerning PL 75, MacVeagh asserted that without Americans in control aid to Greece would "go down a rat hole," while at the same time Acheson told the Senate Foreign Relations Committee that success would require Americans in "the essential key ministries" with the "authority to say to Greece, 'Stop doing that!' "[94] Thus, NSC 5, for example, insisted that the United States should

> Demand as a condition for the continuance of the assistance program, the complete cooperation and aggressive action of the Greek government, including such measures as undertaking necessary political, economic and financial reforms, presenting a united and determined front against Communist aggression, divorcing politics from the conduct of military operations, and . . . improving the efficiency of the administration of the Greek aid program.[95]

But despite such demands, the United States found its leverage limited.

Initially, the problem was how to exercise leverage at arm's length in order to avoid "the charge . . . that this is American imperialism."[96] But as things went from bad to worse, policymakers abandoned such concerns and took more direct measures. Behind the scenes, they threatened the withdrawal of aid if the Greeks did not cooperate. As the Policy Planning Staff put it, "we should not hesitate to make it clear . . . , whenever necessary, that there are limits beyond which it would no

[92] Porter Mission report summary and recommendations, DSB 16 (April 30, 1947), pp. 898–909.

[93] FR, 1947, 5: 89–90.

[94] U.S. House of Representatives, Committee on Foreign Affairs, *Military Assistance Programs*, Part 2, Historical Series, vol. 6 (Washington, D.C.: GPO, 1976), pp. 384, 412–14; and U.S. Senate, *Legislative Origins*, p. 75.

[95] FR, 1948, 4: 6.

[96] Acheson testimony, April 1, 1947, U.S. Senate, *Legislative Origins*, p. 82.

longer be worthwhile for us to proceed."[97] These threats were backed
by the provisions of PL 75 which required termination of aid in the absence of cooperation and by Congress's threat to block future aid if not
satisfied with Greek efforts. More important, however, policymakers
took control of many issues by placing veto-armed Americans in the
Greek government. Thus, by early 1948, the State Department reported that AMAG controlled "almost all segments of the Greek economy, including such matters as governmental administration and procedure, internal budgetary and fiscal controls, control of all foreign
exchange resources, programming and control of imports [and] the
formulation of wage and price policies."[98] But what is extraordinary,
given these controls, is how little effective leverage the United States exercised.

The limits of leverage show clearly in the failure of American efforts
to promote Greek self-sufficiency and the economic redistribution
deemed necessary to undercut the insurgents and solidify a moderate
political center. Because of its dependence on a regressive tax system,
the Greek government's inability to mobilize resources was of central
concern. Thus, the AMAG sought to create new sources of revenue and
shift the system's dependence on indirect taxes to one on direct taxes in
order to redistribute the tax burden and tap the untouched wealth of
the rich. But neither effort succeeded because, despite the appearance
of leverage, AMAG pressure was insufficient to offset that applied by politically powerful interest groups.

The failure of American efforts to create new sources of tax revenue
is neatly illustrated by the surplus Liberty ship fiasco. In order to raise
Greece's foreign exchange earnings and tax base, the United States sold
Greece 109 surplus Liberty ships in 1947. Each ship should have paid
$30,000 per year in taxes and earned $70,000 in foreign exchange. In
fact, while their owners prospered, the ships made almost no contribution to the Greek economy because, as the Porter mission noted in
June 1947, the government feared loss of political support if restrictions were placed on the shippers' activities. It recommended that the
United States force renegotiation of the sales agreements and make future sales contingent upon increased tax rates. AMAG tried, but
achieved nothing until 1950, a year after the end of the insurgency.[99]

AMAG efforts to pressure the Greek government to increase tax revenues and shift the tax burden from the poor to the rich fared no better.

[97] "Aid to Greece," FR, 1948, 4: 203.
[98] Lovett to Hoffman, February 12, 1948, FR, 1948, 4: 76–78.
[99] Amen, *American Foreign Policy in Greece*, pp. 116–18.

Indeed, after a year and a half of futile attempts, the AMAG Director of Public Finance concluded in December 1948 that "the administrative machinery of Greece is simply not up to the job of extracting the maximum contribution from the wealthier elements of the community in support of the military and recovery effort."[100] Since these were deemed critical, however, the United States dropped the reform effort and threw its support behind the Greek government and its wealthy supporters. Tax revenues were raised 45 percent, but only by increasing indirect taxes' share in state revenues to 80 percent. As a result, while the real income of the Greek upper classes doubled between 1939 and 1951, the state's American-backed dependence on indirect taxes reduced their contribution to tax revenues by half.[101] In other words, rather than promoting greater equity, American assistance aided and abetted the Right's assault on the poor majority's standard of living.

Here, as in the Liberty ship fiasco, reverse leverage prevailed. Despite the extraordinary degree of direct American involvement, Greek officials were able to resist and even coopt the American reform effort. Indeed, observes historian Lawrence Wittner, "American aid and supervision did little to reconstruct the shaky underpinnings of the Greek economy, to foster substantial economic growth or to promote the general welfare. Instead, . . . American officials accomplished little beyond fortifying the privileged position of the Greek upper class within a context of economic underdevelopment."[102]

Similar problems plagued efforts to force the creation of a centerist coalition government in Greece. "Ideally," Secretary of State Marshall told AMAG chief Griswold, "members of the government should be drawn from the political parties of the left, the center, and the right, but not so far to the left that they are disposed to make concessions to, or deals with, the Communists, or so far to the right that they would refuse to cooperate with non-communists."[103] Thus, Griswold made clear his belief that "his immediate task should be to change or reorganize the Greek government" and in this he would feel free to use the "club" of Greek dependence on American aid "to force Greek political leaders into a program of unity."[104] Despite the club, however, the

[100] Charles Coombs, December 20, 1948, cited in Wittner, *American Intervention*, p. 175.

[101] Ibid.

[102] Ibid., p. 190.

[103] FR, 1947, 5: 221–22.

[104] FR, 1947, 5: 215–16; and Monthly Report to the Secretary of State from the Chief of the American Mission for Aid to Greece, September 15, 1947, cited in Wittner, *American Intervention*, p. 103.

United States failed to achieve its goal. Indeed, as in the case of economic reforms, American policymakers, coopted by the Greek Right, were eventually made accomplices in actions antithetical to their original intentions.

From the beginning Americans found it impossible to pressure Greek politicians into doing what they wanted. The problem throughout was creating a coalition of centerist Liberals and right-wing Populists that would isolate the left. And, except for a few token representatives, the Liberals refused to participate. Thus, from early 1947 on, the Greek government was, as one observer put it, "manned by people who are merely giving lip service to democracy."[105] Worried by this situation, Griswold and MacVeagh applied heavy pressure (including threats to withdraw U.S. aid) to force creation of a center-right government with a Liberal prime minister.[106] The result, however, was a government nominally headed by the doting Liberal Themistocles Sophoulis but in fact entirely controlled by the Populists and riddled with an unsavory collection of former Nazi collaborators.

With the failure to achieve a center-right government American policymakers—like the Greek Populists they sought to control—began to express concern that democracy itself was at fault. Thus, as George McGhee suggested to Secretary of State Marshall in February 1948, "the effectiveness of the Greek people" as "an instrument of our policy" could be increased by "bringing about the creation of a more authoritarian government."[107] Attention focused on what came to be known as the "Papagos solution": a government headed by General Papagos ruling in the name of the king. This, wrote the State Department's director of Greek, Turkish, and Iranian Affairs, promised Greece "the dynamic, efficient and inspired political leadership . . . the country so surely needs."[108]

The issue came to a head January 3, 1949, when, with Ambassador Grady out of the country, AMAG chief John Nuveen, JUSMAPG commander General James Van Fleet, and visiting ECA Special Representative in Europe Averell Harriman pressured the King to support the Papagos solution. Grady managed to avert the coup by convincing Secretary of State Marshall that "US encouragement" of an "extra-par-

[105] Irving Brown, European representative of the American Federation of Labor, July 7, 1947, cited in Wittner, *American Intervention*, p. 107.

[106] FR, 1947, 5: 324–25.

[107] McGhee to Marshall, February 24, 1948, 868.00/2-2448, cited in Wittner, *American Intervention*, p. 121.

[108] John Jergenson, FR, 1948, 4: 187.

liamentary solution" was inappropriate.[109] A week later, however, Papagos was appointed commander-in-chief of the Greek military and given a virtual carte blanche. In short, in political as in economic reform, reverse leverage prevailed. Not only did Americans fail to achieve the "good government" goals they sought, but they also became the active accomplices of the Greek Right in their subversion.

Beyond the limits of capacity lie the limits of American willingness to exercise leverage. The very decision to become involved signaled the Greeks just how seriously we felt *their* security affected *ours* and convinced them that American security interests dictated continued support regardless of their failure to make reforms. Consequently, the Greek government welcomed all evidence of the U. S. stake in the area and went to great lengths to enmesh the United States even further. As a State Department analyst put it, "Greek officials are obsessed with the idea of getting the United States so deeply committed . . . that it will be unable to withdraw if the Greeks themselves lie down on the job."[110] Americans were not oblivious to the problem and tried to counter it. Thus, for example, Ambassador Grady proposed in December 1948 that

> when budget for Greek program is presented to Congress consideration be given to inclusion statement that Greece is not essential to US security and therefore aid is not requested because our military need. I believe our position vis-à-vis the Greeks would be greatly strengthened if Greek aid program is presented to Congress [as] helping a nation that is helping itself fight the inroads of Communism.[111]

Unfortunately, by the logic of containment Greece *was* essential to U.S. security. Moreover, to assert it was not essential would jeopardize the congressional and public support the Truman administration had created with its "scare hell" tactics. Once committed, in other words, the United States had few "alternatives to collaboration," and its leverage was consequently limited.

The dilemma shows most clearly in American efforts to curb Greek government abuses of political and human rights. From the beginning, the themes of respect for the opposition, due process, and the rights of

[109] FR, 1949, 6: 233–35.
[110] Baxter to Henderson, March 2, 1948, FR, 1948, 4: 56–57. See, too, CIA, "Effects of a US Foreign Military Aid Program," ORE 41-49, February 24, 1949, Appendix A, p. 3. NAMM.
[111] Grady to Marshall, December 7, 1948, FR, 1948, 4: 212.

individuals ran through American policy papers. As Acheson cabled MacVeagh in October 1946,

> US would find it difficult to support strongly any govt by means of which Extreme Right would resort to excessive measures against political opposition expressed through legal and peaceful means or to repression of civil liberties. . . . Proper Greek authorities should be made to understand Dept's view that measures for internal order have not been impartially applied . . . but have instead encouraged lawlessness of the Extreme Right.

In conclusion, the cable declared that "certain notoriously reactionary Rightists" were responsible for "objectionable features of present Govt policy and should be removed from power for the good of the Greek people as a whole."[112] This cable was followed by many more, none of which did any good. To the contrary, the administration was soon justifying or hiding government and government-sanctioned mass arrests, torture, concentration camps, exilings, and summary executions.

The need for United States aid if Greece was to become a "self-respecting democracy" constituted a major rationale for PL 75. Truman, Acheson, and others denied that it signaled approval of Greece's political failings and asserted that American aid would create the conditions "in which the Greek Government can . . . perfect its democratic processes."[113] In Greece, however, the Right applied the new resources to old-fashioned Greek winner-take-all politics of the most violent kind. The government purged the civil service and military, and anybody suspected of republican or leftist leanings was jailed or exiled.[114] In the countryside, rightist mobs lynched suspected leftists, and home guard units murdered others to collect the official bounty for the killing of "bandits." In March a member of the still legal KKE Central Committee was assassinated at noon on a main street in Salonika, and a month later thugs began systematically shooting up "leftist" neighborhoods. In March, too, General Zervas, former head of EDES and now Minister of Public Safety, began a three year campaign of mass arrests. Thousands were banned to desolate islands and more fled to neighboring countries: 25,000 to Yugoslavia; 5,000 to Bulgaria; and 23,000 to Albania.[115] In short, the right took American support to eliminate or intimidate all other contenders, not to form a more perfect union.

[112] October 15, 1946, FR, 1946, 7: 237.
[113] Testimony of Acheson to the Senate Foreign Relations Committee, March 24, 1947, in "Aid to Greece and Turkey," pp. 851–52.
[114] Clogg, *Short History*, p. 168.
[115] Wittner, *American Intervention*, p. 137; Woodhouse, *Struggle for Greece*, pp. 209,

In the face of rightist violence, American leverage proved worthless. Indeed, policymakers were soon drawn willy-nilly into condoning it. As early as mid-1947, Ambassador MacVeagh was insisting that the Greek government "cannot be blamed" for "widespread preventative measures" because of the seriousness of the Communist threat.[116] Similarly, MacVeagh's successor objected to efforts to limit executions since this would "play directly into Soviet hands" and leave untouched the Communist "hard core for future attempts." In fact, he argued, the task should be "to see that nothing prevents Greeks from finishing job well started."[117] Acting Secretary of State Robert Lovett declared that regardless of Greek "lack [of] cooperation," the United States had to "maintain facade of confidence." As the American chargé in Athens insisted, "we can hardly do less than give Greece . . . the kind of support that the cheering section would give their football team if they truly desired victory."[118] The Greeks took this cheering to heart; as a Greek military propaganda leaflet dropped at this time declared: "Bandits! The time has come for you to pay. . . . The revenge will be great and complete. . . . I foretell you this because I have the power of our great country and our great allies, Americans and British."[119]

At home, where the American public received accurate reports of the Greek government's behavior, policymakers attempted to suppress negative press reports or denied the problem. Thus, Ambassador Grady told Congress that reports of arrests, executions, and exilings were "half-truths, distortions of the truth, and down-right lies originating in the propaganda mill of the Kremlin." It was, he said, just a "Big Lie" to discredit the Greek government.[120] Similarly, despite copious OSS and CIA evidence to the contrary, Acting Secretary of State Bohlen dismissed criticism of a "bond of sympathy between the present Greek government and the former Nazi regime or any similarity in their judicial methods" as "wholly unwarranted."[121]

When such denial was insufficient, the government tried other means. Washington bombarded Athens with requests that, for public relations purposes, they be less open about excesses. While in Washing-

---

226; and United Nation, "Report by the Commission of Investigation," pp. 174–79, 231–32.

[116] FR, 1947, 5: 260–61.

[117] Grady to Marshall, August 21, 1948, FR, 1948, 4: 139–40.

[118] Lovett to Embassy Athens, October 30, 1948, ibid., p. 178; and Rankin to the Department of State, April 8, 1948, cited in Wittner, "Defense of Freedom," p. 168.

[119] Cited in Wittner, American Intervention, pp. 152–53.

[120] "Statement on Military Aid to Greece," DSB (August 15, 1949), p. 234.

[121] Bohlen to Vandenberg, April 11, 1948, FR, 1948, 4: 75.

ton to testify in support of PL 75, for example, Ambassador MacVeagh cabled Prime Minister Maximos that though those "in authority realize fully . . . that drastic measures are necessary" but "they are being embarrassed, and the success of the President's proposals is being imperiled, by . . . reports of official toleration of rightist excesses and the application of security measures to non-subversive political opponents of the government."[122] Similarly, Secretary of State Marshall cabled Athens that although "we consider [executions] essential component [of] any plan eventually to restore tranquillity within Greece, simple political expediency requires all executions to be held to absolute minimum pending termination [UN] General Assembly meeting."[123] Finally, policymakers justified Greek government actions. Ambassador Grady explained, for example, that regular executions had been "forced" on the Greek state "in self-protection" against "criminal elements."[124] Acheson commented later, "The only question we should ask is whether they are determined to protect their independence against Communist aggression, and if they are we should recognize our basic unity with them."[125]

INTRAGOVERNMENTAL CONSTRAINTS

The will and capacity of a target government for reform is also critical to U.S. leverage and achievement of the three great oughts. Greece had neither. As for will, Americans were led astray by the unfounded assumption that Greek politicians and military officers had the interests of the nation at heart. Moreover, policymakers assumed that they shared their own assessment of Greece's predicament and the requirements for correcting it. In particular, they assumed that Greek leaders desired and saw the need for an open political system. In fact, they considered such a system antithetical to their interests and wanted nothing to do with it.

The consequences of such crossed purposes show clearly in the derailment of the good government ought. Technical elements of quantitative prescriptions did receive attention, and the Greeks welcomed American aid in professionalizing the bureaucracy. Even here there were problems, however, since Americans assumed that the new state

[122] MacVeagh to Maximos, April 11, 1947, cited in Wittner, "Defense of Freedom," p. 163.

[123] August 6, 1948, FR, 1948, 4: 118–19. See also Marshall to Embassy Athens, March 9, 1948, ibid., pp. 59–60.

[124] Grady to Marshall, August 21, 1948, FR, 1948, 4: 140.

[125] "The Task of Today's Diplomacy," address to the Advertising Council February 16, 1950, in Department of State, General Foreign Policy Series, No. 21, p. 5.

machinery would be apolitical and serve the interests of all. Instead, those in power employed the stronger administrative apparatus to impose their will more effectively than had been possible with the previous weak bureaucracy. As for the qualitative prescriptions, no action was taken at all. Formal elections did go ahead, allowing the government to claim democratic credentials and thus the right to American support. But as then CBS chief European correspondent Howard K. Smith reported, "With all power and armed force in the hands of the right and with the countryside under the terror of . . . rightist bands, the Greek peasant was in no mood to be heroic."[126] Nor was the Right in a mood to relinquish the hold it had finally achieved, expecially because the loss of control would result in leftist purges no less ferocious than its own. Thus, the government showed no will to reform along the lines suggested by the good government ought. To the contrary, leaders ignored all American efforts to promote responsive government and under the guise of "national security" physically eliminated opposition.

Many Americans blamed Greek leaders' venality for their own failed expectations. But such explanations are misleading. They suggest that either "the right man" could have fixed things or, conversely, there were no honorable or capable men (for had there been men of honor, none of this would have happened). The disdain expressed by Americans in their cables is striking, but besides being insulting such an understanding of Greek politics was superficial; it ignored *capacity*. Thus, policymakers insisted that Greek leaders set aside their bickering and unite to defeat the insurgency, but the insurgency was just one of many problems facing the Greeks, and often not the most pressing. In fact, the ability to face the insurgency depended on the prior solution of the problems posed by coalition management. But these could be attained only at the expense of the oughts Americans insisted were essential.

The problem was the weakness of democratic forces in the ruling coalition and the capacity of certain coalition members to impose their aims on the government as a whole. As the CIA noted, "The National Assembly, as such, has had little influence on political events, for the continuance in office of a cabinet has depended on agreement among a few political leaders rather than on a marshaling of voting strength."[127] Moreover, observed Howard K. Smith, elected officials in Athens were "mere figureheads. . . . Real power lies in the bureaucracy, the army and the police, and nothing has been done to purge these instruments of even the most vengeful pro-Nazis not to mention the reaction-

[126] Howard K. Smith, *The State of Europe* (New York: Knopf, 1951), p. 235.
[127] CIA, "Greece," SR-10, March 1948, p. I-5.

ary monarchists."[128] Similarly, the government could neither pass nor implement needed economic reforms. In June 1945, the Minister of Supply, Professor Varvaressos, attempted a bold program to devalue the drachma, control wages, prices and distribution of relief supplies, eliminate the black market, and reform the tax system. The effort failed entirely, and Varvaressos resigned in September, disgusted with a government unwilling and unable to confront resistance by the civil service and commercial classes.[129] Two years later, Paul Porter, too, condemned a "small mercantile and banking cabal" that "is determined above all to protect its financial prerogative, at whatever expense to the economic health of the country."[130] Even in 1949, Prime Minister Sophoulis still complained that the government could not "take the proper measures against the economic and political oligarchy of the country."[131] The stakes of personal survival and regime maintenance were too high.

The consequences of such intragovernmental constraints for American policy show starkly in the case of the Greek National Army (GNA). Policymakers thought aid would be used against the insurgency and professionalization would lead the military out of politics. But the primary concerns of Greek officers were political, not military. Just as during the Second World War SAN preferred politicizing to fighting, so, too, after the war it solidified its political base before turning to the insurgents; and just as the British had guaranteed defeat of the Germans, so, too, the United States now guaranteed defeat of the insurgents. Relieved of concern about martial ability, SAN could insist on loyalty over merit in officer selection. This removed from the army virtually all officers with battlefield experience, since officers who had fought in the resistance were politically suspect. As a result, the GNA was so ill-led it could not defeat the guerrillas on the battlefield despite outnumbering them 263,000 to 23,000.[132] Thus, the GNA confined itself to attacking their civilian supporters and other unarmed political opponents.

GOVERNMENT-POPULATION RELATIONS

Mistaken assumptions concerning the Greek government's relationship to its subjects also diverted American programs from their intended ends. Policymakers defined the Greek government as legitimate,

---

[128] Smith, *State of Europe*, p. 225.

[129] Woodhouse, *Struggle for Greece*, p. 146.

[130] Paul Porter, "Wanted: A Miracle in Greece," *Collier's* (September 20, 1947), p. 106.

[131] *New York Times*, January 18, 1949.

[132] Wittner, *American Intervention*, p. 233.

assumed it embodied a normative order shared by the majority of Greeks, and believed it was dedicated to reconstruction and economic development. Thus, they assumed, too, that more government would result in better government—more efficient delivery of more services—which would raise popular welfare, increase support for the government, and reduce that for the insurgents. Finally, they argued, since government excesses were the result of bad conditions, improved conditions would also improve the quality of government.

But Greek leaders had rather different ideas. Greece had long been a deeply divided society, and governments on neither side of the cleavage had ever shown interest in a rapprochement. The rightist-controlled governments of the immediate postwar period were no exception. Moreover, they also shared a long-standing belief that politics was a matter of control from the top. Therefore, they showed no interest in improving the quality of the lives of citizens; instead, they sought more effective control of the citizenry through the elimination of alternatives, more effective, deeper penetration of their power into the periphery, and the selective provision of relief supplies.[133] Indeed, the government's lack of concern for its citizens was so blatant that JUSMAPG chief General Van Fleet once admitted to a reporter that "the economic and social system . . . sometimes makes him feel like a communist."[134]

This disjunction between American assumptions and Greek realities badly damaged the American program. Considering the security ought, American aid targeted Communist guerrillas, but GNA and paramilitary operations often targeted nonrightist citizens, many of them innocent of insurgent connections. American aid may even have increased the frequency of such attacks by improving the GNA's mobility, size, and capabilities. Second, prescriptions to improve the quality of government-populace relations came to naught, while improvements in the quantity of government simply increased government's ability to impose its will. Finally, governing elites showed no interest in economic development that would either distribute wealth or better integrate the peasant periphery into the national economy and, by extension, national politics. To the contrary, they intended to provide relief aid to surmount the crisis without risking broader participation. As the Deputy Director of the ECA bluntly informed the State Department that "the Greek Government and its representatives . . . have persistently

[133] Ibid., p. 37.
[134] General Van Fleet comment to Cyrus Sulzberger, quoted in Sulzberger, *A Long Row of Candles: Memoirs and Diaries, 1934–1954* (New York: Macmillan, 1969), p. 501.

refused to cooperate wholeheartedly in the work of this organiza-tion."[135]

How They Won

What remains to be explained is how the Greek government won while contravening all the supposed oughts laid down by American policy-makers. Before explaining, it is necessary to dispose of three important but fortuitous considerations. First, in 1948 the insurgents switched from guerrilla tactics to positional warfare. In so doing, they squan-dered their advantages, and maximized the GNA's strengths. This quickened their demise but did not cause it. Second, Tito decided to close the Yugoslav border to the guerrillas in July 1949. Here is a tac-tical lesson: counterinsurgents must eliminate sanctuaries, and insur-gents require them to succeed. But focusing on this point obscures the issues behind the border closing and the role of the Macedonian question in the defeat of the insurgency (described later in this section). Third, analysts tend to exaggerate the role of American military assist-ance. It was essential in expanding the Greek armed forces from 90,000 in 1946 to more than 260,000 by the end of 1948. But, as diplomatic and military observers pointed out, in the face of never more than 25,000 guerrillas, the issue was not numbers but leadership—to which American aid made no contribution. Moreover, according to the *Ma-rine Corps Gazette*, U.S. aid "came too late to have any material effect during the war," and "in all probability the war would have ended where it ended and when it ended had no changes in armaments oc-curred."[136]

The real lessons of the Greek insurgency lie in characteristics of the government, the insurgent leadership, and their contest for support. Considering the government, the key was the military's achievement of its de facto control. Initially, military performance suffered from the of-ficer corps purges, uncontrolled use of the military for private pur-poses, meddling by politicians eager to have their interests protected ir-respective of strategic requirements, and constant breeches of security. Then two things changed. First, in response to a devastating critique by highly successful General Tsakalotos, the armed forces cleaned house. Incompetent officers were removed, offensive spirit was rewarded, and merit was again given weight in promotion decisions (admittedly in an

---

[135] Bruce to Lovett, October 15, 1948, cited in Wittner, *American Intervention*, p. 185.
[136] J. C. Murray, "The Anti-Bandit War: Part II," *Marine Corps Gazette* 38 (February 1954), pp. 57–58.

officer corps of unblushingly rightist orientation).[137] Second, on becoming commander-in-chief in January 1949 General Papagos received "complete control of planning, order of battle, appointments and operations; no interference by the allied missions; martial law throughout the country with strict censorship; and command over the Navy, Air Force and Gendarmerie as well as the Army." [138] In effect, by supplanting political control the military was depoliticized. No longer subject to the paralyzing constraints of coalition management, decisive action was possible. Papagos's orders were neither innovative nor politically sensitive, but they were carried out to the letter.

This bootstrap elevation cannot be viewed in isolation, however. Without guerrilla weaknesses, simple military action would have failed. Ironically, the guerrillas began the war with all the advantages. In fact, initially they enjoyed a marked tactical edge over the GNA. From supporters around the country, the guerrillas received a steady flow of intelligence, supplies, and recruits; until 1948, even in the areas of manpower and equipment, they compared favorably to the GNA since the army's heavy equipment was useless in the mountains and logistics diverted government manpower.[139] But long-term guerrilla success depended on the ability to motivate sufficient popular support to maintain the flows of recruits, intelligence, and supplies. The KKE, however, had no program for the future relevant to the peasants' problems. Instead, the KKE, like the government, sought simply to control the rural population. Despite their dependence on the countryside, the KKE remained committed to a traditional urban proletariat orientation; for the peasantry this merely substituted one form of urban-based control for another. In October 1945, the KKE actually decided to dismantle its structure in the countryside, a move which, as an exmember noted, "disorganized the Party in the rural areas at a time when all its branches should have been strengthened in every way."[140]

Without a rural program capable of motivating popular support, the KKE was reduced to an effort to out-coerce the government. From the beginning, the guerrilla leadership used terror to get support and pursued what one senior KKE official later called "the policy of devastation of the countryside."[141] The KKE, in effect, fought a war on civilians, not

[137] Woodhouse, *Struggle for Greece*, pp. 238, 246.
[138] Ibid., p. 247.
[139] Lt. Col. Edward Wainhouse, "Guerrilla War in Greece, 1946–1949: A Case Study," *MR* 37: 3 (June 1957), p. 22; and Woodhouse, *Struggle for Greece*, pp. 184, 188.
[140] Zizis Zographos, referring to the 7th Party Congress, cited in John Ellis, *A Short History of Guerrilla Warfare* (New York: St. Martin's Press, 1976), p. 172.
[141] Cited in Woodhouse, *Struggle for Greece*, p. 267.

on the GNA. It was an uneven contest in which the guerrillas could win only as long as internal weaknesses constrained the GNA and terror could generate sufficient supplies and manpower. Thus, in November 1948, KKE military leader Markos reported that "since the middle of 1947 recruitment . . . was achieved almost entirely by force."[142] Although such methods produced stable force levels through mid-1948, the quality of guerrilla forces declined rapidly. By early 1949, losses outpaced gains four to one.[143] Terror did not suffice to raise an army.

The guerrilla leadership's failure to develop a political program to motivate forces allowed both the Greek government's victory without one, and General Papagos's success through a blunt, military strategy. This failure, far more than the final, mistaken shift to conventional tactics, doomed the insurgency. Indeed, the switch to positional warfare only confirmed the KKE leadership's belief that the population was the object of conflict, not a source and actor in it. Without a positive political program, the guerrillas faced a simple, brutal contest with the government to control the populace. Given the government's far greater coercive capabilities, the guerrillas lost.

One final question requires attention: the role of Macedonian issues in government success and insurgent failure. There are practical reasons for Macedonia's part in the insurgency. Greater Macedonia—which borders Albania, Yugoslavia, and Bulgaria—provided sanctuary, support, and supplies. As a result, the insurgency was naturally stronger there than in the south. Thus, too, guerrilla forces were heavily Slavo-Macedonian, not Greek, and became more so as defeats in the south raised the proportional representation of Slavo-Macedonians still higher.[144] But considerations of geography and access to sanctuary should not obscure the more important political dynamics of the Macedonian problem.

For many Greeks, border disputes with Slavic neighbors to the north have traditionally rallied nationalist sentiment, irrespective of the regime in power. Discrimination against Slavo-Macedonians is also traditional and flourished after the war. In fact, government and government-sanctioned attacks on Slavo-Macedonians probably exceeded those perpetrated elsewhere and contributed to the exodus of 48,000 Greeks (most of them Slavo-Macedonians) to Albania, Bulgaria, and Yugoslavia where they formed the manpower pool of the insur-

[142] Cited in Kousoulas, *Revolution and Defeat*, p. 252.

[143] Woodhouse, *Struggle for Greece*, p. 263.

[144] In early 1948, Slavo Macedonians constituted 44 percent of guerrilla forces. By mid-1949 they were 70 percent. Ibid., p. 262.

gency.[145] The resulting combination of anti-Slavic sentiment and identification of the insurgency with the Macedonian problem led many to see the insurgency in nationalist terms and to fall in behind the government. The redefinition of the insurgency as a nationalist issue and not a civil war also reduced the political saliency of many offensive government actions, increased its legitimacy, and delegitimized the insurgents, even among many deeply opposed to the regime.

If identification of the insurgency with the Macedonian question helped the government, it posed serious problems for the insurgents. On the one hand, they needed bases in Macedonia to secure their supply lines. On the other, the priority given Macedonia implied a treasonous intent to violate Greece's territorial integrity for traditional enemies. This presented particular difficulties for the KKE. Since the early nineteenth century, control of Macedonia had pitted Greek against Bulgarian against Yugoslav. The involvement of the KKE in the Comintern-sponsored Balkan Communist Federation did little to ease tensions, since the member parties reflected the territorial aspirations of their respective states. The Soviet Union played on this tendency by offering Macedonia to whichever party was currently in favor. Thus, beginning in the 1920s, the KKE faced the problems of Macedonia not only as an issue in Greece but also as one in an intracommunist struggle involving issues of no concern to Greeks, the resolution of which were beyond their control. Still, the KKE followed the Comintern line and championed an independent Macedonian state; consequently, most Greeks branded it traitorous. In 1935, the KKE relaxed its public position in order to improve the standing of the United Front and continued the policy into the war to protect the KKE's position in EAM. Public suspicions continued, however, and with good reason.[146]

In short, Macedonia posed two insurmountable problems for the insurgent leadership. First, the insurgency's attachment to a traitorous, sectional cause reduced its popular appeal, despite widespread hatred for the government, and indeed led many opponents of the regime to support efforts to squelch it. As a result, too, the government was free to act in ways it could not have if the salient issues had been closer to the economic and political mainstream. Second, dependence upon Yugoslavia and Bulgaria necessarily involved the insurgent leadership in the Stalin-Tito struggle which erupted in the summer of 1948.[147]

[145] UN, "Report by the Commission of Investigation," pp. 171–79.

[146] Kousoulas, *Revolution and Defeat*, pp. 54–70; and Woodhouse, *Struggle for Greece*, p. 50.

[147] The following is based on Wittner, *American Intervention*, chapter 9, and Woodhouse, *Struggle for Greece*, chapters 9 and 10.

Ironically, especially given the American assumption that the insurgency was Moscow's doing, a major bone of contention was Stalin's insistence that Tito cease supporting the insurgency because it threatened his relations with the West.[148] The KKE was in a trap, forced to choose between their sanctuaries and Stalin. The KKE attempted to negotiate with Athens first, but when they were rebuffed the leadership split. Vafiades Markos, military leader of the insurgent forces, opted for Tito, and KKE party chief Nikos Zachariades for Stalin. Zachariades then attempted to have Markos murdered. When this failed, he had him removed as military leader and purged his supporters and all those loyal to Tito from the KKE and guerrilla forces. At the same time, Zachariades proclaimed KKE support for an autonomous Macedonia independent of both Yugoslavia and Greece and tied to the Soviet Union. This both broke the morale of the remaining guerrilla forces and finally spurred Tito to abandon the insurgents in return for British and American support against Stalin. He closed the border in July 1949. The insurgency was over.

CONCLUSION

Returning to the comparison of alternative explanations of foreign policy, the Greek case demonstrates both the strengths and limits of each. From a realist perspective, American policy in the Eastern Mediterranean shows a growing recognition of power politics such that when the British withdrew the United States was primed to step in. Presidential politics analysis explains why Truman felt obliged to "scare hell" out of the American people to generate support for the course realism recommended, and hence the dramatic burst of activity unleashed by the Truman Doctrine, its crusading tone, and the reversal of traditional American policy it occasioned. While these approaches point to the importance of Greece, bureaucratic politics analysis explains why policy implementation was often bungled and why, instead of playing as a team, different elements of the American mission often fought each other. But even together, these analyses leave unanswered questions about policy content, the accuracy of policymakers' assessments, and the utility of their prescriptions. These issues are the concern of the cognitive content approach.

Here, contrary to myth, we find not an American success, but an American failure. In fact, the Greek case challenges the utility of coun-

[148] Vladimir Dedijer, *Tito* (New York: Simon and Schuster, 1953), pp. 292–93, 322; and Milovan Djilas, *Conversations with Stalin* (New York: Harcourt, Brace and World, 1962), pp. 181–82.

terinsurgency doctrine both for an outside supplier of assistance to threatened governments and for the governments themselves. On the one hand, doctrine obscured the insurgency's critical features, distorted American perceptions of it, and offered irrelevant or counterproductive prescriptions. Thus, American aid strengthened the Right and the military in Greek politics, but did little to defeat the insurgency. On the other, the Greek government flouted American prescriptions. It did not improve government-population relations, promote development, or control the death squads. It won by brute force. And it was able to do so because of the weaknesses of the insurgent movement, weaknesses undetected by American analysis.

The failure of understanding had serious consequences. It hid the real reasons for the Greek victory and thus smothered the lessons that might have been drawn had events not been misunderstood. Conversely, the mistaken notions underlying American policy would not have been confirmed, reinforced, and perpetuated as universal lessons for indiscriminate application around the world. As a disillusioned Ambassador MacVeagh wrote his brother, "I hope very much that . . . the mistakes made in the guinea pig experiment of Greece will not be repeated on a larger scale, but the auguries don't seem too good."[149] He was right.

[149] *Ambassador MacVeagh Reports*, pp. 733–34 fn.

8

THE PHILIPPINES:
MAGSAYSAY'S MIRACLE

The campaign against the Hukbalahap, or Huks, is the second supposed counterinsurgency success story of the postwar period. Three features distinguish it from the Greek case. First, the Philippines had just gained independence from the United States for which the victory was thus doubly critical: to prove that Communist threats could be defeated in the periphery, the likely battleground of the postwar; and to substantiate American claims to reluctant allies that decolonization, not recolonization, was the wise course. Second, Ramon Magsaysay's winning policies resembled the three oughts more closely than anything undertaken by the Greeks. Third, because the Huks mobilized broad popular support by providing solutions to peasant problems they posed a bigger challenge than the KKE and forced the government, too, to address citizen needs in order to win.

But it is the similarities that command attention, especially concerning the lessons drawn from the Huk defeat. Victory seemed to prove that even in the periphery insurgencies could be dealt with at arm's length and low cost by means of limited economic and military aid, political tutelage, cajolery, and occasional tough talk. To these, victory in the Philippines also added the importance of the "right man" and "responsible statesmanship" to overcome petty politics and effect "reform in crisis."

But American involvement in the Philippines, as in Greece, is less a success story than a cautionary tale. Again, the Huks were defeated, and insofar as this served American interests, the United States benefited. Viewed in terms of American policy, however, the picture is bleak. Policymakers misunderstood the roots of the insurgency in government-populace relations and the intragovernment constraints on reform. Thus, prior to Magsaysay's rise to power, American policies were ignored or subverted. Subsequently, policymakers misunderstood the circumstances which allowed Magsaysay to succeed and thus attributed victory to American initiatives. This, however, overstated the utility of American programs, understated the limits that constrained them, and obscured the local sources of the conflict and its resolution.

CHAPTER 8

BACKGROUND TO REVOLT

Most analysts view the Huk insurgency as the product of immiseration exploited by Communist organizers. Philippine government problems are dismissed as mere political immaturity such that the only link between rebellion and government is governmental inability to provide for citizens' needs or suppress subversive threats to its authority. Yet poverty and weak government characterized the Philippines as a whole, while the Huk insurgency was confined to Central Luzon. Understanding the situation requires analysis of how American colonialism transformed Central Luzon and how peasants and landlords responded. Indeed, the rebellion cannot be understood without reference to American colonialism, nor can the Huks and government be discussed without reference to one another. Their relationship explains Huk motivations, government policies, and the limited choices each possessed for responding to the other.[1]

Two consequences of American colonialism stand out. On the one hand, the commercialization of agriculture that accompanied colonization exposed peasants to greater economic risk, while it gave landlords a disproportionate share of newly available resources and thus reduced peasant bargaining power dramatically. On the other, the legal and administrative institutions of the colonial government offered peasants new means with which to offset the erosion of power caused by commercialization. Conversely, the Filipinos trained to run this new government were those against whom peasants sought to defend themselves. In response, the peasants of Central Luzon organized to counter landlord control of government. When politics failed, their organizations provided the foundation for the Huk insurgency while their absence elsewhere explains the lack of coordinated peasant protest outside Central Luzon.

Prior to Philippine integration into the American economy, landlord-tenant relations were confined to the local community. Tenants, while distinctly weaker, could expect 70 percent of their crops and landlord help in bad times. In return, the landlords controlled the key to economic and political power—people, the essential resource in a country where land was far more available than farmers. But the commercialization of agriculture and rising population changed all this. Between 1900 and 1939 the population in Central Luzon doubled, producing a serious land shortage. Rents rose to 50 percent of a farmer's crop, many small freeholders lost their land, and peasant incomes fell to subsist-

---

[1] The following draws heavily on Benedict Kerkvliet, *The Huk Rebellion: A Study of Peasant Revolt in the Philippines* (Berkeley: University of California Press, 1977).

ence levels or lower. At the same time, as American administration and improved transportation promoted market integration, the locus of political and economic power shifted outward. Landlord dependence on the peasants declined, and as it did they eliminated the traditional services once provided. Sugar and rice production soared, but, since production practices were neither modernized nor intensified, this expansion came from the extension of cultivation and the reduction of peasants' share of the crop.[2]

American colonial authorities observed the peasantry's decline and attempted to reverse it. Their efforts seldom helped, however, and often produced unintended negative consequences. Initially, the United States attacked the land problem by purchasing church estates for resale to peasants. But few tenants benefited because members of the local elite bought most of the land.[3] Similarly, a cadastral survey intended to "rationalize" landholdings, land law, and the land tax system replaced traditional peasant rights to land with legal titles issued to landowners. With this, the courts replaced peasant-landlord bargaining mechanisms for resolution of tenure and rent disputes. Here the landowners profited from their greater capacity to manipulate the system, "fix" land titles, and evict peasant freeholders.[4]

The large landowners did more than manipulate the colonial government: they *became* the government. "As the Americans gradually enlarged the sphere of local government," INR observed, "the landlords . . . gradually acquired a near monopoly of political power."[5] By 1935, when the Philippine Commonwealth raised its flag, offices from the presidency down were filled by large landowners. The most important assets this gave landlords were the courts, police, and Philippine Constabulary (PC). As political appointees, local judges were either beholden to landlords in their districts or were landowners themselves. Thus, the landlords could squelch tenant protests and sabotage implementation of American supported rent, usruy, and tenancy control laws. As for the municipal police, explained J. R. Hayden, a former vice governor, they were the "political henchmen" of the local bosses and were often "the instruments of oppression rather than the agents of the law."[6] In the countryside, the PC guarded landlords' fields, attacked tenant organizations, and generally did the landlords' bidding.

[2] Department of State, Office of Intelligence Research, "The Hukbalahap," OIR Report No. 5209, September 27, 1950, pp. 3–4. DDRS, 1979: 200B.

[3] Ibid., p. 2.

[4] Kerkvliet, *Huk Rebellion*, pp. 22, 36.

[5] "The Hukbalahap," p. 3.

[6] Cited in OSS, "Law Enforcement in the Philippine Islands," R and A Report No. 2330, September 25, 1944, p. 47. NADB, OSS file.

In the face of economic decline and rising landlord control of government, the peasants of Central Luzon counterorganized. In this they were unique and remarkably successful. Although they ultimately failed, the organizational legacy of the 1930s proved critical later. It provided the basis for resistance against the Japanese, the Huk insurgency, and political reintegration under President Magsaysay.

During the 1930s, Central Luzon saw many types of peasant response to declining power and welfare. There were several short-lived uprisings and bouts of rural banditry. More important were such organizations as the General Workers' Union (AMT) and the National Society of Peasants in the Philippines (KPMP). By decade's end, they had wide support and thousands of members. The KPMP, for example, rallied over 15,000 peasants in a May 1939 strike and a year later over 40,000.[7] These were reformist organizations which sought to ameliorate the costs of commercialization and colonization: debt, high interest rates, and falling incomes. At the village level, their leaders focused on consciousness raising and articulation of local grievances, while at the same time they sought to link local peasant groups to those in other areas, making possible large scale protests and political action. At the national level, the organizations found lawyers to represent peasants in the courts and before administrative agencies, and they became active in party politics. In middecade, AMT, KPMP and others joined the Popular Front to back candidates representing peasant interests. By 1940, they ran a full slate of candidates in several Central Luzon provinces and won many mayoral and town councillor races.

Despite these gains (and possibly because of them), landowner-tenant relations went from bad to worse, and violence became endemic. Problems occurred throughout the Philippines, indicating the widespread incidence of agrarian grievances. But more than 70 percent of the total incidents occurred in Central Luzon, evidence of the higher degree of peasant organization and correspondingly greater government and landowner counterefforts.[8] These took several forms. Landowners reduced their need for tenant farmers through mechanization, hired "civil guards" to attack peasant unions, and counterorganized to fight peasant efforts to use the courts and administrative agencies against them.[9] Landlord organizations also promoted "company unions" of

[7] For a description of the organizations, their interests and tactics, see Kerkvliet, *Huk Rebellion*, pp. 26–60.

[8] Ibid., Table 7, pp. 40–41.

[9] In 1937, for example, those in one area formed an "Association of Landowners" "to protect their interests and to get united action in case of litigation arising out of the Land

farm workers and organized the supply of strikebreakers from other, unorganized regions. The largest of them, the Knights of Peace, was led by the Governor of the Central Luzon province of Pampanga and had Manila's support as it attacked AMT and KPMP. Where all else failed, the Commonwealth government used the "mailed fist": it strengthened PC forces in Central Luzon, imposed martial law, and on occasion ordered the PC to take over municipal police forces to deprive Popular Front mayors and town councils of the means to resist landlord attacks on peasant organizations.[10]

War, Resistance, Liberation, Insurgency

Soon after Bataan's fall, several guerrilla groups took up arms against the Japanese. Ironically, the largest of these was not made up of the biggest beneficiaries of American colonial rule—the landed business and political elites. Instead, resistance to the Japanese came from the peasant farmers of Central Luzon, from the *Hukbo Ng Bayan Laban Sa Hapon*, or People's Army (to Fight) Against Japan, called the Hukbalahap or simply "the Huks." Officially formed on March 29, 1942, the Huk movement grew out of discussions begun in December 1941. Included in these talks, under the nominal chairmanship of the Communist Party of the Philippines or PKP, were leaders of such groups as the Civil Liberties Union, Popular Front Party, KPMP, AMT, and other peasant and labor organizations. They agreed to form a United Front to direct resistance against the Japanese and established a military committee to raise a resistance army. Chosen to head the military committee were Casto Alejandrino and Luis Taruc. Both were PKP members, but, more important, both had long been active in peasant organizations in Central Luzon.

The United Front represented a unique event in the Philippines, a joining of the urban political left and the peasant movements. But despite the visibility of the former, peasant organizations provided the core. For as all recognized, resistance required a broad-based movement with deep popular roots and thus depended on the organized, mobilized peasantry of Central Luzon. And once formed, it grew rapidly there. In April 1942, Huk forces stood at less than three hundred. Five months later, they had grown tenfold and by 1944 numbered between ten thousand and twelve thousand. Of these, 75 to 90 percent came

---

Tenancy Act [of 1936]." Similar organizations sprang up across Central Luzon. Ibid., p. 55.

[10] Ibid., p. 55–58.

from the five Central Luzon provinces of Bulacan, Nueva Ecija, Pampanga, Tarlac, and Laguna.[11]

The Huk's rapid growth in Central Luzon can be understood only as an exaggeration of prewar trends. Upon arrival, the Japanese established tight ties with the Philippine elite. "With few exceptions," reported the CIA, "the leading figures in the Philippines accepted and vied for positions of responsibility in the Philippine Executive Committee and the 'Philippine Republic' [the puppet government]. . . . In the economic sphere, many leading businessmen assisted the Japanese by making materiel and supplies available to the Japanese Army and Navy."[12] No less important, government and administrative organs lost their remaining autonomy as the Japanese offered full support to the landlords in the extraction of rice and sugar, including troops to assist the civil guards, police, and PC.[13] Peasants thus confronted a more serious version of the problems they had faced in the 1930s, but without the courts and other peaceful means with which they had defended themselves.

They turned to the Hukbalahap and the organizations they had built during the 1930s. Their function then had been to organize collective self-defense and, in the words of one peasant, "Now, more than ever, we needed to protect ourselves: from the Japanese, from the PC and police, and from bandits."[14] Thus, like its predecessors, the Huk movement articulated common grievances concerning rents, interest rates, evictions, and repression, and sought to turn them into collective action. As INR reported later, "Under the guidance and protection of the Huks, the Central Luzon peasant began to take action to remedy these ills. Ignoring prewar sharecropping arrangements, the peasant kept the entire harvest of the rice fields, after supplying the Huks, instead of supplying the Japanese as ordered by the landlords."[15] More than simply undertaking guerrilla actions, however, the Huks also developed solutions to peasant problems and, despite the war, demonstrated the possibilities for a better life as no previous organizations had.

Against this backdrop, it is important not to ignore the PKP. Communists figured prominently in the Huk leadership, played a critical role in founding the United Front, and supplied much of the Huks'

[11] Ibid., p. 87.
[12] CIA, "Possible Developments Resulting from the Granting of Amnesty to Accused Collaborators in the Philippines," Enclosure A: "Collaboration in the Philippines," ORE 11–48, April 28, 1948, p. 4. NAMM, CIA file.
[13] "Law Enforcement in the Philippine Islands," p. iii.
[14] Cited in Kerkvliet, *Huk Rebellion*, p. 67.
[15] "The Hukbalahap," p. 16.

early capacity for clandestine operations. The Hukbalahap was not primarily a Communist organization, however. The PKP was urban-based, and, although it had had limited contacts with peasant organizations during the 1930s, "radical labor leaders furnished all of the initiatives in the founding of the PKP and the bulk of the early Party leadership."[16] But in the words of Luis Taruc, PKP member and leader of the insurgency, "The resistance movement that sprang up in Central Luzon was unique. . . . The decisive element of difference lay in the strong peasant unions and organization of the people that existed there before the war. It gave the [Huks] a mass base, and made the armed forces indistinguishable from the people."[17] Because the PKP lacked prewar roots in Central Luzon, it neither led nor contributed substantially to rural resistance. Indeed, prior mobilization of the Central Luzon peasantry around their own problems forced the PKP to tailor its program to them, rather than shape peasant interests to the party program.

Liberation and independence dawned cold in the Philippines. Postwar problems began as the returning Americans allied themselves with Filipinos whose wartime credentials were lackluster at best. Landlords and other political elites switched sides with liberation. They convinced the American Counter-Intelligence Corps (CIC) that they, not the Huks, had been the loyal resistance and wrangled appointments as acting mayors, chiefs of police, and town councillors until the 1947 elections. They also convinced Americans that the Huks were but a wing of the PKP. This led Americans to ignore the underlying dynamics of the movement: if peasants belonged to the Huks, it was because of Communist coercion, not self-interest. "So ironclad is their grip and so feared is their power," reported Major Edward Lansdale (then chief of military intelligence), "that the peasants dare not oppose them."[18] Thus, American MP detachments were doubled, placed under the jurisdiction of the Philippines Interior Department, and ordered to raid peasant meetings, break strikes and arrest ex-Huks. Beginning in January 1946 the United States also supplied the police forces of Central Luzon and other government security forces, while the U.S. Army paid and equipped landlords' private armies. The aid gave landlords and their political allies coercive capabilities never before imagined.

Peasant alienation deepened with American support for Manuel Roxas's candidacy for the presidency of the soon to be independent Philippines. Roxas, a prewar politician of note, had served the Japanese

[16] Department of State, Office of Intelligence Research, "The Philippine Communist Party," IR No. 5482, December 4, 1952, pp. 2–3. NADB, OSS file.

[17] Cited in Kerkvliet, Huk Rebellion, p. 83.

[18] Cited in ibid., p. 147.

as Minister Without Portfolio and Director of the Rice Procurement Agency.[19] As such, he organized the extraction of rice from peasant farmers to supply the Japanese military. Roxas was thus among the collaborators most clearly identified in the minds of peasants with the betrayal and abuses suffered during the occupation. General MacArthur, however, liberated Roxas from detention, made him a general on his staff, and in June 1945 relaunched his political career. He was elected the country's first president in April 1946.

Roxas' election gave an ominous signal to the many Filipinos hoping for political change. In the words of an INR report, "His election to the Presidency indicated to the Huks the return to the prewar pattern of [elite] domination."[20] On taking office, Roxas pardoned all Filipinos accused of collaboration. The United States did not object and thus, according to the CIA, alienated ex-Huks who "might otherwise have been friendly to the US," making them "both anti-administration and anti-American."[21] American silence gave Roxas the appearance of American backing, however, while the pardon "gained [him] considerable support among those politically active Filipinos to whom the stigma of collaborationism is attached."[22] So armed, he extended his own influence and tightened the landed elite's grip.

Against this backdrop, peasants in Central Luzon again attempted to mobilize politically. In the place of their old organizations, they formed the National Peasants Union (PKM). (As one peasant put it, however, "KPMP, Hukbalahap, PKM—what's the difference? They're basically all the same anyway.")[23] PKM addressed specific peasant problems, but it focused almost exclusively on the national political arena since, with independence, resolution of peasant problems would be found here, not in the village fields. The PKM participated actively in the Democratic Alliance (DA), a loose coalition party of peasants, progressives, and nationalists formed in July 1945. In the April 1946 election, six DA candidates, all from Central Luzon, won seats in the Philippine Congress. Success was short-lived, however. Roxas refused to seat the DA

[19] OSS, "Personnel of the Philippine Puppet Government," R and A Report No. 1752.1, November 1, 1944 (NADB, OSS file); "The Hukbalahap," p. 25; CIA, "Collaboration in the Philippines"; and David Wurfel, "The Philippines," in *Governments and Politics of Southeast Asia*, ed. George Kahin (Ithaca, N.Y.: Cornell University Press, 1964), p. 697.

[20] "The Hukbalahap," p. 25.

[21] "Possible Developments Resulting from the Granting of Amnesty to Accused Collaborators in the Philippines," ORE 11–48, April 28, 1948, p. 5. DDRS, 1979: 352C.

[22] OSS, "Personalities in the Philippines Political Scene," R and A Report No. 3220, July 30, 1945, p. 2. NADB, OSS file.

[23] Cited in Kerkvliet, *Huk Rebellion*, p. 121.

congressmen. By not seating them, he held a two-thirds majority in the lower house and thus a stranglehold on government. But by closing the door to a political resolution of peasant problems, Roxas opened wide the doors to renewed violence.

Even this might not have provoked armed resistance, however, were it not for rising government and government-sanctioned violence against peasants, the PKM, and the DA. In late 1945, Huk veterans, PKM organizers, and ordinary farmers began to face regular attacks by the police, PC, and civilian guards. Following the April 1946 election both the DA and PKM came under attack: meetings were broken up, members harassed, organizers beaten and occasionally murdered. The repression forced the PKM underground and killed the DA. The violence soon became so widespread that for peasants safety from attack replaced agrarian reform as the most important issue and many joined the new resistance in self-defense.[24] This time, however, they had experience, the confidence born of success against the Japanese, and a program to fight for. They were a formidable opponent.

A REALIST EXPLANATION OF AMERICAN INVOLVEMENT

Several international security concerns commanded policymakers' attention during the Huk crisis and gave this minor local rebellion major significance. In the words of the Joint Chiefs,

> The Philippines are an essential part of the Asian offshore island chain of bases on which the strategic position of the United States in the Far East depends. . . . Soviet domination of these islands would, in all probability, be followed by rapid disintegration of the entire structure of anti-Communist defenses in Southeast Asia and the offshore island chain, including Japan.

"Therefore," they concluded, "the situation in the Philippines cannot be viewed as a local problem." In fact, "the strategic importance of the United States position in the Philippines is such as to justify the commitment of United States forces for its protection should circumstances require" or, at least, "increased United States assistance . . . to remove the Huk threat without further delay." Their views are repeated almost verbatim in NSC 84/2, "The Position of the United States with respect

[24] "The Philippine Communist Party," pp. 9–10. INR attributes the reopening of armed resistance to the February 1948 murder by government agents of Manuel Joven, the outlawing of the PKM and PKP, and the initiation of the government's "mailed fist" policy.

to the Philippines," adopted November 9, 1950, as the basic statement of American policy.[25]

The importance of the Philippines hung on the larger significance of Asia as a whole. But "developments in Asia," wrote John Foster Dulles in a 1950 report to Dean Acheson, "confirm that there is a comprehensive program, in which the Soviet and Chinese Communists are cooperating, designed . . . to eliminate all Western influence on the Asiatic mainland, and probably also [on] the islands of Japan, Formosa, the Philippines and Indonesia."[26] If successful, such "a major political rout" would have repercussions "felt throughout the rest of the world."[27] Thus, following the invasion of Korea, the new *Statement of Policy on Asia* declared that, "in view of the communist resort to armed force in Asia, United States action . . . must be based on the recognition that the most immediate, overt threats to United States security are currently presented in that area."[28]

But if Korea focused attention on aggression by conventional means, the preceding years had given rise to concern for a subversive threat. A 1949 NSC draft report declared:

> Asia is in the throes of political upheaval. The Communist offensive, nationalism, and the revolt against colonial rule, the emergence of new nations, the decline of Western influence, the absence of a stabilizing balance of power, the prevalence of terrorism, economic distress and social unrest, and the repercussions of the struggle between the Soviet world and the Free World are currently disruptive forces.[29]

Moreover, in Mao Moscow had a proven "expert in exploiting the two principal communist issues applicable to East Asia—nationalism in colonial countries and agrarian revolt in independent states."[30] In this context the Huk insurgency against what had been the United States' only Asian colony took on its real, and lasting, importance.

Like their European counterparts, Americans felt it was the duty of the West to see the evolutionary process begun under colonialism com-

[25] "Memorandum to the Secretary of Defense, September 6, 1950, FR, 1950, 6: 1485–86, 1487; and FR, 1950, 6: 1514–20.

[26] November 30, 1950, FR, 1950, 6: 162.

[27] NSC 51, "U.S. Policy toward Southeast Asia," July 1, 1949, p. 6. DDRS, 1975: 276B.

[28] Annex 1 of NSC 48/5, "United States Objectives, Policies and Courses of Action in Asia," May 17, 1951, FR, 1951, 6: 34.

[29] "The Position of the United States with respect to Asia," NSC draft, October 25, 1949, pp. 2–3. NAMM, NSC file.

[30] NSC 51, p. 5.

pleted and prevent its perversion by communism. But American and European policymakers differed over how to proceed. The Dutch and French denied nationalism and stressed instead the need for continued colonial control. As early as 1944, however, an OSS study called for "maximum support for the development of . . . Asia as an autonomous force in world politics" and "rapid progress towards self-government." Failure to do so would "create a resentment toward nations actually or apparently responsible. This, in turn, will create an admirable opportunity for trouble making by any nation with an interest in doing so." Indeed, barring rapid change Asians "would probably . . . seek economic security and political strength through Russian alliances."[31]

Nothing, argued Americans, aggravated the risk more than colonialism, "the greatest single immediate factor contributing to the expansion of Communism in SEA [Southeast Asia]." They recognized the dangers of decolonization. "Can we be sure," asked the authors of NSC 51, "that our Western allies will be able to transfer sovereignty to moderate nationalists [or that] the situation [has not] so deteriorated that the only alternative to imperial rule is chaos . . . and communism?" They concluded that "there *is* no guarantee that these fears will not be realized. But the choice before us for the immediate future is not between hostile tumult and friendly stability. It is between two evils and our task is to estimate which is the lesser." Thus, despite the *need* for further development, the only apparent solution, "even though misgovernment eventuates, . . . must be sought on a non-imperialist plane."[32]

To many Americans, French and Dutch actions in Indochina and Indonesia exemplified how *not* to procede. In the case of Indonesia, the CIA concluded that efforts to crush the nationalist movement "will ultimately release more dangerous social and political forces than those it has brought under control." For the Dutch, the attempt promised to impair reconstruction and leave the Netherlands unable to contribute to the defense of Europe. As for the United States, Dutch actions jeopardized access to Indonesian resources and "other production areas of Southeast Asia," threatened to show the futility of moderation, and identified the United States as "an imperialistic fellow-traveller."[33] Luckily, the Netherland's weakness made it easy to force a United Nations negotiated transfer of power upon it.

[31] OSS, "Political Strategy for the Far East," R and A Report No. 2666, October 28, 1944, pp. 7–11. NADB, OSS file.

[32] NSC 51, pp. 8, 10, 4.

[33] "Review of the World Situation as it Relates to the Security of the United States," CIA 1–49, January 19, 1949, pp. 1–4 (DDRS, 1977: 179A–182A); and NSC 51, pp. 11–12.

No such success graced the tragic case of French Indochina, although the logic was the same. The Truman Administration had no doubts that French colonial control of Indochina spelled disaster for the effort to contain communism in Asia. "Indochina," declared the State Department, "is an example of how nationalism repressed by a Western power has permitted the Kremlin to breach our monopoly on self-determination."[34] Indeed, declared the CIA, "there is almost no effective manner in which Western governments . . . can oppose the trend favoring the Communists, so long as the indigenous, potentially anti-Communist forces accept predominantly Communist leadership in order to eliminate French control."[35] What is more, observed a State Department official, "this shabby business is a mockery of all the professions we have made in the Indonesian case. . . . For the United States to support France in this attempt will cost us our standing and prestige in all of Southeast Asia."[36] Thus, declared NSC 51, the United States had to convince the French to yield control so that moderates would "gravitate away from the present Viet Minh popular front and coalesce in a nationalist, anti-Stalinist organization." Omnisciently, NSC 51 adds, "It would then be necessary . . . for us . . . to ensure, however long it takes, the triumph of Indochinese nationalism over Red imperialism."[37]

Two problems blocked action to force the French to withdraw. First, in Indonesia Americans worried that suppressing moderate nationalists would encourage Communist leadership, but they already believed that "Ho is and will remain a Moscow stooge."[38] Second, policymakers faced a trade-off between European and Asian imperatives. The CIA noted in 1949,

> The essence of this problem since 1945 has been how to satisfy the nationalist aspirations of colonial peoples while . . . maintaining the economic and political stability of European colonial powers. An adequate solution of the first . . . is essential to the protection of long-term US security interests in the Far East. An adequate solution to the second . . . is essential to the support of immediate US

[34] "United States Policy in the Far East," Draft III, October 18, 1949, p. 11. DDRS, Retro: 538C.

[35] "Vulnerabilities of Communist Movements in the Far East," I.M. No. 209, September 20, 1949, p. 27. NAMM, CIA file.

[36] Memo from Raymond Fosdick to Philip Jessup re Charles Yost memo (of November 1, 1949), November 4, 1949, p. 2. DDRS, Retro: 538F.

[37] NSC 51, p. 14.

[38] Memo from Charles Yost to Jessup, Case, and Fosdick, November 1, 1949, p. 2. DDRS, Retro: 538E. See, too, Rusk to Matthews, January 31, 1951, FR, 1951, 6: 20–21.

security interests in Europe. Both . . . are applicable to the relative power positions of the US and USSR on the global scale.[39]

The need to win French acquiescence to German rearmament, however, forced Acheson to support the war in Indochina, while the invasion of Korea convinced the Joint Chiefs that, whatever the long-term costs, failure to do so would result in the rapid "extension of Communism over the remainder of . . . Southeast Asia."[40] With this, American declarations on Indochina softened perceptibly.

It is in this context that policy in the Philippines must be viewed. It was the American "model response" to the need for decolonization and the threats potential in it. "Victory of the Communist-led and dominated Huks," Acheson informed the President, "would place us in a highly embarrassing position vis-à-vis the British, French, and Dutch whom we have been persuading to recognize the realities and legitimacy of Asiatic nationalism and self-determination."[41] Moreover, argued Dean Rusk, then Assistant Secretary of State for Far Eastern Affairs, defeat "would more than any other single factor discredit the United States throughout the length and breadth of Asia. . . . If we fail there, the rest of Asia will surely consider we have nothing to offer elsewhere." Thus, "it is vital that we hold the Philippines whatever the cost—unless we are prepared to write off Asia."[42]

Domestic and Bureaucratic Politics

Domestic politics explain less of American policy in the Philippines than they do in Greece. In fact, domestic concerns seem simply to have reinforced the imperative *not* to lose. Politicians believed that the United States had a special responsibility for the Philippines "arising from the half-century of American sovereignty."[43] But against the backdrop of Chiang Kai Shek's defeat and the invasion of Korea, what mattered was not losing, and that mattered a lot.

Pentagon politics add a new layer of explanation, however. As in Greece, limited resources constrained direct military involvement. The Korean War took precedence over all other concerns and the floundering French in Indochina enjoyed "the highest priority immediately after

[39] "Review of the World Situation," 1–49, p. 2.
[40] Cited in JCS, Historical Division, Walter Poole, *The History of the Joint Chiefs of Staff*, vol. 4, 1950–1952 (December 1979), pp. 413–17, 143.
[41] Acheson to Truman, April 20, 1950, FR, 1950, 6: 1441–42.
[42] Rusk to Matthews, January 31, 1951, FR, 1951, 6: 24.
[43] State Department draft of NSC 84, June 20, 1950, FR, 1950, 6: 1461.

the military effort in Korea."[44] Thus, the Joint Chiefs rejected use of American troops unless "there remained no other means of preventing Communist seizure of the islands." Moreover, intervention would require "a considerable increase" in mobilization.[45] And, reports Edward Lansdale, "Few U.S. officials wanted even to think about going through another experience such as Greece, although they admitted that the Philippine situation seemed to be worsening."[46]

In the Philippines the Joint United States Military Advisory Group (JUSMAG) program reflected the U.S. Army's conception of its mission, not local requirements. JUSMAG aimed to create Philippine forces organized and equipped like those of the United States and trained to fight in the same way—on the plains of Europe. They proved singularly ineffective against guerrillas. Moreover, not only did the officers in JUSMAG "have inadequate knowledge of and experience with political subversion and guerrilla warfare of the type with which the Philippines Government is faced," but they refused to believe that combatting it might have special requirements. As a result, much of the advisory effort was wasted and Filipino officers often refused to associate with JUSMAG.[47]

The Three Oughts in the Philippines

Policymakers shared a common understanding of the Huk insurgency and the American role in combatting it. The parallels to Greece are striking. Indeed, differences simply reflect the guardian-ward character of U.S.–Philippine relations. As the Embassy told President Truman in a memo to prepare him for meeting President Quirino,

> An understanding of the Philippine people is essential and their shortcomings must be appraised against their historic background. A useful analogy is to regard them as precocious children. ... This merely recognizes their relatively recent introduction to the modern world. ... That they have assimilated the superficial

[44] NSC 64, "Progress Report on the Implementation of 'The Position of the United States with respect to Indochina,' " March 15, 1951, p. 1. DDRS, 1977: 196A.

[45] Secretary of Defense Louis Johnson to the NSC, letter of transmittal for NSC 84/2, "The Position of the United States with respect to the Philippines," report of the Secretary of Defense, September 14, 1950, p. 1. DDRS, 1978: 253A.

[46] Edward Lansdale, *In the Midst of Wars: An American's Mission to Southeast Asia* (New York: Harper & Row, 1972), p. 14.

[47] Ibid., pp. 99–100; Chapin to the Secretary of State, April 7, 1950, FR, 1950, 6: 1436; and Heymann and Whitson, *Can and Should the United States Preserve a Military Capability for Revolutionary Conflict?*, pp. 38, 46.

aspects of [our culture] in so short a time is proof of their precocity. Where they fail to grasp its more fundamental implications they are displaying no more than the uncertainty and the bewilderment of [a] national mind in which several strong but incompatible traditions vie for supremacy. As they are today, however, they present no problem that cannot be met by firm patience and sympathetic understanding.[48]

Thus, as the manager of their modernization the United States sought "the establishment and maintenance of: an effective government . . . ; a Philippine military capable of restoring and maintaining internal security; [and] a stable and self-supporting economy."[49]

SECURITY

As islands, the Philippines faced different security risks than Greece. No threat of invasion existed; the issue was internal stability. Policymakers did attribute leadership of the insurgency to outside Communist forces, however. "The Hukbalahap are today the army of Philippine Communism," declared INR in 1950, and their leaders "follow the policies and seek to further the objectives of world Communism." Policymakers noted that the insurgency was "firmly grounded in the peasantry's long-standing and legitimate grievances."[50] Yet, observes Edward Lansdale, they "barely mentioned the political and social factors [and] dwelt almost exclusively on the military situation."[51] In effect, they concurred with President Roxas's assertions that "the only way to fight force is . . . with superior force."[52]

Two problems hindered the Philippine military, however: its incompetence and its tendency to attack civilians. Considering the former, Americans complained that government forces showed a "disinclination to come into close combat with the Huks" and left the initiative to the guerrillas.[53] Americans complained, too, of corruption and officers' tendency to place personal gain before professionalism.[54] They also worried that military involvement in politics damaged the democratic process and impaired the armed forces' martial capabilities, particularly when political loyalty replaced merit in promotion decisions.

[48] Embassy Manila to Rusk and President Truman, August 1, 1951, FR, 1951, 6: 1561–62.
[49] NSC 84/2, NSC staff study, November 9, 1950, FR, 1950, 6: 1514–15.
[50] "The Hukbalahap," pp. iii, 1.
[51] Lansdale, *Midst of Wars*, p. 19.
[52] Cited in Kerkvliet, *Huk Rebellion*, p. 190.
[53] Cowen to the Secretary of State, Feburary 15, 1951, FR, 1951, 6: 1510.
[54] Chapin to the State Department, January 5, 1951, FR, 1951, 6: 1492.

But policymakers were even more concerned about the abuse of civilians. As Douglas Blaufarb notes, "the army and the police, lacking effective tactics, good intelligence, or adequate training, struck out at the nearest available target, the population."[55] Similarly, INR reported that "Poor discipline . . . and their harsh treatment of the civilian population have made the Constabulary at least as feared and hated as the [Huks]. . . . Indeed, peasants are reported to have declared that the only difference between the Constabulary and the Huks is that the Huks did *not* physically injure the farmers and local citizens."[56]

The American response took several forms. Military aid provided equipment, logistic support, and direct budgetary contributions. The United States also established JUSMAG (Philippines) in December 1947 to provide instruction in use of the new equipment, teach new tactics, instill a more aggressive spirit, foster a public spirit orientation, help in depoliticization, root out corruption and professionalize the promotion system to weed out incompetents and encourage "officers showing readiness for combat."[57] When these efforts seemed insufficient, policymakers discussed "the possibility of increasing the personnel of JUS MAG, Philippines, to pattern it generally after the United States Mission in Greece" by placing American officers down to the combat-team level and seeking "American control of the Philippine Army."[58]

GOOD GOVERNMENT

Policymakers agreed with the Joint Chiefs, however, that "military measures . . . can be only a temporary expedient. Remedial political and economic measures must be adopted by the Philippine Government in order to eliminate the basic causes of discontent among the Philippine people."[59] Unfortunately, noted INR, "The political and social policies the Philippine Government has adopted . . . to cope with the Huk problem have been even more dilatory, unconvincing and in-

[55] Blaufarb, *Counterinsurgency Era*, p. 26. Similar concerns show in resistance to Philippine requests for napalm. Cowen, for example, cabled Chairman of the Joint Chiefs General Omar Bradley that its use would only "make more Huks than would be eliminated." FR, 1951, 6: 1549.

[56] "The Hukbalahap," pp. iv–v, 24–25. See, also Blaufarb, *Counterinsurgency Era*, pp. 46–49; and Chapin to the Secretary of State, April 7, 1950, FR, 1950, 6: 1435.

[57] State Department Draft of NSC 84, June 20, 1950, FR, 1950, 6: 1463; Cowen to the Secretary of State, February 15, 1951, FR, 1951, 6: 1510; and "The Hukbalahap," p. 49.

[58] NSC 84/2, p. 4; and Melby draft, January 15, 1951, FR, 1951, 6: 1499. See, too, the memo of conversation, Cowen and Magsaysay, January 22, 1951, FR, 1951, 6: 1504; and General Maloney to the Southeast Asia Aid Policy Committee, January 22, 1951, FR, 1951, 6: 10. JUSMAG expanded in size, but the other proposals were not implemented.

[59] JCS to the Secretary of Defense, September 6, 1950, FR, 1950, 6: 1487.

effectual than its military efforts." Indeed, "the ineffectuality of the government's military measures . . . stems directly from the corruption, abuse of public authority, and incompetence that characterize the Philippine Government's activities in other fields." Luckily INR concluded, "The nature of the problem is well and widely understood [and] the legislative framework for improvement has been set up."[60]

Policymakers were concerned by the poor quality and insufficient quantity of government. Thus, for example, they attributed problems to government mismanagement, inefficiency, and corruption which prevented pursuit of sound goals.[61] They were also worried because, as NSC 84/2 put it,

> The Philippine Government has lacked the courage and initiative to take bold, vigorous measures to wipe out corruption . . . to create a stable administrative system and to encourage confidence in the government and the future of the country. . . . Leadership . . . has been largely in the hands of a small group of individuals representing the wealthy propertied class who . . . have failed to appreciate the need for reform and the pressures generated among less prosperous and more numerous groups of the population.[62]

Moreover, noted INR, "Widespread popular revulsion has been engendered by the administration's resort to fraud and violence in the November 1949 elections and by the public scandals in which high administrative officials have been frequently involved. As a result, many persons who are not active [Huk] supporters have been indifferent towards the government's efforts to stamp out the dissident forces."[63]

Policymakers prescribed better, more responsive leadership and more efficient, less corrupt administration. As the authors of NSC 84/2 admitted, "Owing to the extreme sensitivity of Philippine officials and the people in general on the question of their national sovereignty, the extent and manner in which the necessary influence is brought to bear on the Philippine Government to accomplish essential reforms presents . . . a most difficult and delicate problem." Still, the United States "has no choice" but to reassert "influence to the extent required to eliminate prevalent corruption, provide efficient administrative services, and restore public faith in the concept of government in the best interests of the people,"[64] while, the "present Philippine leadership, by virtue of

[60] "The Hukbalahap," pp. 41, 48, 41.
[61] See Melby, January 15, 1951, FR, 1951, 6: 1499; and Bell, FR, 1950, 6: 1475.
[62] NSC 84/2, FR, 1950, 6: 1518.
[63] "The Hukbalahap," p. iv.
[64] NSC 84/2, FR, 1950, 6: 1519–20.

past malfeasance and demonstrated incompetence, should be strengthened."[65] Thus, the United States sought both to minimize official abuse of the electoral process, voter intimidation, and vote fraud and provide public administration experts to professionalize, depoliticize, and clean up the government bureaucracy.

PROGRESS

Finally, policymakers worried that Manila risked losing popular support to the insurgents for economic reasons. As an American high commissioner noted just prior to the war, economic development had "served but little to ameliorate living conditions among the almost feudal peasantry."[66] The situation was even worse afterward. The Bell Mission, sent to investigate economic conditions in 1950, found that workers' wages provided "much less" than half of a minimum family budget. It found, too, that income inequalities had increased; tenants' and workers' earnings had not regained prewar levels, while those of businessmen and landowners had soared.[67] American observers concluded that substandard wages, racketeering, inadequate labor legislation, and failure to enforce existing regulations contributed to the Huks' appeal in urban areas. In the countryside, they found that Huk support derived from submarginal farm size, exorbitant rents, usurious credit, landlord abuse and nonenforcement of protective legislation.[68]

Although acknowledging these problems as serious, policymakers considered them remediable. In fact, concluded one study, "the tenancy system, the prevalence of absentee ownership and usury, primitive agricultural techniques, and abuses of private and governmental authority are capable of complete or partial solution with the resources now available to the Philippine Government." Thus, the study recommended a package of reforms including the division and resale of estates to tenants, movement of people out of Central Luzon to less densely populated areas, enforcement of fair rent laws, control of loan interest, and establishment of a minimum wage.[69] In this effort, policymakers argued, the United States should offer both advice on land

[65] Melby draft, January 15, 1951, FR, 1951, 6: 1502.
[66] Cited in "The Hukbalahap," p. 3.
[67] Cited in Department of State, Office of Intelligence Research, "Philippine Legislative Implementation of the Report of the Economic Survey Mission to the Philippines," IR No. 5828, May 23, 1952, p. 9 (NADB, OSS file); and U.S. Economic Survey Mission to the Philippines, October 9, 1950, FR, 1950, 6: 1499.
[68] Cowen to the Secretary of State, February 15, 1951, FR, 1951, 6: 1508; and "Philippine Legislative Implementation," pp. 4–5.
[69] "The Hukbalahap," pp. 41, 50.

reform, agricultural development, and labor law and the money to defray the costs of land redistribution, population relocation, and vocational training.[70]

The Limits of Leverage

In the Philippines, as in Greece, leverage was limited. Although the United States had been the colonial master until July 4, 1946, independence eliminated United States control of Philippine policymaking, while the novelty of freedom made Filipinos sensitive to infringements of their sovereignty. As a result, policymakers worried that pressuring Manila would provoke a nationalist backlash or increase the Huks' anti-American appeal. As NSC 84/2 warned, "Extreme care must therefore be exercised in the methods used to persuade the Philippine Government to take the necessary action." This problem was further complicated by the Philippines' role as model for Europe and Asia. Reassertion of control would discredit claims made to the colonial powers that decolonization could work and would damage American credibility in Asia, as "Asiatic opinion generally would prove particularly sensitive to any . . . abridgement or revocation of Philippine independence."[71]

Leverage was thus reduced to cajolery and rational persuasion. Americans tried to convince Philippine officials that their long-term interests required reform and to show that corruption, patronage politics, and maladministration played into Huk hands. They appealed to Philippine officials' "better instincts" and tried simple shaming. For example, it was suggested that President Truman tell President Quirino "to lay aside his petty internal political considerations in favor of the large community of interests which should be the primary concern of responsible statesmen."[72] The officials, and particularly President Quirino, proved impervious. Americans were in a bind.

But as conditions worsened in 1949–1950, policymakers concluded that "this Government has no choice except to attempt to help the Filipinos bring about the necessary reforms since to do nothing would result in disaster."[73] They tried a "Greek response": use of American watchdogs to eliminate corruption, manage aid, and improve admin-

[70] "Philippine Legislative Implementation," p. 8; Cowen to the Secretary of State, February 15, 1951, and State response, April 25, 1951, FR, 1951, 6: 1507–1508 and 1537.

[71] NSC 84/2, FR, 1950, 6: 1518–20. See also, Embassy Manila to Rusk and Truman in preparation for President Quirino's visit, August 1, 1951, FR, 1951, 6: 1561.

[72] Butterworth to Acheson, March 23, 1950, FR, 1950, 6: 1425.

[73] NSC 84/2, FR, 1950, 6: 1520.

istrative capabilities. As Ambassador Cowen put it, "if any reforms are to be effected it will largely come through competent technical advisors scattered profusely through all strategic PhilGovt depts and agencies. . . . We must control to the maximum degree every *centavo* of aid of any character which we send to this country."[74] Similarly, the State Department insisted on the "assignment of United States officers to duty as field observers" to put some backbone in the Philippine army.[75] As in Greece, these measures achieved less than hoped. Despite Americans larded through the bureaucracy, American monetary aid continued to be distributed not as mandated but by local criteria, and corruption continued unabated as did the political manipulation of administration and the military. The sanctions the United States wielded were insufficient to offset the more potent ones imposed by local politics. (See next section for further discussion.)

But besides possessing limited leverage, the United States was also unwilling to exercise that which it had. Policymakers insisted on the extension of aid "in the degree corresponding to progress made toward creating the essential conditions of internal security."[76] But insistence seldom begat action because, insofar as they defined the Philippines as essential to American security and believed a Communist takeover the only alternative to the status quo, threats to curtail aid lacked credibility. Even when government failure to reform led to crisis, Americans felt they had to bail it out, though doing so negated leverage.

Failure of the 1949–1950 effort to force fiscal reform on Manila illustrates this point clearly. When President Quirino visited Washington in August 1949 to plead for more aid, Truman told him that Washington worried "that this money would be largely wasted unless the Philippine Government put its financial house in order."[77] Nothing happened, and four months later Ambassador Cowen remarked that the

> financial situation of the government will have to become substantially worse before President Quirino realizes measures we urge him to take are required by Philippine self-interest. In meantime, any assurance of US aid which he may secure will serve to make him feel that situation is not truly urgent and will . . . delay the

[74] Cowen to Melby, March 27, 1951, FR, 1951, 6: 1526.

[75] Department of State to Cowen, April 25, 1951, FR, 1951, 6: 1538.

[76] NSC Action No. 379, November 1950, cited in JCS, *History*, vol. 4, 1950–1952, p. 433.

[77] Memo of conversation, meeting of President Truman and President Quirino, August 9, 1949, FR, 1949, 7: 598.

time when he may be forced [to] make critical examination of his own administration.[78]

Quirino, he suggested, should be allowed to stew in his own juices until he saw the light. Quirino did nothing, and the Philippines slid toward bankruptcy. By mid-1950, the issue of whether to provide a budgetary bailout dominated the cable traffic. The bailout was provided, and the leverage was lost.

A memo by John Melby to the Director of the Office of Philippine and Southeast Asian Affairs captured the logic of capitulation.

> The argument against it obviously is that such a loan solves no real problem ... unless there is that kind of control which will guarantee its repayment and the development of resources to insure adequate revenues in the future. I think it questionable that the Philippine Government will give us that control. ... On the other hand, the absence of cash creates an immediate crisis situation. School teachers have been unpaid since last spring and the army will not likely tolerate finding itself in the same position. The only alternative to a budgetary loan ... is increased taxation and increased efficiency in tax collection, but this will take considerable time.

Melby concluded: "In the present impossible situation, the long-range program can only succeed if the US makes possible an extended breathing period." Thus, since the presumed cost of *not* caving in was the government's fall and Communist victory, the loan was unavoidable.[79] But under the circumstances, it is not surprising that the State Department found "President Quirino ... supremely confident that no matter what he does the United States will always provide whatever funds are needed to solve his problems."[80]

The problem did not go unnoticed. In the midst of the loan debate, Carlton Ogburn, an analyst in the Bureau of Far Eastern Affairs, criticized aiding any and all self-proclaimed "anti-Communists," since as long as "the United States gives the appearance of a call-girl, we shall ... continue to serve as a refuge for weaklings and incompetents." The Philippines, Ogburn noted,

[78] Cowen to Secretary of State, January 8, 1950, FR, 1950, 6: 1399–1400.

[79] Melby to Lacy, September 28, 1950, ibid., pp. 1493–95. See also, Acheson to Truman, August 31, 1950, pp. 1–2 (DDRS, 1979: 200A); and JCS, *History*, vol. 2, 1950–1952, p. 431.

[80] Department of State, "The Philippines," Section C, October 10, 1950, p. 1. DDRS, 1978: 102C.

give a good example of how our policy betrays us. Without our aid, Quirino's regime will eventually be swept away. It is a weak regime in all save the talents required to retain office by dishonest means, and it should in fact be swept away if the Philippines is to be strong. In exchange for certain "reforms," however—as if a corrupt and dishonest leadership could be reformed—we are going to save this regime from the penalties of its own short comings.

He asked plaintively, "Can we not be a little harder to get and let the favor of the United States be what other peoples aspire to? Darn it, *they* are the ones who are threatened with a fate worse than death—not we."[81] No one listened.

Still, it is essential not to exaggerate the importance of American capacity and willingness. In fact, policymakers' belief in leverage reflected an underestimation of the limits Philippine leaders faced and an overestimation of the likelihood of reform. These intragovernmental constraints on reform, too, affected the leverage the United States could exert. Because policymakers failed to perceive them, however, they could not understand the frustration of leverage nor later appreciate how little American leverage contributed to victory.

INTRAGOVERNMENTAL CONSTRAINTS

As in Greece, policymakers misunderstood the intragovernmental constraints on reform. They blamed failure on Philippine leaders' venality and unwillingness to act like "mature statesmen." Ambassador Cowen, for example, complained that there were "few honest men in Philippine politics" and warned that it "should be kept in mind in interest [of] maintaining [a] realistic perspective [that] majority Philippine politicians are self-seeking and unscrupulous men."[82] In fact, Acheson informed President Truman in April 1950, if the leadership "had demonstrated the capacity and willingness to understand its problems and the required solutions, as well as to accept competent advice, there would have been every reason to assume that the country could have been placed on a stable basis with relative ease, despite the ravages of the Japanese occupation and . . . lack of experience in self-government."[83] But such criticism was misdirected. The difficulty was not that politicians did not understand the need for reform, but that they understood all too well what reform would mean for them.

[81] Ogburn to Rusk, January 15, 1951, FR, 1951, 6: 8–9.
[82] Cowen to Rusk, June 1, 1950, FR, 1950, 6: 1455.
[83] Draft memo Acheson to Truman, April 20, 1950, ibid., pp. 1440–41.

226

Politicians' will to reform is not only a matter of their personalities but also a function of their interests. Americans finessed this point by assuming that as national leaders, Philippine politicians' interests and the national interest were one, and thus that reforms needed to defeat the Huks would also be in their interest. They were not, but instead the reforms struck at the foundations of the political, social, and economic order upon which elite power rested. As noted earlier, American colonial administration created a system of national institutions, control of which was, in turn, taken over by the elite and used to protect their interests against peasant and working class demands. Thus, at the time of independence the government was dominated by members of the upper classes. Furthermore, when the electoral process did throw up peasant or working class representatives, they were barred from participation as in the case of the DA legislators Roxas refused to seat.

Under the circumstances, Philippine leaders had reason to resist the reforms Americans prescribed. In a system where success depended on "*kilala, kapit, and pakikisama* [who you know, good connections, and good personal relationships]," demands for bureaucratic rationalization, merit promotion, and corruption control posed problems. Similarly, calls for the removal of those who had collaborated with the Japanese threatened many in government who had themselves collaborated and the reciprocal ties of family and interest that bound politicians to collaborators outside government. As for curbing the security forces, they were enforcing politicians' interests, often under orders. In short, despite the Huk challenge, the interests of those in power counselled defense of the status quo, not preemptive reform.

But the problem went deeper, for no monolithic elite with common interests opposed reform. Rather, government resembled a balance of power in which many factions struggled to protect their interests. None could impose its will, yet each alone or in coalition could derail the efforts of others. Thus, at issue was not the need for reform, but the potential consequences of reform for others and their possible reconciliation with the interests of key factions. And in the Philippines, where endemic violence raised the stakes of politics to life and death, the room for maneuver was narrow. As a result, the "petty politics" of intragovernmental coalition management, not "responsible statesmanship," prevailed. Ironically, Ambassador Cowen was absolutely correct, when he observed of Quirino, that the Huk threat "evidently seems to him the less immediate danger to his position."[84]

[84] Cowen to Rusk, May 8, 1950, FR, 1950, 6: 1447. Cowen nullifies this observation, however, by continuing that "were he to forget his personal position and begin acting for

The consequent paralysis appears in problems the United States assumed could be solved with technical fixes. Americans, for example, blamed corruption on official venality and the lack of accounting and control mechanisms. But they missed its political function as a means to buy off those needed to hold the system together. In fact, this requirement bound so tight that "by the end of 1949 the government seemed willing to let the military go unpaid and the educational system wither for want of funds, and even to succumb to the Huk rebellion, rather than face up to a minimum responsibility for governmental functions"—corruption control and tax collection.[85] American accounting assistance did nothing to alter this political requirement, and aid merely reduced its costs.

Policymakers' insensitivity to intragovernmental politics shows most clearly in the handling of President Quirino, however. Quirino was corrupt, inept, and infuriating to work with. (He once actually suggested that the U.S. bribe him not to appoint a Japanese collaborator as ambassador to Washington.)[86] One official observed that he addressed his country's problems "by a mental process wherein he identifies his own pronouncements with accomplished fact"—that is, by wishful thinking.[87] His personal style also did not inspire confidence. For example, normally unflappable Ambassador Cowen complained to Washington of a visit which ended when "Quirino seized and shook me by the arms, wept, and said, 'You are a great nation, and if you think it necessary to embarrass me you may do what you will with me!'"[88] They took him at his word and decided to do away with him altogether.

As the Huk threat grew, American frustration with Quirino grew until he became *the* problem. In January 1950, Cowen asserted that it does "not occur to him that, in his preoccupation with domestic politics, he [is] manifesting distressing disregard for his country's interests."[89] In March, the director of the Office of Philippine and Southeast Asian Affairs reported that

> Largely due to the political ineptitude of President Quirino and the complete lack of confidence in him by members of his own party, the overall situation in the Philippines is very disturbing. . . . Pub-

the good of the nation he might largely disarm [the] opposition, but we doubt he has the integrity to appreciate that fact."

[85] Frank H. Golay, *The Philippines: Public Policy and National Economic Development* (Ithaca, N.Y.: Cornell University Press, 1961), pp. 71–72.

[86] Acheson to Truman, February 2, 1950, FR, 1950, 6: 1403.

[87] Melby to Lacy, September 28, 1950, ibid., p. 1494.

[88] Cowen to the Secretary of State, March 28, 1950, ibid., p. 1427.

[89] Cowen to the Secretary of State, January 1, 1950, ibid., p. 1400.

lic order is bad, businessmen badly frightened, and Quirino seems to lack the political courage and political support necessary to restore normal conditions.[90]

An April 20, 1950, memo from Acheson to President Truman went further:

As the [State] Department views it, the first and primary obstacle in the solution of the Philippine problem is President Quirino himself. All our experience . . . with him points to one conclusion, namely, that it is impossible to deal with him successfully. . . . All indications are that he would prefer to see his country ruined rather than compromise with his insatiable ego or accept outside assistance on any terms except his own.[91]

The problems of the Philippines were the fault of one man whose failure "to lay aside his petty internal political considerations" and act like a "responsible statesman" threatened critical American security and other foreign policy interests.[92]

The solution was simple: get rid of Quirino. As Acheson told Truman: "If there is one lesson to be learned from the China debacle it is that if we are confronted with an inadequate vehicle, it should be discarded or immobilized in favor of a more propitious one."[93] In June Ambassador Cowen took up the refrain: "Granting that survival of Philippine Government appears incompatible with Quirino's serving out . . . his current term and that he will use any means—good or evil, but usually the latter—to remain in power, it is probably necessary that the strategy employed against him be plotted by a remorseless mind." He suggested that the United States support Vice President Lopez whose "brainier brother Eugenio" was a "cold-blooded strategist" and behind whom stood the "rest of tightly knit Lopez clan—a group of better-than-average upper class Filipinos but half-enlightened and half-feudal, with demonstrated capacity for ruthless operations against outsiders and not without clan members who understand fact that in Philippines business and politics are complementary activities." In short, Cowen wanted to replace Quirino with his functional equivalent, as if the failure of leverage and reform were due to no more than this one man's personal quirks. As Cowen himself put it,

[90] Lacy to Rusk, March 30, 1950, ibid., pp. 1428–29.
[91] Draft memo, Acheson to Truman, April 20, 1950, ibid., p. 1442.
[92] Butterworth to Acheson, March 23, 1950, ibid., pp. 1424–25.
[93] Draft memo, Acheson to Truman, April 20, 1950, ibid., p. 1442.

we should be under no illusions that the battle against corruption and mismanagement will thereby be wholly won or that Philippine politicians will thereafter abandon their customary struggle for power in favor of harmonious cooperation. What we can legitimately hope is that Philippines . . . can, with reshuffling of the cards be afforded fresh and better opportunity [to] face up to its problems and without help bring them under control.[94]

But neither Cowen nor anyone else suggested why "reshuffling the cards" would actually produce such happy results.

GOVERNMENT-POPULATION RELATIONS

Finally, Americans misunderstood government-population and insurgent-population relations because of misleading expectations concerning the sources and proper leadership of political change. Thus, they failed to ask the critical questions: Security for whom? Defense against what? And more government for whom? As a result, the Americans missed two important facts: the insurgents' superior program accounted for popular support, and government abuse reinforced it.

This shows clearly in an examination of government and Huk relations to the population. American expectations aside, Manila's aim was not to offer peasants the economic and political means to tackle their problems. It sought to control them efficiently, maintain acquiescence to landlord domination, and stymie the organization of peasants' rights groups. As a result, there was little support for increased peasant participation or government responsiveness. While officials welcomed budgetary support and economic aid, they opposed programs which might have redistributive impacts, such as plans to break up large estates, implement rent control laws, or improve rural credit facilities. They welcomed efforts to increase the quantity and efficiency of administration, but only as a means to better enforce their control, not to provide services to common citizens. Similarly, they welcomed administrative decentralization since it played into their hands and reduced American watchdogs' ability to monitor abuses. Finally, they welcomed "security assistance" because it made government and quasi-governmental forces more potent instruments of coercion and cheaper to maintain. And being better armed, the government and landlords had still less reason to listen to American or peasant calls for political and economic reform.

[94] Cowen to Rusk, June 1, 1950, ibid., pp. 1455–56.

Against this backdrop, the insurgents looked very different. The HMB (successor to the Hukbalahap) grew directly from peasant organizations and reflected their interests. (See next section for PKP intentions.) Ironically, the HMB program resembled the American three oughts—except that it recognized the Philippine government's inability to carry them out. Thus, the HMB offered security against the most serious threat peasants faced—official violence. (Contrary to government claims and practice, the insurgents generally restricted their attacks to nonpeasant targets, and few coerced or preyed on villagers.) Beyond security, the HMB sought to improve both the quantity and quality of government available to peasants. On the one hand, they wanted stronger, more numerous government agencies to enforce existing protective legislation and provide greater services. On the other, they wanted respect for their rights as citizens and better access to a more responsive political system that reflected not only landlord but also their own interests. Finally, they sought to secure for tenants enough of their crop to live on, cheap credit to tide them over between harvests, the breakup of the large estates, land redistribution, and the eventual abolition of tenancy.[95]

How They Won

Such was the situation in 1950; two years later INR reported that the insurgency "no longer constitutes a serious threat to the Philippine Government."[96] The HMB could not replace losses, and guerrillas were deserting in droves. The performance of the Philippine armed forces had improved sharply, government reforms had silenced peasant protests, and the ballot box again held sway over the bullet. How was this miracle brought about?

As in the Greek case, it is necessary to dismiss a number of misleading explanations. First, despite claims that victory "was due mainly to the Philippine Government's aggressive military operations against the HMB—operations . . . supported by U.S. military and economic aid,"[97] American military aid was not responsible. Because of the Korean and Indochina wars, equipment deliveries to the Philippine armed forces

[95] See, for example, HMB chief Luis Taruc, cited in Department of State, Office of Intelligence Research, "Philippine Communism from 1953 to 1955," IR No. 6627, March 15, 1955, p. 14. NADB, OSS file. Interviews conducted in Central Luzon by Kerkvliet as well as available documents generally bear out Taruc's position. See *Huk Rebellion*, pp. 168–74.
[96] "The Philippine Communist Party," p. iii.
[97] Ibid.

lagged seriously. The problem was not overcome until 1953, noted the
Joint Chiefs, although "by this time, the worst danger was past."[98]
Moreover, the equipment supplied by JUSMAG was inappropriate, and
its advice was ignored. Instead, against American objections, the Filipinos developed their own tactics and hybrid units.[99] Second, as an is-
land, Luzon offered neither sanctuaries nor the possibility of resupply
by foreign supporters. As a result, the HMB faced constant money,
weapon, and training difficulties. Third, like their KKE counterparts, the
HMB leadership foolishly committed itself to "meet imperialist-puppet
forces in positional warfare," thus negating their strengths and enhancing those of the government.[100] Finally, a government intelligence coup
in October 1950 led to the capture of the PKP's Manila headquarters,
105 top officials, weapons caches, and five tons of documents, codes,
and plans. That haul damaged the entire guerrilla effort.[101]

But these paled against the one insurgent problem that fundamentally affected the government's ability to win: deep differences between
the PKP leaders and peasant guerrillas. The PKP's role cannot be ignored, but it must be carefully qualified because, contrary to policymakers' perceptions, the PKP and HMB were not synonymous. As they
had during the war, PKP leaders brought the organizational resources
and experience needed by the insurgency. Nevertheless, the PKP never
succeeded in converting the HMB into a revolutionary force.[102]

The PKP had two problems. First, the PKP and the peasantry had di-
vergent aims. The former wanted to establish a revolutionary "New
Democracy" (that is, to redistribute the large estates, nationalize the
"commanding heights" of the economy, and throw out the Americans).
But most HMB guerrillas shared the reformist aims long championed by
peasant organizations. They were indifferent to the issue of imperialism, did not fight for nationalized industry, and did not even express

[98] JCS, *History*, vol. 4, 1950–1952, pp. 434–35. See, too, Terry to Cowen, FR, 1951, 6: 1541.
[99] See Blaufarb, *Counterinsurgency Era*, p. 36.
[100] PKP, "Military Strategy and Tactics," circa 1950, cited in Kerkvliet, *Huk Rebellion*, pp. 219–20.
[101] Lansdale, *Midst of Wars*, pp. 63–64.
[102] The following account draws on Kerkvliet, *Huk Rebellion*. Kerkvliet's analysis has been challenged by William Pomeroy, "The Philippine Peasantry and the Huk Revolt," *Journal of Peasant Studies* 5 (July 1978); and James Richardson, "The Huk Rebellion," *Journal of Contemporary Asia* 8:2 (1978). Both argue that the PKP was more central to the insurgency than does Kerkvliet. While the PKP may have played a highly visible lead-ership role, I find little evidence in either article showing a PKP capacity to mobilize peas-ant action in the absence of prior peasant organization.

much desire to see the large estates confiscated; instead, they wanted relief from repression, an equitable share of the crop, cheaper credit, and access to the political process.[103] Second, the PKP lacked strong ties to the peasantry. Its leadership was urban middle- and working-class, its base was Manila, and until the end it kept an orthodox industrial proletariat orientation. As Taruc noted, "Not enough party leaders understood peasants, what they wanted, how they wanted to work for it."[104] In fact, the party shunned mass organization and ignored rising peasant resistance to the government during the critical 1946–1948 period. In 1947, after suppression of the Democratic Alliance, the PKP actually endorsed four senatorial candidates from Roxas's Liberal Party. Only in May 1948 did the PKP politburo recognize the need "to capture the people's uprisings in the provinces."[105] Doing so was another matter.

The PKP aspired to shape the peasantry like "hot iron." But the PKP–HMB tie was at best a precarious alliance, and even the party politburo recognized that many HMB supporters held a "deep prejudice against communism and communists."[106] Even at the rebellion's peak in 1950, "many Huk commanders did not belong to the party and the overwhelming majority of the rank and file did not. In the strong pro-Huk barrios . . . there were only a sprinkling of communists, none in a great many barrios."[107] In fact, reported INR, Huk commanders often "rejected direction by the PKP leadership."[108] Unable to mobilize popular support, the PKP depended on existing peasant organizations and thus possessed little leverage to control the insurgency. This shows most clearly in its repeated failure to spread the insurgency beyond Central

[103] Kerkvliet, *Huk Rebellion*, pp. 223–27. PKP leaders like Jesus Lava recognized the gap. "The great majority of Huks joined because of repression by the Philippine government, American soldiers, and civilian guards. Many felt it was either join or be killed without at least putting up a fight. We didn't have time . . . to educate them politically" (cited, p. 227). Similarly, Luis Taruc observed that most "joined because they had causes—like agrarian reform, government reform, anti-repression . . . and, frequently, because they simply had to defend themselves" (cited, p. 170).

[104] Cited in ibid., p. 233.

[105] Document of December 10, 1949, cited in ibid., pp. 218, 188.

[106] Castro Alejandrino, cited in ibid., p. 229; Politburo document dated November 10, 1949, cited p. 218.

[107] Edwardo Lachia, *The Huks: Philippine Agrarian Society in Revolt* (New York: Praeger, 1971), p. 21.

[108] "The Philippine Communist Party," p. 13. INR claimed that after 1950 changes "greatly improved" this situation. Others, however, suggest that despite them, effective control remained very limited. See Kerkvliet, *Huk Rebellion*, p. 223.

Luzon. Without extant peasant organizations and mobilization around peasant issues, neither the PKP nor the revolt found followers.

The insurgency was thus vulnerable to even minor government concessions targeted to the HMB rank and file. For them, the resort to violence reflected the exhaustion of nonviolent means; it was an act of desperation. While the PKP minority dreamed of a "New Democracy," the HMB's peasant majority knew that long-term solutions to their problems required government acquiescence, especially in the absence of support elsewhere in the country. Their actions were instrumental, intended to wring concessions from the government not to overthrow it. As a result, the insurgency's longevity depended on government intransigence. If the government could manage the effort, even minimal reforms could undo it.

How, then, did Magsaysay win? How did he check violence against the peasantry, improve the combat effectiveness of the armed forces, rejuvenate the electoral process, and convince HMB guerrillas that the government would protect their rights as tenants? The standard answer is "leadership." If Quirino was a bad leader whose venality explained failure, Magsaysay was a good leader who "did what had to be done." And Ramon Magsaysay *was* a leader. He was a man of the people who brought to politics both a reputation unsullied by collaboration or corruption and an understanding of the insurgency's rural roots. He spoke *to* people, and his campaign speeches recounted "his life as a poor man who could have made millions while in office, but who could not, even as a Cabinet member, borrow P2000 from the Philippine National Bank."[109] Magsaysay also made sure things were done right—descending unannounced on hapless bureaucrats, garrisons, and even units in the field, promoting the competent, and demoting the corrupt or lazy on the spot.

But Magsaysay could not operate alone. In part, Magsaysay's success derived from his charismatic ability to unify and mobilize the large number of Filipinos in the countryside, cities, and government who were disgusted by the Roxas and Quirino administrations' performances but whose reformist desires had thus far been stymied by the prevalent intragovernmental constraints. But equally important, his resurrection of the Philippine political process depended on characteristics of the political system and the intergovernmental balance of power which explain why he did not end up dismissed or dead as had many other would-be reformers. Specifically, Magsaysay's success depended on the existence of sufficient residual autonomy in the political

[109] Peterson to the State Department, March 30, 1953. DDRS, Retro: 728J.

system for it to be possible to displace Quirino from within and implement reforms which addressed peasant grievances. In the fixation on Magsaysay, American policymakers at the time (and analysts since) overlooked these enabling conditions. As in the Greek case, they focused on leadership will, not on the political context which defined capacity and the realm of the politically possible.

For Magsaysay and the HMB, the midterm congressional election of November 1951 marked a turning point. Documents captured in the October 1950 raid on PKP headquarters revealed that the insurgent leadership expected a repetition of the fraud and intimidation that accompanied the 1949 Quirino election. This, they were certain, would greatly strengthen their cause by convincing many fence-sitters that the political system was hopelessly corrupt. American diplomats believed the same thing, and with good reason, since for Quirino an honest election meant risking defeat. Thus, he released large "pork barrel" funds to the candidates of his party and sent out goon squads, headed by his brother Antonio, to intimidate, kidnap, and kill opponents.[110]

Quirino's attempt to highjack the election was brought up short, however, by skillful use of the electoral law left by the United States. An independent Commission on Elections was responsible for their conduct and empowered to name any group or institution thought necessary to assure fair elections. In mid-1951, the commission requested the assistance of Minister of Defense Magsaysay. Troops under his command protected the opposition, guarded the polling stations, and carried the ballot boxes back to provincial counting houses. Two citizens' groups, the National Association for Free Elections and the Philippines News Service (a newspaper publishers' organization), also supported the commission. They transported people to the polls, watched for fraud or intimidation, and broadcast the vote counts as soon as the counting was done to prevent doctoring. As a result, the election of 1951 was reasonably honest. Although it cost Quirino dearly, the election produced a surge in popular support for the government and established Magsaysay in the public eye. With this mandate he began an active program of reform. By the time he was elected president two years later, the insurgency was dead.

Magsaysay's counterinsurgency program embodied the three oughts

[110] See, for example, Cowen to State, February 15, 1951, and State to Cowen, April 25, 1951, FR, 1951. 6: 1506–12 and 1536–39; Department of State, "Visit of His Excellency Elpidio Quirino, President of the Philippines," briefing memorandum for President Truman, August 1951, p. 3 (DDRS, 1979: 200C); Office of Intelligence Research, "The Philippine Elections," IR No. 5708, November 8, 1951, pp. 2–4 (NADB, OSS file); and Lansdale, *Midst of Wars*, pp. 118–20.

235

as properly conceived. Run out of the small Ministry of National Defense, it avoided bureaucratization and paralyzing intragovernmental constraints. But even though the actual reforms were small or symbolic, they achieved their effect: they convinced people of the possibility to advance with the government. In these efforts Magsaysay had considerable American, particularly CIA, support and the assistance of Edward Lansdale, a brilliant counterinsurgency tactician.[111] Despite this assistance, it is clear that Maysaysay was neither an American creation nor an American puppet. And more important, without these unique features of the Philippine political system, no amount of American aid could have made Magsaysay a winner.

Magsaysay mounted a two-pronged attack on the security problem. First, he depoliticized the military and transformed it into a competent combat force. To do so required fighting off the political officers and their civilian collaborators. But eventually Magsaysay outflanked the corrupt command structure by wrangling presidential authority to promote or relieve officers in the field, order courts-martial, and control the promotion process.[112] Magsaysay also took care that the troops were paid, fed, and rewarded for good work. At the same time, he pushed professionalization relentlessly, disbanded the civilian guards, and merged the PC with the armed forces to be retrained. And against JUSMAG recommendations, he reorganized the army into units mobile enough to pursue the HMB into the mountains where they were weakest and the risk of civilian casualties was lowest. Second, Magsaysay sharply reduced violence against the peasantry. He insisted that soldiers be "ambassadors of goodwill" and Huk hunters—in that order. When asked about Magsaysay, peasants said such things as: he "cleaned up the PC and Philippine Army"; he "got rid of the civilian guards"; and he "made the soldiers disciplined."[113] The HMB leadership agreed. Jesus Lava, for example, noted that "when Magsaysay started making reforms in the Philippine Army and in the government generally, it had an impact not only on the movement's mass support, but on the [guerrillas] as well. Many left because repression was ending, . . . they were not ideologically committed enough to stay, especially as things grew worse [because of the army's new professionalism]."[114]

While still Minister of Defense, Magsaysay also undertook several

[111] See Lansdale's memoirs, *Midst of Wars.*

[112] Blaufarb, *Counterinsurgency Era,* pp. 29–30. See, too, JCS, *History,* vol. 2, 1947–1949, p. 51.

[113] Cited in Kerkvliet, *Huk Rebellion,* p. 208.

[114] Cited in ibid., p. 238.

critical, if largely symbolic, actions to improve the quality and the quantity of government available to the peasants of Central Luzon. First, Magsaysay's campaign to keep the 1951 election honest convinced many doubters that the political process could work. Second, to undo peasants' conviction that the government was indifferent to them, Magsaysay organized a system whereby anyone could send a reduced rate telegram to complain about anything and get an answer within twenty-four hours. Often the response was a visit by Magsaysay or one of his lieutenants. The office was soon flooded with telegrams. Irrespective of his ability to do anything in any given case, the program gave him a big following and symbolized a new conception of politics. Finally, Magsaysay attempted to improve peasants' ability to use the governmental system. Thus, for example, he ordered the Judge Advocate General's Corps to provide legal assistance to peasants otherwise unable to defend themselves against the landlords because of suppression of the PKM. Later, when president, he quickly established a new peasant's union: that, given the reformist orientation of most HMB guerrillas, brought many back from the forest.[115]

Finally, Magsaysay addressed peasants' economic problems. He provided relief supplies, but more important, he attacked indebtedness, tenancy conditions, and land. Unable to get help elsewhere, Magsaysay (and Lansdale) strong-armed the country's rich but vulnerable Chinese community into improving rural credit facilities and reducing interest rates. At the same time, by disbanding the civilian guards, reforming the PC, and providing lawyers from the Judge Advocate General's Corps, Magsaysay made it possible for peasants to resist landlord efforts to extract more than the legal rent limit. But symbolically most important was the Economic Development Corps program which promised land on Mindanao and government assistance to surrendering HMB guerrillas and their families.[116] In fact, despite much publicity, the program provided only 250 HMB families with land and did little to relieve crowding in Central Luzon. Regardless, the intent was to steal the HMB's thunder. It worked.

In sum, Magsaysay won for three related reasons: the peculiarities of the political system made it possible for a tough, bright leader to break the intragovernmental paralysis and take charge; the majority of the in-

---

[115] Thus, for example, one ex-HMB guerrilla explained that "we didn't give up. . . . I still wanted the same things the PKM had wanted. We've still got a peasant union today— the MASAKA [Free Farmers Union]. It's a continuation of the PKM. To have our own peasant organization was one thing we fought for as Huks. So we won some things out of it." Cited in Kerkvliet, *Huk Rebellion*, p. 209.

[116] Lansdale, *Midst of Wars*, pp. 76–77; and Blaufarb, *Counterinsurgency Era*, p. 36.

surgents remained committed to political, not violent, means to achieve reform, not revolution; and he was able to fashion a counterinsurgency program which addressed the three critical areas of security, governance, and development in such a way as to include all Philippine citizens.

CONCLUSION

In terms of this book's broader purposes, the Philippine case offers several important conclusions. First, as in the Greek case, realist, presidential, and bureaucratic politics approaches partially explain American actions. Realism points to policymakers' perception of a security imperative to defeat the Huks. Presidential politics analysis suggests an obvious domestic corollary for an administration reeling from the loss of China and invasion of Korea. And bureaucratic politics helps explain how, despite the perceived importance of victory, American programs were not implemented as desired. Second, however, analysis shows how actual American policy makes sense only in terms of policymakers misunderstanding Philippine politics and the insurgents. Moreover, despite differences in the international and domestic circumstances of the two insurgencies, policymakers' misperceptions of Greece and the Philippines are virtually identical. This, in turn, suggests a certain autonomy to their analytic framework and hence an added degree of explanatory potency for a cognitive approach.

Finally, the Philippine case points to several important weaknesses in counterinsurgency doctrine. First, for the United States as an outside supplier of assistance to insurgency threatened allies, it is clear that in the Philippines, as in Greece, the American program per se was irrelevant. American explanations of what ought to be done were ignored by Roxas and Quirino who used American aid to do what Americans thought they ought not. Conversely, Magsaysay's success had little to do with American effort. On the one hand, the conditions which made it possible for him to rise, survive, and win went unperceived by policymakers. On the other, while he worked closely with American advisors, there is nothing particularly American about the policies Magsaysay pursued. Indeed, possible antecedents for them can easily be found in the reformist programs offered by the peasant unions since the late 1930s. Thus, as in the case of Greece, the apparent fit between the American counterinsurgency program and victory in the Philippines is spurious. The Philippine case does, however, demonstrate the three oughts' utility for a local government—if capable of implementing them. For unlike the Greeks, Magsaysay pursued a policy which not only beat back the insurgents but also reincorporated them into the body politic. He did so because both the structure of government made it possible and the nature of the insurgency required it.

Understanding these differences—in the nature of the government, insurgency, and their relations which dictate different counterinsurgency strategies and their likelihood of success—is analytically imperative. American policymakers and doctrine obscured them, however, and lumped Greece and the Philippines together as undifferentiated "success stories" for American policy. From them, policymakers drew the wrong lessons and thus faced the future with a confidence born of false promises. In Vietnam they would reap the whirlwind.

9

VIETNAM:
REAPING THE WHIRLWIND

Counterinsurgency failed in Vietnam, just as it failed in Greece and the Philippines. This time, however, no local savior appeared. Instead, failure led to the commitment of combat troops, Americanization of the war, and ultimate defeat. Looking back on this tragic process, the *Pentagon Papers* analysts observed that "the question was what *should* be done, not if anything *could* be done. Defeat was too catastrophic an outcome to bear examination."[1] Realist and presidential politics analysis explain this compulsion to act; bureaucratic politics explain the mismanagement of the actions decided upon. But neither answers the one overriding question: irrespective of why policymakers felt the United States had to intervene, why did policymakers choose policies that could not achieve their goals?

The answer lies in policymakers' understanding of Vietnam. In part, they were misled by the wrong lessons and false promises of the Greek and Philippine success stories. But their assessment of Vietnam and prescriptions for it also embody the same assumptions that shaped policy in Greece and the Philippines in the first place. As a result, many believed the United States could do more, and for less, than was actually the case. This chapter examines how now familiar assumptions produced these misconceptions and flawed policies, the failure of which resulted in the abandonment of arm's-length counterinsurgency for direct American intervention in mid-1965.

REALIST EXPLANATIONS

Realist analysis explains policymakers' compulsion to win, their dismissal of circumstances in Vietnam as irrelevant, and the rough timing of their actions. Considering the first, policymakers displayed an unfaltering attachment to containment and a simple syllogism derived from it: Communist expansion threatened Vietnam; if Vietnam fell to communism other countries would soon follow; this would damage American security and credibility as an ally; thus, the United States had

---

[1] *The Pentagon Papers*, Senator Gravel ed., vol. 2, p. 438. Hereafter this will be cited as PP/I, PP/II, PP/III, and PP/IV.

to stand in Vietnam. They worried, too, that in Vietnam the Soviet Union and China were circumventing containment by new, subversive means against which existing American strategic doctrine was useless. Consequently, the United States, in Dean Rusk's words, had "to show that the 'War of Liberation,' far from being cheap, safe, and disavowable, is costly, dangerous and doomed to failure. We must destroy the myth of its invincibility in order to protect the independence of many weak nations which are vulnerable targets for subversive aggression."[2] At the very least, asserted a senior defense official,

> It is essential—however badly SEA may go over the next 1–3 years—that the US emerge as a 'good doctor.' We must have kept promises, been tough, taken risks, gotten bloodied, and hurt the enemy very badly. We must avoid harmful appearances which will affect judgments by . . . other nations regarding US policy, power, resolve and competence to deal with their problems.[3]

And finally, as then Senator John F. Kennedy put it in 1956,

> Vietnam represents a proving ground for democracy in Asia . . . the alternative to Communist dictatorship. If this democratic experience fails . . . then weakness, not strength, will characterize the meaning of democracy in the minds of still more Asians. The United States is directly responsible for this experiment. . . . We cannot afford to permit [it] to fail.[4]

The consequences of this perspective show in the denial of local circumstances. The realist logic subordinated events in Vietnam to universal concerns and led policymakers to downplay their local causes and import. As Acheson concluded in a 1949 cable, "Question whether Ho as much nationalist as Commie is irrelevant. All Stalinists in colonial areas are nationalists. With . . . independence their objective necessarily becomes subordination state to Commie purposes."[5] Or, as the Joint Chiefs put it in 1950, "the war which is now being waged on Vietnamese territory is only the transposition on a small scale of the clash

[2] Testimony to the U.S. Senate, Committee on Foreign Relations, February 28, 1966, in *The Vietnam Hearings*, introduction by J. William Fulbright (New York: Vintage, 1966), p. 168.

[3] Memo, JTM to MCN [John T. McNaughton to Robert McNamara], "Proposed Course of Action re Vietnam," Annex, "Plan of Action for South Vietnam," draft, March 24, 1965, PP/III, pp. 700–701.

[4] June 1956 address to the American Friends of Vietnam, cited in Guenther Lewy, *America in Vietnam* (New York: Oxford University Press, 1978), p. 12.

[5] May 1949, PP/I, p. 51.

between the USSR and the United States of America."[6] In 1966, General Taylor, then Ambassador to Vietnam, rephrased this view: "we are engaged in a clash . . . with the militant wing of the Communist movement, represented by Hanoi, the Viet Cong and Peking."[7]

Finally, the rough timing of American involvement can be explained by the interaction of perceived security threats and the possibilities of meeting them. In Indochina policymakers faced a dilemma. On the one hand, they believed that continued French control would lead to hypernationalism and Communist subversion. On the other, they feared that pressure for decolonization might hurt American interests in Europe. The latter position prevailed. In 1945 the oss concluded that the United States had no interest in alienating the "European states whose help we need to balance Soviet power in Europe."[8] Two years later, the State Department asserted that "We cannot conceive setbacks to long-range interests France which would not also be setbacks [of] our own." Thus, "in particular, we recognize Vietnamese will for [an] indefinite period require . . . [the] enlightened political guidance which can be provided only by [a] nation steeped like France in democratic tradition . . . respect human liberties and worth individual."[9] Moreover, noted the 1948 "Policy Statement on Indochina," pressure for decolonization would hurt French moderates and so threaten "an immediate and vital interest" in keeping in power "a friendly government to assist in the furtherance of our aims in Europe," which must "take precedence over active steps . . . toward the realization of our objectives in Indochina."[10] Thus linked to France's efforts in Indochina because of concerns for European security, American involvement followed France's need. When the Korean invasion raised the spectre of communist aggression everywhere in Asia, support for the French became imperative for reasons of Asian security, too. With each French setback, American aid increased, ultimately totaling more than $2.6 billion in weapons and budgetary support—about 80 percent of the war's cost.

Against this backdrop, policymakers continued attempts to force

[6] "Viet Nam and the Implementation of the United States Economic and Military Assistance Program," TC-15306, T-10/R-III, French, April 11, 1950, p. 45. DDRS, Retro: 248F.

[7] Testimony to the U.S. Senate, Committee on Foreign Relations, February 17, 1966, in *Vietnam Hearings*, p. 168.

[8] oss, "Problems and Objectives of United States Policy," April 2, 1945, cited in George Herring, *America's Longest War: The United States and Vietnam, 1950–1975* (New York: Wiley, 1979), p. 6.

[9] Department of State guidance to U.S. diplomats Paris, Hanoi, Saigon, May 3, 1947, PP/I, pp. 31–32.

[10] September 27, 1948, FR, 1948, 6: 48.

France to make concessions to non-Communist nationalists but failed. Where the United States sought to contain communism by coopting Indochinese nationalism, the French sought to maintain the empire. As the *Pentagon Papers* note, "France was *not* fighting a long and costly war in order to thereafter completely pull out."[11] Fixated on the short-term, policymakers sacrificed pressure for reform to get on with the war. But as Far Eastern Bureau analyst John H. Ohly warned in late 1950,

> one step after another we are gradually . . . getting ourselves into a position where our responsibilities . . . supplant rather than complement those of the French, and where failures are attributed to us as though we were the primary party at fault and in interest. We may be on the road to being a scapegoat, and we are certainly dangerously close to . . . being . . . committed even to direct intervention. These situations unfortunately have a way of snowballing.[12]

Four years later, one American diplomat commented wryly, "We are the last French colonialists in Indochina."[13] Committed by its commitments, the United States stepped in when the French stepped out.

Presidential and Bureaucratic Politics

If realist analysis explains why intervention seemed necessary, presidential and bureaucratic politics explain why the effort was often half-hearted and mismanaged. As for the former, presidents from Truman to Ford faced a dilemma which kept them from doing even the minimum their advisors told them was necessary to win. On the one hand, they believed the importance of Vietnam to containment, credibility, and national security. As presidents, they also believed that to "lose Vietnam to Communism" would be politically disastrous at home. On the other hand, each had reason to balk at the political costs of devoting scarce resources or troops to Vietnam, particularly given the lesson of Korea—no more land wars in Asia. These contradictory pressures led presidents to pursue not victory, but stalemate, albeit at an escalating level of involvement, as deteriorating conditions in Vietnam required higher levels of commitment to avoid collapse. As Leslie Gelb and Richard Betts put it, until the summer of 1965, "they did what they

[11] PP/I, p. 81.
[12] "Memorandum for the Secretary: Reappraisal of U.S. Position with respect to Indochina," November 20, 1950, pp. 41–42. DDRS, Retro: 553B.
[13] Cited by Max Arnaud, *Le Monde*, November 12, 1953.

deemed to be minimally necessary at each stage to keep Vietnam and later South Vietnam out of Communist hands."[14] In short, policy was dictated not by the imperatives of the international system but by what was possible given the constraints under which presidents responded to them.

Bureaucratic politics analysts argue that counterinsurgency failed because it was bungled by those charged with its implementation. Concerning the military, critics dismiss political constraints and insist that the war was lost because of organizational and doctrinal inflexibility.[15] This intransigence derived from several sources. First, counterinsurgency had no place in the military assistance program which was, noted the *Pentagon Papers*, "dominated by conventional military conceptions."[16] Second, even when difficulties became apparent to advisors in the field, concern that criticism would reflect on their own performance kept them quiet. Nor did development of formal counterinsurgency doctrine help since, even apart from its weaknesses, little of the new doctrinal literature penetrated the military and the officer corps refused to accept that which did.[17] As one general is reported to have exploded, "I'll be damned if I permit the United States Army, its institutions, its doctrine, and its traditions, to be destroyed just to win this lousy war!"[18]

Prior to 1965, the problem showed most clearly in the mirror imaging of American military doctrine and organization in the Army of the Republic of Vietnam (ARVN). Doctrinally, ARVN was taught the four classic functions of the U.S. Army: "find, fix, fight and finish." More specifically, in the words of General William DePuy, they were taught that "the solution in Vietnam is more bombs, more shells, more napalm . . . 'til the other side cracks and gives up."[19] Organizationally, ARVN

[14] Leslie H. Gelb and Richard K. Betts, *The Irony of Vietnam: The System Worked* (Washington, D.C.: Brookings, 1979), p. 25.
[15] The best available bureaucratic study of the U.S. military in Vietnam is *The Army and Vietnam* by Andrew Krepinevich, Jr. See also Blaufarb, *Counterinsurgency Era*, p. 252; and Brian Jenkins, *The Unchangeable War*, RM-6278-1-ARPA (Santa Monica: RAND Corp., 1972), pp. 1–2.
[16] PP/II, p. 408.
[17] See Lewy, *America in Vietnam*, p. 119; Blaufarb, *Counterinsurgency Era*, p. 288; Heymann and Whitson, *Can and Should the United States Preserve a Military Capability for Revolutionary Conflict?*, pp. 27–28; Col. Francis Kelly, *U.S. Army Special Forces, 1961–1971*, Vietnam Studies (Washington, D.C.: Department of the Army, 1973), pp. 163–64.
[18] Jenkins, *Unchangeable War*, p. 3.
[19] Cited in Daniel Ellsberg, *Papers on the War* (New York: Simon and Schuster, 1972), p. 234.

was prepared to refight the Korean war and defeat the "worst case" threat facing South Vietnam: an invasion by the North. Like its American counterpart, ARVN learned to rely on armor, artillery, and transport, although all three limited its ability to fight guerrillas.

Similar explanations focusing on the civilian bureaucracies trace policy confusion to managerial problems. Thus, although strategic and political concerns may have led to involvement, once involved

> the bureaucracy became like a cement block in the trunk of a car—it added tremendous momentum. Cautious, sometimes resistant, in the earlier years, each bureaucratic organization then had its own stakes. The military had to prove that American arms and advice could succeed. The Foreign Service had to prove that it could bring about political stability . . . and build a nation. The CIA had to prove . . . that it could handle covert operations. . . . The Agency for International Development . . . had to prove that pacification could work and that advice and millions of dollars . . . could bring political returns.[20]

Moreover, simply *having* "unexploited counter-guerrilla assets" was itself an incentive for action. ("It is somehow wrong to be developing these capabilities," Walt Rostow said of the Green Berets, "but not applying them in a crucial theater. . . . In Knute Rockne's old phrase, we are not saving them for the junior prom.")[21] The momentum, however, carried different policies in different directions as each organization defined its aims in terms of its organizational mission and available assets. Their efforts might have been coordinated had there been an overarching command structure, but there was none. Instead, with only unimportant exceptions, noted Robert Komer, "not a single senior level official above the rank of office director or colonel in any U.S. agency dealt full-time with Vietnam before 1969."[22]

Such analysis thus echoes Robert McNamara's 1966 conclusion that the cause of counterinsurgency failure "undoubtedly lies in bad management."[23] The resultant fixation on management is reflected in the constant organizational tinkering, name changes, and turf fights of the

[20] Gelb and Betts, *Irony of Vietnam*, p. 239.

[21] Walt Rostow to John Kennedy, March 29, 1961, Kennedy Papers, National Security File, Box 192, Kennedy Library.

[22] Cited in Colonel Harry G. Summers, Jr., *On Strategy: A Critical Analysis of the Vietnam War* (Novato, Calif.: Presidio Press, 1982), p. 147. See, too, Blaufarb, *Counterinsurgency Era*, p. 233; and Hilsman, *To Move a Nation*, pp. 465–66 for the "Eyes Only" annex of the Forrestal-Hilsman report.

[23] October 14, 1966, PP/IV, p. 351.

1960s. Again, as with presidential politics analysis, the key is that a managerial focus assumes that *what* to do posed no problem if the question of *how* to do it could be answered. Yet, as in Greece and the Philippines, the assessments and prescriptions which drove policy were often incorrect. Even perfect implementation might not have produced the desired results, but made things worse. To understand why, however, requires another shift of analytic focus.

The Three Oughts

By mid-1955 France was gone, and the United States had assumed its new role as guarantor of the regime of Ngo Dinh Diem. It had been a rough transition. For the French, it marked a final humiliation by their supposed inferiors and recognition of France's fall from imperial stature. For the Americans, however, it marked the beginning of a new era and the chance to undo the harm done by the French. What was needed was enlightened, arm's-length guidance. Thus, as the *Pentagon Papers* note, "the tone of USG internal documents and of its dealings with the GVN was that of a benevolent big brother anxious to see little brother make good on his own—but with the benefit of extensive advice."[24]

After an initial period of distrust, Americans came to see Diem as the local manager of modernization. Not everyone agreed with Vice President Johnson's 1961 claim that he was the "Winston Churchill of Asia," but in the late 1950s and early 1960s most viewed him as a strong leader bent on modernizing his country. Diem, declared Ambassador Kenneth Young in 1961,

> is a humanist who always thinks in terms of the people involved; . . . a planner with a "blueprint" bias and a detailed engineering approach to problems; . . . a traditionalist who takes many of his cues from Vietnamese history and customs; . . . [and] a modernist who wants to graft Western technology onto Eastern methodology. He is the single key to generating action in Viet Nam. His word is a command. He is obeyed.

And, Young asserted, Diem represented those who mattered, "the young professional intelligentsia in the civil service, private organizations and the faculties"[25] who, policymakers assumed, shared Ameri-

[24] PP/II, p. 303.
[25] Ambassador Young, "Vietnam: Some Suggestions for Dealing with the Crisis and President Ngo," memorandum to McGeorge Bundy and W. W. Rostow, April 29, 1961, pp. 1–3. DDRS, 1975: 317C.

can goals.[26] Focus on the moderns also led policymakers to consider the peasantry irrelevant. What mattered, declared Ambassador Young, was to give Diem "the motivation and confidence to do many stern, disagreeable things." The State Department's Office of Intelligence Research concluded that the "most urgent" tasks are "(1) to maintain and strengthen the military and security apparatus; (2) to improve the government's capacity to organize the population to serve its current programs; and (3) to keep the people fed and supplied at a level sufficient to avert unrest."[27]

SECURITY

"He who protects, governs," declared Ambassador Young in 1961 and so summed up the priority of security.[28] In part, the emphasis reflected fears in Washington and Saigon of an invasion by North Vietnamese and/or Chinese forces, as well as subversion. But Americans also believed there was a direct link between the regime's military strength and its political viability. As MAAG chief General John O'Daniel reported in August 1955, "A position of military strength is basic to . . . popular support of Diem government."[29] Secretary of State Dulles agreed and insisted that the development of a modern military represented the first, essential step toward stable government in Vietnam.

Diem's forces did not meet American policymakers' standards, however. First, they worried that ARVN was too small and ill-equipped to meet the threat they faced. Second, they argued that Diem impaired ARVN performance by maintaining too tight a political rein. Finally, they fretted that ARVN lacked the professional competence and the aggressive spirit needed to win, while ARVN indiscipline and attacks on civilians damaged popular support for the regime. Thus, the South Vietnamese armed forces were expanded, reequipped with American weapons, and reorganized along American lines. At the same time, training programs were established to raise their professional competence and sensitize them to the political necessity of strict discipline.[30]

[26] As Morton Halperin notes, "there was a tendency to take seriously reports from South Vietnamese officials. . . . Almost no one studied the possibility that the South Vietnamese were supplying information which they hoped would lead the United States to do what the government of South Vietnam wanted." *Bureaucratic Politics and Foreign Policy*, pp. 142–43.

[27] Young, "Vietnam," p. 1; and "The Outlook for North and South Vietnam," IR No. 8008, May 5, 1959, p. 4. NADB, OSS file.

[28] Young, "Vietnam," p. 4.

[29] Gen. John O'Daniel, Chief of Military Advisory Assistance Group (Indochina) to Commander-in-Chief, Pacific, August 9, 1955. PVII: 5.

[30] Krepinevich, *The Army and Vietnam*, Part 1; NSC 5612/1, "Statement of Policy on

CHAPTER 9

GOOD GOVERNMENT

Despite the short-term primacy of security, policymakers considered political development the key to long-term success. As the 1962 "Action Program for Vietnam" observed, "massive infusions of external aid and advice will not in themselves win the war. Rather the outcome . . . will depend primarily upon the ability of the GVN to enlist the loyalties and organize the efforts of the Vietnamese people."[31] Or, as John Kenneth Galbraith put it to President Kennedy: "The key and inescapable point, then, is the ineffectuality . . . of the Diem government. This is the strategic factor."[32]

American concerns took several forms. Policymakers worried over the "inescapable fact that there is no tendency toward team play or mutual loyalty . . . among many of the leaders and political groups within South Vietnam."[33] They criticized "over-concentration of governmental power and authority," "lack of government efficiency," officials' insensitivity and corruption, and the lack of an "unifying spirit or cause" to mobilize popular support.[34] Thus, policymakers demanded first "that South Vietnamese leaders declare a moratorium on their bickering and knuckle down to the increased effort needed to defeat the Viet Cong."[35] Second, they sought to convince Diem "to broaden the base of political power . . . coupled with a strengthening of the civilian bureaucracy."[36] Third, the GVN should "demonstrate visibly and dramatically its continuing concern for the welfare of the Vietnamese people," and "saturate the minds of the people with some socially conscious and attractive ideology."[37]

U.S. Policy in Mainland Southeast Asia," September 5, 1956 (PVII: 22); and Hilsman, "General Taylor's Recommendations on South Vietnam," memorandum to the Secretary, November 16, 1961, pp. 5–6. DDRS, Retro: 808F.

[31] Department of State, "Action Program for Vietnam: General," August 14, 1962, p. 1. DDRS, 1978: 113A.

[32] "Policy in Vietnam," cable to Kennedy, November 21, 1961, p. 3. DDRS, Retro: 39A.

[33] Gen. Maxwell Taylor, "The Current Situation in South Vietnam—November 1964," excerpts printed in the *New York Times*, June 14, 1971.

[34] Nolting to the Secretary of State, July 14, 1961, p. 3 (DDRS, Retro: 787B); and *Vietnam Hearings*, p. 6.

[35] Dean Rusk, "Vietnam," memorandum for July 2, 1965 meeting on U.S. military and political options in South Vietnam, July 1, 1965, p. 3. Johnson Library.

[36] Hilsman, "General Taylor's Recommendations," p. 10. See, too, Nolting to the Secretary of State, June 12, 1961, p. 2 (DDRS, Retro: 784G); Bowles to Nolting, November 4, 1961, pp. 1–2 (DDRS, Retro: 799E); and Durbrow to Diem, October 14, 1960 (PVII: 75–8).

[37] "Action Program for Vietnam," pp. 1–2; and PP/II, p. 530.

PROGRESS

Finally, Americans worried that poverty and the trauma of modernization made the rural masses of Vietnam vulnerable to Communist appeals. Thus, the United States sought to meet short-term relief needs and long-term developmental ones. For example, NSAM 111 of November 22, 1961, authorized support "to permit the GVN to pursue a vigorous flood relief and rehabilitation program" and any aid needed "in support of the security effort." More generally, the ICA and later AID (USOM) built roads, hospitals, and schools, distributed fertilizer, improved rice seed, pigs, and so on. Some, such as President Johnson, even dreamed of a "TVA on the Mekong" to transform the Delta as rural electrification had transformed central Texas.

PUTTING THE OUGHTS INTO PRACTICE

These policy prescriptions remained largely uncoordinated until early 1960 when increasing VC activity and decreasing GVN performance led to preparation of an integrated "Counter-Insurgency Plan" (CIP) for Vietnam. It was never implemented. The CIP fell victim to both the new administration's desire to develop its own plan and a feud between MAAG and the American Embassy in Saigon.[38] Most important, however, Diem's intransigence forced American capitulation. Diem refused to unify the military chain of command, tightened personal control over decisionmaking, promoted politicization of the bureaucracy, and blocked all social and political reform measures proposed in the CIP to improve popular support.

Against this backdrop, President Kennedy established the Vietnam Task Force in April 1961 to develop a new "Program of Action." Its "Presidential Program for Vietnam" called for "initiating on an accelerated basis . . . actions of a political, military, economic, psychological and covert character, designed to create . . . a viable and increasingly democratic society and to keep Vietnam free."[39] The Task Force accepted MAAG's assertion that "the chief threat to the viability of President Diem's administration is, without a doubt, the fact of Communist insurgency and the government's inability to protect its own people." Bearing in mind the futility of efforts to force CIP reforms on Diem, the Task Force sought "to win Diem over with a strong display of personal confidence in him."[40] As a result, NASM 52, which ordered action on the

[38] PP/I, p. 269; PP/II, p. 27.
[39] Department of State, Task Force on Vietnam, "Presidential Program for Vietnam," May 23, 1961, p. 1. DDRS, 1978: 112A.
[40] PP/II, pp. 52–54.

Presidential Program, authorized increased military assistance but only "confidence building" measures in the political realm.[41] Within months, however, the Presidential Program was in trouble. vc attacks increased sharply in the late summer and fall, and in September insurgents seized and briefly held a provincial capitol just fifty-five miles from Saigon. In October, the President dispatched two trusted advisors, General Maxwell Taylor and Walt Rostow, to reassess the situation.

The Taylor–Rostow report marked a turning point in American involvement. Where previous position papers had emphasized arm's-length measures, their analysis recommended use of American combat troops and a high-profile commitment to South Vietnam. No less important, it reinforced the assumption that the needed reforms could be easily achieved. Indeed, observed the *Pentagon Papers* analysts, "The question of an overall strategy to defeat the insurgency came very close to being regarded as a problem in the organization and management of resources."[42]

In Vietnam, Taylor and Rostow found "a double crisis in confidence: doubt that U.S. is determined to save Southeast Asia; [and] doubt that Diem's methods can frustrate and defeat Communist purposes and methods."[43] Without more aid, they argued, Vietnam could not continue the fight; without American backing Vietnamese morale would crumble, and Vietnamese resistance would fail. Moreover, a visible American commitment was needed to impress Moscow to "use its influence with Ho Chi Minh to call his dogs off, mind his business, and feed his people."[44] Thus, Taylor and Rostow recommended a Greek response: "what is now required is a shift from U.S. advice to limited partnership and working collaboration with the Vietnamese. The present war cannot be won by direct U.S. action; it must be won by the Vietnamese. But . . . Vietnamese performance in every domain can be substantially improved if Americans are prepared to work side by side with [them]." In fact, Taylor and Rostow wanted to supply "a generous infusion of American personnel to all levels of the Vietnamese government and army [to] instill [them] with the right kind of winning spirit

[41] NSAM 52, May 11, 1961, PP/II, pp. 642–43. For criticisms of the "Presidential Program," see NSC, Robert W. Johnson, "Program of Action for Vietnam," memorandum for Mr. Rostow, April 28, 1961, pp. 1–2 (DDRS, 1975: 277C); and R.W.K. [Robert W. Komer], "Comments on *Program of Action for Vietnam*," memorandum for WWR [Walt W. Rostow], April 28, 1961, pp. 1–2 (DDRS, 1975: 330A); and PP/II, p. 54.

[42] PP/II, p. 137. See, too, pp. 98–99.

[43] Initial cable summary from the Philippines, Taylor to Kennedy, cited in PP/II, p. 88.

[44] Taylor-Rostow report, cited in PP/II, p. 99.

and reform the regime 'from the bottom up.' "[45] Wherever Diem had balked before, they recommended direct American involvement: "individual administrators for insertion into the governmental machinery," "a joint effort ... to improve the military-political intelligence system," "a joint survey of the conditions in the provinces to assess the social, political, intelligence and military factors bearing on ... counter-insurgency," and "a joint effort ... to free the Army for mobile, offensive operations."[46]

In the military area, the Taylor–Rostow report was optimistic. Taylor's original cable to Kennedy "focused on the insurgency as a problem reducible to fairly conventional military technique and tactics,"[47] and the main report tended "even more to conveying an essentially optimistic picture of the opportunities for a vigorous American effort to provide the South Vietnamese government and Army with the élan and style needed to win." This optimism paralleled the report's analysis of the GVN's security problems as "a pretty straight-forward case of external aggression. There is no indication ... that Diem might not be able to defeat the Viet Cong even if infiltration were largely cut off."[48] Although Kennedy, for reasons of presidential politics, ignored his advisors' call for the immediate deployment of troops, he did enlarge the advisory effort. Within two years there were more than 23,000 military personnel in Vietnam and thousands of civilians on government contracts. Even these efforts failed, however, and for the same reasons similar policies failed in Greece and the Philippines.

The Limits of Leverage

American efforts in Vietnam were hampered by acutely limited leverage. Indeed, policymakers seldom raised the issue. When the United States replaced France, no specific conditions for continued American aid were spelt out, while in 1961, note the *Pentagon Papers* analysts, policymakers still assumed that advice and "leadership by example" would suffice: leverage was "rarely discussed, much less practiced." Even the "limited partnership" intended to overcome Diem's resistance to reform "finessed the whole issue of sanctions by assuming ... that no problem existed."[49] Americans *talked* about reciprocity, of course,

---

[45] Cited in PP/II, pp. 94, 4.

[46] Initial cable summary from the Philippines, Taylor to Kennedy, cited in PP/II, p. 89.

[47] PP/II, p. 92.

[48] PP/II, p. 98. See, too, Rusk and McNamara, memorandum for the President, November 11, 1961, cited in PP/II, pp. 110–16.

[49] PP/II, pp. 452–53 and 411.

but never achieved it. As President Eisenhower wrote Diem in 1954, aid
was contingent on GVN "assurances as to the standards of performance
it would be able to maintain in the event such aid were supplied."[50]
When the United States attempted to collect on his assurances, however, the effort backfired. Eisenhower's ambassador urged Diem that
unless he broadened his government, appointed a new cabinet, ended
censorship, and restored rural elections, the insurgents would win.
Diem arrested opposition politicians, tightened his control of the military and increased censorship. When the Kennedy administration tried
to make its aid program contingent upon reform, it too failed. Diem
informed Ambassador Nolting that Vietnam "did not want to be a pro-
tectorate," and he did nothing.[51] Kennedy backed down. As in Greece
and the Philippines, capitulation left the United States supporting policies believed to sustain the insurgency while committing American
prestige to its defeat.

The leverage dilemma began with limited capacity born of the need
for an arm's-length involvement. In part, policymakers feared a nationalist backlash. As Ambassador Nolting warned, "Strong and evident
US support has brought to the government side a certain number of
fence-sitters. . . . It has at the same time made Diem an even more vulnerable target of Communist attack which has, I fear, carried some
people into the enemy's camp."[52] Policymakers also argued that an
arm's-length relationship was necessary if the Vietnamese were to learn
to manage for themselves, and so they insisted that "we must strike a
fine balance between vitalizing GVN operations by influence of US officials and anything which might be construed as US attempt to take
command."[53] Finally, policymakers argued, the very nature of the war
made it necessary for the Vietnamese to fight it themselves. The problem, explained the State Department's Sterling Cottrell, was that

> The Communist operation starts from the lowest social level—the
> villages. The battle must be joined and won at this point. . . . For-
> eign military forces cannot themselves win the battle at the village
> level. Therefore, the primary responsibility for saving the country
> must rest with the GVN. . . . This rules out any treaty or pact which

[50] October 1, 1954, *Public Papers of the Presidents of the United States: Dwight D. Eisenhower, 1954*, p. 383.
[51] Nolting to the Department of State, November 18, 1961. Kennedy Papers, National Security File, Box 165, Kennedy Library.
[52] Nolting to the Secretary of State, July 14, 1961, p. 1. Diem also used this argument. See Nolting to State, November 25, 1961. DDRS, Retro: 787B and PVII: 148–49.
[53] Joint Embassy/USOM/MACV cable to the Secretary of State, June 25, 1964, p. 1. DDRS, 1979: 206A.

either shifts ultimate responsibility to the U.S., or engages any full U.S. commitment to eliminate the Viet Cong threat.[54]

The cumulative effect of these arm's-length restrictions, however, left the United States limited capacity to push Diem toward achieving the three oughts.

The United States was also unwilling to exercise the leverage it did possess for reasons reflecting two variants of the no "alternatives to collaboration" problem. First, policymakers saw no alternative to victory. Declared Dean Rusk, "we are in Vietnam because the issues posed there are deeply intertwined with our own security and because the outcome of the struggle can profoundly affect the nature of the world in which we and our children will live."[55] Accordingly, Diem concluded that there was no reason to make sacrifices; the United States would. It had no choice, its own interests—real and imagined—left no alternative to collaboration. Thus, every time a crisis offered the chance to apply pressure, policymakers opted to "get on with the war" rather than hold out for reforms. Moreover, whereas in Greece and the Philippines policymakers had to weigh new commitments against the requirements of containment elsewhere, in Vietnam no such constraints existed. No other major crises demanded attention, and the buildup of forces begun in the late 1950s meant the United States was prepared as never before to play an active part. The deeper the commitment, however, the less credible were the alternatives to collaboration. American strength and Vietnamese weakness bred a perverse reverse leverage.

Second, Americans believed they had no alternative to Diem. As Ambassador Heath put it in December 1955, "we will continue to support Diem because there is no one to take his place who would serve U.S. objectives any better."[56] (He was, in LBJ's phrase, "the only boy we got out there.") As the *Pentagon Papers* analysts observe, Diem fully exploited this dependency and adeptly played the

> role of offended lover . . . secure in the knowledge that ultimately the U.S. would not abandon him no matter what he did. . . . No amount of pressure or suasion was likely to be effective in getting Diem to adopt ideas or policies which he did not find to his liking, since we had communicated our unwillingness to consider the ul-

[54] Appendix to the Taylor–Rostow report, cited in PP/II, p. 96.
[55] Testimony to the U.S. Senate, Committee on Foreign Relations, February 28, 1966, in *Vietnam Hearings*, pp. 228–29.
[56] Cited in PP/I, p. 227.

timate sanction—withdrawal of support for his regime. We had ensnared ourselves in a powerless, no alternatives policy.[57]

This problem was exacerbated by fear that pressure for reform might itself topple Diem and with it hopes for a non-Communist Vietnam. Warned Ambassador Heath, "we would assist a Communist takeover by a withholding of our aid, even if it must necessarily be given to a government which is less than perfect."[58] Diem, in short, occupied what Bernard Fall rightly labeled an "unassailable position of total weakness."

The paralysis of leverage efforts continued until mid-1963 when conditions had so deteriorated that policymakers began to consider "the ultimate sanction." But when they did, they did not examine the causes of paralysis, nor did they ask what constrained the ability of *any* Vietnamese leader to promote reform. They focused on Diem. They were certain they knew what had to be done, and if Diem would not do it, someone else would—particularly if impressed by American willingness to unseat the uncooperative. Before turning to the decision to remove Diem, however, it is essential to understand intragovernmental constraints on reform and government-populace relations. Neither were appreciated by policymakers, but both contributed to Diem's intransigence and the disastrous consequences of his ouster.

INTRAGOVERNMENTAL CONSTRAINTS

Behind policymakers' assumptions about leverage were further assumptions about Vietnamese leaders' willingness and capacity to promote reform. As in the Philippines, they saw no fundamental limits to leadership capacity, just a freak unwillingness on the part of a specific leader. Thus, they focused on Diem's personal idiosyncrasies and assumed that his refusal to reform reflected a mandarin preference for paternalism and anachronistic attachment to premodern forms of governance. It was a critical assumption, for as the *Pentagon Papers* note, "it is a matter of record that [Diem] did not reform his government. . . . What remains at issue is whether he could have. . . . If he could not, the U.S. plan to end the insurgency was foredoomed."[59] Examination of intragovernmental constraints suggests it is unlikely that Diem or any leader could have successfully pursued a markedly more reformist course.

Diem's incapacity to reform his government began with the political

[57] PP/II, p. 228–29.
[58] Cited in PP/I, p. 227.
[59] PP/II, p. 410.

structure left by the French. Like all colonial systems, it was designed for ruling a subject people. Thus, in Saigon Diem inherited a "national assembly" whose function was not representation, but cooptation of the powerful. Similarly, in the countryside his administrators, like the *Prefèts* they replaced, depended on local elites to maintain order, collect taxes, and supply conscripts. This wedded Diem to the existing local economic and political power structure and tied his interests to those of the village and provincial notables. As one villager put it, "If you protect the villagers' interests, you cannot help hurting the interests of some very influential men. If you try to please these men, you must harm the villagers' interests."[60] The very influential men had the sharper teeth, and thus, even as VC strength increased, Diem could not consider reforms to meet the challenge. Likewise, despite American pressure and a desperate need for revenue, Diem refused to raise taxes or practice austerity, since as the *Pentagon Papers* note, these "looked more risky than holding out for the Americans to provide a few more millions out of their vast resources."[61]

Diem's system of palace politics further limited the possibility for reform. Americans argued that overcentralization, inefficiency, nepotism, and corruption hampered the GVN's ability to combat the insurgency and perform like a modern government; they also assumed that Diem shared these goals and hence that, offered the chance, he would attack the problems. But Diem did not wish them undone. They were his means of survival in a fragmented political system, his solution to the dilemma of relying on subordinates who might reach for power at any time. Thus, Diem filled the most sensitive positions in government with family members whose loyalty was unquestioned, and elsewhere he employed fellow Catholics, refugees from the North, and others who lacked local political bases. Diem also "deconstructed" the government to insure that no two parts of the bureaucracy or units of the army could cooperate—and so conspire against him. For example, he created ten separate intelligence agencies, none of which communicated with the others and all of which devoted more energy to spying on one another than the VC.[62] Finally, Diem used corruption to buy off the potentially troublesome, on the safe assumption that those served by the system would not attack it. And as Colonel Nguyen Huy Loi put

[60] Samuel Popkin, "Pacification: Politics and the Village," AS 10: 8 (August 1970), p. 668.

[61] PP/II, p. 62.

[62] Dennis Duncanson, *Government and Revolution in Vietnam* (New York: Oxford University Press, 1968), pp. 255–56.

it later, "to benefit from corruption was actually the principal motivation of a substantial part of the military and civilian leadership."[63]

But while palace politics reduced short-term threats, it aggravated long-term ones. First, as Americans never ceased to point out, bureaucratic divide-and-rule led to uncoordinated policies which did not achieve their ends and demoralized the bureaucrats. Similarly, centralization of decision making in Diem's office reduced governmental capacity to that of one man, while corruption limited its resources and offended the public. These impaired the GVN's ability to mount counterinsurgency operations. Second, and more important for Diem, they also undermined his ability to hold the palace. This was the backside of palace politics. For while Diem's system met the immediate needs of political survival in a fragmented political system, it also increased fragmentation, hardened cleavages, reduced room for maneuver, raised the costs and, more important, the stakes. Diem's system was comprised of the very elements which threatened him and thus depended on the continued ability to placate them. With the rising costs of corruption and the conflict, however, this became increasingly difficult. Furthermore, this vision of the GVN as simply a means of distributing goodies made it an ever more valuable prize, for through it "national" resources (and American aid) could be funneled into the victor's pockets. This ultimately undid both Diem himself and American hopes that someone else could shore these fragments against the ruin.

The consequences of palace politics for American counterinsurgency prescriptions show most clearly in the politicized military. Trouble began with a misassessment of the security threat facing Vietnam and naive assumptions about the supposedly apolitical nature of a modern military. In 1954 policymakers judged a Korea-like invasion to be *the* threat and prescribed the development of a large, conventional American-style army.[64] They saw this endeavor in strictly technical terms, and MAAG officers "deluded themselves" into ignoring both the local political impact of their "gift-bearing role [and] the often adverse consequences of their 'purely technical' assistance on the military as well as the larger political authority structure."[65] Thus, in 1960 official spokesmen proclaimed that the United States had achieved a "minor

[63] Cited in Stephen Hosmer, Konrad Kellen, and Brian Jenkins, *The Fall of South Vietnam: Statements by Vietnamese Military and Civilian Leaders*, R-2208-OSD (HIST) (Santa Monica: RAND Corp., 1978), p. 31.

[64] For the story of the American advisory effort, see Krepinevich, *The Army and Vietnam*, Part 1.

[65] Heymann and Whitson, *Can and Should the United States Preserve a Military Capability for Revolutionary Conflict?*, p. 47.

miracle," transforming what had been "little more than a marginal collection of armed men" into a modern army.[66] The real situation was rather different. ARVN's organization and doctrine were inappropriate for counterinsurgency, while its size, status, and infrastructure requirements swamped the budget and starved civil administration and economic development of investment capital, operating funds, and quality personnel. Most important, however, American aid increased the danger of military coups. As the *Pentagon Papers* observe, ARVN developed "a potentially effective institutional framework under U.S. tutelage, but that effectiveness ... Diem realized, could potentially be transferred into effectiveness against himself."[67]

Diem went on the offensive. To frustrate conspiracies against him, he attacked the chain of command, creating overlapping jurisdictions, multiple channels of communication with the palace, and bypassing the chief of staff altogether.[68] Similarly, he promoted interservice rivalries and civil-military conflicts. Finally, he manipulated the promotion system to weed out charismatic, independent officers and reward Catholics, other displaced Northerners, relatives, and loyal incompetents such that "before long, the upper echelons of the officer corps were preponderantly from these groups and closely netted to the Diem family web of preferment,"[69] that is, sanctioned corruption.

While these measures fulfilled Diem's purpose until October 1963, they destroyed ARVN. Political manipulation left it incapable of fighting effectively. No less important, ARVN's rapid growth, increased rural presence, and the militarization of rural administration provoked hostile reactions from the citizenry as the high command came to regard itself as an army of occupation in its own country. Moreover, military administrators often plundered their charges, while the troops lived off the peasants because corrupt officers sold their rations on the black market. As a result, a MACV study reported in December 1963, "The arrogant, inconsiderate treatment of civilians by soldiers has caused many civilians to support the Viet Cong."[70]

[66] Judson Connor, "Teeth for the Free World Dragon," *Army Information Digest* (November 1960), p. 33.

[67] PP/II, p. 134.

[68] Note the *Pentagon Papers*, "the division and confusion of military authority served a real purpose for a ruler ... with no broad base of support: it lessened the chance of a coup that would throw him out." PP/II, p. 24.

[69] PP/I, p. 323.

[70] Cited in Kelly, *Special Forces*, p. 62. See, too, PP/I, p. 256; J. J. Zasloff, *Origins of the Insurgency in South Vietnam, 1954–1960: The Role of the Southern Vietminh Cadres*, RM-5163/2/ARPA (Santa Moncia: RAND Corp., 1967); Lewy, *America in Vietnam*, pp. 177–79; and W. P. Davison, *Some Observations on Viet Cong Operations in*

In sum, quite apart from Diem's mandarin unwillingness to reform, there is little reason to believe he could have even had he wanted to. To the contrary, intragovernmental constraints limited his room for maneuver, while his responses to them and American programs made things worse. But it is also necessary to look beyond the GVN. The ultimate issues were relations to the population: not only could the government act, but also did its actions respond to the challenge it faced. Here, too, however, misassessment of government- and insurgent-population relations bred bad policy.

GOVERNMENT-POPULATION RELATIONS

Convinced of the Diem government's legitimacy, American policymakers sought to *reinforce*, not reshape, it. To them, popular nonsupport of the government indicated that, although the system was not functioning well, improvements would fix the problems. Conversely, they dismissed the insurgents as illegitimate, ignored the issues they raised, and attributed their successes to organizational technique, propaganda, and coercion. That picture will not bear scrutiny, however.

The problems appear first in policymakers' focus on infiltration. Both American and Vietnamese officials believed that VC strength depended on forces infiltrated from the North. General Bruce Palmer, Jr., for example, former commander of U.S. Army, Vietnam, argued that "cut off from substantial out-of-country support, the Viet Cong was bound to wither on the vine." Similarly, General Truong argues that Vietnam could easily have solved its internal problems "if the infiltration could have been brought under control."[71] At least for the Diem era, however, such claims are misleading since even United States government figures indicate that the number of infiltrators was minimal, particularly in relation to total VC strength. Moreover, based on his study of Long An, Jeffrey Race concludes that by the time significant infiltration started in 1959, the local VC was already "well on its way" to "destroying the government's local apparatus." Finally, by this time, Diem's "Denounce Communists" campaign had all but wiped out the "stay-behind" cadres who were to have mounted a "sponsored" take-

---

the Villages, RM-5267/2-ISA/ARPA (Santa Monica: RAND Corp., 1968), pp. 41–42. Similar problems plagued the police assistance program. See Blaufarb, *Counterinsurgency Era*, pp. 216–17.

[71] Cited in Summers, *On Strategy*, p. 123; and Hosmer et al., *Fall of South Vietnam*, p. 45.

over from within.[72] Enough remained to organize the insurgency, but the manpower had to be local. This posed no problem, however, noted the *Pentagon Papers* analysts, since conditions in the countryside created by Diem's policies "could have underwritten a major resistance movement even without North Vietnamese help."[73]

Policymakers also focused on terrorism to explain support for the insurgents: peasants would not support the GVN while subject to VC coercion, and the GVN could not win if it could not "terrorize at will" as could the VC.[74] But there are two problems. The VC were careful *not* to attack peasants and instead targeted GVN officials, landowners, and rent collectors. Insofar as these were corrupt and abusive, many peasants were grateful, or at least not offended by VC "terror."[75] Conversely, the GVN did use terror tactics, including indiscriminate artillery and ground attacks on supposedly Communist villages, mass arrests, and random violence which terrorized but nothing else.[76] More important, such actions suggest that the logic of the security ought was wrong. For many, greater security for the GVN meant tougher enforcement of a status quo decidedly unfavorable to them. Thus, they did not welcome the effort to promote security, and some joined the VC to fight it.

Against this backdrop, security assistance was bound to fail without achievement of the good government ought, which aims to bind the government and people together with shared values. But palace politics imposed severe limits on the likelihood of its realization. In the face of these limits, Americans asserted the desirability of democracy, but in practice they supported central control. Their reasons for doing so derived from a distorted vision of a traditional Vietnamese peasantry. Because of their supposed malleability and vulnerability to unscrupulous outsiders, peasants required guidance by modern elites at the center

[72] Jeffrey Race, *War Comes to Long An: Revolutionary Conflict in a Vietnamese Province* (Berkeley: University of California Press, 1972), pp. 197–98. Government figures for South Vietnam as a whole indicate that in 1959 and 1960 approximately 2,000 infiltrators entered the country. This figure rose to 3,700 in 1961 and more than 5,000 in 1962. William Duiker, *The Communist Road to Power in Vietnam* (Boulder, Col.: Westview Press, 1982), pp. 213, 183–84.

[73] PP/I, p. 242. See, too, Gen. Tran Van Don, *Our Endless War* (San Rafael, Calif.: Presidio, 1978), p. 66.

[74] Race, *War Comes to Long An*, p. 196. (Citing official government statements.)

[75] F. J. West, Jr., *Area Security*, P-3979-1 (Santa Monica: RAND Corp., 1969), p. 5; Race, *War Comes to Long An*, pp. 151–52; Blaufarb, *Counterinsurgency Era*, p. 98; and Duiker, *Communist Road*, p. 180.

[76] Nathan Leites, *The Viet Cong Style of Politics*, RM-5487-1-ISA/ARPA (Santa Monica: RAND Corp., 1969), pp. 63–64.

and traditional notables in the villages. These assumptions—and their weaknesses—show clearly in policymakers' focus on Communist organizational techniques and propaganda and belief in the "myth of the village."

Americans attributed much of the vc's success to organizational innovation—a means of mobilizing the peasantry that both used their passivity to control them and played on their potential for violence. However, by focusing intently on technique, policymakers failed to ask *who* was organizing *whom* for *what*, and thus they were misled. The problem shows clearly in a comparison of vc and gvn efforts. vc organizers were peasants, dressed like peasants, and lived with them. The issues they organized around were peasant issues, the organizations they created were of peasants and for peasants, and they gave peasants a sense of pride and control. The vc, in short, changed the quality of peasants' relationship to political power and offered them organizational tools for coping with problems beyond their reach as individuals.[77] Conversely, Diem's rural organizers were members of the urban elite, qualified for their jobs by a Western education. They did not understand or sympathize with the peasants, and their agenda was set by the Ministry of Interior, the Office of the President, or the High Command for whom the aim of rural organization was better control of the peasantry. For peasants, in other words, the Diem program of more government meant merely more of the same. Indeed, note the *Pentagon Papers*, it meant that the gvn "became visible—and resented—at the village level as it had never been before."[78]

An equally unfavorable comparison can be made in the case of propaganda. Policymakers attributed vc success to a seductive ideology and simple slogans even peasants could grasp. Conversely, they argued that "the people don't know the government's story," that a failure of communication across the modern-traditional gap led peasants to mistrust the gvn, and that the peasantry lacked sufficient national consciousness. Thus, Americans devoted their attentions to developing "propaganda programs emphasizing national symbols such as the flag, photographs of national leaders, and the duty of 'loyalty to the state' "[79] and then supplied the material requirements for them.

[77] It may be argued that this concern was intended merely to capture the peasantry until the communists were strong enough to control them. But intentions are not the issue. What matters is that the vc mobilized widespread and dedicated support from peasants convinced that they could provide solutions to problems created or aggravated by the gvn and its constituents. Americans and their allies could not.

[78] PP/I, p. 312.

[79] Cited in Race, *War Comes to Long An*, p. 206. See, for example, Ambassador

Policymakers assumed, in effect, that any ideology, like any con-
sumer good, could be sold to the gullible peasantry if properly mar-
keted. But as the *Pentagon Papers* analysts observed later, "the sales-
men were less at fault than the product"[80] which had two critical flaws.
First, the assumption that peasants distrusted the government because
they misunderstood it was simply wrong. They were painfully aware of
those government policies relevant to them: for instance, reinforcement
of inequitable land distribution; aid to landlords and money lenders in
collecting rents and loans; refusal to punish abuses by soldiers and local
officials. Second, in a contest between potential *Vietnamese* state systems, what mattered for peasants was how and under what conditions
they would be part of the state. In this, Diem's program had little appeal, while the vc's seemed to offer dignity, the possibility of power,
and practical solutions to daily problems. Thus, the American investment in propaganda only led the regime "to make a fool of itself more
loudly."[81]

The most damaging misassessment of government-population relations, however, derived from the "myth of the village." The traditional
village, policymakers argued, was badly shaken by colonialism and
capitalism. In Samuel Popkin's summary version of the myth, the
French

> changed the traditional methods for selecting village notables and
> chiefs. This destroyed the . . . sense of collective obligation, . . . led
> to abusive village administration, [and] paved the way for eco-
> nomic stratification and inequality: The good notables . . . were
> driven from public service . . . ; they were replaced by less worthy
> men who lacked legitimacy and who profited from their office at
> the expense of the poor. Eventually, this opened the way for a rev-
> olutionary elite to emerge and replace these new "illegitimate" no-
> tables.[82]

Destruction of the traditional village also supposedly left "a deep cultural craving for the restoration of the lost unity of the peasant's world
with a larger world outside the village and, beyond that, with the mys-
tical forces governing the universe."[83] This combination of desire for
authority and abuse by "bad" notables made peasants susceptible to

Lodge's "Ten Point Program for Success," PP/II, p. 530; and CIA, "Improvement of In-
formational-Psychological Program in South Vietnam," n.d., DDRS, 1978: 29C.
[80] PP/I, p. 308.
[81] Duncanson, *Government and Revolution*, pp. 321–22.
[82] Popkin, *Rational Peasant*, p. 137.
[83] Blaufarb, *Counterinsurgency Era*, pp. 93–94.

totalitarian appeals. The alternative was to restore the traditional village and link it to Diem's modern state.

But this vision of the traditional village was, indeed, mythical. It misrepresented its structure and workings, the interests of peasants and notables in it, and the appeal of the insurgency to those subject to it. In fact, at the heart of the traditional village were practices that enforced inequality and marginalized the majority. French rule exaggerated this stratification, not because good old notables were replaced by bad new ones but because the old ones turned French policies to their own advantage in intravillage struggles. Diem's system strained things further. Weaker than the French, yet more ambitious, Diem depended on local notables more and offered them more. Despite nominal reorganization, he did not alter the composition of village government. Positions had to be bought and were thus restricted to the notables who had always ruled. But Diem's greater demands for conscripts, forced labor, and taxes, as well as the bureaucratization of daily life, increased the notables' power over peasants' lives and offered new opportunities for graft.[84]

This perspective offers a rather different picture of peasant motives in the insurgency. As Popkin noted, "the conflict is not between a traditional peasantry and a modernizing state but between a politically sensitive peasantry and a state that is jealous of its own power and prerogatives" and depends on those groups responsible for peasants' "sensitivity."[85] Thus, a policy predicated on loyalty to the existing village system and intended to reinforce it necessarily alienated a large portion of the rural population. Here insurgent and American assessments and policies differed most drastically. Contrary to the United States–GVN strategy of reinforcement, the VC targeted the hierarchy and institutions of the traditional village. In fact, the VC gave precedence to poverty and peasantness, and it changed peasants' relationship to authority by giving them a voice in village councils such that in the insurgency peasants felt they possessed the means to attack their problems, including land redistribution, taxes, conscription, and forced labor. No less important, the VC offered peasants dignity and appealed to their sense of justice.[86] This promise of the dignity, prestige, and mastery denied

[84] Popkin, *Rational Peasant*, pp. 33, 139–65.

[85] Samuel L. Popkin, "Pacification: Politics and the Village," AS 10: 8 (August 1970), p. 671.

[86] As Nathan Leites argued, to many "the difference between the VC and the GVN is more than between the attacker and the defender of a certain social order. It is also the difference between unworthy and noxious men in power and better men aspiring to replace them." *Viet Cong Style of Politics*, pp. 6–7. See also Popkin, *Rational Peasant*, p.

peasants in the traditional village evoked a powerful response. Notes Jeffrey Race, it

> ensured that when the conflict crossed into the military phase the majority . . . would choose to fight against the government in defense of its own interests, or would at least not . . . fight against the revolution. . . . While the government could effectively motivate the minority . . . in the social classes whose interests would be harmed under the society represented by the revolutionary movement, every attempt to demand counterrevolutionary efforts from the [peasantry] simply drove them into the arms of the revolutionary movement.[87]

Indeed, while draft evasion plagued ARVN, the steady stream of VC volunteers shows that many peasants were willing to invest even their lives in the future the VC promised.

These problems could not be solved by the simple prescriptions of the progress ought. Again, perception and policy failed to distinguish among different classes and their different interests. Despite references to social and economic inequities, progress prescriptions largely assumed that "the peasants" simply wanted *more* (food, fertilizer, etc.) and would be loyal to whoever provided it. (Noted Milton Taylor of the Michigan State University team, "American aid represents a large scale relief project more than an economic development program.")[88] But two serious problems stand out. First, GVN and American aid programs were not contingent upon behavior, but targeted as many people as possible assuming that loyalty would follow automatically. VC programs, on the other hand, were contingent and applied only to supporters. Moreover, the GVN provided the contingency since failure to support the VC meant a return to the unfavorable *status quo ante*. Likewise, because government aid recipients faced no such dilemma and owed no such loyalty, large amounts of that aid went to the guerrillas. VC supporters happily passed on a portion of what they received, and many others found it expedient to do so. In fact, aid made it easier to pay off the VC than stand with the GVN against them, thus inverting the intended results of aid.

Second, progress prescriptions did not address redistribution. They

---

60; David Elliott and W. A. Steward, *Pacification and the Viet Cong System in Dinh Tuong: 1966–1967*, RM-5788-ISA/ARPA (Santa Monica: RAND Corp., 1969), pp. 14–15; Jeffrey Race, "How They Won," AS 10: 8 (August 1970), pp. 641–42.

[87] Race, *War Comes to Long An*, p. 150.

[88] Milton Taylor, "South Vietnam: Lavish Aid, Limited Progress," *Pacific Affairs* 34: 3 (Fall 1961), p. 243.

offered incremental absolute gains, but people joined the vc to win a redistribution of power and status, as well as possessions. Thus, notes Jeffrey Race, "those unsympathetic to the government were glad to have dispensaries, roads, loans and farmers' associations, but they went right ahead and cooperated with the revolutionary movement, for *the same groups were still going to be at the bottom no matter how much assistance the government provided.*"[89] The Diem regime understood; this was the flip side of its reasons for fighting. But Americans failed to perceive it at all. In 1970 after detailing American largesse, one official commented, "Of course, increased agricultural income is far from evenly distributed."[90] The "of course" is telling: to Americans, uneven distribution was of no interest compared to the quantity of aid; to peasants mobilized around the redistribution, it was *the* issue.

Nowhere does the clash show more clearly than in the question of land. Here one would think redistribution would receive consideration: 10 percent of the rural population in the Central Lowlands and 44 percent in the Mekong Delta were landless tenants. In the Central Lowlands, an additional 58 percent rented half or more of their land as did 28.5 percent in the Delta. In neither area did they possess security of tenure. Average rents in the Lowlands were 50 percent of the anticipated gross crop and in the Delta 34 percent, although the average plot in the Delta would feed a family only if rent were 21 percent or less.[91] Yet while land reform received limited attention, land redistribution was ignored until the late 1960s. To understand the reasons and results, it is necessary to compare GVN and vc land policies.

The Viet Minh and vc addressed peasants' problems directly: landlessness, high rents, indebtedness, and high taxes. During the war against the French, the Viet Minh confiscated the land of collaborators and absentee landlords and redistributed it to the landless. At the same time, they reformed the traditional system whereby village notables controlled communal lands, established local courts (thus depriving large landowners of the advantage they had possessed in the French court system), attempted to fix maximum interest rates, and replaced the repressive land tax system with a progressive income tax. The vc

[89] Race, *War Comes to Long An*, p. 176. Emphasis in original.

[90] R. W. Komer, *Impact of Pacification on Insurgency in South Vietnam*, P-4443 (Santa Monica: RAND Corp., 1970), p. 15.

[91] Roy L. Prosterman, "Land-to-the-Tiller in South Vietnam: The Tables Turn," AS 10: 8 (August 1970), pp. 752–54 and fn. pp. 753–54; Race, *War Comes to Long An*, pp. 7–8; and William Bredo, "Agrarian Reform in Vietnam: Vietcong and Government of Vietnam Strategies in Conflict," AS 10: 8 (August 1970), p. 741.

reinstituted these policies in areas they controlled, thus capturing the good will earned by the Viet Minh throughout the countryside.[92]

The Diem program had different goals and very different consequences. Between 1955 and 1960, the GVN undertook three reform programs: land redistribution, tenancy reform, and land development. None achieved its declared aim, although all three probably achieved their real target: solidification of support among landlords. Land development projects improved the infrastructure serving large landowners at public (and American) expense, while tenancy reform laws answered American pressure, but were never enforced. More important, Ordinance 2, the "rent limitation program," required peasants to sign an official contract to receive protection. This, however, also forced them to acknowledge "that the land they had been granted by the Viet Minh still belonged legally to the landlords."[93] Ordinance 57, the government's land distribution program, required peasants to purchase their land and produced few results. In fact, Ordinances 2 and 57 restored landlord domination, stripped peasants of the land given them by the Viet Minh, and reimposed high rents. Moreover, since these efforts went furthest in areas where the GVN was strongest, the political consequences were disastrous as the VC gained popular support by promising to defend Viet Minh land reforms.[94]

Americans were indifferent to the land issue. Insofar as they were concerned, it was because Diem's program, admirable in principle, was, as a senior CIA official put it, "notably weak in execution."[95] In part, this reflected policymakers' fear that land reform might threaten the landed classes' support for Diem. But according to Robert Sansom, "the basic reason land reform was not pursued was that U.S. officials did not believe that land-based grievances were important."[96] In fact, between 1960 and 1965, "no support whatsoever, either financial or in terms of advisory assistance, was given to the Government of Vietnam to help carry through this most fundamental of social measures."[97]

[92] Popkin, *Rational Peasant*, pp. 225–27, 236–38; Bredo, "Agrarian Reform," pp. 744–46; Race, *War Comes to Long An*, pp. 127–28, 166–67; and Davison, *Viet Cong Operations*, pp. 95–96.

[93] Race, *War Comes to Long An*, p. 91.

[94] According to senior VC defectors, the VC dates its recovery from the near disaster of Diem's anticommunist campaign from the implementation of Ordinances 2 and 57. Ibid., p. 97.

[95] George Carver, "The Faceless Viet Cong," *Foreign Affairs* 44: 3 (April 1966), p. 360.

[96] Robert Sansom, *The Economics of Insurgency in the Mekong Delta of Vietnam* (Cambridge: MIT Press, 1970), p. 229.

[97] Bredo, "Agrarian Reform," p. 743.

Only the findings of the 1966 Stanford Research Institute (SRI) study of land tenure and reform shook this indifference and underscored the failure to understand the issues as perceived by peasants. Thus, William Bredo, head of the SRI team, reported of interviews with farmers:

> It had been *presumed* that villagers would stress . . . public works including schools. Instead, the desire to own land was at the top of the list, and credit was a close second among farmer respondents. It was *revealing* that the provision of agricultural technical assistance ran a very poor third, and even peace and security were far down the list behind the desire to own land.[98]

In short, for the majority of Vietnam's population, the American program was irrelevant.

STRATEGIC HAMLETS

This irrelevance shows most clearly in the failure of the strategic hamlets program. Although hatched by Diem and his brother Ngo Dinh Nhu, the *Pentagon Papers* note that "by early 1962 . . . there was apparent consensus among the principal participants that the Strategic Hamlets Program . . . represented the unifying concept for a strategy designed to pacify rural Vietnam (the Viet Cong's chosen battleground) and to develop support among the peasants for the central government."[99] Americans expressed pleasure that the program seemed intended to achieve the three great oughts by means of a strategy

> which, beginning with clearing the insurgents from an area and protecting the rural populace, progressed through the establishment of GVN infrastructure and thence to the provision of services which would lead the peasants to identify with their government. The strategic hamlet program was, in short, an attempt to translate the newly articulated theory of counter-insurgency into operational reality.[100]

The program had a meteoric rise and an equally rapid demise. Things went so fast that by the time a national plan had been released in April 1962, 1,300 hamlets—10 percent of the country—had supposedly been completed. When promulgated, the plan called for the construction of 11,316 strategic hamlets. By October Diem and Nhu boasted that more than 3,000 had been completed. By April 1963, the figure

[98] Ibid., pp. 740–41. Emphasis added.
[99] PP/II, p. 128.
[100] Ibid. See, for example, CIA/OSD/McCone Memo for the Secretary of Defense, July 13, 1962, PP/II, pp. 684–85.

266

stood at 5,900 and in July 7,200. By October, 8.7 million peasants had been "hamletized."[101] But when the November coup forced a closer look, it was clear that all was illusion. In Hau Nghia Province, for example, only 8 of 52 reported strategic hamlets were "viable," and the province was 75 percent VC-controlled; in Binh Long only 4 of 41 strategic hamlets had been completed, and of these 3 were "considered populated and controlled by the VC"; and in Pleiku only 44 of 181 supposedly completed hamlets had weapons, the "great majority" were "wide open to VC," and many others had been "destroyed by hamlet residents themselves."[102]

Explanations for the failure abound. The program lacked an integrated national plan sensitive to government capabilities and local requirements. In the rush to complete the program, the GVN overextended itself: critical supplies were often lacking, inventory controls were poor, material leaked to the VC or the black market, peasants were not reimbursed for the homes they gave up, and government services never arrived. Finally, many officials simply did not understand the program or gave it a low priority. But although these problems contributed to failure, such explanations are insufficient. As the *Pentagon Papers* note, a strictly managerial perspective "finesses the problem" since it assumes that "the strategic hamlet program would lead to effective pacification if only Diem would make it work."[103] This assumption is false, however, for reasons of intragovernmental contraints and government-population relations.

The problems of intragovernmental constraints appear first in the divergence of American and GVN aims. For the United States, security took priority as a precondition for the achievement of good government and progress. Diem simply wanted to increase his control over the political system. And as the *Pentagon Papers* analysts point out,

> The Strategic Hamlet Program offered a convenient vehicle for this purpose. . . . It put achieving security before winning loyalty—in an operational context in which it was difficult to differentiate between *security for* the rural populace and *control of* that populace, since many of the actions to achieve one were almost identical to the acts to realize the other.[104]

[101] Blaufarb, *Counterinsurgency Era*, pp. 114–15, 120.

[102] CIA, William Colby, "Appreciation of the Situation in South Vietnam," February 18, 1964, p. 2 (DDRS, 1975: 246C); CIA, "Initial Report of the CAS Group Findings in South Vietnam," February 10, 1964, p. 2 (DDRS, Retro: 39D); and American Consul Helble, Hue, to the Secretary of State, March 11, 1964, pp. 1–2 (DDRS, Retro: 838A).

[103] PP/II, pp. 158, 152.

[104] PP/II, p. 147. Emphasis in original.

When they perceived what was happening many Americans protested, but to no avail. For Diem and Nhu the switch was a logical extension of palace politics. The failure to foresee this occurrence and the assumption that the United States possessed the leverage to change it simply reflects the extent of policymakers' blindness.

In fact, palace politics explains much of the program's apparent mismanagement and the ends to which it was put. The strategic hamlets gave Diem and Nhu an opportunity to subvert the ministries of the central government by creating a special strategic hamlets bureaucracy of their own.[105] This explains the refusal to tailor hamlet construction to bureaucratic capabilities, pursue administrative reform to improve program management, or decentralize authority to increase flexibility and efficiency. Similarly, at the local level the program helped Diem and Nhu destroy opposition groups and consolidate their control by putting party loyalists in command of both the hamlets and the provincial strategic hamlet programs. Chosen for their loyalty, the new representatives' behavior toward the peasantry was of little concern and at least some corruption was encouraged as loyalty's reward.

But beyond intragovernmental politics, it is also necessary to consider the nature of the government-population relationship embodied in the strategic hamlets program. Considered in this light, the program was foredoomed. The incentives for moving into the strategic hamlets were irrelevant to most peasants: they did not need protection, but government officials and landlords did; they did not desire a reinforced status quo, but the GVN and local elites did. Thus, not surprisingly, the program often divided not the insurgents and peasants but the rural population and government. As one American advisor put it, "No wonder the Vietcong looked like Robin Hoods when they began to hit the hamlets."[106]

THE COUP AGAINST DIEM

Dominance of infamous men over the state is like a goiter on the
neck of some unlettered rustic; he cannot stand it, stabs it rashly
with a knife, and then dies of the wound he has given himself.
SU TUNG-P'O, circa 1080

---

[105] Duncanson, *Government and Revolution*, p. 314. "I was forced," he told one American official, "to take charge of many new areas of government myself." John Mecklin, *Mission in Torment* (Garden City, N.Y.: Doubleday, 1965), p. 45.

[106] Cited in David Halberstam, *The Making of a Quagmire* (New York: Random House, 1965), p. 187.

As things fell apart in the first half of 1963, Americans responded as they had in the Philippines: they blamed the leader. Counterinsurgency could work; the flaw was Diem. As Secretary of State Rusk cabled Ambassador Lodge, "the Nhus are by all odds the greater part of the problem in Viet-Nam, internally and for American public opinion."[107] But no Magsaysay appeared to make the system work from within and avert the perceived need to "change horses." This time policymakers went all the way.

The idea of replacing Diem was not new in 1963. In November 1961, President Kennedy's adviser and Ambassador to India, John Kenneth Galbraith, had argued that the United States ought to get rid of him. In an "eyes only" cable to Kennedy, Galbraith laid Vietnam's troubles at Diem's feet. "Given even a moderately effective government and putting the relative military power into perspective, I can't help thinking the insurgency might very soon be settled." Indeed, were ARVN "well deployed on behalf of an effective government it should be obvious that the Viet Cong would have no chance of success or takeover." The problem was Diem who "holds far too much power in his own hands, employs his army badly, has no intelligence organization worthy of the name, arbitrary or incompetent subordinates [and] a poor economic policy."[108] Galbraith argued that "Diem will not reform . . . because he cannot. It is politically naive to expect it. He senses that he cannot let power go because he would be thrown out." (pp. 4–5) Thus, he concluded, "the only solution must be to drop Diem. . . . He has run his course. He cannot be rehabilitated." As for who would replace him, Galbraith was unconcerned. "It is a cliché that there is no alternative to Diem's regime. . . . It is a better rule that nothing succeeds like successors." (pp. 6–7)

The same blithe spirit infused American thinking in the late summer of 1963. Confronted with protesting Buddhists, the Nhus turned American-trained ranger units loose on the pagodas of Saigon. The August 21 attacks outraged both many in Washington and the newly appointed Ambassador Henry Cabot Lodge who arrived the following day. On August 24 he cabled the State Department and placed blame squarely on the palace. Lodge's cable prompted an immediate response. It instructed him to give Diem "the chance to rid himself of of Nhu" but added that "we must face the possibility that Diem himself cannot be preserved. . . . You may also tell appropriate military com-

---

[107] Rusk to Lodge, August 29, 1963. PVII: 189–90. See also PP/II, p. 153.
[108] Galbraith, "Policy in Vietnam," pp. 2–3.

manders we will give them direct support in any interim period of breakdown central government mechanism."[109] The fat was in the fire.

By Monday, August 26, the United States was committed to a coup. On August 29, Chief of the U.S. Military Mission General Harkins received authorization to tell the Vietnamese generals that "the USG supports the movement to eliminate the Nhus," and Ambassador Lodge received clearance to "announce suspension of aid [to] Diem Government at a time and under conditions of your choice."[110] The same day Lodge cabled Rusk that

> We are launched on a course from which there is no respectable turning back: the overthrow of the Diem government. . . . There is no possibility . . . that the war can be won under a Diem administration, still less that Diem . . . can govern the country in a way to gain the support of the people who count, i.e., the educated class in and out of government service, civil and military. . . . We should proceed to make all-out effort to get Generals to move promptly.[111]

Four weeks of confusion followed. The generals proved to be fainthearted, divided, and indecisive. In Washington pro- and anticoup factions struggled for the president's ear. General Taylor and Defense Secretary McNamara concluded in early October that if Diem could be managed better, the insurgency would be "little more than organized banditry" by 1965.[112] A fact-finding mission by General Victor Krulak and the State Department's Joseph Mendenhall produced contradictory recommendations. Krulak argued that unstinting support for Diem would win the war; Mendenhall declared there was "a virtual breakdown of the civil government in Saigon." A perplexed President Kennedy asked, "You two did visit the same country, didn't you?"[113]

While the generals shuffled their feet and Washington chased its tail, Ambassador Lodge remained a believer. On October 25, he cabled McGeorge Bundy that "we should not thwart a coup" since "it seems at least an even bet that the next government would not bungle and stumble as much as the present one has."[114] On October 30 he added that "the U.S. is trying to bring this medieval country into the 20th Century. . . . We have made considerable progress in military and eco-

[109] PP/II, p. 734.
[110] Rusk to Lodge and Harkins, August 29, 1963. DDRS, Retro: 823E,F.
[111] Lodge to the Secretary of State, August 29, 1963. PVII: 188–89.
[112] Taylor-McNamara Mission Report, October 2, 1963. PP/II, pp. 751–66.
[113] Hilsman, *To Move a Nation*, p. 502.
[114] Lodge to Bundy, October 25, 1963. PVII: 210–12.

nomic ways but to gain victory we must also bring them into the 20th Century politically, and that can only be done by either a thoroughgoing change in the behavior of the present government or by another government."[115] On the night of November 1, the generals finally seized control. Diem and Nhu were murdered the next day.

When the blood had dried, Secretary of State Rusk sent Ambassador Lodge a telegram of congratulations. "I want to express my highest esteem," he declared, "for your superb handling of a very complex and difficult series of events."[116] But ditching Diem had been the easy part; the troubles had just begun. As Diem himself had warned, "*Après moi, le déluge*!"[117]

The Coup's Consequences

Diem's death marked the beginning of the end for the counterinsurgency phase of the Vietnam war. The Diem regime disintegrated overnight. With the kingpin gone, the palace politics system flew apart, flinging the once carefully counterbalanced factions into violent confrontation. In the melee, there were only losers. What little stability had existed disappeared, and with it the little military, political, and economic capacity the GVN possessed. The North Vietnamese immediately recognized the opportunity they had been offered and in December decided to escalate the conflict. As insurgent pressure mounted and both the GVN and ARVN withered, the United States faced the critical decision. Counterinsurgency, with its emphasis on arm's-length aid to an autonomous government no longer made sense. There no longer *was* a government worth mentioning, let alone one capable of defeating the insurgents. The choices were quit or take over. But "losing" was never an option. When the GVN went under for the third time, the United States jumped in, too.

The coup's impact registered immediately. By December Defense Secretary McNamara had concluded that "there is no organized government in South Vietnam at this time."[118] In a memorandum for President Johnson, he explained that "current trends, unless reversed in the next 2–3 months, will lead to neutralization at best and more likely to a Communist-controlled state."[119] By February 1964 South Vietnam had its second military government; many more were to follow. Out in

[115] Lodge to Rusk, October 30, 1963. PVII: 214.

[116] Rusk to Lodge, November 4, 1963. DDRS, Retro: 830D.

[117] Cited in Thompson, p. 58.

[118] Memorandum for the record, December 21, 1963. PVII: 232–34.

[119] Memorandum for the President, December 21, 1963, PP/III, pp. 494–96.

the provinces, military commanders and civilian administrators came and went equally fast as each government turned out its predecessor's appointees and rewarded its own supporters with lucrative posts.[120] By mid-1964 the VC controlled more than 40 percent of South Vietnam. ARVN desertion rates and draft dodging rose sharply, and morale fell while VC recruiting soared.[121] At the same time, ARVN behaved more than ever like an army of occupation. Reform stalled entirely, and aid sat in warehouses or disappeared into the black market or VC hands. Factionalism advanced "almost to the point of anarchy."[122] Graft and abuse of the peasantry rose to new heights as officials extracted the utmost from very short-lived opportunities. Too weak to rule and too engrossed in plundering to try, the generals abandoned Diem's efforts to secure central power in the countryside. Instead, they gave power to the sects and openly relied on the coercive powers of local elites. In one blow Diem's ouster undid the GVN as a viable ally, added to the forces driving the insurgency, further reduced the prospects of developing policies to mobilize popular support for the government, and all but eliminated the possibility reforms would be implemented if per chance they were attempted.

Policymakers appreciated the magnitude of the disaster, but their surprise that it happened reveals how little they had understood Diem's predicament or the real prospects for counterinsurgency. The collapse of the GVN exposed the naiveté of Galbraith's "better rule" that "nothing succeeds like successors" and Lodge's "even bet" that the next government "would not bungle and stumble" like Diem's. But most revealing was policymakers' surprise at ARVN's disintegration, for it shows how completely they had misunderstood what Diem had been doing and why. As the *Pentagon Papers* note, they

> had failed to appreciate the deeply corrosive effect on internal allegiance and discipline . . . that Diem's loyalty based promotion and assignment policies had had. They did not foresee that in the wake of a coup senior officers would lack the cohesiveness to hang together and that the temptations of power would promote a divisive internal competition among ambitious men at the expense of the war against the VC.[123]

[120] CIA, William Colby, "Appraisal of the Situation in South Vietnam," February 14, 1964, p. 1. DDRS, 1975: 246C. See, too, McNamara, Memorandum for the President, March 16, 1964. PVII: 249–51.

[121] McNamara, memorandum for the President, March 16, 1964. PVII: 249–58.

[122] CIA, "The Situation in South Vietnam," Special National Security Estimates, SNIE 53-2-64, October 1, 1964. PVII: 323.

[123] PP/II, p. 205.

Following the coup, these hidden weaknesses appeared immediately. The generals were revealed in their full glory: politically immature, administratively inexperienced, and militarily incompetent. Direct access to wider fields for corruption (especially U.S. aid) only spurred further conflict and dereliction of duty among officers, while it gave them a new interest in resisting professionalization and reform of the command structure to suit the fighting.

The coup's consequences did not produce any analytic breakthroughs. Policymakers haggled over how heavily military or political counterinsurgency programming should be. McNamara and the Pentagon believed that "the military tools and concepts of the GVN/US effort are generally sound and adequate. Substantially more can be done in the effective employment of military forces in the economic and civic action areas."[124] State Department and other civilian officials criticized too tight a focus on military issues, but like the military they continued to believe in the basic program. As Roger Hilsman, an advocate of the "political" approach, wrote Secretary of State Rusk, "In my judgment, the strategic concept that was developed for South Vietnam remains basically sound. If we can ever manage to have it implemented fully and with vigor, the result will be victory."[125]

Policymakers clung to their belief that the lack of leadership was the main problem. Neither aid nor advice took new directions in the year and a half that followed Diem's murder. Instead, past failures and present problems were blamed on Diem, while policy proceeded as before. When nothing happened, Secretary of State Rusk was reduced to asking Ambassador Lodge plaintively, "Is there any way in which we can shake the main body of leadership by the scruff of the neck and insist that they put aside all bickering and lesser differences in order to concentrate on the defeat of the Viet Cong?" There was not, and as the CIA reported "no Magsaysay has yet appeared."[126]

Policymakers also blamed mismanagement for the failure of otherwise well-conceived policies. But if GVN collapse made improved Vietnamese implementation impossible in the short-term and the VC threat precluded long-term solutions, how could the recommended policies be put in place? The only answer was direct involvement. Already in January 1964 the Joint Chiefs had concluded that the United States "must be prepared to put aside many of the self-imposed restrictions which now limit our efforts" and "undertake bolder actions which may em-

[124] McNamara, memorandum for the President, March 16, 1964.
[125] "South Vietnam," memorandum for the Secretary, n.d., p. 1. DDRS, 1978: 295D.
[126] Rusk to Lodge, May 21, 1964 (PVII: 270–72); and CIA, "The Situation in South Vietnam," Special National Security Estimate, SNIE 53-2-64, October 1, 1964. PVII: 325.

body greater risks." They recommended that the United States take over "the actual tactical direction of the war" and "commit additional US forces, as necessary, in support of combat action."[127] In May, Secretary of State Rusk's special assistant, William Sullivan, presented a list of possible initiatives to National Security Advisor McGeorge Bundy. Because "more stress has been placed upon the fragile framework of the Vietnamese government than it can stand," he suggested the "encadrement" of American officers and "coadministrators" to manage the war and pacification.[128] On the same day, Rusk cabled Ambassador Lodge that mobilization of the GVN "can only be done with a pervasive intrusion of Americans into their affairs."[129]

The Great Society and the Goldwater challenge stood between such recommendations and their implementation. But the Johnson landslide of November 1964 and continued GVN deterioration brought them into the Oval Office in January 1965. Six months later, the Marines landed in Danang. Intervention had replaced counterinsurgency.

CONCLUSION

In sum, Vietnam demonstrates the interdependence and distinctness of our alternative explanations of foreign policy. On the one hand, realist analysis explains the otherwise incredible importance attributed to Vietnam, presidential politics the rejection of "win" strategies, bureaucratic politics the muddling of what was done, and cognitive content what policymakers thought ought to be done. Conversely, however, without prior reference to the latter, the former are misleading. Policymakers' fear of Communist expansion in Asia, for example, may have driven American involvement in Vietnam, yet realist analysis says nothing about the accuracy of their threat assessment or the possibility of intervening successfully. In fact, their fears and actions were shaped by a distorted view of Vietnam which, if different, might have had quite different consequences. Similarly, bureaucratic analysis implies that policy failed because of managerial problems. But in Vietnam policymakers set out to do the wrong things. No amount of managerial manipulation could have cured this and might have made things worse.

Turning, then, to our second theme, Vietnam demonstrates again counterinsurgency doctrine's failure. For the United States, it promised the impossible and obscured the issues critical to analysis of the pros-

[127] JCS, memorandum No. JCSM-46-64, January 22, 1964. PVII: 235–37.

[128] William H. Sullivan, Special Assistant to the Secretary of State, memorandum to McGeorge Bundy, May 21, 1964. PVII: 268–70.

[129] Rusk to Lodge, May 21, 1964. PVII: 270–72.

pects for success: the limits of leverage, intragovernmental constraints on reform, and the nature of government- and insurgent-population relations. For the GVN, it was irrelevant, impossible, or counterproductive. For both, doctrine failed because it explained what *ought* to happen, not what would happen or what policymakers could make happen. Policy was thus blind, but bold. The combination was fatal.

10

CONCLUSION:
FACING THE FUTURE

> One is bound by one's commitments; one is committed even by
> one's mistakes. The United States may be free to avoid new and
> mistaken entanglements in the future. It is not free to tear out of
> its scrapbook the political misjudgments of the past. Nor is it free
> to avoid entanglements altogether.
>
> STANLEY HOFFMANN

In the above quote, Hoffmann captures both the story and the
challenge of his book, "Restraints and Choices. . . ."[1] In Greece, the
Philippines, and Vietnam, the United States spent lives, money, and
prestige in defense of its commitments. Yet, though our allies won in
Greece and the Philippines, American policy per se failed in all three.
Despite past failures, however, future commitments are unavoidable.
Thus, the challenge is to understand old mistakes with the hope that
through understanding, tomorrow's inevitable commitments can be
more wisely chosen and better managed. But analysis of past debacles
unfortunately offers little comfort. To the contrary, it seems likely that
the underlying causes of failure will remain unchanged.

This pessimistic conclusion derives from this book's key findings.
Stated succinctly, American policymakers misunderstood past insurgency situations, prescribed inappropriate solutions to them, and overestimated the United States' role in the process. They did so because of
the distorting impact of widely shared and unquestioned assumptions
concerning the sources, nature, direction, and potential consequences
of political change in the Third World. These assumptions shaped policymakers' "definition of the situation" by incorrectly focusing their attention on certain issues and causing them to ignore more important
ones. Similarly, these assumptions led policymakers to pursue inappropriate, often counterproductive, policies while closing off other courses
of action not consistent with them. The continuity of such ideas across
four decades and in many different cases suggests they are relatively autonomous and, as such, unlikely to improve much in the near future.

Before turning to the ideas directly, it is necessary to relocate the
claims of a cognitive content approach among those of alternative ex-

---

[1] Hoffmann, "Restraints and Choices in American Foreign Policy," p. 678.

276

planations of foreign policy. As argued in chapters 1 and 2, claims for a cognitive content approach must demonstrate not only that policymakers' ideas and actions are consistent with one another but also that their ideas had an independent impact large enough to merit attention. To do so, this book compared realist, presidential, and bureaucratic politics with American exceptionalist and cognitive content explanations of the motivation, content, and timing of postwar American counterinsurgency involvements. This comparison revealed three things. First, examination of American actions in Greece, the Philippines, and Vietnam clearly showed the important, independent impact of a very durable set of ideas. Second, to a certain extent the case studies pointed not to the exclusivity of these competing approaches but to their complementarity. Each, in effect, refines our understanding another degree by answering questions the others do not address. But third and most important, the case studies also proved the *indeterminacy* of alternative explanations of foreign policy without reference to the policymakers' ideas. These approaches are not truly additive, each illuminating shadowed sections of the previous one's picture of events. Rather, assessments of international threats, presidential calculations of politically feasible responses, and bureaucratic turf battles over who will do it and how make sense only when examined in the light of a specific set of assumptions. In the presence of another set, very different assessments, calculations, and bureacratic coalitions might have prevailed. By the same token, predictive statements about future foreign policy actions and their prospects for success also depend on policymakers' shared ideas, their accuracy, and their perfectability.

To review, then, realist analysis paints with the broadest brush stroke, but also sets the overarching policy environment in which decision makers operate. In Greece, the Philippines, and Vietnam, the United States seemed to face variants of the same security threat. At issue was how a nonimperial hegemonic power could manage threats to weak allies undergoing rapid political change in the context of the bipolar postwar world. In Greece, Britain's withdrawal led American policymakers to assume its role in the Great Game (for which "containment" was but a new name). In the Philippines, the United States feared Communist expansion and, more generally, Communist subversion in the colonial periphery; thus, Americans sought to defeat the Huks in a manner which would also serve as a model to our still-imperial allies. Finally, in Indochina, the United States violated its own precepts by supporting the French in order to meet a more pressing security threat in Europe. With the French defeat, Americans tried to stem what was seen as the tide of Communist expansionism in Asia by aiding "Free Vietnam" directly.

In the case of Greece and Vietnam, presidential politics analysis explains important anomalies in how and when the United States responded to these security threats. Although throughout World War II observers in both the state and war departments warned of American–Soviet conflict over the Northern Tier, President Roosevelt stuck with the Wilsonian idealism of the Atlantic Charter to deny isolationists a weapon with which to attack him. For two years after the war President Truman continued to repudiate spheres of influence, to the near despair of such advisors as Ambassador MacVeagh. When he finally acted, the result was a sudden change of direction announced in the Truman Doctrine. But more than simply aligning American policy with the dictates of containment, the "scare hell" tactics Truman used to convert the public to globalism had consequences for policy. Thus, domestic political considerations first delayed the adjustment of policy to changing international imperatives and then caused it to overcompensate.

Similar considerations mark the course of American involvement in Vietnam. First, although presidents from Truman to Ford believed that not "losing" Vietnam was vital to national security and domestic political success, they refrained from doing even the minimum needed to win because they feared devoting limited resources and political capital to a distant war would damage the rest of their programs. Instead, they pursued a policy of stalemate—doing jut enough not to lose. Second, although policy changed in part with conditions in Vietnam, the major shifts followed another logic: the electoral cycle. President Kennedy came to office with a team of advisors fascinated by counterinsurgency and predisposed to lavish attention on such conflicts; President Johnson delayed the decision to Americanize the war until after he had won a personal electoral mandate; and President Nixon was elected with a mandate to Vietnamize it.

Although analyses of realist and presidential politics explain the motivations of policy and timing, the case studies also show the extent to which bureaucratic politics shaped implementation. In each, policy—defined as "what happened"—reflected not only what policymakers thought *ought* to be done but what the implementing agencies could and would do. Thus, in Greece and the Philippines the American military commitment was constrained because the Pentagon considered both less important than alternative uses for limited American manpower. Conversely, the absence of other crises and greater military capabilities help explain the relative lack of resistance to a Vietnam commitment in the mid-1960s. Similarly, each case demonstrates how large

278

bureaucracies' institutional repertoires and "essence" constrain action. Hence, in the Philippines and Vietnam, the American military resisted adaptation to Third World counterinsurgency conditions and instead duplicated its own organization, doctrine, and tactics. Finally, because each agency concerned had its own resources and sense of mission, American policy in Greece, the Philippines, and Vietnam was often the uncoordinated aggregate of their independent "policies."

Although realist, presidential, and bureaucratic politics approaches seem to explain policymakers' sense of compulsion, the timing of their actions, and the muddling of policy implementation, a cognitive approach is required to understand how policymakers perceived security threats, assessed possible responses to them, and what they actually sought to do. Here it is essential to emphasize the autonomy and impact of the ideas embodied in security and development, and counterinsurgency doctrines. Thus, despite important differences among them, in Greece, the Philippines, and Vietnam, policymakers saw weak, would-be modern governments struggling against a Communist threat from without and a popular one from below. In each, too, they prescribed a mix of assistance to meet the immediate security threat to the regime and the longer-term requirements of political and economic development. In all three, the United States offered aid and advice to expand and train the military, enlarge and improve the government, and promote economic development—in short, to achieve the three counterinsurgency oughts.

More generally, the cases demonstrate how policymakers' "definition of the situation" and choice of responses to it must be understood as products of how they saw and analyzed "reality." In each case, the perception of threat, presumed nature of the threatened countries' vulnerability, identities of enemies and allies, and choice of variables to manipulate, as well as the means for doing so, are comprehensible only in terms of a specific analytic framework. Had policymakers shared a different, more accurate, framework it is possible that they would have acted differently—and still their actions would have fit the expectations of the other approaches. In short, the alternative explanations are indeterminate in the absence of an understanding of what policymakers think and how what they think shapes what they do. Put differently, realist, presidential, and bureaucratic politics explanations stand alone only if one can assume that policymakers perceive the world accurately or at least without systematic bias. And as the case studies reveal, they do not.

This, then, raises this book's second major theme: Why did certain explanations of these situations prevail? Why was the same package prescription chosen for each? And why were other, possibly more accurate assessments and more fruitful courses of action not considered? Or, more succinctly, where did policymakers' ideas come from, and why have they endured despite failure?

Examination of policymakers' ideas reveals neither a uniquely American product as the exceptionalists contend nor a blueprint provided by academic political development theorists. Instead, their ideas are readily traceable to the much older histoire raisonnée tradition of universalistic developmentalism. It is perhaps most clearly visible in political development theory, the inheritor of histoire raisonnée via the nineteenth-century comparative method, classical sociology, anthropology, and psychology. But while during their formal education most policymakers were surely exposed to many of these disciplines, academia alone does not explain their participation in the tradition. In fact, these ideas infuse even everyday understandings of what happens in the Third World and why. Thus, despite the general absence of direct links between academics and policymakers, political development theory and security and development doctrine virtually replicate one another.

This familiarity, combined with explanatory, prescriptive, and ideological utility, explains these ideas' endurance despite academic attacks and real world failure. Precisely because "everybody knows them" these ideas are like Sherlock Holmes's "dog that didn't bark"; their very familiarity leads people to accept them unquestioningly and, conversely, resist alternatives. This set of ideas also possesses a trio of utilities which have greatly enhanced their "shelf life." They appear to provide parsimonious explanations of Third World complexity. These explanations, in turn, suggest readily available policy prescriptions for managing it. Finally, they serve important ideological functions, justifying an American "white man's burden," confirming American self-satisfaction, and providing theorists and policymakers alike an heroic and worthwhile role. Furthermore, the recursive relationship between social scientists and policymakers reinforces this familiarity and the appearance of utility. For rather than challenging each other to question and refine their ideas, they influenced each other only when they reconfirmed shared ideas.

While these characteristics explain theory's and doctrine's popularity and longevity, their most important substantive characteristic is the tendency toward contentless universalism. Both assume a single "normal growth curve" along which all societies progress by means of an equally universal development process. Thus, focused on process, not substance, and on universals, not specifics, they gain the appearance of explanatory and prescriptive power at the cost of an ability to distinguish among cases. Furthermore, the reduction of politics to process dehumanized this quintessentially human activity and directed attention away from real people making creative decisions about their own lives. The result was a critical failure for both social scientists and policymakers: neither theory nor doctrine shed any light on which people or states under which conditions would do what, why, and when.

This weakness shows most clearly in the identical analysis and treatment of the insurgencies in Greece, the Philippines, and Vietnam. In each case, the insurgency was defined as an illegitimate challenge to a legitimate government struggling to manage both the trauma of modernization and the subversive efforts to exploit it. Thus, policymakers prescribed assistance to improve threatened governments' performance in three areas: physical control of territory and populations; penetration of authority into the periphery; and promotion of economic and social development. But this pat assessment obscured the issues critical to an outside power contemplating intervention in support of an insurgency-threatened ally: the constraints on leverage; intragovernmental limits on reform by the would-be ally; and the nature of relations between government and populace and, conversely, insurgents and populace. Without the analytic tools to assess these or to tailor programs to the specific circumstances of individual countries which such assessment would have allowed, American policy in Greece, the Philippines, and Vietnam was blind and consequently irrelevant or counterproductive.

When examined carefully, the three case studies suggest that there is no counterinsurgency "master key" and that efforts to apply one will fail. For policymakers contemplating involvement for whatever reason, the issue is not what threatened governments *ought* to do, but rather sober analysis of what they *can* do and what leverage the United States possesses to make them do it. As for the latter, the case studies demonstrate the need for careful assessment of American capacity, weighed against the necessity for an arm's-length relationship, and American willingness, weighed against the alternatives to collaboration. More important, however, the case studies indicate the need for new, more discerning analytic tools with which to assess intragovernmental constraints on reform (or action) and government-population and insurgent-population relations.

In light of these three variables, analysis of counterinsurgency in Greece, the Philippines, and Vietnam reveals the striking differences among them that are obscured by doctrine. Thus, in Greece the keys were the nature of the insurgent movement and the issues it raised. On the one hand, the KKE did not offer a program to mobilize popular support, but it aimed instead to impose control on the population. On the other, its embrace of Macedonian separatism led to a redefinition of the insurgency as a nationalist issue, not a struggle over the nature of the government. This reduced the political saliency of government abuses, increased its legitimacy (at least on this critical issue), and delegitimized the insurgents, even among many opposed to the regime. In the resulting contest, American prescriptions were ignored and, in fact, contributed to rightist abuses. What mattered was achievement of sufficient military autonomy to out-coerce the insurgents.

The Philippine case differed in important ways. Again, the ability to overcome intragovernmental constraints on action was essential to Magsaysay's miracle. Analytically what is critical, however, is the very different insurgent-population relationship. In the Philippines, the Huks (though not the PKP) had deep popular ties and offered practical solutions to peasants' most pressing problems. Magsaysay was obliged to respond in kind. The resultant intragovernmental constraints were thus far greater than those facing the Greeks while the programs he was forced to mount turned not on coercion but cooptation.

Finally, in Vietnam Diem faced both insurmountable intragovernmental constraints and an insurgent movement which had preempted control of the majority of the rural population. On the one hand, Diem's rule depended on the support of elites whose actions were an important source of insurgent support. This dependence, however, forced a policy of elite reinforcement, not reform. Moreover, the system of palace politics with which he controlled his always dangerous supporters further reduced his ability to act while increasing the strength of his rivals for power. On the other hand, the VC mobilized the peasantry around a program of peasant solutions to peasant problems and deftly used government reinforcement policies to solidify support for their cause. The result was a no-win trap. Diem could either not act and lose by default or act in politically acceptable ways and add oil to the fire. No less important, it was not just *his* problem. As the GVN's collapse following his ouster demonstrated, the intragovernmental constraints on action overshadowed the qualities of individual leaders. Even Magsaysay would have lost.

Here, then, lies the challenge. The key to successful policymaking is the matching of ends and means in a specific context. And as Stanley Hoffmann observes, the more ambitious a policy, "the more indispensible it is to analyze . . . each case with critical rigor before applying to it one's concepts or preconceptions, for otherwise the statesman will trip into the pitfalls of irrelevance, adventurism or unreality."[2] Just as management of Third World insurgency has been an American goal for the past thirty-five years, so it will likely remain one in the future. But as crises arise, warns Douglas Blaufarb, the United States must "scrutinize the terrain with care, with an eye to the underlying fundamentals, and with a disabused realism in regard to its own abilities to provide suitable assistance."[3] In short, the United States needs a new, more accurate triage mechanism, an analytic tool for assessing "the realities of each case" lest blind application of the failed policies of the past once again commit us to an unwinnable war. What are the prospects such a doctrine can and will be developed in the near future? Unfortunately, as Ambassador MacVeagh observed in 1949, "the auguries don't look too good."[4]

FACING THE FUTURE

Counterinsurgency—now part of "low-intensity warfare"—is back in vogue and again attracting the high-level attention that propelled the counterinsurgency era of the 1960s. In fact, as one expert put it recently, the 1980s "ushered in a new counter-insurgency era."[5] Perhaps nothing demonstrates this better or offers a better opportunity to assess new American thinking on counterinsurgency than the January 1986 Conference on Low-Intensity War sponsored by Secretary of Defense Caspar Weinberger.[6] Under Secretary of Defense for Policy Fred Iklé, chaired the conference, which featured papers by the Secretary of Defense, Secretary of State George Shultz, Ambassador Jean Kirkpatrick, and a who's who of American counterinsurgency experts; it was attended by senior representatives of the Defense Department, all four armed services, Congress, the White House, State Department, and CIA, as well as ranking foreign diplomats and military officers. Examining the proceedings, however, is a sobering experience, for they show no evidence that any underlying analytic problems of past doctrine have been recognized, let alone corrected. Indeed, what is most striking

[2] In Richard Pfeffer, ed., *No More Vietnams? The War and the Future of American Foreign Policy* (New York: Harper & Row, 1968), p. 116.

[3] Blaufarb, *Counterinsurgency Era*, p. 310.

[4] *Ambassador MacVeagh Reports*, ed. Iatrides, pp. 733–34, fn.

[5] Sam C. Sarkesian, "Commentary on 'Low-Intensity Warfare: Threat and Military Response,' " in *Proceedings of the Low-Intensity Warfare Conference*, sponsored by the Secretary of Defense, January 14–15, 1986, Fort McNair, Washington, D.C., p. 38.

[6] *Proceedings of the Low-Intensity Warfare Conference.*

about the proceedings is the extraordinary continuity of the ideas expressed.[7]

There is no mistaking either the importance attached to low-intensity conflict or conference participants' sense of urgency that something be done about it. Shultz spoke in words reminiscent of the 1962 USOIDP: the challenge of low-intensity warfare is "one of the most pressing problems in U.S. foreign and defense policy"; indeed, "the future of peace and freedom may well depend on how effectively we meet it."[8] And again, as in the 1960s, one and all agreed with Weinberger that "if we are to deal with [this challenge], we must understand it and understand the circumstances which gave rise to it." "We must decide,"— and must have the means to decide—he observed,

> if our interests justify intervention . . . if the leadership of the country threatened is capable of using our assistance to proper effect, which is to say for the security and well-being of the nation, rather than merely to sustain itself in power and to reinforce those abuses which may have contributed to the nation's difficulties from the beginning. We must decide whether an existing leadership is better or worse for its people and our interests than possible alternatives. . . . We must decide what form intervention should take, if we are to intervene, and by what means, and through which agencies.[9]

But it is here that the difficulties lie, for the new thinking on counterinsurgency—like the old—hinders rather than helps this necessary diagnostic endeavor.

The new counterinsurgency remains as tightly focused on Soviet meddling as its predecessor. Indeed, Weinberger opened the conference by declaring: "Tonight, one out of four countries around the globe is at war. In virtually every case, there is a mask on the face of war. In virtually every case, behind the mask is the Soviet Union and those who do its bidding."[10] Later General Paul Gorman warned that some such conflicts "arise from causes remote from the influence of [the superpowers]," while Sam Sarkesian noted that "unconventional conflicts

[7] Equally extraordinary is the continuity of personnel. Among those presenting papers were, for example, Brian Jenkins, Sir Robert Thompson, and Charles Wolf, Jr., all of whom figured importantly in the counterinsurgency debate of the 1960s, and General Paul Gorman, Ret., who served Secretary of Defense McNamara as Special Assistant for Counter-Insurgency.

[8] George Shultz, "Low-Intensity Warfare: The Challenge of Ambiguity," speech to the Low-Intensity Warfare Conference, *Proceedings*, pp. 9, 12.

[9] Caspar Weinberger, "The Phenomenon of Low-Intensity Warfare," speech to the Low-Intensity Warfare Conference, *Proceedings*, pp. 3, 6.

[10] Ibid., p. 3.

are not necessarily triggered by Soviet power projections or machinations" and may "evolve from the political, social and economic turmoil in Third World States."[11] Yet both warnings were ignored even by those who issued them[12] and analysis presented at the conference followed Iklé's admonition to focus on "the Soviet role in each specific situation and the Soviet role globally towards low-intensity conflict."[13] Thus, like policymakers in the 1950s and 1960s, conference participants explained low-intensity conflict as a Soviet effort to subvert the existing balance of power. As Shultz put it, "the ironic fact is, these new [*sic*] and elusive challenges have proliferated, in part, *because* of our success in deterring nuclear and conventional war. . . . Low-intensity warfare is . . . a flanking maneuver. . . . [It] has exposed a chink in our armor."[14] And how have the Soviets done so? By means, declared Weinberger, of "a strategy proven in the takeover of Russia herself, and refined in the enslavement of Eastern Europe."[15] Therefore, asserted Iklé in his summary comments at the end of the conference, there are no "obscure political forces" to be understood in analyzing a low-intensity conflict situation. To the contrary, "as we look more closely, we will find a body of theory behind it . . . called Leninism."[16]

The consequences of this focus on Soviet tactics are as devastating in the 1980s as they were in the 1960s. The very definitions of "low-intensity warfare" stress the tactics used (e.g., bombings and assassinations), not the underlying circumstances.[17] Even where an effort is made to be more analytic, the definitions offered are too broad to be useful and maintain the voluntarist assumption that revolutions are made by revolutionaries wielding a tested revolutionary doctrine.[18] As a result, critical distinctions among cases are obscured and the whole of

---

[11] Paul Gorman, "Low-Intensity Conflict: American Dilemma," *Proceedings*, pp. 13–14; and Sarkesian, "Commentary," p. 51.

[12] Sarkesian, for example, closed his presentation on the following note: "As Leon Trotsky said, 'The road to Paris and London lies through the towns of Afghanistan, the Punjab and Bengal.' Were he alive today, it is conceivable that Trotsky might have added, 'The road to Washington is through the towns of Havana, San Salvador, Managua and Mexico City.' " "Commentary," p. 55.

[13] *Proceedings*, p. 97. This quote is from the unedited transcript of the conference. Subsequent uses of this material will be marked (Transcript).

[14] Shultz, "Challenge of Ambiguity," p. 9. Emphasis in original.

[15] Weinberger, "Phenomenon," p. 4.

[16] *Proceedings*, p. 191. (Transcript)

[17] See, e.g., Shultz, "Challenge of Ambiguity," p. 9.

[18] Thus, Sarkesian, for example, defines "revolution" as being "designed to achieve a strategic goal, with both strategic and tactical dimensions. It encompasses political-psychological, social and economic components aimed at the entire political-social order of the existing system." "Commentary," p. 42.

the Third World is reduced to a featureless lump that is universally vulnerable to insurgency. As Iklé put it, the 150 countries of the Third World "have perhaps only two things in common—the name and the fact it is an arena for low-intensity warfare."[19] Conversely, as Brian Jenkins and Sir Robert Thompson agreed in one exchange, despite the possibly "unique history, . . . unique culture, . . . unique government situation, unique laws, unique military situation, [and] unique circumstance" of any given case, "we can in fact talk about a [counterinsurgency] doctrine that is fungible from one country to another" because all insurgencies and insurgency-threatened countries are fundamentally alike.[20] A similar, and familiar, universalism informed conference participants' assurance that they already understood the essential issues involved in developing such doctrine, for as Weinberger put it, "there is . . . no gainsaying the argument that we know something about nation-building, having built one ourselves."[21]

The problems posed by such crude generalization show clearly in the picture of insurgency offered at the conference. On the one hand, where explanations refered to local causation, they merely repeated those offered in earlier eras. Sam Sarkesian, for example, referred in passing to insurgencies' roots in "modernization, political change and internal instability," and Sir Robert Thompson to insurgents' use of governments' "shortcomings . . . in policy, performance and behavior."[22] On the other, most explanations portrayed insurgency as requiring no more than "death and destruction"[23] to "instill fear, to institutionalize anxiety . . . and make . . . craven survival the ultimate value," so as to create a situation in which "the better part of wisdom consists of resignation to the will of the insurgents, be they ever so small in number, brutal in behavior, or unrepresentative in their goals."[24]

As the case studies demonstrate, however, these explanations of the roots of revolution are seriously misleading. As for the former, it is clear that such generic assessments of the "trauma of modernization" impede the careful diagnosis necessary before counterinsurgency assistance can safely be contemplated. In particular, they blind policymakers to which countries under what conditions may be subject to insurgency. Thus, on the one hand, they give the frightening, but false,

[19] Summary comments, *Proceedings*, p. 188. (Transcript)
[20] *Proceedings*, pp. 181–182. (Transcript)
[21] Weinberger, "Phenomenon," p. 7.
[22] Sarkesian, "Commentary," p. 40; and Sir Robert Thompson, "Civic Action in Low-Intensity Warfare," *Proceedings*, p. 74.
[23] Gorman, "American Dilemma," p. 15.
[24] Weinberger, "Phenomenon," p. 5.

impression that all Third World countries are vulnerable, while on the other they give the comforting, but no less false, impression that all threatened allies are equally aidable. As for the latter, insurgents *may* pursue policies of "death and destruction," but as the KKE's demise indicates, they are a mark of weakness and the kiss of death. Indeed, if observed, counterinsurgents should take heart, for such tactics indicate a movement without solid support and vulnerable to relatively modest government initiatives. Conversely, neither the Huks nor the VC pursued purely destructive policies. In fact, the seriousness of the challenge they posed was a direct result of the constructive possibilities they offered peasants.

This double failure of explanation is reflected in misprescription. In the absence of improved analytic acuity, no one at the conference questioned the classic "three oughts" or the prescriptions deriving from them. In fact, Sir Robert Thompson unblushingly repeated—sometimes verbatim—precisely the same prescriptions he offered in his 1966 book *Defeating Communist Insurgency*.[25] Thus, both analysts and members of the audience called for increased security assistance, training programs to professionalize and depoliticize the military, the promotion of civic action by American and allied forces, efforts to raise the quantity and quality of threatened governments, and the provision of aid to generate economic development. Despite occasional references to the possible sensitivity of the required reforms, no attention was paid to either the essential questions of leverage,[26] intragovernmental constraints on reform, and government-population relations or the implications of these for the likely success or failure of American counterinsurgency assistance if offered. To the contrary, in the absence of any changes in the assumptions about the target countries, attention focused exclusively on *American* problems in the implementation of policies presumed to be correct.

Contemplating the supposedly world-wide challenge of Soviet-sponsored low-intensity conflicts, Ambassador Kirkpatrick told the conference, "I've my own version of that old Pogo canard, and [it] is, 'I have seen the problem and it is us.' "[27] She and other speakers stressed three

[25] Thompson, *Defeating Communist Insurgency*.

[26] Indeed, Sir Robert Thompson stated that the interests, problems and potential solutions for threatened governments "apply to a foreign power assisting that government," therefore in effect denying the need for leverage altogether. "Civic Action," p. 74.

[27] Jean Kirkpatrick, "The Role of the Soviet Union in Low-Intensity Warfare," speech to the Low-Intensity Warfare Conference, *Proceedings*, p. 130. Similarly, Gen. Gorman approvingly cited a forthcoming article in *Army* by Gen. William DePuy in which DePuy asserts that "the political heart of the matter" is that "we are self-constrained by our own

aspects of this problem in particular: American culture, domestic political structure, and bureaucratic, especially Pentagon, politics.[28] First, declared Kirkpatrick, "Our whole world view and view of history predisposes us to believe that peace is a norm and that war and violence are abnormal."[29] Thus, echoed Weinberger and Shultz, "the American nation [is] culturally disposed to quick conclusions"—impossible in low-intensity warfare—and bound by "moral scruples that discipline our power"—and so "paralyze" us before unscrupulous enemies.[30] Others worried that as a democracy the United States is "at a distinct disadvantage in responding to unconventional conflicts," while the memory of Vietnam has divided American public opinion on the use of force, left "a legacy of contention between the executive and legislative branches and a web of restrictions on executive action," and bred a press that makes the prosecution of protracted and inconclusive wars impossible.[31] Finally, many argued that counterinsurgency failure in Vietnam resulted from the inapplicability of American general purpose forces, the propensity of military leaders "to define the United States out of low-intensity conflict," its relegation to "the periphery of military education and professionalism," distrust of counterinsurgency units by the regular military, an approach to military assistance that makes Third World forces the mirror image of ours, and continued attachment to a philosophy of "laying ordinance on target," especially with "high tech weapons used at a distance" which in insurgency situations "is like using a sledge-hammer to swat flies and is highly counterproductive."[32]

Not surprisingly, the conference focused largely on prescriptions for

---

history and political processes, and therefore vulnerable to failure." Gorman, "American Dilemma," pp. 16–17.

[28] Put differently, they repeated the new revisionist explanation for American defeat in Vietnam that blames a lack of will, too much democracy, betrayal by the press, and political constraints on the military.

[29] Kirkpatrick, "Role of the Soviet Union," p. 131.

[30] Weinberger, "Phenomenon," p. 4; Schultz, "Challenge of Ambiguity," pp. 9–10.

[31] Sarkesian, "Commentary," p. 40; Brian Jenkins, Proceedings, pp. 175–76 (Transcript); Shultz, "Challenge of Ambiguity," p. 11; and Patrick Buchanan, Proceedings, pp. 152–53 (Transcript).

[32] Gorman, "American Dilemma," pp. 15–18; Sarkesian, "Commentary," p. 38; and Bill Taylor, "A Comment" [on Gorman, "American Dilemma"], Proceedings, pp. 60–61. Indeed, such criticisms are so widespread in the counterinsurgency community that Secretary Weinberger had to go out of his way to praise "the most selfless segment of America's public servants" and assert that "contrary to what some have said, it is not preeminently the role or object of our military to preserve hallowed doctrine, nor to preserve honored tradition, nor to preserve budgets. It is to preserve freedom." Weinberger, "Phenomenon," p. 5.

removing these constraints on our ability to implement agreed upon counterinsurgency policies. Some such prescriptions were straightforward (though ironically no attention was paid to the problems of implementing them): if the Pentagon procurement system makes it difficult to develop cheap, rugged equipment for use in the Third World, change the procurement system; if the U.S. military cannot train Third World armed forces for counterinsurgency, hire civilian contractors to do so; if the current organization of the Joint Chiefs of Staff discourages interservice cooperation in counterinsurgency planning, organization and implementation, reorganize the JCS; if counterinsurgency requires special units and a new kind of military man trained in political warfare, set up such units and revamp military training.[33] Many other prescriptions were but vague wish-lists perhaps best exemplified by Sam Sarkesian's assertion that

> Within the American body politic, a new realism must emerge regarding . . . the challenge of unconventional conflicts. Within military and civilian policy circles, in the world of elected officials, and the body politic, particularly the media, there must grow an understanding . . . of the nature of the Third World and a recognition of the long range threat of unconventional conflicts. Without this new realism, it is unlikely that the necessary national will, political resolve, and staying power can be developed to effectively respond to unconventional conflicts.[34]

Specific or vague, the key point is that attention focused on how to better implement the three oughts. There is no suggestion that either the classic prescriptions or the analysis behind them might be wrong. To the contrary, the old assumptions remained unchallenged, despite the logical flaws in them detailed by this book and the real world failures of policies based on them.

If such a gathering can do no better than this, what are the prospects for the development of a new, improved means of weighing and, if necessary, undertaking future counterinsurgency involvements in the Third World? If the analysis presented here is correct, there seems to be little chance we will avoid falling into Hoffmann's "pitfalls of irrelevance, adventurism, [and] unreality." On the one hand, policymakers' perception of both international and domestic imperatives will likely lead them to assess and respond to Third World insurgencies as they

[33] Gorman, "American Dilemma"; Sarkesian, "Commentary"; and Taylor, "A Comment."
[34] Sarkesian, "Commentary," pp. 53–54.

have in the past. On the other, the requirements of a better analytic tool for assessing potential counterinsurgency involvements conspire against its development and acceptance. For it must overcome not only the inertia of familiar ideas, but its own "anti-utility." Explanatory complexity, prescriptive limits, and ideological ambiguity are not the stuff of popular new policy paradigms. Thus, looking back to Greece, the Philippines, and Vietnam, Gaddis Smith's rejoinder to Santayana comes to mind: "One of the most somber aspects of the study of history is that it suggests no obvious ways by which mankind could have avoided folly."[35] Future historians may well make the same observation regarding our new commitments.

[35] Cited in Summers, *On Strategy*, p. 84.

BIBLIOGRAPHY

Document Collections

Agency for International Development:
  Office of Public Safety archives
Carrollton Press, Inc.
  Declassified Documents Reference System
Central Intelligence Agency:
  National Intelligence Estimates
  Review of the World Situation as It Relates to the Security of the
    United States
  Situation Reports
Department of State:
  Foreign Relations of the United States
  General Foreign Policy Series
  Near Eastern Series (also Near and Middle Eastern Series)
National Archives:
  Modern Military Branch
    Joint Chiefs of Staff papers
    National Security Council Papers
  Diplomatic Branch
    Office of Strategic Services series (also Bureau of Intelligence Re-
      search, Department of State)
    Policy Planning Staff papers
*The Pentagon Papers: The Defense Department History of United
  States Decisionmaking in Vietnam.* Senator Gravel edition. 4 vols.
  Boston: Beacon Press, 1971.
Porter, Gareth, ed. *Vietnam: The Definitive Documentation of Human
  Decisions.* 2 vols. Stanfordville, N.Y.: Earl M. Coleman, 1979.

Books and Articles

Acheson, Dean. *Present at the Creation: My Years in the State Depart-
  ment.* New York: W. W. Norton, 1969.
Ake, Claude. "Modernization and Political Instability: A Theoretical
  Explanation." wp 26: 4 (July 1974): 576–91.
———. "Political Integration and Political Stability: A Hypothesis."
  wp 19: 3 (April 1967): 486–99.

Allard, Général de Corps de Armée J. "Vérités sur l'Affaire Algérienne." RDN 26 (January 1958): 5–41.

Allison, Graham T. "Conceptual Models and the Cuban Missile Crisis." APSR 63: 3 (September 1969): 689–718.

———. *Essence of Decision: Explaining the Cuban Missile Crisis.* Boston: Little Brown, 1971.

Allison, Graham T., and Morton H. Halperin. "Bureaucratic Politics: A Paradigm and Some Policy Implications." WP 24 (Supplement, Spring 1972): 40–79.

Almond, Gabriel A. "A Developmental Approach to Political Systems." WP 17: 2 (January 1965): 183–214.

———. *The American People and Foreign Policy.* New York: Praeger, 1965.

———. "Anthropology, Political Behavior, and International Relations." WP 2: 2 (January 1950): 277–84.

———. *The Appeals of Communism.* Princeton: Princeton University Press, 1954.

———. *Political Development: Essays in Heuristic Theory.* Boston: Little Brown, 1970.

Almond, Gabriel A., and James S. Coleman, eds. *The Politics of Developing Areas.* Princeton: Princeton University Press, 1960.

Almond, Gabriel A., and Stephen J. Genco. "Clouds, Clocks and the Study of Politics." WP 29: 4 (July 1977): 489–522.

Almond, Gabriel A., and G. Bingham Powell, Jr. *Comparative Politics: A Developmental Approach.* Boston: Little, Brown, 1966.

Almond, Gabriel A., and Sidney Verba. *The Civic Culture: Political Attitudes and Democracy in Five Nations.* Boston: Little, Brown, 1965.

Ambler, John Steward. *The French Army in Politics, 1945–1966.* Columbus: Ohio State University Press, 1966.

Amen, Michael Mark. *American Foreign Policy in Greece, 1944/1949: Economic, Military and Institutional Aspects.* Frankfurt am Main: Peter Lang, 1978.

Amphioxu, Capitaine. "La Guerre en Algerie: Regards de l'Autre Côte." RDN 28 (January 1959): 82–91.

L'Année politique, economique, sociale et diplomatique, 1947. Paris: Presses Universitaires de France, 1948.

Arnold, Hugh M. "Official Justifications for America's Role in Indochina, 1949–67." *Asian Affairs* (September–October 1975): 31–48.

Aron, Robert. *Les origines de la guerre d' 'Algérie.* Paris: Fayard, 1962.

Auty, Phyllis, and Richard Clogg, eds. *British Policy Towards Wartime*

Resistance in Yugoslavia and Greece. New York: Macmillan, 1975.

Baldwin, David A. "Foreign Aid, Intervention, and Influence." WP 21: 3 (April 1969): 425–47.

———. "Power Analysis and World Politics." WP 31: 2 (January 1979): 161–94.

Barber, Bernard. *Science and the Social Order.* London: George Allen & Unwin, 1953.

Barber, Bernard, and Walter Hirsch, eds. *The Sociology of Science.* New York: Free Press, 1963.

Bates, Robert H. "People in Villages: Micro-Level Studies in Political Economy." WP 31: 1 (October 1978): 129–49.

Bell, Daniel. "The End of American Exceptionalism." *Parameters* 10: 2 (June 1980): 2–18.

———. "Ten Theories in Search of Reality: The Prediction of Soviet Behavior in the Social Sciences." WP 10: 3 (April 1958): 327–65.

Bell, J. Boyer. *The Myth of the Guerrilla: Revolutionary Theory and Malpractice.* New York: Alfred A. Knopf, 1971.

Bellah, Robert. "Meaning and Modernization." *Religious Studies* 4: 1 (October 1968): 37–45.

Bendix, Reinhard. *Nation Building and Citizenship.* New York: Wiley, 1964.

Ben-Dor, Gabriel. "Institutionalization and Political Development: A Conceptual and Theoretical Analysis." CSSH 17 (July 1975): 309–25.

Benedict, Ruth. *Patterns of Culture.* New York: Mentor Books, 1959.

Bennett, John W. "Anticipation, Adaptation, and the Concept of Culture in Anthropology." *Science* 192: 4242 (28 May 1976): 847–53.

Berger, Peter L., and Thomas Luchman. *The Social Construction of Reality: A Treatise in the Sociology of Knowledge.* Garden City, N.Y.: Anchor, 1967.

Berman, Larry. *Planning a Tragedy: The Americanization of the War in Vietnam.* New York: W. W. Norton, 1982.

Bernstein, Marver H. "The Appeal of Communism in Arab Countries." WP 9: 4 (July 1957): 623–29.

Betts, Raymond. *Assimilation and Association in French Colonial Theory, 1890–1914.* New York: Columbia University Press, 1961.

Betts, Richard K. *Soldiers, Statesmen, and Cold War Crises.* Cambridge: Harvard University Press, 1977.

Bienen, Henry. "What Does Political Development Mean in Africa?" WP 20: 1 (October 1967): 128–41.

Binder, Leonard. *Iran: Political Development in a Changing Society.* Berkeley: University of California Press, 1962.

Binder, Leonard, James S. Coleman, Joseph Lapalombara, Lucian W. Pye, Sidney Verba, and Myron Weiner. *Crises and Sequences in Political Development.* Princeton: Princeton University Press, 1971.

Bjelajac, Slavko N. "Psywar: The Lessons from Algeria." MR 42: 12 (December 1962): 2–7.

Black, C. E. *The Dynamics of Modernization: A Study in Comparative History.* New York: Harper Torchbooks, 1966.

Blaufarb, Douglas. *The Counterinsurgency Era: U.S. Doctrine and Performance.* New York: Free Press, 1977.

Blum, John Morton. *The Promise of America: An Historical Inquiry.* Boston: Houghton Mifflin, 1966.

Bonnet, Col. Gabriel. *Les guerres insurrectionnelles et révolutionnaires.* Paris, 1958.

———. "Mao Tsé-Toung et la Stratégie Révolutionnaire." RDN (January 1955): 22–33.

Bramson, Leon. *The Political Context of Sociology.* Princeton: Princeton University Press, 1961.

Bray, Charles. "Toward a Technology of Human Behavior for Defense Use." *American Psychologist* 17: 8 (August 1962): 527–41.

Brazzaville: 30 janvier–8 fevrier, 1944. Published by the Ministère des Colonies.

Brecher, Michael. *The Foreign Policy System of Israel: Setting, Images, Process.* New Haven, Conn.: Yale University Press, 1972.

Bredo, William. "Agrarian Reform in Vietnam: Vietcong and Government of Vietnam Strategies in Conflict." AS 10: 8 (August 1970): 738–50.

Brown, Seyoum. *The Faces of Power: Constancy and Change in United States Foreign Policy from Truman to Johnson.* New York: Columbia University Press, 1968.

Bullington, James R., and James D. Rosenthal. "The South Vietnamese Countryside: Non-Communist Political Perceptions." AS 10: 8 (August 1970): 651–61.

Burrowes, Robert. "Theory Si, Data No! A Decade of Cross-National Political Research." WP 25: 1 (October 1972): 120–44.

Carr, Edward Hallett. *The Twenty Years' Crisis, 1919–1939: An Introduction to the Study of International Relations.* New York: Harper Torchbooks, 1964.

Carver, George. "The Faceless Viet Cong." *Foreign Affairs* 44: 3 (April 1966): 347–72.

Caude, Capitaine R. "Propagande et Guerre Psychologique." RDN (August–September 1955): 176–85.

Chang, David. "Military Forces and Nation-Building." MR 50: 9 (September 1970): 78–88.

Charrasse, Pierre. "L'Armée et l'Algérie de Demain." RDN 28 (March 1959): 420–32.

———. "L'Intégration Algérienne dans l'Histoire." RDN 28 (September 1959): 1386–1400.

Chassin, Général L.-M. "Guerre en Indochine." RDN (July 1953): 3–22.

———. "Insuffisance de la stratégie nucléaire." RDN 16 (July 1960).

———. "Du rôle idéologique de l'armée." Revue Militaire d'Information. (October 10, 1954): 13–19.

———. "Technique de l'Insurrection." RDN (May 1957): 696–713.

Cherns, Albert. "The Use of the Social Sciences." Human Relations 21 (November 1968): 313–25.

Chomsky, Noam. American Power and the New Mandarins. New York: Pantheon Books, 1969.

———. Towards a New Cold War: Essays on the Current Crisis and How We Got There. New York: Pantheon Books, 1982.

Clogg, Richard. A Short History of Modern Greece. New York: Cambridge University Press, 1979.

Connor, Judson. "Teeth for the Free World Dragon." Army Information Digest (November 1960): 32–43.

Connor, Walter. "Nation-Building or Nation-Destroying?" WP 24: 3 (April 1972): 319–55.

Courand, André, and Michael Meyer. "The Scientist's Code." Minerva 14 (Spring 1976): 79–96.

Crahan, Margaret, and Brian Smith, eds. Human Rights and Basic Needs in the Americas. Washington, D.C.: Georgetown University Press, 1982.

Crick, Bernard. "What is Truth in Social Science?" New Society (4 June 1964): 20–21.

Cruise O'Brian, Donal. "Modernization, Order, and the Erosion of a Democratic Ideal: American Political Science 1960–1970." Journal of Development Studies (1972): 351–78.

Dahl, Robert A. "The Science of Politics: New and Old." WP 7: 3 (April 1955): 479–89.

Daniels, Jonathan. The Man of Independence. New York: W. B. Lippincott, 1950.

Debray, Régis. Revolution in the Revolution? Armed Struggle and Political Struggle in Latin America. New York: Grove Press, 1967.

Decalo, Samuel. *Coups and Army Rule in Africa: Studies in Military Style*. New Haven, Conn.: Yale University Press, 1976.

Dedijer, Vladimir. *Tito*. New York: Simon and Schuster, 1953.

Deitchman, Seymour J. *The Best Laid Schemes: A Tale of Social Research and Bureaucracy*. Cambridge: MIT Press, 1976.

————. *Limited War and American Defense Policy*. Cambridge: MIT Press, 1964.

Deschamps, Hubert. "Et Maintenant, Lord Lugard?" *Africa* 33: 4 (October 1963): 293–306.

Destler, I. M. *Presidents, Bureaucrats and Foreign Policy: The Politics of Organizational Reform*. Princeton: Princeton University Press, 1972.

Deutsch, Karl. "The Growth of Nations: Some Recurrent Patterns of Political and Social Integration." WP 5: 2 (January 1953): 168–95.

————. "Social Mobilization and Political Development." APSR 55 (September 1961): 493–514.

Djilas, Milovan. *Conversations with Stalin*. New York: Harcourt, Brace and World, 1962.

Dodd, Joseph W. "Faction and Failure in South Vietnam." *Asian Affairs* (January–February 1975): 173–78.

Donnell, John C. "Expanding Political Participation: The Long Haul from Villagism to Nationalism." AS 10: 8 (August 1970): 688–704.

Doob, Leonard. "The Utilization of Social Scientists in the Overseas Branch of the Office of War Information." APSR 41: 4 (1947): 649–67.

Dube, S. C. "Bureaucracy and Nation-Building in Transitional Societies." *International Social Science Journal* 16 (1964): 229–39.

Duiker, William J. *The Communist Road to Power in Vietnam*. Boulder, Col.: Westview Press, 1982.

Duncanson, Dennis J. *Government and Revolution in Vietnam*. New York: Oxford University Press, 1968.

Dunn, Lewis A. "Past as Prologue: American Redemptive Activism and the Developing World." WP 27: 4 (July 1975): 612–27.

Durkheim, Emile. *The Division of Labor in Society*. New York: Free Press, 1964.

————. *The Rules of Sociological Method*. New York: Free Press, 1965.

Easton, David. "An Approach to the Analysis of Political Systems." WP 9: 3 (April 1957): 383–400.

————. *A Framework for Political Analysis*. Englewood Cliffs, N.J.: Prentice-Hall, 1965.

Eberstein, William. "The Study of Totalitarianism." WP 10: 2 (January 1958): 274–88.

Eckstein, Harry, ed. *Internal War: Problems and Approaches*. New York: Free Press, 1964.

Eigen, Manfred, and Ruthild Winkler. *Laws of the Game: How the Principles of Nature Govern Chance*. New York: Knopf, 1981.

Eisenstadt, S. N. "Approaches to the Problem of Political Development in Non-Western Societies." WP 9: 3 (April 1957): 446–58.

———. "Breakdowns of Modernization." EDCC 12: 4 (July 1964): 345–67.

———. "Modernization and Conditions of Sustained Growth." WP 16: 4 (July 1964): 576–94.

Ellis, John. *A Short History of Guerrilla Warfare*. New York: St. Martin's Press, 1976.

Ellsberg, Daniel. *Papers on the War*. New York: Simon and Schuster, 1972.

Ely, Général d'Armée P. "Les Problèmes Français de l'Equilibre Mondial." RDN 28 (November 1959): 1709–25.

———. "Vers une Evolution Possible de l'Occident." RDN 28 (February 1959): 213–18.

Embree, John F. "Standardized Error and Japanese Character: A Note on Political Interpretation." WP 2: 3 (April 1950): 439–43.

Emerson, Rupert. *From Empire to Nation*. Boston: Beacon Press, 1960.

Enloe, Cynthia H. *Police, Military and Ethnicity: Foundations of State Power*. New Brunswick, N.J.: Transaction Books, 1980.

Evans, Ernest. "The U.S. Military and Low-Level Conflict." Center for International Affairs, Harvard University, 1981.

Falkowski, Lawrence S., ed. *Psychological Models in International Politics*. Boulder, Col.: Westview Press, 1979.

Fallers, Lloyd. "Africa: Scholarship and Policy." WP 9: 2 (January 1957): 287–94.

Feit, Edward. "Military Coups and Political Development: Some Lessons from Ghana and Nigeria." WP 20: 2 (January 1968): 179–93.

———. "Pen, Sword, and People: Military Regimes in the Formation of Political Institutions." WP 25: 2 (January 1973): 251–74.

Finifter, Ada, ed. *Political Science: The State of the Discipline*. Washington, D.C.: American Political Science Association, 1983.

Fitch, John Samuel. "The Political Impact of U.S. Military Aid to Latin America: Institutional and Individual Effects." *Armed Forces and Society* 5: 3 (Spring 1979): 360–86.

FitzGerald, Frances. *Fire in the Lake: The Vietnamese and the Americans in Vietnam.* New York: Vintage Books, 1973.

Forrer, John O. "The Sources of Communist Appeal." WP 16: 3 (April 1964): 521–38.

Foster, George M. *Traditional Cultures and the Impact of Technological Change.* New York: Harper and Brothers, 1962.

Froelich, J. C. "La Situation Politique Actuelle d'Afrique d'Expression Française." RDN (November 1960): 1788–1801.

Furniss, Edgar S., Jr. *De Gaulle and the French Army: A Crisis in Civil-Military Relations.* New York: Twentieth Century Fund, 1964.

Gabriel, Richard A. "No Light in the Tunnel: Can U.S. Conventional Forces Meet the Future?" *Conflict Quarterly* (Fall 1981): 4–8.

Gache, Paul. "La Subversion en Afrique Orientale." RDN 28 (July 1959): 1258–72.

Gaddis, John Lewis. *Strategies of Containment: A Critical Appraisal of Postwar American National Security Policy.* New York: Oxford University Press, 1982.

Galula, David. *Counterinsurgency Warfare: Theory and Practice.* New York: Praeger, 1964.

de Gaulle, Charles. *The Complete War Memoirs of Charles de Gaulle.* New York: Simon and Schuster, 1967.

———. *Discours et messages: dans l'attente, 1946–1958.* Paris: Plon, 1970.

Geertz, Clifford, ed. *Old Societies and New States: The Quest for Modernity in Asia and Africa.* New York: Free Press, 1963.

Gelb, Leslie H., and Richard K. Betts. *The Irony of Vietnam: The System Worked.* Washington, D.C.: Brookings, 1979.

George, Alexander. "American Policy-Making and the North Korean Aggression." WP 7: 2 (January 1955): 209–32.

———. "The 'Operational Code': A Neglected Approach to the Study of Political Leaders and Decision-Making." ISQ 13 (June 1969): 192–222.

Gillert, Lt. Col. Gustav, Jr. "Counterinsurgency." MR (April 1965): 25–33.

Girardet, Raoul. *La crise militaire française, 1945–1962.* No. 123. Paris: Cahiers de la Fondation Nationale des Sciences Politiques, 1964.

Girault, Arthur. *Principes de colonisation et de législation coloniale.* 3d ed. Paris, 1927.

Golay, Frank H. *The Philippines: Public Policy and National Eco-*

nomic Development. Ithaca, N.Y.: Cornell University Press, 1961.

Goldhamer, Herbert. "Fashion and Social Science." WP 6: 3 (April 1954): 394–404.

Goodman, Allan E. "The Political Implications of Rural Problems in South Vietnam: Creating Public Interests." AS 10: 8 (August 1970): 672–87.

Gould, Stephen Jay. *The Mismeasure of Man*. New York: W. W. Norton, 1981.

Grady, Henry F., Ambassador to Greece. "Statement on Military Aid to Greece." DSB (15 August 1949).

Greene, Lt. Col. T. N., ed. *The Guerrilla: And How to Fight Him*. New York: Praeger, 1962.

Grindle, Merilee S., ed. *Politics and Policy Implementation in the Third World*. Princeton: Princeton University Press, 1980.

Grinter, Laurence E. "How They Lost: Doctrines, Strategies and Outcomes of the Vietnam War." AS 15: 12 (December 1975): 1114–32.

Groth, Alexander J. "The Institutional Myth: Huntington's Order Revisited." *Review of Politics* 41: 2 (April 1979): 203–34.

Guevara, Ernesto Che. *Guerrilla Warfare*. New York: Vintage Books, 1961.

Gurr, Ted. "Psychological Factors in Civil Violence." WP 20: 2 (January 1968): 245–78.

Gusfield, Joseph R. "Mass Society and Extremist Politics." *American Sociological Review* 27: 1 (February 1962): 19–30.

———. "Tradition and Modernity: Misplaced Polarities in the Study of Social Change." *American Journal of Sociology* 72 (January 1967): 351–62.

Hagen, Everett. "How Economic Growth Begins: A Theory of Social Change." *Journal of Social Issues* 19 (January 1963): 20–34.

Halberstam, David. *The Making of a Quagmire*. New York: Random House, 1965.

Halperin, Morton H. *Bureaucratic Politics and Foreign Policy*. Washington, D.C.: Brookings, 1974.

———. "Why Bureaucrats Play Games." *Foreign Policy* (Spring 1971): 70–90.

Halperin, Morton H., and Arnold Kanter, eds. *Readings in American Foreign Policy: A Bureaucratic Perspective*. Boston: Little, Brown, 1973.

Halpern, Manfred. *The Politics of Social Change in the Middle East and North Africa*. Princeton: Princeton University Press, 1965.

Halpern, Manfred. "Toward Further Modernization of the Study of New Nations." WP 17: 1 (October 1964): 157–81.

Hammer, Major Kenneth. "Huks in the Philippines." MR 36: 1 (April 1956): 50–54.

Harris, Errol. *Hypothesis and Perception*. London: Allen & Unwin, 1970.

Harrison, Christopher. "French Attitudes to Empire and the Algerian War." *African Affairs* 82: 326 (January 1983): 75–95.

Harsanyi, John C. "Rational-Choice Models of Political Behavior vs. Functional and Conformist Theories." WP 21: 4 (July 1969): 513–38.

Hartz, Louis. *The Liberal Tradition in America: An Interpretation of American Political Thought Since the Revolution*. New York: Harcourt, Brace, 1955.

Heclo, Hugh. *Modern Social Politics in Britain and Sweden*. New Haven, Conn.: Yale University Press, 1974.

Heeger, Gerald A. "Bureaucracy, Political Parties, and Political Development." WP 26: 4 (July 1973): 600–607.

———. "Politics in the Post-Military State: Some Reflections on the Pakistani Experience." WP 29: 2 (January 1977): 242–62.

———. *The Politics of Underdevelopment*. New York: St. Martin's Press, 1974.

Heilbrunn, Otto. *Partisan Warfare*. New York: Praeger, 1962.

Hermassi, Elbaki. "Toward a Comparative Study of Revolutions." CSSH 18: 2 (April 1976): 211–35.

Herring, George C. *America's Longest War: The United States and Vietnam, 1950–1975*. New York: Wiley, 1979.

Heymont, Colonel Irving. "Armed Forces and National Development." MR (December 1969): 50–55.

Hilsman, Roger, Jr. "Intelligence and Policy-Making in Foreign Affairs." WP 5: 1 (October 1952): 1–45.

———. *To Move a Nation: The Politics of Foreign Policy in the Administration of John F. Kennedy*. New York: Dell, 1967.

Hirschman, Albert O. "Exit, Voice, and the State." WP 31: 1 (October 1978): 90–107.

———. "The Search for Paradigms as a Hindrance to Understanding." WP 22: 3 (April 1970): 329–43.

Hoagland, John. "Changing Patterns of Insurgency and American Response." *Journal of International Affairs* 25: 1 (1971): 120–41.

Hoffmann, Stanley. *Contemporary Theory in International Relations*. Englewood Cliffs, N.J.: Prentice-Hall, 1960.

————. *Gulliver's Troubles, Or the Setting of American Foreign Policy*. New York: McGraw-Hill, 1968.

————. "International Relations: The Long Road to Theory." WP 11: 3 (April 1959): 346–77.

————. *Primacy or World Order*. New York: McGraw-Hill, 1978.

————. "Restraints and Choices in American Foreign Policy." *Daedelus* 91 (Fall 1962): 668–704.

————. *The State of War: Essays on the Theory and Practice of International Politics*. New York: Praeger, 1965.

Hofstadter, Douglas R. "Mathematical Themas: Virus-Like Sentences and Self-Replicating Structures." *Scientific American* (January 1983): 14–22.

Hofstadter, Richard. *The American Political Tradition and the Men Who Made It*. 25th anniversary ed. New York: Knopf, 1979.

Hogard, Jacques. "L'Armée Française devant la Guerre Révolutionnaire." RDN 24 (January 1957): 77–89.

————. "Cette Guerre de Notre Temps." RDN 27 (August–September 1958): 1304–19.

————. "Guerre Révolutionnaire et Pacification." *Revue Militaire d'Information* (January 1957): 7–24.

————. "Guerre Révolutionnaire ou Révolution dans l'Art de la Guerre." RDN (December 1956): 1497–1513.

————. "Le Soldat dans la Guerre Révolutionnaire." RDN 24 (February 1957): 211–26.

Hopkins, Raymond F. "Securing Authority: The View from the Top." WP 24: 2 (January 1972): 271–92.

Horowitz, Irving Louis, ed. *The Rise and Fall of Project Camelot: Studies in the Relationship Between Social Science and Practical Politics*. Rev. ed. Cambridge: MIT Press, 1974.

————. "Social Science Mandarins: Policymaking as a Political Formula." *Policy Sciences* 1 (Fall 1970): 339–60.

————. "Social Science Yogis and Military Commissars," *Trans-Action* (May 1968): 29–38.

Hoselitz, Bert F., and Wilbert E. Moore, eds. *Industrialization and Society*. The Hague: UNESCO-Mouton, 1966.

Hough, Richard. *Economic Assistance and Security: Rethinking US Policy*. Washington, D.C.: National Defense University Press, 1982.

Howard, Michael. "The Use and Abuse of Military History." *Parameters* 11:1 (March 1981): 9–14.

Huntington, Samuel P. "The Change to Change: Modernization, Development and Politics." CP (April 1971): 283–322.

Huntington, Samuel P. *Military Interventions, Political Involvement and the Unlessons of Vietnam.* Chicago: Adlai Stevenson Institute of International Affairs, 1968.

———. "Political Development and Political Decay." WP 17: 3 (April 1965): 386–430.

———. *Political Order in Changing Societies.* New Haven: Yale University Press, 1968.

Iatrides, John O., ed. *Ambassador MacVeagh Reports: Greece, 1933–1947.* Princeton: Princeton University Press, 1980.

Inkeles, Alex, and David H. Smith. *Becoming Modern: Individual Change in Six Developing Countries.* Cambridge: Harvard University Press, 1974.

Janowitz, Morris. *Military Institutions and Coercion in the Developing Nations.* Chicago: University of Chicago Press, 1977.

Jervis, Robert. *Perception and Misperception in International Politics.* Princeton: Princeton University Press, 1976.

Johnson, Chalmers A. "Civilian Loyalties and Guerrilla Conflict." WP 14: 4 (July 1962): 646–61.

Johnson, U. Alexis. "Internal Defense and the Foreign Service." *Foreign Service Journal* (July 1962): 20–23.

Jones, Joseph Marion. *The Fifteen Weeks.* New York: Harcourt, Brace and World, 1955.

Kahin, George, ed. *Governments and Politics in Southeast Asia.* Ithaca, N.Y.: Cornell University Press, 1964.

Kahler, Miles. *Decolonization in Britain and France: The Domestic Consequences of International Politics.* Princeton: Princeton University Press, 1985.

Kalleberg, Arthur L. "The Logic of Comparison: A Methodological Note on the Comparative Study of Political Systems." WP 19: 1 (October 1966): 69–82.

Katzenbach, Major Edward L., Jr. "Indochina: A Military-Political Appreciation." WP 4: 2 (January 1952): 186–218.

Katzenbach, Major Edward L., Jr., and Gene Hanrahan. "The Revolutionary Strategy of Mao Tse-Tung." *Political Science Quarterly* 70: 3 (September 1955): 321–40.

Kecskemeti, Paul. "The Policy Sciences: Aspiration and Outlook." WP 4: 4 (July 1952): 520–35.

Kelly, Colonel Francis J. *U.S. Army Special Forces, 1961–1971.* Vietnam Studies, Department of the Army. Washington, D.C., 1973.

Kelly, George Armstrong. *Lost Soldiers: The French Army and Empire in Crisis, 1947–1962.* Cambridge: MIT Press, 1965.

Kennan, George F. *American Diplomacy, 1900–1950.* New York: Mentor Books, 1951.

———. *Memoirs, 1925–1950.* Boston: Little, Brown, 1967.

Kennedy, John F. *A Compilation of His Statements and Speeches During His Service in the United States Senate and House of Representatives.* Washington, D.C.: GPO, 1964.

Keohane, Robert O., and Joseph S. Nye. *Power and Interdependence: World Politics in Transition.* Boston: Little, Brown, 1977.

Kerkvliet, Benedict J. *The Huk Rebellion: A Study of Peasant Revolt in the Philippines.* Berkeley: University of California Press, 1977.

Kesselman, Mark. "Order or Movement? The Literature of Political Development as Ideology." WP 26: 1 (October 1973): 139–54.

Kissinger, Henry A. *American Foreign Policy.* Expanded ed. New York: W. W. Norton, 1974.

Kluckholm, Clyde. "Politics, History, and Psychology." WP 8: 1 (October 1955): 112–23.

Komer, Robert W. *Bureaucracy at War: U.S. Performance in the Vietnam Conflict.* Boulder, Col.: Westview Press, 1986.

———. "Clear, Hold and Rebuild." *Army* (May 1970): 16–24.

———. "Impact of Pacification on Insurgency in South Vietnam." *Journal of International Affairs* 25: 1 (1971): 48–69.

———. "Pacification: A Look Back and Ahead." *Army* (June 1970): 20–29.

Kousoulas, D. George. *Revolution and Defeat: The Story of the Greek Communist Party.* London: Oxford University Press, 1965.

Krasner, Stephen D. "Are Bureaucracies Important? (Or Allison Wonderland)." *Foreign Policy* 7 (Summer 1972): 159–79.

Krepinevich, Andrew F., Jr. *The Army and Vietnam.* Baltimore, Md.: Johns Hopkins University Press, 1986.

Kuhn, Thomas S. *The Structure of Scientific Revolutions.* 2d ed. Chicago: University of Chicago Press, 1970.

Kuniholm, Bruce Robellet. *The Origins of the Cold War in the Near East: Great Power Conflict and Diplomacy in Iran, Turkey and Greece.* Princeton: Princeton University Press, 1980.

Labin, Suzanne. "La Guerre Politique des Soviets." RDN (June 1960): 1028–39 and (July 1960): 1248–62.

Lacheroy, Col. Charles. "La Guerre Révolutionnaire." *La Défense Nationale.* (1958): 307–30.

Lachia, Edwardo. *The Huks: Philippine Agrarian Society in Revolt.* New York: Praeger, 1971.

Lafeber, Walter. *America, Russia, and the Cold War, 1945–1975.* 3d ed. New York: Wiley, 1976.

Lansdale, Edward G. *In the Midst of Wars: An American's Mission to Southeast Asia*. New York: Harper & Row, 1972.

LaPalombara, Joseph, ed. *Bureaucracy and Political Development*. Princeton: Princeton University Press, 1967.

———. "Macrotheories and Microapplications in Comparative Politics." CP 1 (October 1968): 52–78.

Laqueur, Walter. *Guerrilla: A Historical and Critical Study*. Boston: Little, Brown, 1976.

Lasswell, Harold D. "Personality, Prejudice, and Politics," WP 3: 3 (April 1951): 399–407.

———. "The Policy Sciences of Development." WP 17: 2 (January 1965): 286–309.

Lazarsfeld, Paul, William Sewell, and Harold Wilensky, eds. *The Uses of Sociology*. New York: Basic Books, 1967.

Leeper, Sir Reginald. *When Greek Meets Greek*. London: Chatto and Windus, 1950.

Lefever, Ernest W. *Spear and Scepter: Army, Police, and Politics in Tropical Africa*. Washington, D.C.: Brookings, 1970.

Leites, Nathan. "Psycho-Cultural Hypotheses About Political Acts." WP 1: 1 (October 1948): 102–19.

Leites, Nathan, and Charles Wolf, Jr. *Rebellion and Authority: An Analytic Essay on Insurgent Conflicts*. Chicago: Markham, 1970.

Lerner, Daniel. *The Passing of Traditional Society: Modernizing the Middle East*. New York: Free Press, 1958.

Lerner, Daniel, and Harold Lasswell, eds. *The Policy Sciences: Recent Developments in Scope and Method*. Stanford, Ca: Stanford University Press, 1951.

Lerner, Daniel, and Richard D. Robinson. "Swords and Ploughshares: The Turkish Army as a Modernizing Force." WP 13: 1 (October 1960): 19–44.

Lewy, Guenther. *America in Vietnam*. New York: Oxford University Press, 1978.

Lindblom, Charles E., and David K. Cohen, *Usable Knowledge: Social Science and Social Problem Solving*. New Haven: Yale University Press, 1979.

Lipset, Seymour Martin. *Political Man: The Social Bases of Politics*. Garden City, N.Y.: Anchor, 1963.

Loewenstein, Karl. "Report on the Research Panel on Comparative Government." APSR 38: 3 (June 1944): 540–48.

Lowenthal, Abraham. "Armies and Politics in Latin America." WP 27: 1 (October 1974): 107–30.

Lyons, Gene M. *The Uneasy Partnership: Social Science and the Federal Government in the Twentieth Century.* New York: Russell Sage, 1969.

MacRae, Duncan J. *The Social Function of Social Science.* New Haven: Yale University Press, 1976.

Macridis, Roy, and Richard Cox. "Research in Comparative Politics: Seminar Report." APSR 47: 3 (September 1953): 641–57.

Maechling, Charles, Jr. "Our Internal Defense Policy—A Reappraisal." *Foreign Policy Journal* (January 1969): 19–27.

———. "Insurgency and Counterinsurgency: The Role of Strategic Theory." *Parameters* 14: 3 (Autumn 1984): 32–41.

Maitland, Ian. "Only the Best and the Brightest?" *Asian Affairs* (March–April 1976): 263–72.

Malinowski, Bronislaw. *The Dynamics of Cultural Change: An Inquiry into Race Relations in Africa.* New Haven: Yale University Press, 1961.

Marchand, Général Jean. "Les Origins du Drame Indochinois." RDN 21 (October 1952): 310–21.

———. "Perspectives Africaines." RDN 28 (November 1959): 1749–58.

Marchat, Lieutenant Philippe. "Rappelé en Algérie." RDN 26 (December 1957): 1827–52.

Maslow, Abraham. *Motivation and Personality.* New York: Harper and Row, 1954.

May, Ernest. *"Lessons" of the Past: The Use and Misuse of History in American Foreign Policy.* New York: Oxford University Press, 1973.

———. "The Nature of Foreign Policy: The Calculated versus the Axiomatic." *Daedelus* 91 (Fall 1962): 653–67.

Mazrui, Ali. "From Social Darwinism to Current Theories of Modernization: A Tradition of Analysis." WP 21: 1 (October 1968): 69–83.

McClelland, David C. *The Achieving Society.* New York: Van Nostrand, 1961.

McCuen, Lt. Col. John J. *The Art of Counter-Revolutionary War: The Strategy of Counter-Insurgency.* Harrisburg, Penn.: Stackpole Books, 1966.

McNeill, W. H. *The Greek Dilemma: War and Aftermath.* Philadelphia: J. B. Lippincott, 1947.

Mecklin, John. *Mission in Torment.* Garden City, N.Y.: Doubleday, 1965.

305

Melanson, Philip H. "The Political Science Profession, Political Knowledge, and Public Policy." *Politics and Society* 2 (Summer 1972): 489–501.

Merk, Fredrick. *Manifest Destiny and Mission in American History: A Reinterpretation*. New York: Vintage Books, 1966.

Merye, Jean. "Considérations Militaires sur la Guerre d'Algérie." RDN 28 (May 1959): 807–21.

Migdal, Joel S. "The Individual and Rapid Change." Paper presented at Annual Conference of the International Society of Political Psychology, New York, September 2, 1978.

———. *Peasants, Politics and Revolution: Pressures Toward Political and Social Change in the Third World*. Princeton: Princeton University Press, 1974.

———. "Why Change? Toward a New Theory of Change Among Individuals in the Process of Modernization." WP 26:2 (January 1974): 189–206.

Millikan, Max, and Walt Rostow. *A Proposal: Key to an Effective Foreign Policy*. New York: Harper, 1957.

Mollet, Guy. *Bilan et perspectives socialistes*. Paris: Plon, 1958.

Moore, Barrington, Jr. "The New Scholasticism and the Study of Politics." WP 6: 1 (October 1953): 122–38.

Morgenthau, Hans. *Scientific Man vs. Power Politics*. Chicago: University of Chicago Press, 1946.

Muller, Colonel J. "La Subversion Menace-t-elle Aussi l'Afrique Noire Française?" RDN 26 (May 1958): 754–70.

Murray, J. C. "The Anti-Bandit War: Part I." *Marine Corps Gazette* 38 (January 1954): 14–23.

———. "The Anti-Bandit War: Part II." *Marine Corps Gazette* 38 (February 1954): 50–59.

———. "The Anti-Bandit War: Part III." *Marine Corps Gazette* 38 (March 1954): 48–57.

———. "The Anti-Bandit War: Part IV." *Marine Corps Gazette* 38 (April 1954): 52–60.

Nelson, Joan M. *Access to Power: Politics and the Urban Poor in Developing Nations*. Princeton: Princeton University Press, 1979.

Nemo, Général. "La France et l'Afrique." RDN 28 (December 1959): 1939–49.

———. "La Guerre dans le Milieu Sociale." RDN 25 (May 1956): 605–28.

Nettle, J. P. "The State as Conceptual Variable." WP 20: 4 (July 1968): 559–92.

Neubauer, Dean E., and Lawrence D. Kastner. "The Study of Compliance Maintenance as a Strategy for Comparative Research." WP 21: 4 (July 1969): 629–40.

Nieberg, H. L. "The Threat of Violence and Social Change." APSR 56 (December 1962): 865–73.

Nighswonger, William. *Rural Pacification in Vietnam*. New York: Praeger, 1966.

Nisbet, Robert. *Social Change and History: Aspects of the Western Theory of Development*. New York: Oxford University Press, 1969.

Nordlinger, Eric A. "Political Development: Time Sequences and Rates of Change." WP 20: 3 (April 1968): 494–520.

Nougues, Chef de Bataillon J., and Chef de Bataillon G. Galzy. "A Propos des Enseignements de la Guerre d'Indochine." RDN (April 1956): 427–35.

Oberschall, Anthony R. "Rising Expectations and Political Turmoil." *Journal of Development Studies* 6: 1 (October 1969): 5–22.

Odell, John S. *U.S. International Monetary Policy: Markets, Power, and Ideas as Sources of Change*. Princeton: Princeton University Press, 1982.

Olson, Mancur, Jr. "Rapid Growth as a Destabilizing Force." *Journal of Economic History* 23 (December 1963): 529–52.

———. *The Rise and Decline of Nations: Economic Growth, Stagflation and Social Rigidities*. New Haven: Yale University Press, 1982.

Packenham, Robert. "Approaches to the Study of Political Development." WP 17: 1 (October 1964): 108–20.

———. *Liberal America and the Third World: Political Development Ideas in Foreign Aid and Social Science*. Princeton: Princeton University Press, 1973.

———. "Political Development Doctrines in the American Foreign Aid Program." WP 18: 2 (January 1966): 194–235.

Paget, Julian. *Counter-Insurgency Operations: Techniques of Guerrilla Warfare*. New York: Walker and Company, 1967.

Papathanasiades, Col. Theodossios. "The Bandits' Last Stand in Greece." MR 30: 11 (February 1951): 22–31.

Paret, Peter. *French Revolutionary Warfare from Indochina to Algeria: The Analysis of a Political and Military Doctrine*. Princeton Studies in World Politics, no. 6. New York: Praeger, 1964.

Parsons, Talcott. "Social Structure and Political Orientation." WP 13: 1 (October 1960): 112–28.

Pauker, Guy J. "Southeast Asia as a Problem Area in the Next Decade." WP 11: 3 (April 1959): 325–45.

307

Perlmutter, Amos. "The Presidential Political Center and Foreign Policy: A Critique of the Revisionist and Bureaucratic-Political Orientations." WP 27: 1 (October 1974): 87–106.

Perrin, J. "L'Algérie et l'Information." RDN 27 (December 1958): 1935–44.

Pfeffer, Richard M., ed. No More Vietnams? The War and the Future of American Foreign Policy. New York: Harper & Row, 1968.

Pierre, Andrew J. The Global Politics of Arms Sales. Princeton: Princeton University Press, 1982.

Pike, Douglas. The Viet Cong Strategy of Terror. Cambridge: MIT Press, 1970.

Platig, E. Raymond. "Foreign Affairs Analysis: Some Thoughts on Expanding Competence." ISQ 13: 1 (March 1969): 19–30.

Polanyi, Michael. Knowing and Being: Essays by Michael Polanyi, ed. Marjorie Green. London: Routledge & Kegan Paul, 1969.

———. "The Republic of Science: Its Political and Economic Theory." Minerva 1 (Autumn 1962): 54–73.

Pomeroy, William J., ed. Guerrilla Warfare and Marxism. New York: International Publishers, 1968.

———. "The Philippine Peasantry and the Huk Revolt." Journal of Peasant Studies 5: 4 (July 1978): 497–517.

Pool, Ithiel de Sola, ed. Contemporary Political Science: Toward Empirical Theory. New York: McGraw-Hill, 1967.

———. "Who Gets Power and Why." WP 2: 1 (October 1949): 120–34.

Popkin, Samuel L. "Pacification: Politics and the Village." AS 10: 8 (August 1970): 662–71.

———. The Rational Peasant: The Political Economy of Rural Society in Vietnam. Berkeley: University of California Press, 1979.

Porter, Paul. "Wanted: A Miracle in Greece." Colliers (September 20, 1947): 14–15, 106–107.

Prosterman, Roy L. "Land-to-the-Tiller in South Vietnam: The Tables Turn." AS 10: 8 (August 1970): 751–64.

Public Papers of the Presidents of the United States, John F. Kennedy, 1962. Washington, D.C.: GPO, 1963.

Public Papers of the Presidents of the United States, Harry S. Truman, 1947. Washington, D.C.: GPO, 1963.

Pye, Lucian. "Armies in the Process of Political Modernization." Archives Européenes de Sociologie 2 (1961): 82–92.

———, ed. Communications and Political Development. Princeton: Princeton University Press, 1963.

———. "The Concept of Political Development." Annals of the Amer-

ican Academy of Political and Social Science 358 (March 1965): 1–13.

———. "Communist Strategies and Asian Societies." WP 11: 1 (October 1958): 118–27.

———. "Eastern Nationalism and Western Policy." WP 6: 2 (January 1954): 248–65.

———. *Guerrilla Communism in Malaya: Its Social and Political Meaning.* Princeton: Princeton University Press, 1956.

———. *Politics, Personality, and Nation Building.* New Haven: Yale University Press, 1962.

———. "The Roots of Insurgency and the Commencement of Rebellions." Cambridge: Center for International Studies, MIT, June 1962.

Race, Jeffrey. "How They Won." AS 10: 8 (August 1970): 628–50.

———. "The Origins of the Second Indochina War." AS 10: 5 (May 1970): 359–82.

———. "Vietnam Intervention: Systematic Distortion in Policy-Making." *Armed Forces and Society* 2: 3 (May 1976): 377–96.

———. *War Comes to Long An: Revolutionary Conflict in a Vietnamese Province.* Berkeley: University of California Press, 1972.

Randolph, S. Sean. "The Limits of Influence: American Aid to Thailand, 1965–70." *Asian Affairs* (March–April 1979): 243–66.

Recuil des délibérations du Congrès Colonial National, Paris, 1889–90. Paris, 1890.

Redfield, Robert. *The Little Community: Viewpoints for the Study of a Human Whole.* The Gottesman Lectures, Uppsala University. Stockholm: Almquist an Wiksells Boktrykeri AB, 1955.

———. *A Village That Chose Progress: Chan Kom Revisited.* Chicago: University of Chicago Press, 1950.

Reicken, Henry W. "Social Sciences and Social Problems." *Social Science Information* 8 (February 1969): 101–29.

Richardson, James. "The Huk Rebellion." *Journal of Contemporary Asia* 8: 2 (1978): 231–37.

Rieff, Philip. "Psychology and Politics: The Freudian Connection." WP 7: 2 (January 1955): 293–306.

Riggs, Fred W. "The Theory of Developing Politics." WP 16: 1 (October 1963): 147–72.

de Rivera, Joseph. *The Psychological Dimension of Foreign Policy.* Columbus, Ohio: Charles E. Merrill, 1968.

Rockefeller, Nelson. *The Rockefeller Report on the Americas.* Official Report of the United States Presidential Mission for the Western Hemisphere. Chicago: Quadrangle, 1969.

The Role of Popular Participation in Development. Cambridge: Center for International Studies, MIT, 1968.

Rondot, Pierre. "Les Musulmans et l'Islam devant le Technique." RDN (June 1960): 1011–27.

Rose, Hilary, and Steven Rose, eds. *Ideology of/in the Natural Sciences.* Boston: G. K. Hall, 1980.

Rose, Richard. "Dynamic Tendencies in the Authority of Regimes." WP 21: 4 (July 1969): 602–28.

———. "The President: A Chief But Not an Executive." *Presidential Studies Quarterly* 7 (Winter 1977): 5–20.

Rosen, Stephen P. "Vietnam and the American Theory of Limited War." *International Security* 7: 2 (Fall 1982): 83–113.

Roskin, Michael. "From Pearl Harbor to Vietnam: Shifting Generational Paradigms and Foreign Policy." *Political Science Quarterly* 89 (Fall 1974): 563–88.

Rostow, W. W. "Guerilla Warfare in the Underdeveloped Areas." DSB (7 August 1961): 233–38.

Roth, Guenther. "Personal Rulership, Patrimonialism, and Empire-Building in the New States." WP 20: 2 (January 1968): 194–206.

Rothchild, Donald. "Ethnicity and Conflict Resolution." WP 22: 4 (July 1970): 597–616.

Rourke, Francis E. *Bureaucracy and Foreign Policy.* Baltimore: Johns Hopkins University Press, 1972.

Roussel, Lieutenant-Colonel J. "A Propos de Subversion et d'Insurrection." RDN (March 1960): 498–506.

Rowe, A. P. "From Scientific Idea to Practical Use." *Minerva* 2 (Spring 1964): 303–19.

Rudolph, Lloyd I., and Susanne Hoeber Rudolph. "Authority and Power in Bureaucratic and Patrimonial Administration: A Revisionist Interpretation of Weber on Bureaucracy." WP 31: 2 (January 1979): 195–227.

Rustow, Dankwart A. "New Horizons for Comparative Politics." WP 9: 4 (July 1957): 530–49.

Salter, MacDonald. "The Broadening Base of Land Reform in South Vietnam." AS 10: 8 (August 1970): 724–37.

Sansom, Robert. *The Economics of Insurgency in the Mekong Delta of Vietnam.* Cambridge: MIT Press, 1970.

Sartre, Jean Paul. *Critique de la raison dialectique.* Paris: Gallimard, 1960.

Sayigh, Yusif A. "Development: The Visible or the Invisible Hand?" WP 13: 4 (July 1961): 561–83.

Schmeltz, Guy-Willy. "L'Europe devant le Sous-Développement Economique: I." RDN 26 (May 1958): 729–42.

———. "L'Europe devant le Sous-Développement Economique: II." RDN 26 (June 1958): 945–57.

———. "L'Europe devant le Sous-Développement Economique: III." RDN 26 (July 1958): 1175–84.

Schmidt, Steffen W., and Gerald A. Dorfman. *Soldiers in Politics*. Los Altos, Calif.: Geron-X, Inc., 1974.

Schneider, Colonel F. "La Stratège Révolutionnaire de Mao Tsé-Toung." RDN (October 1960): 1633–50.

Scoville, Thomas W. *Reorganizing for Pacification Support*. Washington, D.C.: Center for Military History, United States Army, 1982.

Shils, Edward. *Center and Periphery*. Chicago: University of Chicago Press, 1975.

———. "The Concentration and Dispersion of Charisma." WP 11: 1 (October 1958): 1–19.

———. "The Intellectuals in the Political Development of the New States." WP 12: 3 (April 1960): 329–68.

———. "Intellectuals, Public Opinion, and Economic Development." WP 10: 2 (January 1958): 232–55.

———. *Political Development in the New States*. The Hague: Mouton, 1962.

Shiner, L. E. "Tradition/Modernity: An Ideal Type Gone Astray." CSSH 19 (April 1975): 245–52.

Skocpol, Theda. *States and Social Revolutions: A Comparative Analysis of France, Russia, and China*. New York: Cambridge University Press, 1979.

———. "Wallerstein's World Capitalist System: A Theoretical and Historical Critique." *American Journal of Sociology* 82: 5 (March 1977): 1075–90.

Smith, Howard K. *The State of Europe*. New York: Alfred A. Knopf, 1951.

Smith, Tony. *The French Stake in Algeria, 1945–1962*. Ithaca: Cornell University Press, 1978.

Snyder, Richard, H. W. Bruck, and Burton Sapin, eds. *Foreign Policy Decision-Making*. New York: Free Press, 1962.

Souyris, Captain André. "An Effective Counterguerrilla Procedure." Translated from the original and reprinted. MR 36: 12 (March 1957): 86–90.

Steel, Ronald. *Pax Americana*. Rev. ed. New York: Viking, 1970.

Sulzberger, Cyrus. *A Long Row of Candles: Memoirs and Diaries, 1934–1954*. New York: Macmillan, 1969.

Summers, Colonel Harry G., Jr. *On Strategy: A Critical Analysis of the Vietnam War.* Novato, Calif.: Presidio Press, 1982.

Tanham, George K., and Dennis J. Duncanson. "Some Dilemmas of Counterinsurgency." *Foreign Affairs* 48 (January 1970): 113–22.

Taylor, Milton. "South Vietnam: Lavish Aid, Limited Progress." *Pacific Affairs* 34: 3 (Fall 1961): 242–56.

Thaxton, Ralph. "On Peasant Revolution and National Resistance: Toward a Theory of Peasant Mobilization and Revolutionary War with Special Reference to Modern China." WP 30: 1 (October 1977): 24–57.

Thillaud, Chef de Bataillon. "Vaincre sans Trahir." RDN 26 (April 1958): 643–53.

Thompson, Sir Robert. *Defeating Communist Insurgency: Experiences from Malaya and Vietnam.* London: Chatto and Windus, 1966.

Thompson, James Clay. *Rolling Thunder: Understanding Policy and Program Failure.* Chapel Hill: University of North Carolina Press, 1980.

Tillema, Herbert K. *Appeal to Force: American Military Intervention in the Era of Containment.* New York: Thomas Y. Cromwell, 1973.

Tilly, Charles. "Does Modernization Breed Revolutions?" CP (April 1973): 425–47.

Tipps, Dean C. "Modernization Theory and the Comparative Study of Societies: A Critical Perspective." CSSH 15 (March 1973): 199–226.

Tönnies, Ferdinand. *Community and Society.* Translated and edited by Charles P. Loomis. New York: Harper Torchbooks, 1963.

Toulmin, Stephen. "From Form to Function: Philosophy and History of Science in the 1950's and Now." *Daedelus* (Summer 1977): 143–62.

Tran Van Don. *Our Endless War.* San Rafael, Calif.: Presidio Press, 1978.

Trinquier, Roger. *Modern Warfare: A French View of Counterinsurgency.* Translated by Daniel Lee. New York: Praeger, 1964.

Useem, Michael. "Government Influence on the Social Science Paradigm." *Sociological Quarterly* 17 (Spring 1976): 146–61.

Van der Slik, Jack R. "The President in a Paradigm of Policy Making." *Presidential Studies Quarterly* 9 (Winter 1979): 65–71.

Vandenberg, Arthur H., Jr., and Joe Alex Morris, eds. *The Private Papers of Senator Vandenberg.* Boston: Houghton Mifflin, 1952.

Verba, Sydney. "Political Behavior and Politics." WP 12: 2 (January 1960): 280–91.

Wainhouse, Lt. Col. Edward R. "Guerrilla War in Greece, 1946–49: A Case Study." MR 37: 3 (June 1957): 17–25.

Wall, Irwin M. "The French Communists and the Algerian War." *Journal of Contemporary History* 12 (1977): 521–43.

Waterbury, John. "Endemic and Planned Corruption in a Monarchical Regime." WP 25: 4 (July 1973): 533–55.

Weber, Max. *The Theory of Social and Economic Organization*. Translated and edited by A. M. Henderson and Talcott Parsons. New York: Free Press, 1964.

Weiner, Myron. "India's Political Future." WP 12: 1 (October 1959): 103–19.

———. "The Macedonian Syndrome: An Historical Model of International Relations and Political Development." WP 23: 4 (July 1971): 665–83.

———. "Political Integration and Political Development." *Annals of the American Academy of Political and Social Science* 358 (March 1965): 52–64.

Whitaker, C. S., Jr. "A Disrhythmic Process of Political Change." WP 19: 2 (January 1967): 190–217.

Williams, William Appleman. *America Confronts a Revolutionary World: 1776–1976*. New York: William Morrow, 1976.

Willner, Ann Ruth. "The Underdeveloped Study of Political Development." WP 16: 3 (April 1964): 468–82.

Windle, Charles, and T. R. Vallance. "Optimizing Military Assistance Training." WP 15: 1 (October 1962): 91–107.

Wittner, Lawrence S. *American Intervention in Greece, 1943–1949*. New York: Columbia University Press, 1982.

———. "The Truman Doctrine and the Defense of Freedom." *Diplomatic History* 4: 2 (Spring 1980): 161–88.

Wolf, Charles, Jr. "Insurgency and Counter-Insurgency: New Myths and Old Realities." *Yale Review* 56: 2 (December 1966): 225–41.

———. "Some Aspects of the 'Value' of Less-Developed Countries to the United States." WP 15: 4 (July 1963): 623–35.

Wolf, Eric R. *Peasant Wars of the Twentieth Century*. New York: Harper Torchbooks, 1969.

Wolfers, Arnold. *Discord and Collaboration: Essays on International Politics*. Baltimore: Johns Hopkins Press, 1979.

Woodhouse, C. M. *The Struggle for Greece, 1941–1949*. London: Hart-Davis, MacGibbon, 1976.

"XXX." "Pourquoi L'Indochine." RDN (June 1954): 645–55.

"Ximenes." "Revolutionary War." MR 37: 5 (August 1957): 103–8.

Yergin, David. *Shattered Peace: The Origins of the Cold War and the National Security State.* Boston: Houghton Mifflin, 1977.

Zolberg, Aristide. "The Military Decade in Africa." wp 25: 2 (January 1973): 309–31.

———. "The Structure of Political Conflict in the New States of Tropical Africa." APSR 63 (March 1968): 70–87.

Zorthian, Barry. "Where Do We Go From Here?" *Foreign Service Journal* (February 1970): 16–19.

RAND CORPORATION PAPERS

Averch, Harvey, and John Koehler. *The Huk Rebellion in the Philippines: Quantitative Approaches.* RM–6254–ARPA. August 1970.

Brown, Seyoum. *Political Development as a Policy Science—A Polemic.* P–3650. August 1967.

Cohen, Joel E. *Social Research among the Estates of Science.* P–3927. February 1969.

Davison, W. P. *Some Observations on Viet Cong Operations in the Villages.* RM–5267/2–ISA/ARPA. May 1968.

Dror, Yehezekel. *Prolegomena to Policy Sciences.* P–4283. January 1970.

Elliott, David, and Mai Elliott. *Documents of an Elite Viet Cong Delta Unit: The Demolition Platoon of the 514th Battalion Part Four: Political Indoctrination and Military Training.* RM–5851–ISA/ARPA. May 1969.

Elliott, David, and W. A. Stewart. *Pacification and the Viet Cong System in Dinh Tuong: 1966–1967.* RM–5788–ISA/ARPA. January 1969.

Gurtov, Melvin, and Konrad Kellen. *Vietnam: Lessons and Mislessons.* P–4080. June 1969.

Heymann, H., Jr., and W. Whitson. *Can and Should the United States Preserve a Military Capability for Revolutionary Conflict?* R–940–ARPA. January 1972.

Hosmer, Stephen, Konrad Kellen, and Brian Jenkins. *The Fall of South Vietnam: Statements by Vietnamese Military and Civilian Leaders.* R–2208–OSD (HIST). December 1978.

Jenkins, Brian. *The Unchangeable War.* RM–6278–1–ARPA. September 1972.

Kecskemeti, P. *Insurgency as a Strategic Problem.* RM–5160–PR. February 1967.

Kellen, Konrad. *A Profile of the PAVN Soldier in South Vietnam.* RM–5013–1–ISA/ARPA. June 1966.

———. *A View of the VC: Elements of Cohesion in the Enemy Camp in 1966–1967.* RM–5462–1–ISA/ARPA. November 1969.

Koehler, John. *Explaining Dissident Success: The Huks in Central Luzon.* P–4753. January 1972.

Komer, R. W. *Impact of Pacification on Insurgency in South Vietnam.* P–4443. August 1970.

———. *The Malayan Emergency in Retrospect: Organization of a Successful Counterinsurgency Effort.* R–957–ARPA. February 1972.

Leites, Nathan. *The Viet Cong Style of Politics.* RM–5487–1–ISA/ARPA. May 1969.

Leites, Nathan, and Charles Wolf, Jr. *Rebellion and Authority: Myths and Realities Reconsidered.* P–3422. August 1966.

Menges, Constantine. *Democratic Revolutionary Insurgency as an Alternative Strategy.* P–3817. March 1968.

Mitchell, Edward. *The Huk Rebellion in the Philippines: An Econometric Study.* RM–5757–ARPA. January 1969.

Pauker, Guy. *Sources of Insurgency in Developing Countries.* P–5029. June 1973.

———, Steven Canby, A. Ross Johnson, and William Quandt. *In Search of Self-Reliance: U.S. Security Assistance to the Third World under the Nixon Doctrine.* R–1092–ARPA. June 1973.

Ronfeldt, David, and Luigi Einaudi. *Internal Security and Military Assistance to Latin America in the 1970's: A First Statement.* R–924–ISA. December 1971.

West, F. J., Jr. *Area Security.* P–3979–1. August 1969.

Wolf, Charles, Jr. *Controlling Small Wars.* P–3994. December 1968.

———. *The Logic of Failure: A Vietnam "Lesson."* P–4651–1. October 1971.

Zasloff, J. J. *Origins of the Insurgency in South Vietnam, 1954–1960: The Role of the Southern Vietminh Cadres,* RM–5163/2/ARPA. 1967.

———. *Political Motivation of the Viet Cong: The Vietminh Regroupees.* RM–4703/2–ISA/ARPA. May 1968.

U.S. GOVERNMENT DOCUMENTS

U.S. Arms Control and Disarmament Agency. *World Military Expenditures and Arms Transfers, 1970–1979.* Washington, D.C., March 1982.

U.S. Department of Defense. *Proceedings of the Low-Intensity Warfare Conference.* Sponsored by the Secretary of Defense, 14–15 January 1986. Fort McNair, Washington, D.C.

U.S. Department of Defense, Defense Security Assistance Agency. *Foreign Military Sales, Foreign Military Construction Sales and Military Assistance Facts as of September 1981*. Data Management Division, DSAA. December 1981.

U.S. General Accounting Office. *Issues and Observations on the Purposes of Special Security Supporting Assistance Programs: Departments of Defense and State, Agency for International Development*. Report to the Committee on International Relations, U.S. House of Representatives, by the Comptroller General. GAO ID–76–11. September 12, 1975.

———. *Foreign Military Sales—A Growing Concern*. Report to the Congress by the Comptroller General. GAO ID–76–51. June 1, 1976.

———. *Stopping U.S. Assistance to Foreign Police and Prisons*. Report to the Congress by the Comptroller General. GAO ID–76–5. February 19, 1976.

U.S. House, Committee on Foreign Affairs. *Soviet Policy and United States Response in the Third World*. Congressional Research Service report to Congress. March 1981.

———. Committee on Foreign Affairs, Subcommittee on Asian and Pacific Affairs. *The Treatment of Political Prisoners in South Vietnam by the Government of the Republic of South Vietnam*. Hearings, 93rd Cong., 1st sess., September 13, 1973.

———. Committee on International Relations, Subcommittee on International Security Affairs. *Conventional Arms Transfer Policy: Background Information*. 95th Cong., 2nd sess. February 1, 1978.

U.S. Military Assistance Command, Vietnam. *Handbook for Military Support of Pacification*. February 1968.

U.S. Senate, Committee on Foreign Relations. *Economic Development Versus Military Expenditures in Countries Receiving U.S. Aid: Priorities and the Competition for Resources*. Report by the Agency for International Development. 96th Cong., 2d sess., December 1980.

———. *Legislative Origins of the Truman Doctrine*. Hearings. 80th Cong., 1st sess., 1973.

———. *Report on Human Rights Practices in Countries Receiving U.S. Aid*. Prepared by the Department of State. February 8, 1979.

———. *The Vietnam Hearings*. Introduction by J. William Fulbright. New York: Vintage Books, 1966.

———. Special Committee to Study the Foreign Aid Program. *Report on Military Assistance and the Security of the U.S., 1947–1956*. Prepared by the Institute of War and Peace Studies, Columbia University. Washington, D.C.: GPO, 1957.

INDEX

Academics and foreign policy, 9–12, 44; cost-benefit counterinsurgency, 127–128; counterinsurgency policy, 111–115; in Kennedy administration, 21

Acheson, Dean, 38 n. 57, 166, 241; balance of power politics, 175; on Greek right wing, 193; on President Quiniro, 226, 229; supports Indochina war, 217; U.S. involvement in Greece, 176–177

Adequacy, of paradigm, 37–39, 47. *See also* Perfectability, of paradigm

Administrative capacity in Third World, 64, 117; programs to improve, 126–127

Afghanistan, 83

Agriculture, commercialization in Philippines, 206–207

Albania, 193, 201

Alejandrino, Casto, 209

Algeria: end of war in, 162–164; French greatness linked with, 141, 144–146; French resettlement policies, 157; nationalism, 150–151, 161; oil in, 143; psychological warfare, 159; Socialists in, 146

Allard, J. (Gen.), 150, 154

Alliance for Progress, 94

Allies: benefactor relationship with, 130–131; as buffer against instability, 84–85

Allison, Graham, 29

Almond, Gabriel, 13, 51, 56, 61, 66, 68, 69, 71, 135

AMAG. *See* American Mission to Aid Greece

Ambiguous data, foreign policy and, 37–38

American exceptionalism: American foreign policy, 135–165; explanatory limits of, 7; French vs. American counterinsurgency policy, 15; low-intensity warfare theories, 288–289

American Mission to Aid Greece (AMAG), 182, 184–185, 189–190

American Political Science Association (APSA), 51–52; Panel on Comparative Government (1944), 51–52; political ultimacy theory, 55–56; Seminar on Comparative Politics (1953), 52

American self-esteem, political development theory, 65–66

Amphioxu (Capt.), 151

AMT. *See* General Workers' Union

Angola, 83

Anthropology and political development theory, 51, 52–53

Anticommunism as positive social doctrine, 65

APSA. *See* American Political Science Association

Arendt, Hannah, 61

Argentina, 96 n. 67

Army of the Republic of Vietnam (ARVN), 244–245; after Diem coup, 271–274; assessment of, 247; desertion rates, 272; destruction by Diem, 256–257; draft evasion, 263

Aron, Robert, 146

ARVN. *See* Army of the Republic of Vietnam

Assimilation and French colonialism, 141

Association and French colonialism, 141

"Association of Landowners" (Philippines), 207 n. 9

Atlantic Charter, 174–175, 278

Auriol, Vincent, 146 n. 27

Authority: legitimacy of, 131; political development theory, 51; revolution as attack on, 152

Azerbaijan crisis, 176

Balance of power: East-West perspective, 167–175, 178–179; Greek civil war, 174–175; Huk rebellion, 213–214; Vietnam, 240–241

Balance of terror, 149–151

Balkan Communist Federation, 202

Venizelist Party, 167
Venizelos, Eleftherios, 167
Viet Cong: assessment of, 246–247, 249, 251; control of Vietnam, 272; organization innovation, 260–261; penetration of strategic hamlets, 267–268; relations with peasants, 260, 262–265; U.S. assessment of, 258–259; village support for, 262–263
Viet Minh popular front, 216; peasants and, 264–265
Vietnam: counterinsurgency policy failure in, 240–275; Diem coup, 268–274; government-population relations, 258–266; intragovernmental constraints in, 254, 258, 282; limits U.S. leverage, 251–254; military failure in, 24; myth of the village in, 125 n. 47, 261–263; palace politics, 254–257; peasants in, 259–260; police training in, 89; presidential and bureaucratic politics, 243–246; rent limitation program, 265; revisionist theories on U.S. defeat, 288; social science role in policy, 73; stalemate policy in, 278; U.S. counterinsurgency policy in, 15
Vietnam Task Force, 249–250
Villages: Greek civil war, 173; in Vietnam, 261–263. See also "Myth of the village"
Violence: American counterinsurgency policy, 137–138; in French colonial policy, 143; in French counterinsurgency policy, 156–157; in Greece, 173–174; in Philippines, 213, 220; in Vietnam, 257, 259
Vulnerability to insurgency, 105–115

Warren, Robert (Gen.), 91–92
Wars of national liberation, 111, 241
Weber, Max, 49–51
Weinberger, Caspar, 283–286, 288
Weiner, Myron, 64
Western culture: French defense of, 160–161; policy, ideology, and, 9; political development theory, 49
Westernization of Third World, 54–55; instability and, 80–81; of ruling elites, 84–85
White man's burden as policy justification, 46–47, 280
White, T. H., 34
Willingness: intergovernmental constraints upon, 120–122 (in Greece, 195; in Philippines, 226–227; in Vietnam, 254); leverage and, 119–120 (in Greece, 192–195; in Philippines, 224–226; in Vietnam, 253–254). See also Capacity
"Window of vulnerability" concept, 83
Wittner, Lawrence, 190–191
Wolf, Charles, Jr., 127–128, 284 n. 7
Wolfers, Arnold, 32

"Ximenes" (psychological warfare), 158
"XXX," 149

Young, Kenneth, 246–247
Yugoslavia, Greek refugees in, 193–194, 199–200

Zachariades, Nikos, 203
Zaire, military aid to, 91
Zervas (Col.), 169–170, 193
Zolberg, Aristide, 73

Library of Congress Cataloging-in-Publication Data

Shafer, D. Michael, 1953-
Deadly paradigms.

Bibliography: p.   Includes index.
1. United States—Foreign relations—1945-
2. Counterinsurgency—United States. I. Title.
E744.S475 1988   327.73   87–25873
ISBN 0–691–07774–6 (alk. paper)

Rev.